READING WITH MEANING
Strategies for College Reading

Dorothy Grant Hennings

Kean College of New Jersey

PRENTICE HALL, Englewood Cliffs, New Jersey 07632

Library of Congress Cataloging-in-Publication Data

Hennings, Dorothy Grant.
    Reading with meaning : strategies for college reading / Dorothy
Grant Hennings.
        p.   cm.
    Includes index.
    ISBN 0-13-753492-2
    1. Reading (Higher education)--United States. 2. College readers.
I. Title.
LB2395.3.H46 1990
428.4'2'071173--dc20   89-34652
                                                       CIP

Editorial/production supervision and interior design: Jan Stephan
Cover design: Maureen Eide
Manufacturing buyer: Ray Keating/Mike Woerner
Photo Research: Kay Dellosa
Cover Art: Michael Quackenbush/Image Bank

Chapter Opening Art

Contents: Public Relations Office, Kean College. **Preface:** Cynthia Dopkin/Photo Researchers. **Chapters 1 and 2:** Public Relations Office, Kean College. **Chapter 3:** Robert A. Isaacs/Photo Researchers. **Chapters 4, 5, 6, and 7:** Laima Druskis. **Chapter 8:** Boston Universtiy Photo Service. **Chapters 9 and 10:** Laima Druskis. **Chapter 11:** Ken Karp. **Chapter 12:** University of Arkansas, Division of Information. **Chapter 13:** Laima Druskis. **Chapter 14:** Courtesy of Apple Computer, Inc. **Chapter 15 and Summary:** Ken Karp.

Printed in the United States of America

10 9 8 7 6 5 4 3 2 1

ISBN 0-13-753492-2

Prentice-Hall International (UK) Limited, *London*
Prentice-Hall of Australia Pty. Limited, *Sydney*
Prentice-Hall Canada Inc., *Toronto*
Prentice-Hall Hispanoamericana, S.A., *Mexico*
Prentice-Hall of India Private Limited, *New Delhi*
Prentice-Hall of Japan, Inc., *Tokyo*
Simon & Schuster Asia Pte. Ltd., *Singapore*
Editora Prentice-Hall do Brasil, Ltda., *Rio de Janeiro*

Acknowledgements appear on p. 352, which constitutes a continuation of the copyright page.

To my sister, Barbara Moll Grant,
who introduced me to the pleasures of teaching
college reading

Contents

PREFACE   ix

PART I: INTRODUCTION TO READING

1   GETTING READY TO READ   1

Introduction—Getting Ready to Read   2
The Getting-Ready-to-Read Strategy   3
Selection 1: A Nation on the Move   4
Selection 2: The Signs of Life   11
Selection 3: The New Colossus   15
Extending What You Have Learned   17

PART II: VOCABULARY AND READING

2   UNLOCKING THE MEANING OF WORDS:
USING CONTEXT CLUES   19

Introduction—Unlocking the Meaning of Unfamiliar Words   20
Practicing Using Context Clues   21

More Practice with Context Clues   23
Selection 1: Niagara   25
Selection 2: The Computer as Mind Tool   28
Chapter Vocabulary Review: More Practice with Context Clues   30
Extending What You Have Learned   33

3   UNLOCKING THE MEANING OF WORDS: USING WORD-STRUCTURE CLUES   34

Introduction—Unlocking the Meaning of Unfamiliar Words   35
Common Word-Building Elements   36
Common Prefixes   39
Suffixes   42
Selection 1: Attacking Words in Science   43
Selection 2: Brushing Up on Dinosaurs   47
Selection 3: Heterotrophs and Autotrophs   50
Extending What You Have Learned   54

PART III: BASIC COMPREHENSION

4   READING FOR MAIN IDEA   56

Introduction—Reading for Main Ideas   57
Distinguishing Between General and Specific   57
Working with Main Ideas and Supporting Details   61
Selection 1: Summer of Destiny   65
Selection 2: James Michener   71
Identifying the Main Idea of an Extended Selection   77
Selection 3: The Secret of America   78
Extending What You Have Learned   83

5   THINKING ABOUT DETAILS   85

Introduction—Thinking about Details   86
Practicing the Strategies: Seeing the Significance of Details   89
Practicing the Strategies: Making Inferences Based on Details   92
Selection 1: The Dream at Panama   95
Extending What You Have Learned   108

6   USING CLUE WORDS TO ANTICIPATE AN AUTHOR'S THOUGHTS   110

Introduction—Using Clue Words   111
Recognizing Sentence Relationships   123
Applying What You Know in Writing   127
Selection 1: The Nature of Scientific Investigation   129
Extending What You Have Learned   135

PART IV: EFFICIENT STUDY READING

7   HANDLING TEXT STRUCTURE: SQ3R PART ONE   **136**

Introduction to Elements of Text Structure   137
Strategies for Working with Text Structure   139
Selection 1: Physical Geology   141
Selection 2: The Northwest Ordinance of 1787   143
Extending What You Have Learned   151

8   REMEMBERING THROUGH RECITING AND REVIEWING: SQ3R PART TWO   **153**

Introduction—Remembering What You Have Read   154
Selection 1: Black Folk Music   157
Selection 2: The Education of Richard Rodriguez   161
Taking an Examination on What You Have Read   164
Extending What You Have Learned   167

9   INCREASING YOUR READING RATE   **168**

Introduction—Increasing Your Reading Rate   169
Selection 1: One Writer's Beginnings   176
Selection 2: Big Brother Is Watching You   179
Selection 3: Language and Communication   181
Selection 4: The Microbial Environment   182
Thinking about Your Reading Rate   184
Keeping a Reading Log   185

PART V: CRITICAL AND CREATIVE READING

10   CRITICAL THINKING: COMPARING, INFERRING, CONCLUDING, JUDGING   **186**

Introduction—Comparing, Inferring, Concluding, and Judging   187
Selection 1: American Indian Myths and Legends   192
Selection 2: Haydn and Mozart   200
Extending What You Have Learned   210

11   INTERPRETING STYLE, TONE, AND MOOD   **212**

Introduction—Style, Tone, and Mood   213
Selection 1: The Gettysburg Address   216
Selection 2: I Have a Dream   218
Selection 3: Dream Poems by Langston Hughes   225
Extending What You Have Learned   228

PART VI: READING WITH DIVERSE PURPOSES

12   UNDERSTANDING DEFINITIONS AND EXPLANATIONS   230

Introduction—Reading Definitions and Explanations   231
Definitions   231
Selection 1: Diffusion and Osmosis   234
Selection 2: Energy Value of Food   237
Explanations   239
Selection 3: Evolution by Means of Natural Selection   242
Selection 4: Natural Selection—The Peppered Moth   246
Extending What You Have Learned   251

13   UNDERSTANDING DESCRIPTIONS AND NARRATIVES   254

Introduction—Reading Descriptions and Narratives   255
Description   255
Selection 1: Florence the Magnificent   259
Narration   267
Selection 2: Muhammad the Prophet   272
Extending What You Have Learned   284

14   UNDERSTANDING OPINIONS AND PERSUASIVE WRITING   285

Introduction—Reading Opinions   286
Selection 1: The Eight Best Presidents—and Why   290
Selection 2: Soviet Reform Reflects Tragedy of the Revolution   296
Maya Angelou's School Thoughts   303
Extending What You Have Learned   307

15   INTERPRETING CHARTS, GRAPHS, AND DIAGRAMS   309

Introduction—Charts, Graphs, and Diagrams   310
Charts and Tables   310
Selection 1: Land and Populations   315
Selection 2: The Fifty States of the United States   317
Pictographs   320
Circle (or Pie) Graphs   322
Bar Graphs   324
Selection 3: Immigration to the United States   325
Line Graphs   327
Selection 4: Weather in New Delhi and Santiago   329
Line Drawings   331
Selection 5: Rose versus Cobb   332
Extending What You Have Learned   334

SUMMATION: READING WITH MEANING   335

GLOSSARY: WORDS FEATURED IN THE TEXT   340

APPENDIX: CALCULATING YOUR READING RATE: READING RATE TABLES AND EXPLANATIONS   336

Preface

Reading experts define reading as an active process of thinking. To read with understanding is to develop relationships among ideas. Reading experts also explain that what you bring to the reading of a selection is as important to your understanding of it as what the author put into it. To the reading of a text, you bring knowledge of and attitudes toward the sciences, social sciences, and humanities. You bring a purpose for reading. You bring understanding of vocabulary, your ability to figure out meanings, and your attitudes toward reading.

PURPOSE OF THE TEXT

Reading with Meaning: Strategies for College Reading is a book that incorporates this view of reading. It is designed to help you, the college student, create meaningful ideas as you read. It emphasizes

- active reading in which you respond while reading. As you read this book, you will be actively involved in thinking, talking, and writing.
- strategic reading in which you learn specific strategies for understanding written passages. For example, you will learn to preview before reading, brainstorm what you know before reading, set your own purposes for reading, distinguish main from subordinate ideas, use clue words to anticipate

the author's train of thought, visualize, predict, infer, conclude, and judge as you read.

- vocabulary development in which you expand your vocabulary through actual reading so that you can use your growing understanding of words to make future reading more successful. As you read, you will learn to use context and word-structure clues to unlock the meaning of unfamiliar words.
- expansion of the knowledge you bring to reading so that future reading is more meaningful.

Reading with Meaning: Strategies for College Reading contains many selections similar to ones you will read in your college courses in history, English, biology, earth sciences, and other subjects. To succeed in college, you must know how to read this type of content. The primary purpose of the book, therefore, is to prepare you to function successfully in college.

ORGANIZATION OF THE TEXT

The overall organization of *Reading with Meaning: Strategies for College Reading* reflects these emphases. Take time to study the Contents. This is something you should do before reading any college text. You will see that this book starts with basic reading strategies for working with vocabulary, main ideas, and significant details, which lead into more advanced strategies for study, critical, and creative reading.

Part One has one chapter. Its purpose is to teach you a strategy, or an approach, to use in preparing to read.

Part Two focuses on vocabulary. It has two chapters. The first chapter teaches you how to use the surrounding words in a sentence to unlock the meaning of an unfamiliar word; the second teaches you how to use word parts to figure out word meanings, especially the meanings of technical terms important in college reading.

Part Three helps you understand what you read. The three chapters in this part teach you (1) how to find the main idea of paragraphs and selections, (2) how to make sense out of details, and (3) how to use clue words to anticipate the author's train of thought.

Part Four deals with study reading and introduces you to a study plan called *SQ3R*. The first chapter in this part teaches strategies for surveying a text and organizing your thoughts before reading. The second chapter shows you how to remember what you read and gives suggestions for taking tests. The third deals with increasing your reading rate.

Part Five involves you in critical and creative reading. The first chapter in this part introduces you to comparing, inferring, concluding, and judging. The second chapter helps you handle style, tone, and mood in reading—aspects of reading particularly important in the reading of novels, plays, poems, and speeches.

Part Six helps you understand the kinds of diverse selections you will read in college courses. The first chapter in this section provides practice in comprehending definitions and explanations, which are commonly found in college textbooks, especially those in the natural and social sciences. The second chapter introduces strategies for comprehending descriptions and narratives, which are often found in humanities as well as science textbooks. The third chapter provides practice in reading opinions and persuasive writing, a kind of writing you will encounter very often in history and the humanities as well as in newspapers and magazines. And the last chapter introduces strategies for reading charts, graphs, and diagrams.

At the back of the book is a glossary of vocabulary words featured in the text. It contains a pronunciation guide as well as an explanation of how to use a glossary. You can use this glossary as a dictionary, checking meanings and pronunciations of unfamiliar words. For each entry in the glossary, there is a sample sentence.

ORGANIZATION OF THE CHAPTERS

Very often in college textbooks—including this one—there is a pattern to the development of chapters. It generally helps to identify the pattern before you start to read. Turn now to Chapter 4 and identify the component parts of a typical chapter.

In *Reading with Meaning: Strategies for College Reading,* each chapter begins by asking you to look through the chapter before reading to identify the topic and then to jot down what you already know about that topic and what you hope to find out through reading the chapter. Each chapter then presents a statement of what you will learn through the chapter—the objective. Next comes an introductory discussion of the strategy to be taught in the chapter and practice using the strategy.

Following this instructional segment are one or more selections in which you apply what you have learned in the opening segments of the chapter. Accompanying most selections are two kinds of activities to do before reading: "Expanding Your Vocabulary for Reading" and "Getting Ready to Read." "Expanding Your Vocabulary" introduces featured vocabulary from the selection in a sentence so that you get continued practice in using your understanding of context and word structure clues to unlock the meaning of unfamiliar words. "Getting Ready to Read" encourages you to look over, or survey, a selection before reading. You can complete these activities by yourself or with class members during class time.

Next is a selection to be read. Selections are from magazines, books, and textbooks. Exercises follow that you can use to check your understanding. These are either short answer or short essay. In each case, however, you must apply the strategies learned earlier in the chapter. In other words, if the chapter builds strategies for finding the main idea, you will answer questions dealing with finding main ideas. Additionally, as you read, you will often be asked to record key words, main ideas, significant details, or descriptive words as margin notes or to circle or underline parts of the text—something that you should do in college reading. In some instances, you will find the number of words contained within a selection written at the end of it. If you want to check your reading rate on a selection, you can use that number and the reading rate chart in the appendix to calculate your reading rate.

At the ends of selections, you will find exercises for reviewing featured vocabulary. In many cases, the exercises include sentences using the featured words; they provide more practice in using sentence clues to unlock the meaning of words.

At the ends of selections, you will also find suggestions for writing. Sometimes you will be asked to write using knowledge from the selection. Sometimes you will write using the same writing approaches used by the author of the selection. Research shows that writing is a good way to learn content and develop reading skills.

The final segment of each chapter provides an opportunity for you to extend your understanding of the content and vocabulary and to practice the reading strategies taught in the chapter. In some chapters, you will be asked to review the steps in the strategies with which you have been working. You will be asked to find a similar kind of selection to read independently and to keep a vocabulary notebook to help you make the words featured in the chapter a part of your everyday vocabulary. At times, you will also be asked to locate on a map places mentioned in the selection. By doing this, you are building your knowledge base for future reading.

ACKNOWLEDGEMENTS

The author wants to thank the fine reviewers who read the manuscript for this book in each of its drafts and provided suggestions that proved invaluable. She sends her thanks to

Ellen Kaiden, Ramapo College

Thomas L. Franke, Lansing Community College

Mary Lou Palumbo, Community College of the Finger Lakes

Janet Elder, Richland College

Gail Ziros Benchener, De Anza College

Anita Podrid, Queens College

The author recognizes the help of the public relations office at Kean College in providing the photographs at the beginning of some chapters. She sends her appreciation as well to Jan Stephan, production editor at Prentice Hall who handled the manuscript with efficiency. It was a pleasure working with her and with Phil Miller, the Humanities Editor-in-Chief. Thanks are also due to Kay Dellosa for the Photo Research which produced many of the chapter opening art pieces.

In addition, the author thanks Barbara M. Grant of William Paterson College of New Jersey, who has taught college reading courses for many years, who introduced her to the excitement of teaching college reading, and who contributed numerous ideas. Her suggestions proved most helpful.

The author also thanks George Hennings, helpmate and husband, who contributed by locating reading selections, compiling the glossary, criticizing the manuscript, introducing her to word processing, and providing encouragement when the work load became heavy.

Dorothy Grant Hennings
Warren, New Jersey

1

Getting
Ready
to Read

Before reading the chapter, read the title, the stated objective, and the head-ings and subheadings. Ask yourself: What is this chapter about? What is the topic of the chapter? In the space above and beside the chapter number, jot down what you already know about that topic. Then in the space below the chapter number, jot down at least two questions you hope to answer through reading the chapter.

OBJECTIVE

In this chapter, you will develop strategies for getting ready to read. Specifically, you will learn how to

1. make a general survey of a selection before reading,
2. review what you know about a topic before reading about it, and
3. set a purpose for your reading.

INTRODUCTION—GETTING READY TO READ

Reading is a thinking process that sets two people in action together—an author and a reader. The author has a purpose in writing and a message to communicate to his or her audience. In writing a piece, the author chooses the facts and ideas to include in it, chooses the words to express those facts and ideas, and organizes them into a clear sequence. In so doing, the author draws upon his or her knowledge and feelings about the topic. Obviously, what the author writes in a text determines to a great extent what you get out of it.

But what you make out of a text depends also on your purpose for reading and on what you bring to the reading of that text (see Figure 1.1). One thing that you may bring to the reading of a selection is factual knowledge about the topic. You have a storehouse of knowledge that you have built up through firsthand experience and through prior reading. As you read, you relate what is in the text to what you already know about the topic; you make connections between what you already know and what is in the text. The more connections you can make, the more you get out of a selection when you read.

For that reason, to improve your reading, you must build your storehouse of knowledge. You can do that by reading. You must keep reading about important subjects. You must read science, history, and geography. You must read about art and music. You must read novels and poems. The more you read about the world around you, the better reader you will become.

There is something else you can do to make yourself a better reader. Because what you get out of a text depends on what you already know about the topic, take three steps before reading a selection.

Step 1—Previewing Before Reading

The first step is to preview, or look through, the selection you are going to read. A major question to keep in mind as you preview a selection before reading is: What is the topic of this selection (or what is it generally about)? To answer this question, look at the **title**. The title often provides a good clue as to the topic. Look for the name of the **author** if one is given. What topics does this author typically write about? Look at the **headings** that may divide the piece into sections. Look at the **terms the author repeats at the beginnings of paragraphs or**

Figure 1.1 *Reading with Meaning*

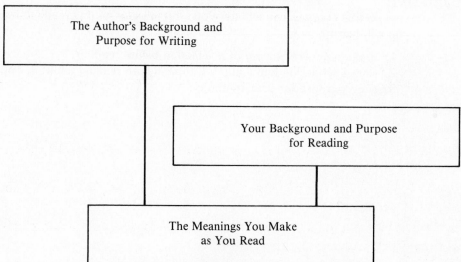

that are in italics or in bold print. Quickly read the **first paragraph** and the **last.** What clues do they provide as to the topic? What clues do they provide as to the subtopics, or the aspects of the topic included? Look at the **illustrations**—the photographs, maps, and charts that accompany the selection. They generally help the reader get an idea as to the major focus, or concern, of a selection.

Step 2—Thinking About What You Already Know

The next step is to think about what you already know on the topic. Sometimes it pays to jot down on paper a few words that sum up what you know before reading. In a way, what you are doing at this stage is brainstorming; to brainstorm, you write down words and thoughts that come to mind about the topic of the selection. Useful here are the key questioning words: *who, what, when, where, how,* and *why.* In relation to the topic, ask yourself: Who is or was involved in this? When does or did this happen? Where does or did this happen? What is or was involved? How is it or was it important? Why does or did this happen?

Step 3—Setting Your Purpose for Reading

The third step is to set your purpose for reading. At this point, knowing what the topic of the selection is and what you already know about that topic, you should ask: What do I want to get out of reading this piece? What do I want to find out? What do I want to learn?

With books you choose yourself for personal reading, you probably have a good idea of what you want to get from your reading before you start to read. You may have chosen a popular novel to enjoy the pleasure of reading or to escape from your own problems. You may have chosen a book because everyone is talking about it and you want to be knowledgeable about the topic.

On the other hand, you may be dealing with an assigned reading. As a college student, you will have to read textbooks and references that your professor has assigned. You will read these books to get information, to know more about the topic. In this case, setting one or more specific purposes for reading can guide you as you read. Your purposes give direction to your reading.

THE GETTING-READY-TO-READ STRATEGY

In sum, a useful strategy to apply before reading includes these three steps:

1. Preview the selection by
   - looking at the title, author, and headings;
   - reading terms that repeat at the beginning of paragraphs or that are in italics or bold type;
   - reading quickly the first and last paragraphs;
   - studying the illustrations;
   - asking: What is this selection going to be about? What is the topic of the selection?
2. Review what you already know about the topic. Ask: What do I know about the topic?
3. Set a purpose to guide your reading. Ask: What do I want to learn from reading this selection?

In this chapter, you will apply these strategies as you read three selections similar to the kinds of selections you will be asked to read in your college classes: a selection from a history textbook, a selection from a biology book, and a poem of the kind you will read in English courses. To do well in college, you must learn how to attack material like this. Keep that in mind as you read the selections.

SELECTION 1: A NATION ON THE MOVE

A. Getting Ready to Read

1. *Preview the selection that follows to figure out what it is about. Turn to pages 6–9. Quickly read, or skim, the title and the subheadings. Look at the name of the author. Look at the photographs. Then return to this page and answer the questions in the space provided.*

- What is the main topic of the selection? (What is it about?) _____
- What subtopics does the selection cover? _____

_____

- What clues did you use to determine the topics and subtopics? _____

_____

_____

2. One way to think about what you already know is to make an "idea web" related to the topic and subtopics of the selection. To make a web as part of previewing a selection, you write the topic of the piece in the center of a sheet of paper. You draw lines outward from this hub. At the ends of the lines, you write the subtopics you have found by previewing the subheads. Next to the subtopics, you write questioning words: what, when, where, who, how, and/or why. Next to the questioning words, you record what you already know on the topic and subtopics before reading.

   Figure 1.2 is an example of an idea web that you could have prepared based on a preview of the selection "Americans Move West After the War of 1812." Explain how this idea web relates to the selection. Write your explanation here.

   Before reading, apply the second step of the Getting-Ready-To-Read Strategy: Think about what you already know. If you know anything (what? when? where? why?) about the national road, canals, steamboats, or railroads, jot down a few words that sum up your knowledge under the appropriate term in Figure 1.2. If you do not know anything about one of these, such as the national road, just leave it blank.

3. Set your purpose for reading. Thinking about what you know on this topic, you may have discovered that you have little knowledge about some aspect

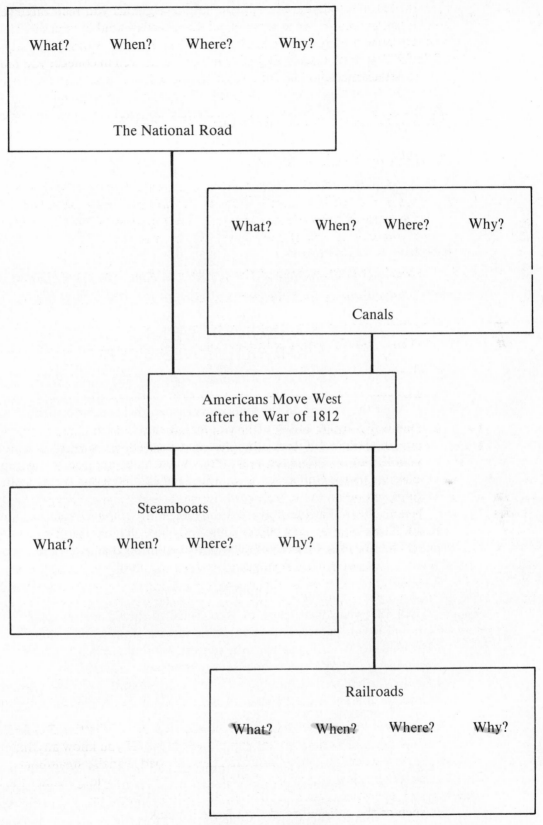

Figure 1.2 *Idea Web*

of the topic. What areas will you have to emphasize in your reading? What do you want to find out through reading the selection? In this case, questions you may try to answer through your reading are: What was the national road? How was it used?

Before reading, write several more questions that you will try to answer through reading. Use the idea web in Figure 1.2 to help you to write questions. Write your questions in the space provided here. Writing questions to answer through reading sets a purpose for your reading.

Reading with Meaning

Now read Selection 1. Keep your pencil in hand. Add information that answers your purpose-setting questions directly to the idea web in Figure 1.2

A NATION ON THE MOVE— AMERICA MOVES WEST

Henry Graff

After the War of 1812, Americans turned their attention from the problems of Europe to the promise of a growing nation. Vast changes had begun to take place. One of the most exciting of these was the migrating of people into the region between the Appalachians and the Mississippi. One visitor to the United States said in wonder, "America seems to be breaking up and moving westward."

A problem that faced every family deciding to move west was how to go. There was no easy, direct route to follow. Recognizable roads either did not exist or were of such poor condition that after a heavy rain, wagons and horses simply bogged down in the mud.

The National Road

In 1811 the construction of a road, called the Cumberland or National Road, began. This road would stretch from Cumberland, Maryland, to Wheeling, a town in western Virginia. When the road opened seven years later, people by the thousands traveled on it, seeking a new life farther west. Conestogas, or covered wagons, filled with goods bound for market used the road in both directions.

Canals

In the early 1800s shipping goods from one section of the country to another was expensive. The National Road had helped to lower this cost. Still, American business people searched for ways to move freight across the country even more cheaply. A way truly to link the East and the West had to be found. The answer, some thought, was the *canal,* a waterway dug across land for ships to sail through.

DeWitt Clinton, the governor of New York, began in 1817 to push

Collection of the Maryland Historical Society, Baltimore.

Figure 1.3   *The National Road—As each part of the National Road was finished, hundreds of families in Conestoga wagons moved farther west. The road is now called United States Highway 40.*

Figure 1.4   *The Erie Canal—Boys walked alongside boats in the Erie Canal, guiding them with ropes to keep them from hitting the banks.*

I. N. Phelps Stokes Collection Miriam and Ira D. Wallach Division of Art, Prints and Photographs, the New York Public Library, Astor, Lenox and Tilden Foundations.

for the construction of a canal linking the Great Lakes with the Atlantic Ocean. Many people considered Clinton's "Big Ditch," as the project was nicknamed, doomed to failure. Finally the massive project got underway. Eight years later the canal stretched from Buffalo, New York, to Albany, New York, on the Hudson River. The Erie Canal, costing $7 million, paid for itself within nine years. Its immense success encouraged other states to begin canal projects.

Steamboats

Americans had always used the natural waterways to transport themselves and their goods from one place to another. When a boat was forced to sail against the current of a river, however, it was impossible to be sure how long the trip would take.

Several Americans worked on an invention—the steamboat—that would greatly aid river travel. They believed that a boat powered by steam engines would be able to move upstream readily against a strong current. When Robert Fulton's *Clermont* sailed up the Hudson River from New York City to Albany in 1807, a new age in travel and transport was born. What was also needed was a faster means of transportation across land.

Railroads

Some Americans were convinced that steam engines could also be used to move wagons faster on land. In 1828 investors in the city of Baltimore began to build a railroad to the Ohio River. The first spadeful

Figure 1.5   *The First Passenger Railroad in the United States—With the connection between Baltimore and Wheeling, West Virginia, completed in 1853, the Baltimore & Ohio became the first passenger railroad in America. No north-south line was built until after the Civil War.*

Chicago Historical Society Photo, Baltimore and Ohio R.R. "Atlantic" showing engine and two cars. ICH: 09067.

of earth was turned by Charles Carroll, the last surviving signer of the Declaration of Independence. The merchants of Baltimore hoped that the railroad would give faster, cheaper service to the West than was then available.

By the 1840s railroad building was going on everywhere. During the 1850s, the amount of railroad track in the United States increased from 9021 miles (14,434 kilometers) to 30,626 miles (49,002 kilometers). The East Coast was now joined to the land beyond the Appalachian Mountains by the iron rails. (594 words)

C. Checking for Understanding

Select the best answer to each question. Refer to your idea web in thinking about your answers.

1. The national road stretched from
   a. Maine to California.
   b. Maryland to western Virginia.
   c. Maine to Florida.
   d. New York to Chicago.

2. Why was the national road important?
   a. Thousands of people traveled west on it in search of a new life.
   b. Goods bound for market were carried west on it.
   c. Goods bound for market were carried east on it.
   d. All of the above are true.

3. Clinton's Big Ditch was a name given to
   a. the first steamboat.
   b. the first steam engine.
   c. the national road.
   d. the Erie Canal.
   e. the first railroad.

4. Of the following, which is true about the Erie Canal?
   a. It was an idea that paid off.
   b. It was an idea that never came into being.
   c. It was a bad idea that never paid off.
   d. It was a project that was stopped before it was completed.

5. The *Clermont* was the name of
   a. the first steamboat.
   b. the first steam engine.
   c. the national road.
   d. the Erie Canal.
   e. the first railroad.

6. What was a disadvantage of boats not powered by steam?
   a. They would not go against the current of a river.
   b. It was impossible to be sure how long a trip would take when boats were forced to go against the current.
   c. They were very unstable, especially when forced to go against the current of a river.
   d. They used much more coal than a steamboat.

7. Who was Charles Carroll?
   a. the inventor of the steamboat
   b. the inventor of the railroad
   c. the person who developed the idea for the Erie Canal
   d. the person who turned the first spadeful of earth in the building of the railroad that joined the East Coast to the land beyond the Appalachians

8. In the period from 1840 to 1860, railroad building was
   a. almost nonexistent.
   b. taking place, but on a very limited scale.
   c. taking place on a large scale.

9. Of the following events, which happened last?
   a. The East Coast was connected to land beyond the Appalachian Mountains by a railroad.
   b. The Erie Canal was completed, connecting Buffalo, New York, to Albany, New York, on the Hudson River.
   c. The first trip by steamboat was made.
   d. The National Road was completed.

10. Of the following events, which happened first?
   a. The East Coast was connected to land beyond the Appalachian Mountains by a railroad.
   b. The Erie Canal was completed, connecting Buffalo, New York, to Albany, New York, on the Hudson River.
   d. The first trip by steamboat was made.
   e. The National Road was completed.

D. Thinking and Writing with What You Know

Answer the following in complete sentences. Think (or talk about the questions with a classmate) before writing.

1. Which do you think was the biggest accomplishment: The building of the National Road? The building of the Erie Canal? The building of the railroad between Baltimore and Wheeling, West Virginia? Give your reasons.

2. On the map in Figure 1.6 circle the following sites: Cumberland, Maryland; Wheeling, West Virginia; the Great Lakes; Buffalo, New York; Albany, New York; New York City; and Baltimore, Maryland. Label the Appalachian Mountains (that extend from West Virginia into Pennsylvania) and the Atlantic Ocean. Label the Hudson River that runs from Albany to New York City.

3. Study the locations you have circled on the map. Then use what you have learned from the selection and your map study to answer this question. Why was each of the following important to the growth of the United States?

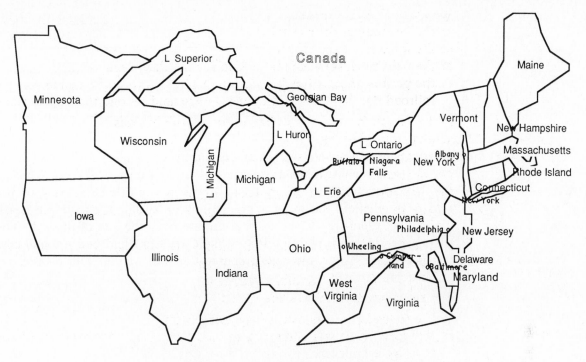

Figure 1.6 *The Northeastern United States*

a. the National Road

b. the Erie Canal

c. the steamboat

d. the railroad across the Appalachians

SELECTION 2: THE SIGNS OF LIFE

Getting Ready to Read

1. *Preview the selection that follows to figure out what it is about. Turn to page 12 and quickly read, or skim, the title and the first paragraph. Skim the paragraphs, looking for words that repeat at the beginning of each paragraph. Then return to this page and answer these questions.*

- What words does Curtis repeat in each paragraph that are clues to the topic?

  _____

- What is the main topic of the selection? _____

- How many characteristics of living things is the author going to discuss?
  How do you know? _____

  _____

2. Think about what you already know about living things. Based on what you know, predict what the characteristics of living things are. Ask: What are the "signs of life"? Notice that you are using the title to guide your pre-reading prediction. Write your predictions on the lines of this idea web. Notice that there are seven lines that radiate from the hub of the web. That is because a preview of the selection indicates that there are seven characteristics of life. You could have prepared this idea web on your own as part of your preview.

Signs of Life

3. Now set your purpose for reading. Write a question that you will try to answer through your reading. To do this, start your question with the words "What are . . . ." Record your question here:

   What are. . . .

Reading with Meaning

Now read Selection 2, keeping a marker in hand. Underscore the sentences in the text that tell you the characteristics of living things. You should underscore approximately seven sentences. When you have finished reading, go back to the idea web, correct the predictions you made, add points that you learned through reading, and answer the question you wrote before reading.

THE SIGNS OF LIFE

Helena Curtis

Biology is the "science of life." But what do biologists mean when they use the word "life"? Actually, there is no simple definition for this common word. Life does not exist in the abstract. There is no "life," only living things. And living things come in a great variety of forms, from tiny bacteria to giant sequoia trees. All of these, however, share certain properties that, taken together, distinguish them from nonliving objects.

The first characteristic of living things is that they are highly organized. In living things, atoms—the particles of which all matter is composed—are combined into a vast number of very large molecules called macromolecules. Each type of macromolecule has a distinctive structure and a specific function in the life of the organism. Some macromolecules are linked with other macromolecules to form the structures of an organism's body. Others participate in the dynamic processes essential for the continuing life of the organism; among the most significant are the large molecules known as enzymes. Enzymes, with the help of a variety of smaller molecules, regulate all of the processes occurring within living matter. The complex organization of both structures and processes is one of the most important properties of living things.

The second characteristic is closely related to the first: Living systems maintain a chemical composition quite different from that of their surroundings. The atoms present in living matter are the same as those in the surrounding environment, but they occur in different proportions and are arranged in different ways. Although living systems constantly exchange materials with the external environment, they maintain a stable and characteristic internal environment.

A third characteristic of living things is the capacity to take in, transform, and use energy from the environment. For example, in the process of photosynthesis, green plants take light energy from the sun and transform it into chemical energy stored in complex molecules. The energy stored in these molecules is used by plants to power their life processes and to build the characteristic structures of the plant body. Animals, which can obtain this stored energy by eating plants, change it into still other forms, such as heat, motion, electricity, and chemical energy stored in the characteristic structures of the animal body.

Fourth, living things can respond to stimuli. Bacteria move toward or away from certain chemical substances; green plants bend toward light; cats pounce on small moving objects. Although different organisms respond to widely varying stimuli, the capacity to respond is a fundamental and almost universal characteristic of life.

Fifth, and most remarkably, living things have the capacity to reproduce themselves so that, generation after generation, organisms produce more organisms like themselves. In each generation, however, there are slight variations between parents and offspring and among offspring.

Most organisms have a sixth characteristic: They grow and develop. For example, before hatching, the fertilized egg of a frog develops into the complex, but still immature, form that we recognize as a tadpole; after hatching, the tadpole continues to grow and undergoes further development, becoming a mature frog. Throughout the world of living things, similar patterns of growth and development occur.

A seventh characteristic of living things is that they are exquisitely suited to their environments. Moles, for instance, are furry animals that live underground in tunnels shoveled out by their large forepaws. Their eyes are small and sightless. Their noses, with which they sense the worm and the other small animals that make up their diet, are fleshy and enlarged. This most important characteristic of living things is known as adaptation.

These characteristics of living things are interrelated, and each depends, to a large extent, on the others. At any given moment in its life, an organism is organized, maintains a stable internal environment, transforms energy, responds to stimuli, and is adapted to its external environment; the organism may or may not be reproducing, growing, and developing, but it possesses the capacity to do so. (660 words)

Checking for Understanding

Put a check in front of the items that are characteristics of all living things.

_____ ✓   1. They are highly organized.

_____   2. They maintain a chemical balance that is similar to that of their surroundings.

_____ ✓   3. They can take in, transform, and use energy from their environment.

_____   4. They transform light energy from the sun into chemical energy.

_____ ✓   5. They can respond to stimuli.

_____   6. They respond to the same stimuli.

_____   7. They very rarely exchange materials with the external environment.

_____ ✓   8. They can reproduce themselves.

_____ ✓   9. They are well suited to their environments.

_____   10. Offspring do not vary from their parents.

_____   11. They can travel from location to location.

_____   12. They have feelings.

Thinking and Writing About What You Have Learned

Answer the following in complete sentences. Think (or talk about the questions with a classmate) before writing.

1. In reading material that contains technical terms, the reader sometimes has to work on understanding the meanings of those terms. A good strategy is to make your own glossary of terms with definitions to use in study. Write definitions of the following terms. Refer to the selection in writing answers.
   a. atoms

b. enzymes

c. macromolecules

d. photosynthesis

2. Write a paragraph in your notebook in which you explain in your own words one characteristic of living things. Pick the characteristic that to you is the most striking one. You may be asked to read your paragraph to the class and tell why you picked that characteristic as the most striking one.

SELECTION 3: THE NEW COLOSSUS

Getting Ready to Read

1. *Preview the selection that follows to figure out what it is about. Read the title and the information about the author. Then answer the questions below in the spaces provided.*

- What is the meaning of the adjective *colossal?* If you do not know its meaning, check in the glossary before reading. _____
- Check the glossary (under the term *colossus*) to find out what the Colossus of Rhodes was. What was it? Where did it stand? _____
  _____
  _____

  Read the paragraph that introduces the poem.

- Who wrote the poem? What was her background? Why do you think she wrote this poem? _____
  _____
  _____
- Predict: What is the "New Colossus"? _____
- What is the topic of the selection? _____
2. Next think about what you already know about the topic. What does the topic make you think of? Why is the topic important? Make an idea web in the following space. Put the topic in the center. Extending outward from the center, record what you already know about this topic.

Topic: _____

3. Now set your purpose for reading. Remember that this is a poem that you are going to read, and in writing poetry rather than prose, authors are often more concerned about expressing feelings than expressing facts. Because the author's purpose is different, your purpose may be something other than to get information. Write your purpose for reading here. _____

_____

As you read Selection 3, keep your purpose in mind.

Reading with Meaning

THE NEW COLOSSUS

Emma Lazarus

Emma Lazarus was born in New York City. Throughout her life, which was short, Ms. Lazarus had two major interests: the Jewish people who had come to America and poetry. Her poem "The New Colossus" is engraved on the base of the Statute of Liberty, which is located in New York Harbor near Ellis Island.

Not like the brazen giant of Greek fame,
With conquering limbs astride from land to land;
Here at out sea-washed, sunset gates shall stand
A mighty woman with a torch, whose flame
Is the imprisoned lightning, and her name
Mother of Exiles. From her beacon-hand
Glows world-wide welcome; her mild eyes command
The air-bridged harbor that twin cities frame.
"Keep, ancient lands, your storied pomp!" cries she
With silent lips. "Give me your tired, your poor,
Your huddled masses yearning to breathe free,
The wretched refuse of your teeming shore.
Send these, the homeless, tempest-tost to me,
I lift my lamp beside the golden door!"

Checking for Understanding

1. Who is the "mighty woman with a torch"? *Statue of Liberty*
2. What name does Emma Lazarus give to this "mighty woman"? *Mother of Exiles*
3. Why do you think Ms. Lazarus gave the "mighty woman" this name? Think about Ms. Lazarus's background and interests as you answer this question.

   _____

   _____

   _____

4. To whom is Ms. Lazarus referring when she writes about the "huddled masses yearning to breathe free"? *people*
5. How does the poet feel about those "huddled masses"? _____

   _____

   _____

6. How did this poem make you feel? _____

   _____

   _____

Thinking and Writing Based on What You Have Read

In the poem "The New Colossus," Emma Lazarus speaks for the Statue of Liberty. Try your hand at poetry. Write a few lines in which you pretend to be an inanimate, or nonliving, object, such as Niagara Falls, The Golden Gate Bridge in San Francisco harbor, the ship *The Queen Elizabeth II,* the faces cut in the rock at Mt. Rushmore. Do not worry about rhyming or producing a perfect poem; your purpose as a writer is to try to get down some thoughts and feelings.

EXTENDING WHAT YOU HAVE LEARNED

Reviewing the Strategies

In this chapter, you have been applying the three steps of the Getting-Ready-to-Read Strategy. What are those three steps? Outline them here:

1.

2.

3.

Reread the directions in the introductory paragraph on the first page of this chapter. If you followed those directions before reading the chapter, you were applying the Getting-Ready-to-Read Strategy. You will find similar directions at the beginning of each chapter to encourage you to preview, or survey, the chapter before reading it.

Incidentally, most college textbooks leave some blank space at the beginning of chapters. You can use that space to jot down what you know about the topic before reading and some questions you hope to answer through reading. In short, fill the blank space found at chapter beginnings with an idea web as described in Chapter 1.

Applying the Strategies to Your Independent Reading

Find a selection that you want to read or one that has been assigned to you in a course you are taking. Apply the three steps of the Getting-Ready-to-Read Strategy before reading it.

- Record here the topic of the selection. _____

- Make an idea web. Record the topic of the selection in the middle of a page. From that hub, draw lines outward. At the ends of the lines, write down the subtopics. Next to the subtopics, record what you already know about them before reading.

- Establish a purpose before reading based on your idea web. _____

2

Unlocking the Meaning of Words: Using Context Clues

Before reading the chapter, read the title, the stated objective, and the headings and subheadings. Ask yourself: What is the topic of the chapter? In the space above and beside the chapter number, jot down what you already know about that topic. Then in the space below the chapter number, jot down at least two questions you hope to answer through reading the chapter.

OBJECTIVE

In this chapter, you will develop strategies for figuring out the meaning of an unfamiliar word through the use of context clues, or the surrounding words in a sentence. Specifically you will learn how to use

1. definitions built directly into a sentence,
2. synonyms placed near the word,
3. explanations and descriptions given in the paragraph,
4. words that express contrasting, or opposite, meanings,
5. the overall sense, or meaning, of a sentence.

INTRODUCTION—UNLOCKING THE MEANING OF UNFAMILIAR WORDS

As you read, at times you may meet a word that is unfamiliar to you. How do you approach such a word? What can you do to figure out its meaning?

One approach is to use the **context** (or the surrounding words in the sentence) as a clue to meaning. Sometimes clues are very explicit; the author of a text builds a definition of a difficult term into the sentence or sets a synonym, a word with almost the same meaning, near the unfamiliar term.

For example, what is a synonym? In the previous paragraph, the phrase "a word with almost the same meaning" defines the term *synonym*. Similarly, the definition of the word *context* is built directly into the text and is set off by parentheses—"the surrounding words in the sentence."

In other cases, clues are not set forth so clearly. You must consider the entire sentence in which a word is used and even surrounding sentences to figure out the meaning of an unfamiliar word. For example, study the sentence in the second paragraph in which the word *explicit* is used. The sentence reads, "Clues are very explicit; the author has built a definition of a difficult term right into the sentence." What does that explanation tell you about the meaning of the word *explicit?* Does it not hint to you that when things are explicit, they are very clear, very apparent?

But there is another clue to the meaning of "explicit" incorporated in the text. The fourth paragraph begins, "In other cases, clues are not so clearly set forth." Here is a contrast to the sentence, "Sometimes clues are very explicit." Working with the two sentences together, you begin to get the idea that *explicit* means "clearly set forth." To figure out the meaning of *explicit* by using context clues, you would have had to use opposite, or contrasting, expressions as well as the overall meaning of the sentence.

Sometimes the only clue to the meaning of a word is the overall meaning of the sentence. In this case, you may find it helpful to substitute a word that you know for the unfamiliar one to see whether it makes sense. What you are actually doing is seeing whether the word you know works in that context. If it does, it can give you a clue to the meaning of the unfamiliar word. For example, in the sentence "The thirsty man yearned for a drink of water," you might say to yourself: "I can substitute the word *craved* for *yearned*. Therefore, *yearned* may mean the same as *craved;* the thirsty man wanted a drink very badly." Figure 2.1 summarizes useful types of context clues and examples of each.

In sum, when you encounter an unfamiliar word in reading, you should look at the surrounding words in the sentence. You should study

- definitions, synonyms, and explanations built directly into a sentence;
- contrasting phrases and words of opposite meaning (antonyms) found close by; and
- the overall meaning of the sentence in which the word occurs.

If you are still not sure of the meaning of an important word, check the glossary of the book or a dictionary.

The Clue	An Example	Notes About the Example
Definition	*Archaeology* is the scientific study of prehistoric cultures by excavation of their remains.	Definition is given directly in the sentence.
	Through *archaeology,* the scientific study of prehistoric cultures by excavation of their remains, we have learned much about our human ancestors.	Definition is given next to the term, set off by commas.
	Through *archaeology*—the scientific study of prehistoric cultures by excavation of their remains—we have learned much about our human ancestors.	Definition is given next to the term, set off by dashes.
	Through *archaeology* (the scientific study of prehistoric cultures by excavation of their remains), we have learned much about our human ancestors.	Definition is given next to the term, set off in parentheses.
Description	A *paramecium* is a microscopic organism. Made up of one small cell, the paramecium is shaped like a slipper and has a deep groove down its side. It lives in fresh water.	A complete description is included that gives a complete picture of the object being defined.
Synonym (word with the same meaning)	Reducing the blood cholesterol has a number of *beneficial* results. One positive outcome is a lessening of the chances of heart attack.	The word *positive* is set near its synonym, *beneficial.* You can relate *beneficial* to *positive,* and in that way figure out the meaning of *beneficial.*
Antonym (word with the opposite meaning)	Her taste tends toward *pastels.* In contrast, I prefer sharp colors like bright red or deep purple.	The word *pastels* is set near a phrase with nearly the opposite meaning. Using the words *in contrast,* you can pick up the contrast and reason that pastels are less bright, more muted.

Figure 2.1 *Context Clues*

PRACTICING USING CONTEXT CLUES

Use the context of these sentences to figure out the meaning of each italicized word. Circle the term that is closest in meaning to the italicized one. Jot down next to each item the sentence clue you used to find the meaning (e.g., definition, synonym, or explanation given in the text; word of opposite meaning found close by; the overall meaning of the sentence). Reread Figure 2.1 if you have trouble using context clues.

1. She took some deep breaths to *alleviate* the nervousness she felt before the swim meet.
   a. lessen
   b. motivate
   c. elevate
   d. evoke

2. He *brooded* over the loss of his summer job, wondering if anything he might have said had made a difference.
   a. forgot
   b. paid a great deal of money
   c. worried
   d. hatched

3. He felt *contempt* for all those who would not stand up for their beliefs.
   a. respect
   b. scorn
   c. love
   d. concern

4. She did her exercises each day at the hour *designated;* when she became sick, however, she could not exercise when she was supposed to.
   a. that was assigned
   b. that she requested
   c. that was best for her
   d. that was part of her design

5. It's hard to do an *improvisation* in drama class, because you have to make up your lines as you go along.
   a. bad performance
   b. a good performance
   c. a performance without preparation
   d. a performance done alone

6. The shy boy spoke so softly, his voice was practically *inaudible.*
   a. unable to be heard
   b. unable to be enjoyed
   c. unable to be seen
   d. without variation

7. We saw the axe neatly *cleave* the board in two.
   a. make into something else
   b. split
   c. hold up
   d. make clean

8. When she first began training, she was a *novice* at the sport.
   a. an expert
   b. a young woman
   c. a beginner
   d. a helper

9. As the wind grew even stronger, the mountain climber came *perilously* close to losing his grip.
   a. dangerously
   b. practically

    c. permanently

    d. ridiculously

10. His movements were so *subtle,* I was hardly aware that he was moving at all.

    a. clear

    (b.) slight

    c. extreme

    d. wonderful

11. The paintings in her collection appealed to my *aesthetic* sense.

    a. philosophical

    b. mathematical

    c. scientific

    (d.) artistic

12. The cat jumped from one window ledge to the next with amazing *agility;* we were impressed at the ease with which the animal made the difficult jumps.

    (a.) nimbleness

    b. speed

    c. clumsiness

    d. care

MORE PRACTICE WITH CONTEXT CLUES

Here are some sentences from the introduction to a college physical science textbook. In each segment of text, there is an italicized word or phrase. Use the context to figure out the meaning of that word. Write the meaning in the space provided. Then write down an explanation of how you unlocked the meaning. The first two are completed as a model of how to think out the meaning.

ON GEOLOGY

1. It is morning and you are having breakfast in the kitchen. You test your cup of coffee to see how hot it is and *leisurely* unfold the newspaper.

    "Leisurely—it is breakfast time, morning. It appears that you are getting ready to drink your coffee and that you are relaxing, because you are going to read the newspaper. *Leisurely* must mean 'taking your time'—in a relaxed, unhurried way."

2. As usual, you think, there is bad news in the world. An earthquake in Chile has left many dead and thousands homeless. They say the *intensity* of the earthquake was 8.1 on the Richter scale, whatever that means.

    "The Richter scale must be a scale for measuring earthquakes. The intensity on this scale was 8.1. The 8.1 must tell how great the earthquake was—how powerful. *Intensity* must mean strength of force."

3. Hawaii is *bracing* for the arrival of large sea waves triggered by the quake.

4. Another item catches your eye: "Flooding in the Midwest. Several towns *inundated,* and men paddling boats through the streets."

5. At the bottom of the page the newspaper notes that scientists are still observing a new volcano that appeared a few days ago in the North Atlantic. The volcano is *spewing* out ash and cinders amid thunderous explosions.

6. You turn the page and take another sip of coffee. Ah, here are, perhaps, more *relevant* matters on the local news front.

7. In addition to the *furor* over the severe pollution of the lake, a manufacturer is accused of polluting the groundwater supply by pumping acids and other wastes into a disposal well.

8. In this *hypothetical* situation you started your day, perhaps without realizing it, by reading a series of geological reports.

9. All the items noted share one thing in common: They involve geology. *Geology* is the study of the earth.

10. The *overall* objective of the geologist is to try to answer questions concerning the earth's physical nature, both past and present.

11. Of equal concern to the geologist is the application of this knowledge to certain problems that beset human beings as they *wrest* from the earth the things that they need (e.g., oil, gas, water, metals, construction materials) while still trying to maintain harmony with the environment.

12. In attempting to understand the nature of the earth, geologists study the rocks that make up its outer *crust*.

13. These rocks might be thought of as documents that have *survived* through millions of years yet carry within them the clues to past events.

14. Geologists seek to unlock these secrets by careful study of rock records, not only in their natural outdoor settings, but by subjecting samples of these rocks to further *scrutiny* in the laboratory.

15. In addition the geologist must pay close attention to forces *operative* at the earth's surface (e.g., wind, wave, and stream action) and forces *operative* within the earth.

In the next two sections of this chapter, you will read two selections that contain some words that may be new to you. Use the context in which these words are used to figure out, or analyze, their meanings as you read.

SELECTION 1: NIAGARA

Getting Ready to Read

*Preview the selection that starts on this page. Read the title and first para-
graph. Then answer the following questions.*

- What is the topic of the selection? _Niagara_
- What do you already know about that topic? _It is
a great water fall._
_____

- What kind of information do you think this article will tell you about the
topic? _____
_____
_____

Reading with Meaning

*Read the article. Think about the italicized words as you read. Use the con-
text in which they are used to predict their meaning. Write that meaning in the
margin as you go along. If you have trouble, you may want to check the glossary.*

NIAGARA

In 1678 LaSalle led an *expedition* through the Great Lakes region.
On the way from Lake Erie to Lake Ontario an extraordinary scene
awaited the party. From a distance they heard a thunderous roar and saw
great billowing clouds *shrouding* the landscape. At closer range they
watched in horror and amazement as the Niagara River plunged head-on
into a "fearful *abyss*" they estimated to be 500 to 600 feet deep.

News of Niagara Falls spread throughout Europe after LaSalle's
chaplain, Louis Hennepin, published two widely read accounts in 1683
and 1697. The latter contained an imaginative picture of Niagara Falls
which remained the only representation of the *cataract* for the next
several decades. Few reports of the New World fascinated readers as
Hennepin's did; even after eighteenth-century explorers had noted his
exaggerations (the cataract is about 160 feet high, rather than 500 or 600),
Niagara Falls retained its grip on the European imagination.

Subsequent travelers agreed with Hennepin that Niagara's fearful
drop, impressive breadth, and thunderous waters made it "the finest and
at the same time the most awful *cascade* in the world."

Widely considered the most *sublime* landscape on earth, Niagara
gradually shed its fearful aspect and took on holy meaning. James
Fenimore Cooper described the Falls in 1848 as a "signal instance of the
hand of the Creator." Others had profound religious experiences at
Niagara: Harriet Beecher Stowe, who visited in 1834, was among those
who claimed to have entered a *trance-like* state in which she sensed God's
presence in the cataract's rushing water and ever-present rainbow.

Niagara Falls was thought to *embody* national as well as religious

New York State Department of Commerce.

Figure 2.2 *Niagara Falls—How does Niagara Falls differ today from the Falls as seen by the early explorers?*

qualities. A *symbol* of the New World from the time of Hennepin, Niagara's great size and vitality *manifested* the unique features of America; after visiting in 1834, John Quincy Adams declared patriotically that Americans should be proud to have at their doorstep "what no other nation on earth has . . . one of the most wonderful works of God." No traveler felt he had seen America until he had seen Niagara, and many trips to this country were made with the sole object of seeing the great cataract.

Attracted by Niagara's *scenic* splendor and *profound* significance, artists and writers flocked to the cataract with the intention of capturing its *"essence."* The Falls became the subject of Charles Dickens and Walt Whitman (both of whom visited in the 1840s), and of virtually every member of the Hudson River School of landscape painting. Nevertheless, most people agreed with *ornithologist* John James Audubon, who, after visiting in 1824, declared that "not all the pictures ever made, or all the descriptions ever written, could *evoke* more than a glimmer" of Niagara's splendor. (447 words)

Checking Understanding of Featured Words

Circle the definition for each item. Base your answers on the way the words are used in the selection. Reread the sentence in the selection if you hit a snag. Then check the glossary.

1. expedition
   a. show or display of various things
   b. a slowing-down process
   c. a group of persons making a journey for a purpose
   d. the act of releasing air from the lungs through the nose or mouth

2. shrouding
   a. planting with bushes
   b. making loud noises with the vocal cords and mouth
   c. moving one's shoulders or arms to indicate not knowing
   d. covering or cutting off from view

3. abyss
   a. a seemingly bottomless pit or depth
   b. a person associated with a monastery or religious home
   c. an infected wound or sore
   d. the use of someone or something to injure or damage

4. cataract
   a. an extreme misfortune or tragic event
   b. a large waterfall over a cliff, or precipice
   c. a religious question-and-answer list
   d. a legal paper that promises certain things will be done

5. exaggeration
   a. an overstatement, or misrepresentation, beyond the truth
   b. an abnormal sense of power or importance
   c. a large collection of things
   d. an annoyance

6. subsequent
   a. related
   b. coming later or after
   c. coming before
   d. falling short of the standard

7. cascade
   a. a barrel-shaped container or a box for burial
   b. a holder for audio- or videotape
   c. something rushing forth or falling in quantity
   d. a spectacle

8. sublime
   a. fine in purity or excellence
   b. ugly
   c. crafty
   d. covered with lime

9. trance
   a. a windowlike structure over a door
   b. a state of profound absorption
   c. a disastrous event
   d. a temporary state

10. embody
    a. throw into disorder
    b. involve in a conflict

c. represent, or personify

d. put into the human body

11. symbol
    a. a speech sound that is part of a word
    b. a musical instrument
    c. a person lacking in common sense
    d. something used to represent something else

12. mainfested
    a. showed clearly
    b. showed a list of cargo, as on a ship
    c. put together from parts, as in a factory
    d. infected with bacteria

13. scenic
    a. appearing very thin or drawn
    b. having an odor
    c. relating to views of nature
    d. sinful, amoral

14. profound
    a. extravagant, lavish
    b. abusive, vulgar
    c. having depth, extending far below the surface
    d. discovered in earlier times

15. essence
    a. the most significant property of a thing
    b. a material that produces an odor when burned
    c. an example of something
    d. an agreement with someone's actions

16. ornithologist
    a. a dentist that straightens teeth
    b. an artist who works with ornamental objects
    c. a person who interprets handwriting
    d. a person who specializes in the study of birds

17. evoke
    a. annoy or bother
    b. speak out of turn
    c. awaken suddenly
    d. call forth, or summon

SELECTION 2: THE COMPUTER AS MIND TOOL

Getting Ready to Read

Rapidly look over the following selection before reading: Quickly read the title and first paragraph. Then return here and answer these questions:

• What is the topic of the selection? _____

• What thoughts does this topic bring to your mind? _____

_____

_____

Reading with Meaning

Now read the selection, keeping this special question in mind: What is the meaning of each technical term used? To answer this question, relate the term to the context in which it occurs.

THE COMPUTER AS A MIND TOOL
Patrick McKeown

In *Megatrends,* his popular book on the direction of Western society, John Naisbitt discusses the many trends that currently affect our lives. One important concept that he presents is the **information society**—that is, a society in which the majority of the workers are involved in the transmittal, or sending, of information. Naisbitt notes that we have undergone a transition from an agrarian society to an industrial society to the current information society.

The tools for such a society have existed for some time. These tools include the adding machine, the typewriter, the file cabinet, the television, and the telephone. The adding machine helps us work with numbers, the typewriter facilitates our work with characters, the file cabinet stores information in an easily retrievable fashion, the television portrays our ideas in pictures, and the telephone allows us to communicate with others instantaneously.

However, the key element in the transition from an industrial society to an information society is a ''wonder'' called a computer. The agrarian society depended on the metal plow and wheel, and the industrial society depended on the steam engine. The information society depends on the computer. Because the computer facilitates the work of the mind rather than manual labor, we refer to it as a mind tool—that is, a tool that extends, but does not replace, the human mind.

The key idea behind the computer as a mind tool is that it performs all of the operations performed by the adding machine, typewriter, file cabinet, television, and telephone. On a computer, we can manipulate numbers as we do on a calculator (add, subtract, divide, multiply, and so on), we can manipulate letters of the alphabet as we do on a typewriter, and we can have the computer draw pictures based on these manipulations. Any of these symbols may be stored within the computer. Finally, we can communicate with other computer users over a telephone line. If a computer can do all of these things, just exactly how would it be described? Briefly, a **computer** is a machine that stores and manipulates symbols based on a series of user instructions called a program. This ability to execute a list of instructions differentiates the computer from a calculator or other office machines.

In addition to the computer's ability to perform all these tasks, two important characteristics of the computer make it the catalyst that generated the information society. These characteristics are speed and accuracy. The speed of a computer's operations is measured in *nanoseconds*—billionths of a second—and the computer does *exactly* what it is instructed to do. These two characteristics can also lead to problems when the computer is given the wrong instructions. In this case, the computer quickly performs incorrect operations! (463 words)

Checking for Understanding of Words

In the selection, circle the nine words or phrases listed below. Then circle the phrases in the selection that give you clues as to the meaning of each of the circled items. Write the definitions in the space below. If you are unsure of a meaning, check the glossary. Be ready to tell how you unlocked the meaning of each word or phrase.

Being able to figure out the meanings of technical terms is very important as you read college texts. You can use this same strategy in your college reading:

- Circle each unfamiliar term.
- Circle words or phrases that are clues to the meaning of the term.
- Write in your notebook or in the margin of your textbook definitions of words you will need to know.

1. an information society _____

_____

2. a mind tool _a nick name for a computer_

3. manipulate numbers _add, subtact_

4. a computer _____

5. nanosecond _a billion of a second_

6. a computer program _tool use by a computer_

7. agrarian (The definition is not given explicitly. You must figure it out from words used in relation to it—"plow and wheel.")_____

_____

8. manual labor (The definition is not given explicitly. You must figure it out by contrasting manual labor with "the work of the mind.") _____

_____

9. catalyst (Figure this one out based on the meaning of *generated*. If you run into problems, check the glossary.) _____

_____

CHAPTER VOCABULARY REVIEW: MORE PRACTICE WITH CONTEXT CLUES

Using Context Clues

Select the word from the list that best fits the context of each sentence. Use each word only once. Consult the glossary for help if you need it.

a. abyss   d. exaggeration   g. profound
b. cataracts   e. expedition   h. scenic
c. essence   f. manifested   i. shrouded

1. The _____ of the Magna Carta between King John of England and the barons was that the King agreed that English people had civil and political liberties.

2. The signing of the Magna Carta in 1215 A.D. had a/an *profound* effect on government in England and later in America.

3. To say that the Magna Carta is one of the major documents of political history would not be a/an *exaggeration*

4. Lewis and Clark explored the Louisiana territory and the lands extending to the Pacific; their *expedition* took place between 1803 and 1806.

5. Before the Lewis and Clark expedition, members of Congress *manifested* _____ great interest in the western regions of North America.

6. The members of the Lewis and Clark expeditionary force marveled at the *scenic* _____ wonders they saw.

7. The explorers looked down into a seemingly bottomless pit, a/an _____ that was dark and frightening.

8. The land was _____ with thick mist. The mist covered the land so thoroughly that the members of the expeditionary force had to make camp.

9. The explorers encountered many _____ in the Yellowstone region. The men were amazed at the great heights from which the water fell.

Using More Context Clues

Put one of these words in each sentence blank.

a. cascade   c. ornithologist   e. subsequent
b. evoked   d. trancelike   f. symbol

1. On *subsequent* visits, he investigated the problems he had not solved on previous visits.

2. My visit to his home *evoked* many happy memories of previous visits.

3. The American flag is the *symbol* of our country.

4. Her eyes were glazed as she stood in *trancelike* wonder.

5. His interest in birds led him to become a/an *ornithologist*

6. When he jerked the dish towel, a/an *cascade* of dishes crashed to the floor.

Using Words in Sentences

   Try to write a sentence with a context clue that hints at the meaning of the word. If you have a problem, model your sentences after the sentences on pages 22–23 or those in the glossary.

1. alleviate _____

_____

2. brooded _____

_____

3. contempt _____

_____

4. designated _____

_____

5. improvisation _____

_____

6. inaudible _____

_____

7. cleave _____

_____

8. novice _____

_____

9. perilously _____

_____

10. subtle _____

_____

11. aesthetic _____

_____

12. agility _____

_____

Doing More with Context

Put these words into the sentence blanks. Use the context to decide. Use each word only once. Be ready to explain the sentence clue you used.

a. bracing	e. leisurely	h. scrutiny
b. hypothetical	f. operative	i. spewing
c. intensity	g. relevant	j. wrest
d. inundated		

1. Our trip was a _____ one; we took our time. As a result we returned home relaxed and full of energy.

2. Make sure that all the information you put into your report is _____; unrelated ideas will confuse the reader.

3. The weather reporter predicted a storm of great _____ with much rain and wind.

4. Because the volcano was _____ out lava, we could not go near it.

5. The professor subjected the students' papers to careful _____ before assigning a grade.

6. I tried to _____ the gun from his hand, but I could not get it away.

7. Because we were _____ for a severe storm, we were pleasantly surprised when there was only a little shower.

8. On the exam, we had to devise a _____ plan telling what we would have done if we had been there.

9. Near the end of the semester, students often feel _____ with work; so much work comes their way that they do not know where to begin.

10. We studied the forces _____ within society during the Civil War.

EXTENDING WHAT YOU HAVE LEARNED

Reviewing Your Understanding of Context Clues

In your notebook, write a paragraph in which you present at least three steps to use in attacking new words you meet in reading. Be sure to talk about context clues.

Applying the Strategies to Your Reading

1. Read a column from the editorial page of a newspaper. As you read, underline three or four words that are rather new to you. In the margin of the article, jot down the meanings of the words as you figured them out from the context. Be ready to share your new words with the class and tell how you figured out the meanings.

2. Starting in Chapter 4, before each selection to be read, you will find sentences with new words from the selection. Use your understanding of context clues to unlock the meanings of these words as you work through this text during the semester.

Building a Knowledge Base for Reading

Circle the names of Niagara Falls, Lake Erie, and Lake Ontario on the map on page 11. Locate and label the St. Lawrence River.

3

Unlocking the Meaning of Words: Using Word-Structure Clues

Before reading the chapter, read the title, the stated objective, and the headings and subheadings. Ask yourself: What is the topic of the chapter? In the space above and beside the chapter number, jot down what you already know about the topic. Then in the space below the chapter number, jot down at least two questions you hope to answer through reading the chapter.

OBJECTIVE

In this chapter, you will develop strategies for figuring out the meaning of an unfamiliar word through the use of word structures, or the parts that make up the word. Specifically you will learn how to use

1. roots (or basic word parts) and
2. affixes (prefixes and suffixes).

INTRODUCTION—UNLOCKING THE MEANING OF UNFAMILIAR WORDS

Understanding how words in our language are constructed can help you become a better reader, especially when you deal with content filled with technical terms. That is because the English language contains many words built from roots and affixes. A root is a basic unit of meaning in the language. Some English roots—*sing,* for example—can function as a word; from that root word, we can build *singing* and *singer.* Some word parts come from other languages, such as Latin and Greek; we generally do not use these roots as words in our language, but we put them together to form words.

Affixes include both prefixes (meaningful units added to the beginnings of words and roots) and suffixes (meaningful units added to the ends of words and roots).

An example of a commonly used root that is from Latin is *astro,* which means "star." Words formed from this root include

astronomy—scientific study of the heavens;

astronaut—traveler beyond the earth;

astrology—pseudoscientific study of the effects of heavenly bodies on people's lives;

asterisk—star-shaped symbol (*).

aster—star-shaped flower.

Based on your understanding of the root *astro* and your ability to use context clues, what is the meaning of the underlined word in this sentence?

He asked an *astronomically* high price for towing my car to the garage.

To figure out, or analyze, the meaning of *astronomically,* you might reason in this way: *Astro* means "star." Stars are very high in the sky. *Astronomically* must mean "high as the stars." That fits the context of the sentence. An astronomically high price is a very, very high one. Both word structure and context clues help you unlock the meaning of *astronomically.*

What is the meaning of the word *astronomer?* Analyzing the structure of the word, you might reason in this way: *Astro* means "star," *astronomy* is the study of stars and heavenly bodies, *-er* is a suffix that sometimes means "a person who." *Astronomer* is someone who studies the stars and heavenly bodies. Analyze the word *astrologer.* What is its meaning?

Agri is another Latin root used in English. In the last chapter, you learned that the word *agrarian* refers to the land or agriculture. From that usage, you can predict that the root *agri* means "of the land or soil."

A widely used root is *graph* or *grapho.* It means drawn or written. Predict the meanings of the italicized words using both word structure and context clues.

1. She described the accident in such *graphic* terms that I felt I had been there. *Graphic* means
    a. clear or vivid.
    b. terrible.
    c. boastful.
    d. unpleasant.

2. Her brother decided to study *graphic arts* because he could draw well. The *graphic arts*
    a. involve physical activity.
    b. relate to driving a car.

Root	Meaning	Example of Word
astro	star	astronomical, astronaut
agri	of land or soil	agrarian, agriculture
graph	written	graphic, phonograph
tele	distant	telegraph, telephone

Figure 3.1 *Summary Chart of Word Parts*

    c. relate to drawing, etching, or painting.
    d. relate to a mathematical graph.
3. Guglielmo Marconi was the inventor of the first successful wireless *telegraph*. The *telegraph* is a
    a. device for sending messages or signals over a distance.
    b. picture tube.
    c. computer.
    d. television set.

In figuring out the meaning of *telegraph,* you may want to draw on the meaning of another very commonly used root—*tele.* It means "distant," or "sent over a distance." Other words that are built with *tele* include *telegram* (a message sent by telegraph), *telescope* (an instrument for making distant objects appear nearer), *television* (the broadcasting of a moving image over a distance). Think about the meanings of these words: *telethermometer, telepathy, teletypewriter.*

As you read and encounter unfamiliar words, especially technical terms, try to break those words into component parts. Doing that may help you figure out the meanings of the words you do not know.

COMMON WORD-BUILDING ELEMENTS

Memorizing word parts and their meanings will not help you become a better reader. Being aware that words are made up of meaningful parts and using that awareness to figure out the meaning of words as you read will increase your comprehension.

Increasing Your Awareness of Word Parts

Here is a list of commonly used word parts and their meanings as well as the definition of one word built from the part. In the blank column, write the word that fits the definition. Remember that you have already learned that bio- *means "life."*

Word Part	Meaning of Part	Word	Meaning of the Word
1. -scope	instrument for viewing	_____	an instrument for viewing the heavens
2. micro-	very small	_____	an instrument for viewing small things
3. -ology	the study of	_____	the study of living things

4. -ologist	one who studies	_____	one who studies small living things (Note: You must use both *bio-* and *micro-*)
5. anthropo-	human person	_____	study of the development of humankind
6. archeo-	ancient times	_____	one who studies life in ancient times
7. astro-	star	_____	study of heavens to predict human events
8. chrono-	time	_____	study of time
9. geo-	earth	_____	one who studies the earth and its forms
10. hydro-	water	_____	study of water
11. neuro-	nerves	_____	a doctor who specializes in study of the nervous system
12. patho-	disease	_____	a person who studies tissues for evidence of disease
13. psycho-	mind	_____	study of human behavior
14. socio-	social	_____	a person who studies human society
15. theo-	god	_____	study of religion

Working with Word Parts

Some word elements are clues to number meanings. For example,

mono-	means	one	*deca-*	means	ten
bi-	means	two	*cent-*	means	hundred
tri-	means	three	*mille-*	means	thousand
quadri-	means	four	*multi-*	means	many
quint-	means	five	*omni-*	means	all

Based on the meanings given above, choose the correct answer.

1. In feudal times, the king was *omnipotent*.
   a. everywhere
   b. all powerful
   c. respected
   d. feared

2. In 1876, the United States celebrated the nation's *centennial*.
   a. ten-year anniversary
   b. hundred-year anniversary
   c. two hundred-year anniversary
   d. thousand-year anniversary

3. In 1976, the United States celebrated the nation's *bicentennial.*
   a. ten-year anniversary
   b. hundred-year anniversary
   c. two hundred-year anniversary
   d. thousand-year anniversary

4. How many *centimeters* are in a meter?
   a. one
   b. ten
   c. one hundred
   d. one thousand

5. How many *milliliters* are in a liter?
   a. one
   b. ten
   c. one hundred
   d. one thousand

6. The *decade* ending in 1870 saw the end of the Civil War. How long is a *decade?*
   a. one year
   b. ten years
   c. twenty years
   d. forty years

7. Because my friend is *bilingual,* he got a job as a translator. *Bilingual* means
   a. able to speak two languages.
   b. able to travel.
   c. very intelligent.
   d. born outside the country.

8. Great Britain, France, and the United States entered into a *trilateral* trade agreement. *Trilateral* means
   a. having to do with business.
   b. three-way.
   c. having to do with war.
   d. having to do with a triumphant victory.

9. Mr. Fitzpatrick fainted when he heard his wife had given birth to *quintuplets.* How many children were born?
   a. three
   b. four
   c. five
   d. six

10. The *quadricentennial* of the United States will take place in
    a. 2076.
    b. 2176.
    c. 2276.
    d. 2376.

11. The popular leader had a *multitude* of friends.
    a. ten
    b. one hundred
    c. one thousand
    d. a great number

12. No one can live for a *millenium*. How long is a *millenium?*
    a. ten years
    b. one hundred years
    c. two hundred years
    d. one thousand years

13. For each of the word parts given, write a word based on the part and the definition of the word. Use a dictionary if you have trouble building words. Do not use words from the sentences above.

Part	Word	Meaning
a. mono-	_____	_____
b. bi-	_____	_____
c. tri-	_____	_____
d. quadri-	_____	_____
e. quint-	_____	_____
f. deca-	_____	_____
g. cent-	_____	_____
h. mille-	_____	_____
i. multi-	_____	_____
j. omni-	_____	_____

COMMON PREFIXES

A prefix is a letter or group of letters added to the beginnings of words. An example of a common prefix is *re-*, which means "again." To *reconsider* is simply to consider again. What meanings do you assign to these words?

readjust _____

reappoint _____

reattach _____

reassure _____

Seeing the prefix at the beginning of these words and assigning the meaning of "again" to it, helps you unlock the meaning of the whole word. However, not all words that begin with *re-* are built from the prefix. Cases in point are *read, ready,* and *reason.*

Seeing Prefixes in Words

See if you can figure out the meanings of the prefixes underlined in these sentences:

1. Astrology is often considered <u>pseudo</u>science because astrologers try to predict human events based on the stars.
   a. before

    b. after
    c. against
    d. false
    e. not

2. As part of his <u>pre</u>operative treatment, he had to take antibiotics so that he would be ready for surgery.
    a. before
    b. after
    c. against
    d. false
    e. not

3. During the <u>post</u>war period, many people joined in to clear away the rubble.
    a. before
    b. after
    c. against
    d. false
    e. not

4. The man joined the <u>anti</u>war movement because he was against violence in any form.
    a. before
    b. after
    c. against
    d. false
    e. not

5. Because of his illness, he was <u>un</u>able to come.
    a. before
    b. after
    c. against
    d. false
    e. not

6. Two-year-old children are often <u>hyper</u>active.
    a. between
    b. within
    c. over
    d. not

7. Although I wanted to go, it became <u>im</u>possible; I had to stay home.
    a. between
    b. within
    c. over
    d. not

8. Because she was so unfriendly, I began to <u>dis</u>like her.
    a. between
    b. within
    c. over
    d. not

9. When I traveled from New Hampshire to Massachusetts, I took the <u>inter</u>state highway.
    a. between
    b. within

    c. over

    d. not

10. Because he hauled products only from Los Angeles to San Francisco, he was said to be involved in <u>intra</u>state commerce.

    a. between

    b. within

    c. over

    d. not

11. Because the ship was completely <u>sub</u>merged, we could not see it.

    a. under

    b. above

    c. around

    d. across

    e. before

12. The <u>trans</u>continental railroad connected the west and east coasts.

    a. under

    b. above

    c. around

    d. across

    e. before

13. The Revolutionary War <u>ante</u>dates the Civil War.

    a. under

    b. above

    c. around

    d. across

    e. before

14. The <u>super</u>intendent was in charge of the entire operation.

    a. under

    b. above

    c. around

    d. across

    e. before

15. Magellan's ship was the first to <u>circum</u>navigate the globe.

    a. under

    b. above

    c. around

    d. across

    e. before

Making a Table of Prefixes

Using the answers to the previous exercise, complete this summary chart of prefixes. Make your sample word one not used in the sentences above.

Prefix	Prefix Meaning	Sample Word	Word Meaning
1. pseudo-	_____	_____	_____
2. pre-	_____	_____	_____
3. post-	_____	_____	_____
4. anti-	_____	_____	_____

Prefix	Prefix Meaning	Sample Word	Word Meaning
5. un-	_____	_____	_____
6. im-	_____	_____	_____
7. hyper-	_____	_____	_____
8. dis-	_____	_____	_____
9. inter-	_____	_____	_____
10. intra-	_____	_____	_____
11. sub-	_____	_____	_____
12. trans-	_____	_____	_____
13. ante-	_____	_____	_____
14. super-	_____	_____	_____
15. circum-	_____	_____	_____

SUFFIXES

A suffix is a letter or a group of letters that is added to the end of a word and may change the part of speech of that word. An example of a common suffix is *-ness*. It means "the state of." You have seen it on nouns formed from adjectives, such as *loveliness* (the state of being lovely), *thoughtfulness* (the state of being thoughtful), and *softness* (the state of being soft).

A second suffix you probably know is *-ical* or *-al,* which simply turns a noun into a word that can serve as an adjective. You have seen it on adjectives such as *practical* (adapted for actual use), *societal* (pertaining to society), and *theoretical* (based on theory).

Another common suffix is *-ize,* which means "to make." You have seen it on verbs such as *civilize* (to make civil), *personalize,* (to make personal), and *categorize* (to put into categories).

Still another very common suffix is *-ion,* which means "state of" or "process of." You have seen it on nouns such as *invention* (the process of inventing), *limitation* (the state of being limited), and *innovation* (the process of innovating, or creatively changing).

Here are a few other suffixes. For each suffix, give the meaning of the sample word, reasoning from the meaning of the suffix. Then give an example of another word that contains the suffix.

Suffix	Meaning	Word	Meaning	Word
-able	able to be	likable	_____	_____
-ous or ious	full of	joyous	_____	_____
-ful	full of	peaceful	_____	_____
-y	state of being	rainy	_____	_____
-ify	to make	simplify	_____	_____
-er or -or	a person who	banker	_____	_____

Suffix	Meaning	Word	Meaning	Word
-ist	one who does, is concerned with, or holds certain beliefs	communist	_____	_____

As you read, keep alert for suffixes that may give you a clue to the meaning of an unfamiliar word. Try to see the component parts of the word.

Circle the suffixes in the underlined words. Then write the definition of each word, using word structure and context clues.

1. It was a memorable occasion. I will always remember it. _____
   _____

2. Without innovation the world would stand still. Progress is dependent on innovation. (Reminder: You already know the meaning of novice.) _____
   _____

3. There must be some way of joining the work of the two committees. Good articulation is necessary. _____
   _____

4. The oval arch was a radical departure from the way it was done before. In that respect it was an innovation. _____
   _____

5. Surface changes are not enough. Deep structural changes are required. ___
   _____

6. Scientists are concerned with theoretical ideas as well as with practical applications. _____
   _____

7. Do not confuse him. Try to clarify the situation instead. _____
   _____

In the next three sections of this chapter, you will read three selections. The first deals with roots used in science. The second is a general selection that includes many words built from roots. The third is a selection from a science textbook that also has numerous words built from roots. In reading the last two selections, use your growing familiarity with word parts to unlock complex words as you meet them in context.

SELECTION 1: ATTACKING WORDS IN SCIENCE

Getting Ready to Read

Read the title and the first paragraph of this selection, which is from a paperback book from the National Science Teachers Association called The Language of Science.

- What is the topic of the selection? _____
- What do you already know about that topic? Add words, phrases, and ideas you already know about the topic to this idea web, or cluster.

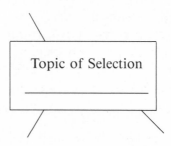

Topic of Selection
_____

Reading with Meaning

Now read the selection, looking particularly for examples of how word meanings can be unlocked through understanding of word parts.

ATTACKING WORDS IN SCIENCE
Alan Mandel

To unlock the meanings of complex scientific words, such as *infraphotodensitometer* and *bathythermograph,* or even to learn to spell them correctly, may appear to be a nearly impossible task. Yet, using some of the clues and word-attack skills to be discussed in this article, you should be able to conquer words such as these and most of the other scientific words you encounter.

Analyzing Words for Meaning

You are familiar with root words, prefixes, and suffixes from your language studies. Most science terms are words composed of a root word and prefixes or suffixes or both. Consider the word *photosynthesis.* Here the root "photo," meaning light, and the root "synthesis," meaning to put together are combined to produce a term which signifies "putting together through the use of light." You probably know photosynthesis as a term which describes the processes by which green plants make food materials in the presence of light. If you didn't know that, the word itself, thus analyzed, would give you a clue to its meaning.

Think of some other "photo" words. *Photograph* implies writing (graphein = to write) by light; add an "er" and we have *photographer. Photometer* suggests a device to measure (meter = measure) light. Indeed, a photometer is used by photographers (people who write or record with light) to determine the amount of light available in order to take a good picture. Going back to *infraphotodensitometer,* we identify "infra" as near the limits of the light spectrum (i.e., infrared) and "density" as referring to the thickness or denseness of a material. Our word then becomes an understandable term which describes a device that measures the density of a material to infrared light energy.

When we look again at *bathythermograph,* we get a clue to "thermo" from the word *thermometer,* which we know is a temperature-measuring instrument. If we know that "bathy" refers to depths under water, we can see that bathythermograph signifies a device that records (writes) the temperature in deep waters.

From these examples, it should be apparent that knowing the meanings and uses of some of the more commonly used scientific root words, prefixes, and suffixes is of primary importance in becoming adept with the scientific vocabulary. Figure 3.2 lists some common combining terms, their meanings, and uses.

Analyzing the Sequence of Word Parts

The arrangement of the parts of a complex word is often an important clue to its meaning. Consider, for example, *photomicrography* and *microphotography.* Knowing the meanings of "photo" and "graphy" and adding that "micro" pertains to very small objects, we can see that both terms are concerned with written records of light energy on a very small scale. Word analysis, using the relative positions of the parts of the word, suggests that microphotography means "small, light-written, recording." It is the process of making extremely small photographic records (on microfilm) of normal-size materials. Photomicrography, on the other hand, indicates "light-written records of tiny materials" and is used generally to describe taking pictures through the microscope.

Origin of Word Parts

Scientific terms and symbols come from Greek, Latin, Arabic, and many other languages. Historically, Greek and Latin were the languages of the learned world, so it is not surprising that much scientific terminology derives from word roots of these languages. Some scientific terms have mixed Greek and Latin roots. (558 words)

Checking for Understanding

Using the information in Figures 3.1 and 3.2, circle the root or roots in each word, indicate the meaning of each root, and propose the meaning of the term.

1. anthropologist _____

_____

2. antibiotic _____

_____

3. genetic _____

_____

4. geology _____

_____

5. aquaphobia _____

_____

Term[a]	Meaning	Example of Use
alb	white	albino
anti	against	antitoxin (opposes poisons)
anthrop	human being, man	anthropology (study of man)
aqua	water	aqueous (watery)
archeo	ancient	archaeology (study of ancient remains)
bar	weight, heaviness	barometer (measures weight of atmosphere)
bio	life	biology
centr	center	centrifuge
claus	an enclosed place	claustrophobia (fear of being confined)
dem	people	demography (study of human populations)
derm	skin	ectodermis
ect	outer	ectodermis (outer skin layer)
end	inner	endodermis (inner skin layer)
ep	upon, atop	epicenter (above the center)
gene	birth, descent	genealogy
ge	earth	geography (mapping of the earth)
graph	write	geography
hydr	water	hydrometer (water meter)
is	equal	isotope (same place in atomic table)
logy	study of	biology, anthropology
lun	moon	lunar (pertaining to the moon)
mes	middle	mesodermis (middle skin layer)
meter	measure	metrology (study of measurement)
muta	change	mutate, mutation
morph	shape, form	morphology (study of form and structure)
nym	name	pseudonym (false name)
omni	all, total	omniscient (all-knowing)
phil	love	aquaphila (love of water)
phob	fear	claustrophobia (fear of being confined)
phon	sound	phonograph
phot	light	photograph
phyt	plant	epiphyte (a plant growing upon another)
pod	foot	pseudopodium ("false foot" of single-celled animal)
prot	early, first	protozoa (first animals)
pseud	false	pseudonym
scien	knowledge	science, omniscient
therm	heat	thermometer
top	place	topography
tox	poison	toxic (poisonous)
zo	animal	zoology

[a]In forming words from these terms, connecting vowels are often used, as will be clear from the examples given. Dictionaries and various authorities may give slightly different forms for terms or roots.

Figure 3.2   *Some Common Combining Terms Used in Science*

Chart courtesy of Alan Mandell and the National Science Teachers Association.

6. photometer _____

_____

7. antonym _____

_____

8. prototype _____

_____

9. dermatology _____

_____

10. omnipresent _____

_____

SELECTION 2: BRUSHING UP ON DINOSAURS

Expanding Your Vocabulary for Reading

In the selection you will read next, you will meet some interesting words. You probably already know the word *dinosaur.* It is made up of two Greek roots, *dino* meaning "terrible" and *saur* meaning "lizard." You can see how that prehistoric animal (an animal living before the days of written records) received its name.

In the selection, you will meet *Tyrannosaurus rex,* who also has an appropriate name. *Tyranno* is a Greek root that means "absolute ruler." *Rex* means "king." Can you define the word *tyrant?* Check the glossary to be sure.

Another root that is important to your understanding of the selection is *paleo.* It means ancient, or old. You probably already know that the suffix *-ology* means "the study of." Based on the meaning of the root and the suffix, you should be able to figure out the meaning of *paleontology.* Again, check the glossary to be sure. Why would someone who studies dinosaurs be called a paleontologist?

Another root is *eco.* It means home, abode, or habitat. *Ecology* is the branch of biology that focuses on the relations between organisms and their environment. An *ecologist* is a person who studies ecology. *Ecological* means "of or relating to organisms and their environment." *Ecological niche* refers to the role of an organism in a community of plants and animals.

Getting Ready to Read

Preview this selection by reading the title, introductory phrase, and first paragraph.

• What does the title "Brushing Up on Dinosaurs" and the first paragraph

tell you about the topic of the selection? _____

_____

• What does the phrase "brushing up" suggest? _____

_____

_____

• What do you already know about that topic? _____

_____

_____

• Read the selection to see if you can use your understanding of word parts to figure out the meanings of complex words in the selection.

Reading with Meaning

Now read the selection. Keep your purpose in mind: to use your understanding of word parts to increase your comprehension. Also read to find out how scientists of today view dinosaurs as compared to the way scientists of the past viewed them.

BRUSHING UP ON DINOSAURS
Stefi Weisburd

When art and science combine, the result can be a remarkably vivid and accurate glimpse into prehistoric life

Robert Bakker met his first dinosaurs in the spring of 1955 in his grandfather's sun room, and he fell in love. There on the coffee table, a terrifying *Tyrannosaurus rex* glowered at a long-necked *Apatosaurus* supping in a swamp—both surrounded by a menagerie of wonderfully exotic creatures that roamed the prehistoric landscape hundreds of millions of years ago. Ten-year-old Bakker had discovered Rudolph Zallinger's Pulitzer prize-winning mural, reproduced that week on the cover of *Life*.

"As soon as I saw it I decided I was going to spend the rest of my life studying dinosaurs," says Bakker, who went on to do just that, becoming a renowned paleontologist and artist in his own right. "That was the first really great color dinosaur mural. It launched an awful lot of careers, including mine."

Figure 3.3 *One of the Great Dinosaurs—Tyrannosaurus rex and the other great dinosaurs of prehistoric times became extinct. Scientists disagree as to why these mighty reptiles died out.*

American Museum of Natural History, New York.

While many, like C. P. Snow in *The Two Cultures,* have lamented the growing abyss between science and the arts, the two are inexorably merged in paleontology, particularly in the reconstruction of dinosaurs and their habitats and behavior. This union of art and science is what makes ancient bones of long-extinct animals come alive. Paintings and sculptures not only spark the public imagination and inspire new ranks of paleontologists, but for scientists they are also an effective means of communicating ideas and exploring new theories.

"Paleontology is a very visual inquiry," notes Bakker. "All paleontologists scribble on napkins at coffee breaks, making sketches to explain their thinking." If they are not artists themselves, most dinosaur paleontologists work closely with artists, some of whom have published scientific works of their own.

Museums have presented displays of dinosaurs. In many of the early displays, dinosaurs were portrayed as violent, clumsy and slovenly beasts, dressed in drab greys, browns and dark greens and standing by themselves. Newer paintings and sculptures project quite a different image of sleeker, more varied and lively animals that lived in socially complex communities and had adapted to almost every ecological niche now occupied by modern mammals and birds.

One of the most important changes that has taken place in the portrayal of dinosaurs is in their posture. Until fairly recently, the convention was to draw many large dinosaurs with their front legs splayed out and bent at the elbows like lizards. But in pictures today, the elbows are straight and the front legs have been pulled under the body, closer to the animal's center of gravity.

The physical portrayal of many dinosaurs has changed in other ways as well. Recent studies have shown that the *Stegosaurus,* which had been portrayed with two rows of bony plates down its back for 100 years, really had just one row. And contemporary illustrators have started to use more vivid colors: mauve, pink, metallic blues and reds. While there is no direct physical evidence to show that dinosaurs were indeed colorful creatures, "this makes a lot of sense," says Bakker, "because dinosaurs are closely related to birds. Colors were undoubtedly used, especially in the mating season."

By studying the mass and distribution of muscles, the mechanics of limbs, fossilized footprints and the newly characterized posture of the dinosaurs, some scientists have concluded that the animals could move at greater speeds than once thought. Bakker, in particular, has championed the idea that dinosaurs were much nimbler than earlier paleontologists believed. His 1969 drawing of a running *Deinonychus* (or "terrible claw," for the lethal, sickle-shaped claws on its feet) shows a very sleek, fast-moving animal.

Bakker has presented evidence that some dinosaurs averaged a walking speed of about 3 miles per hour—about four times as fast as that of present-day lizards and turtles, and comparable to the speeds of moose, deer, bulls and other warm-blooded animals. Because the average cruising speed reflects an animal's metabolism, Bakker argues that many dinosaurs were warm-blooded.

Another perception that has evolved dramatically is that of the social behavior of dinosaurs, which paleontologists have inferred from various kinds of physical evidence. These clues—such as bone beds, created when a group of animals was killed *en masse* by a flood, volcano, or other catastrophe, and fossilized trackways—suggest that both predators and prey traveled in packs or herds. One painting by a Baltimore artist, Gregory Paul, illustrates that the prey were by no means defenseless: A herbivorous *Diplodocus* is rearing up like an elephant to protect the rest of its herd against a carnivorous *Allosaurus,* and is swinging a thick, very lethal, whip-like tale. Trackways also show that some dinosaurs walked side by side as they traveled. Other tracks indicate that meat-eating dinosaurs could swim, leaving the herbivores little chance of escaping in the water, as some scientists had once believed they could.

There is also growing evidence that dinosaurs, like present-day crocodiles, cared for their young after they hatched. Dinosaur eggs were first discovered in the 1920s in the Gobi desert, but it wasn't until a few years ago that communal nesting grounds were found. Paleontologist John Horner discovered a series of nests in Choteau, Montana, that had belonged to duckbilled *Maiasaura.* Because young *Maiasaura* of different ages and sizes were found in nests, some scientists have concluded that parents were protecting and feeding their young until they were large enough to fend for themselves. (890 words)

Checking for Understanding

Give the meaning of each term, based on its structure.

a. paleontology _____

_____

b. ecology _____

_____

c. prehistoric _____

_____

d. dinosaur _____

_____

e. carnivore _____

_____

SELECTION 3: HETEROTROPHS AND AUTOTROPHS

Expanding Your Vocabulary for Reading

As you read the next selection, you will note some words that are built from roots. An example is the word *biosphere,* built from two Greek roots, *bio* meaning "life" and *sphere* meaning "globe." *Biosphere,* or "living globe," refers to the whole surface of the earth where there is life.

As you read, look out for words made up of roots. Circle them as you read. See if you can figure out their meaning using both context and word structure. In the margin, write the meanings of words you circle.

Getting Ready to Read

Preview this selection, which is from an environmental science book, by reading the title and first paragraph and by studying the illustrations.

- What is the topic of the selection? _____
- What do you already know about that topic? _____

  _____

  _____

- What two questions should you be able to answer by the time you finish reading the selection? Use the title to help you write the questions. _____

  _____

  _____

Reading with Meaning

Now read the selection keeping in mind your purpose: to figure out the meaning of technical terms through use of word structure clues.

HETEROTROPHS AND AUTOTROPHS

Daniel Chiras

Living organisms can be categorized by the way they obtain their organic nutrients and energy. Accordingly, they fit into one of two categories: autotrophs and heterotrophs. The common root of these words, *troph* means to feed or nourish.

Autotrophs, or "self-feeders," are organisms capable of making their own foodstuffs. Plants are the major autotrophic organisms in the biosphere, making their own food during photosynthesis.

Another interesting but minor group of autotrophs is the *chemotrophs,* or *chemosynthetic organisms.* These bacteria are capable of capturing energy from certain chemical reactions called oxidation reactions. In chemistry an oxidation reaction is one in which electrons are lost from an atom or molecule. Energy is released during these reactions. The chemotrophs capture energy from the oxidation of a number of chemicals.

All other organisms are called heterotrophs (*hetero = other*). Whereas plants acquire energy from the sun, heterotrophs get their energy by consuming organic matter (plants and animals). Heterotrophs—especially the animals—can be further categorized on the basis of the food source. For instance, heterotrophs that feed exclusively on plants are called herbivores. Deer, elk, and cattle are good examples. Heterotrophs

Figure 3.4   *The Autotrophs—Plants such as these are autotrophs; they make their own food through photosynthesis.*

Figure 3.5   *The Heterotrophs—Animals such as these are heterotrophs; they get their energy by consuming organic matter.*

such as the mountain lion that feed only on other animals are called carnivores. Those heterotrophs that feed on both plants and animals are called omnivores. We human beings are a classic example of omnivores. Heterotrophic organisms such as fungi that feed strictly on dead organic matter are called saprobes, or saprophytes.

Survival of the entire ecosystem ultimately depends on the autotrophs. Without them, herbivores, carnivores, omnivores, and saprobes would have nothing to eat. But autotrophs also depend on heterotrophs in many different ways. Autotrophs and heterotrophs are highly interdependent. Autotrophs capture solar energy and use it to make living tissue, in the process giving off oxygen as a waste product. Heterotrophs consume the plants and oxygen. The plant matter is broken down in a series of carefully controlled reactions that yield small amounts of energy. These reactions produce carbon dioxide and water, both needed by autotrophs to make organic materials. Thus, a full circle is made. The products of one type of organism are essential to the survival of the other. (362 words)

Checking Your Understanding of Word Parts

1. *Here is a list of roots from words in Selection 3. Next to each is the meaning of the root. In the third column, write a word from the selection that contains the root. In the fourth column, write the meaning of the word based on the context and the word structure.*

Root	Meaning of Root	Word with the Root	Meaning of the Word
auto	self	_____	_____
troph	feed	_____	_____
hetero	other	_____	_____
herb	grass	_____	_____
vore	eat, devour	_____	_____
carn	flesh, meat	_____	_____
omni	all	_____	_____
sapro	dead	_____	_____
synthetic (synthesis)	make, or place together	_____	_____
phot	light	_____	_____
chemo	chemical	_____	_____
bio	life	_____	_____
sphere	globe	_____	_____

2. *Match the following items. You may place more than one number in each blank in the left column.*

_____	a. human being	1.	saprobe
_____	b. mountain lion	2.	omnivore
_____	c. fungus	3.	carnivore
_____	d. green plant	4.	herbivore
_____	e. elk	5.	heterotroph
_____	f. cow	6.	autotroph

Writing

Write two paragraphs in your notebook, one in which you tell about autotrophs and one in which you tell about heterotrophs. Writing after reading is an effective way to review what you have read and to firm up your understanding of new terms.

EXTENDING WHAT YOU HAVE LEARNED

Handling Unfamiliar Words in Reading

In Chapters 2 and 3, you have been learning ways of handling unfamiliar words in reading. Here, in summary, are the steps in a strategy for unlocking the meaning of new words.

1. Look at the unfamiliar word in relation to the sentence in which it appears. Ask: Is there something in the sentence that provides a clue to the meaning of the word?
   * Is there a definition built directly into the sentence? If so, what does it say?
   * Is there a synonym in the sentence that provides a clue to the meaning? If so, what is it?
   * Are there explanations or descriptions that relate to the unfamilar word? If so, what do they tell you about the meaning of the unfamiliar word?
   * Are there words in the sentence that express contrasting meanings? If so, what do they tell you about the unfamiliar word?
   * Can you get any clue from the overall meaning of the sentence?
2. Look at the word itself. Can you break the word into parts? If so, do you know any of the word parts? Do the word clues give you a clue as to meaning?
3. Ask yourself whether you need to check the glossary or a dictionary.

The word-unlocking strategy just outlined is particularly important as you read textbooks that contain important new technical terms. You need to know those terms to understand important ideas. In contrast, when doing recreational reading, you do not need to know the meaning of all the terms used; you often can get the main ideas without considering the meaning of every word.

Applying the Strategy

Read three editorials in your local newspaper. Locate six words from the editorials that you can define based on your understanding of roots, prefixes, and suffixes. Circle them. In the margin of the article, note the meanings of the circled words. Your instructor may ask you to share an editorial and the circled words with the class.

Building Your Vocabulary

Because a large vocabulary is important in reading, you should also develop a strategy for building your personal vocabulary. The strategy introduced in this chapter is keeping a vocabulary notebook.

As you read and encounter a useful new word, record it in a personal vocabulary notebook. Record also the meaning of the word and a sample sentence using that word. For example, you could begin your vocabulary notebook with the words *clarify* and *innovation,* from this chapter. As you add words to your notebook, you may find it helpful to section it alphabetically. Keep a page for words that begin with the letter *a,* another page for *b* words, and so forth.

This vocabulary-building strategy will work only if you think about the words you record after you have entered them in your personal notebook. For example, today as you walk around, consider where you might apply the word *innovation.* Where do you see examples of innovation? When have you been innovative?

If you record and keep thinking about two new words each day, your vocabulary will grow. Research shows that one or two encounters with a word are not enough for you to learn a word. To own a word—to make it yours—you must encounter that word many times. You must work at increasing your vocabulary. Therefore, from time to time, thumb through your personal vocabulary notebook and think about your entries. Make an effort to use those words when appropriate in speaking and writing.

4

Reading
for Main Ideas

Before reading the chapter, read the title, the stated objective, and the headings and subheadings. Ask yourself: What is the topic of the chapter? In the space above and beside the chapter number, jot down what you already know about that topic. Then in the space below the chapter number, jot down at least two questions you hope to answer through reading the chapter.

OBJECTIVE

In this chapter you will develop a strategy for identifying the main idea of paragraphs and selections.

INTRODUCTION—READING FOR MAIN IDEAS

When authors write, they have an idea in mind that they are trying to communicate to their readers. This is especially true as authors compose paragraphs. They organize each paragraph around one topic. The topic is what the paragraph is about. They make one major point about the topic. That major point is the *main idea*.

Sometimes writers state their main idea somewhere in the paragraph—at the beginning, in the middle, or at the end. The sentence in which they state the main idea is the *topic sentence*. Or writers may leave the idea unstated. In that case, you must infer, or figure out, the main idea for yourself.

DISTINGUISHING BETWEEN GENERAL AND SPECIFIC

To identify the main idea of a paragraph, you must distinguish between the main idea and specific details related to that idea found in the paragraph. Here is an example. One of the four sentences below is a general idea. The other three provide details, or specific points, that support the idea. Which is the main idea sentence?

a. In Philadelphia a visitor can see the Liberty Bell, a symbol of that time in history when citizens sought liberty even at the expense of their own lives.

b. A visitor can stand before the Philadelphia State House, a stately old building that hints at what happened that summer of 1787.

c. A visitor to Philadelphia can stand in the very chamber where the delegates to the Constitutional Convention discussed issues and eventually signed the historic document.

d. A visit to Philadelphia more than 200 years since the signing of the Constitution still provides evidence of what happened there.

Which is the most general statement? The answer is "d." It talks of a visit today to Philadelphia giving evidence of the events of 200 years ago. What specific evidence would that be? The other statements give the supporting detail. The specific evidence is the Liberty Bell, the Philadelphia State House, and the chamber in which the Constitution was born. Statements "a," "b," and "c" are details that support the main idea. Figures 4.1 and 4.2 visually show the relationship between the main idea statement and the statements giving supporting details.

In each group of sentences that follow, one sentence states the main idea. The other sentences give supporting details. In each group, circle the sentence that states the main idea. In doing this, keep asking yourself: Which is the most general sentence? Which provide specific details? Be ready to tell why you answered as you did.

1.

a. In the Treaty of Paris, Great Britain recognized the United States as a free and independent nation.

Main Idea:
A visit to Philadelphia more than 200 years since the signing of
the Constitution still provides evidence of what happened there.

Supporting Detail: In Philadelphia a visitor can see the
Liberty Bell, a symbol of that time in history when citizens
sought liberty even at the expense of their own lives.

Supporting Detail: A visitor can stand before the
Philadelphia State House, a stately old building that hints at
what happened in that summer of 1787.

Supporting Detail: A visitor can stand in the very chamber
where the delegates to the Constitutional Convention discussed
issues and eventually signed the historic document.

Figure 4.1   *A Diagram, or Relational Map, Showing Main Idea and Supporting Details—Note
that the details support the main idea by telling specific things the visitor to Philadelphia can
see today.*

   b. The treaty established the borders of the United States, which extended north
to Canada, west to the Mississippi, and south to east and west Florida.

   c. Under the terms of the treaty, the British agreed to withdraw all their troops
from the United States.

   d. The Treaty of Paris, which officially ended the war between the British and
Americans, was generally favorable to the Americans.

2.

   a. The war had forced people to act toward one another in a more democratic
way.

   b. After the war, because of the labor shortage, people's religion was no longer
considered a factor in hiring.

   c. The war had brought changes to the country now called the United States
of America.

   d. People had many more opportunities to get ahead.

3.

   a. After the Revolution, slavery was still practiced in the United States.

   b. Unfortunately, inequities remained.

   c. Jewish people, who had contributed greatly to the war effort, could not hold
public office because they were Jews.

   d. Women could not vote and in some places could not own property.

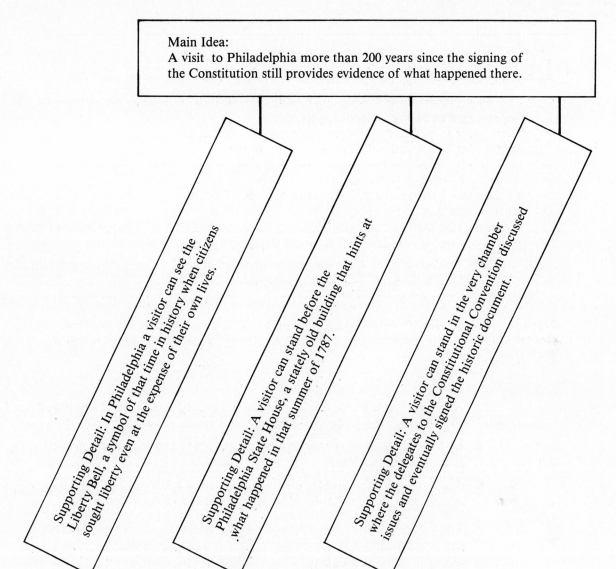

Main Idea:
A visit to Philadelphia more than 200 years since the signing of the Constitution still provides evidence of what happened there.

Supporting Detail: In Philadelphia a visitor can see the Liberty Bell, a symbol of that time in history when citizens sought liberty even at the expense of their own lives.

Supporting Detail: A visitor can stand before the Philadelphia State House, a stately old building that hints at what happened in that summer of 1787.

Supporting Detail: A visitor can stand in the very chamber where the delegates to the Constitutional Convention discussed issues and eventually signed the historic document.

Figure 4.2 *Another Way to Map Main Idea and Supporting Details*

4.

a. The citizens of the new country recognized that they must have a plan for administering the government of the land.

b. A Pennsylvanian named John Dickinson was selected to write the plan for a central government.

c. Dickinson's job was to set forth a government that retained power in the individual states yet established a central government to manage relations between the state and represented the country in foreign relations.

d. Dickinson's plan, the Articles of Confederation, was approved by the Continental Congress in 1777.

5.

a. The Congress could raise an army or navy and wage war.

b. The Congress was responsible for managing Indian affairs.

c. The Articles of Confederation gave certain important powers to the Congress of the United States.

d. The Congress could make treaties and send representatives to other countries.

6.

a. The Articles of Confederation—by establishing a "firm league of friendship" between the individual states—kept the states united as a nation.

b. The Articles of Confederation provided for a Congress, which determined how new states would be admitted to statehood.

c. The Articles of Confederation was a significant document in that it had lasting effects on the nation.

d. The articles provided for a Congress to manage disputes between the states.

7.

a. Great Britain kept its forts in the northwest territories and did not live up to the terms of the Treaty of Paris.

b. Because—under the Articles of Confederation—the national government was essentially weak, foreign governments did not respect it.

c. Spain, which controlled the port of New Orleans, began to tax goods using that port.

d. The Congress could raise an army only by asking the states for troops, but the states would not contribute; other governments did not respect a government without an army.

8.

a. The great American minds of the 1780s realized that a strong federal government was needed to represent the nation before foreign governments.

b. The great minds of the day knew that a strong federal government was needed to solve the financial problems that plagued the new nation.

c. The leaders of the day knew that disputes between states could be handled only by a strong central government.

d. James Madison and other great leaders of the day realized the need for a strong central government.

9.

a. Others, such as Patrick Henry, were leery of ideas for a strong central government.

b. They feared that a central government would curtail the rights of the individual states.

c. They feared the loss of individual liberty and freedom.

d. These statesmen had become doubtful as to whether a national unity could ever be achieved.

10.

a. The convention was held in Annapolis, Maryland, in September 1786.

b. A convention was called by the Virginia legislature to discuss trade problems between the states.

c. Leaders of this convention were Alexander Hamilton from New York, James Madison from Virginia, and John Dickinson from Delaware.

d. The convention did not last long because so few states sent representatives; however, a report was drafted calling for a new convention.

WORKING WITH MAIN IDEAS AND SUPPORTING DETAILS

Paragraphs have a structure that can help you identify the main idea. In this section, you will learn about different ways that authors structure their paragraphs.

Getting the Main Idea from a Chart

Study this chart. As you look at it, ask yourself: What point is it making about the early presidents of the United States?

Early Presidents of the United States

Name	No. of President	Birthplace	Other Data
George Washington	1	Westmoreland County, Virginia, 1732	Called the Father of His Country; lived at Mt. Vernon in Virginia
Thomas Jefferson	3	"Shadwell" in Goochland (now Albemarle) County, Virginia, 1743	Founded the University of Virginia at Charlottesville, Va.; lived at Monticello in Virginia
James Madison	4	Port Conway, Virginia, 1751, member of the Virginia planter class	Helped to draft the constitution for the state of Virginia
James Monroe	5	Westmoreland County, Virginia, 1758	Educated at the College of William and Mary in Williamsburg, Va.; studied law under Jefferson

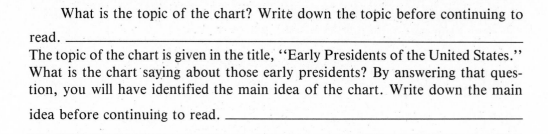

What is the topic of the chart? Write down the topic before continuing to read. _____

The topic of the chart is given in the title, "Early Presidents of the United States." What is the chart saying about those early presidents? By answering that question, you will have identified the main idea of the chart. Write down the main idea before continuing to read. _____

Sifting through the details in the chart, did you see any way in which most of the facts were related? In what respect were these early presidents similar? What feature of their background was the same? One clue to noting relationships within a chart like this (or within a paragraph, which is like a body of data) is to see whether there are any words or phrases that keep repeating. What word repeats in the chart on the early presidents? If you saw that *Virginia* was repeated and that these early presidents were all Virginians, you found the main idea of the chart.

Finding the Main Idea in a Paragraph

Now read the following paragraph. As you read, keep sifting through the data given to see how each fact relates to others. Look for repeating words. Look, too, for a sentence that may state the main idea. As soon as you identify the main idea, jot it in the margin at the left.

> In the early days of our country, Virginia served as the breeding ground of presidents. Of the first five presidents, four were Virginians. The Father of His Country and the first president was George Washington. He was born in Westmoreland County, Virginia, and spent his later years at Mt. Vernon, his estate in Virginia. The third President, Thomas Jefferson, was also a native Virginian. Raised in what is now Albemarle County, Virginia, he founded the University of Virginia. His home in later years was Monticello, near the University. James Madison, the fourth president, was born in Port Conway, Virginia, and helped draft the constitution for the state of Virginia. James Monroe, the fifth president, was born, like Washington, in Westmoreland County; he was educated at the College of William and Mary in Williamsburg and studied law under Thomas Jefferson.

Did you decide that the main idea was that Virginia was the birthplace of many of the early presidents? This main idea was stated in the first sentence. Underline that sentence in the paragraph. It is called the topic sentence because it develops the topic of the paragraph; it states the main idea.

Each sentence that follows the topic sentence supports the main idea. Each sentence tells something about a president that relates to his origins in Virginia. Notice that other facts about these presidents that do not relate to their beginnings in Virginia (for example, the names of their wives) are not included in the paragraph. That is because a well-written paragraph focuses on one main idea.

The structure of the paragraph about the Virginia presidents can be diagrammed like this:

```
┌─────────────────────────────────────────┐
│  Main idea (or topic sentence)           │
│  ┌──────────────────────────────────────┤
│  │  Supporting detail sentence           │
│  │  Supporting detail sentence           │
│  │  Supporting detail sentence           │
│  │  Supporting detail sentence           │
│  │  Supporting detail sentence           │
│  │  Supporting detail sentence           │
└──┴──────────────────────────────────────┘
```

A paragraph constructed in this way is a *deductive paragraph*. Deductive paragraphs begin with a general statement and then continue with specific facts to support the point. The deductive structure is a tidy design for paragraph writing. It makes reading easier, because the main idea is stated at the beginning to guide your reading of the paragraph.

Now read this revised paragraph about the early presidents. The topic is the same as that in the first version. The main idea is the same. When you find a sentence that states the main idea, underline it. Think also as you read: How does the paragraph differ from the first version?

> George Washington, the Father of His Country and the first president, was born in Westmoreland County, Virginia, and spent his later years at Mt. Vernon, his estate in Virginia. Thomas Jefferson, the third president, was also a native Virginian. Raised in what is now Albemarle County, Virginia, he founded the University of Virginia, and his home in later years was Monticello, near the university. James Madison, the fourth president, was born in Port Conway, Virginia, and helped draft the constitution for the state of Virginia. James Monroe, the fifth president, was born, like Washington, in Westmoreland County; he was educated at the College of William and Mary in Williamsburg and studied law under Thomas Jefferson. Clearly, Virginia supplied more than its share of presidents in the early days of the nation.

Did you identify the last sentence as the topic sentence of the paragraph? It expresses the idea that Virginia was the home of many of our early presidents. The design of the paragraph is shown here.

```
┌─────────────────────────────────────────┐
│  ┌──────────────────────────────────────┤
│  │  Supporting detail sentence           │
│  │  Supporting detail sentence           │
│  │  Supporting detail sentence           │
│  │  Supporting detail sentence           │
│  │  Supporting detail sentence           │
│  ├──────────────────────────────────────┤
│  Main idea (or topic sentence)           │
└─────────────────────────────────────────┘
```

This design is an inductive one. An *inductive paragraph* provides a series of examples and gives the general, or main, idea at the end.

When you read a paragraph in which the main idea is not stated in the first sentence, your job as a reader is more difficult. You must keep relating each new piece of information to those already given in the paragraph. Sifting through each new sentence, you must ask yourself: In what way is this new piece of data like the ones that have gone before it? What are the sentences saying about the topic? A repeating term (in this case, the word *Virginia*) may provide a hint as to the main idea as you read through the paragraph. The last sentence—the topic sentence—confirms the main idea.

Some paragraphs have no topic sentence. The paragraph is simply a string of interrelated sentences. You, the reader, must figure out what the main idea is. You must reason from the specific details as to the general point the paragraph is making.

Here is the same paragraph about early presidents of the United States written without a topic sentence.

> George Washington, the Father of His Country and the first president, was born in Westmoreland County, Virginia, and spent his later years at Mt. Vernon, his estate, in Virginia. Thomas Jefferson, the third president, was also a native Virginian. Raised in what is now Albemarle County, Virginia, he founded the University of Virginia. His home in later years was Monticello, near the university. James Madison, the fourth president, was born in Port Conway, Virginia, and helped draft the constitution for the state of Virginia. James Monroe, the fifth president, was born, like Washington, in Westmoreland County; he was educated at the College of William and Mary in Williamsburg and studied law under Thomas Jefferson.

To get the main idea of this paragraph, you must sift through each piece of data as it is presented and ask the questions: How does this sentence relate to the ones before it? What point is this sentence making about the topic?

The design of the paragraph is simply this:

```
Supporting detail sentence
Supporting detail sentence
Supporting detail sentence
Supporting detail sentence
Supporting detail sentence
```

Writing Paragraphs with Topic Sentences

Here is another data chart. Study it to determine the main idea.

Name	No. of President	Birthplace	Other Data
John Adams	2	Born in Braintree, Mass., 1735	Graduated from Harvard in Mass.; on the drafting committee of the Declaration of Independence

Name	No. of President	Birthplace	Other Data
John Quincy Adams	6	Born in Braintree, Mass., 1767	Son of John and Abigail Adams

What is true of both the second and sixth presidents of the United States? Can you see from the chart that both men were from the same state and the same family? They were both Adamses from Massachusetts.

Now, in your notebook, write a paragraph that communicates that point. Begin with a topic sentence. You may model it after the topic sentence about the presidents from Virginia. Follow your topic sentence with one or two sentences giving details about John Adams. Follow that with a sentence or two about John Quincy Adams. When you do this, you will be writing a deductively designed paragraph.

Revise your paragraph so that it is structured inductively. Begin with some details about John Adams. Follow with details about his son, John Quincy Adams. Then write a sentence at the end that states the main idea, the important relationship you are stressing in the paragraph. Write your inductive paragraph in your notebook.

Share your paragraphs with a classmate. See whether he or she can identify the topic sentence with the main idea.

A Strategy for Main Idea Reading

In this section you have been learning a strategy, or procedure, for sifting through information given in a paragraph to find the main idea. Your strategy has been to

- Identify the topic of the paragraph—what it is about.
- Ask as you read each sentence: How is this detail related to the one before it? What are these details telling me about the topic? What is the point the author is making in the paragraph?
- Ask: Is there a sentence that states the main idea?

Keep asking these questions as you sift through pieces of information. Do not wait until you reach the end of the paragraph.

Reading the next selection, you will have the opportunity to apply this strategy.

SELECTION 1: SUMMER OF DESTINY

The paragraphs in this section are from an article entitled "Summer of Destiny," by Hubert Pryor.

Identifying Main Idea

Now read this paragraph, the first in Pryor's article. As you read it, decide on the topic of the paragraph—what it is about. Think also about the main idea of the paragraph. Keep asking yourself: What is the paragraph saying about the topic? What point is the author trying to make? Where are all the details leading?

> The United States of America, many contend, was born, not in 1776, but in the summer of 1787. It was in the late spring of 1787 that delegates from 11 of the original states gathered in the Pennsylvania State House in Philadelphia, then America's largest city. (The New Hampshire delegation arrived in late July.) In the paneled assembly room of the graceful red-brick building topped by white clock tower and steeple—the place we now call Independence Hall—they sweated through four months of arduous, inspired, sometimes bitter, and almost disastrous deliberations. The result: the most brilliant document for human government in world history.

What is the topic? If you said the paragraph was about the birth of our nation or about the Constitution of the United States, you were on target. What

Figure 4.3 *An Early Bill of Rights from Virginia—The Constitution and the Bill of Rights drew upon ideas from previous documents such as this one.*

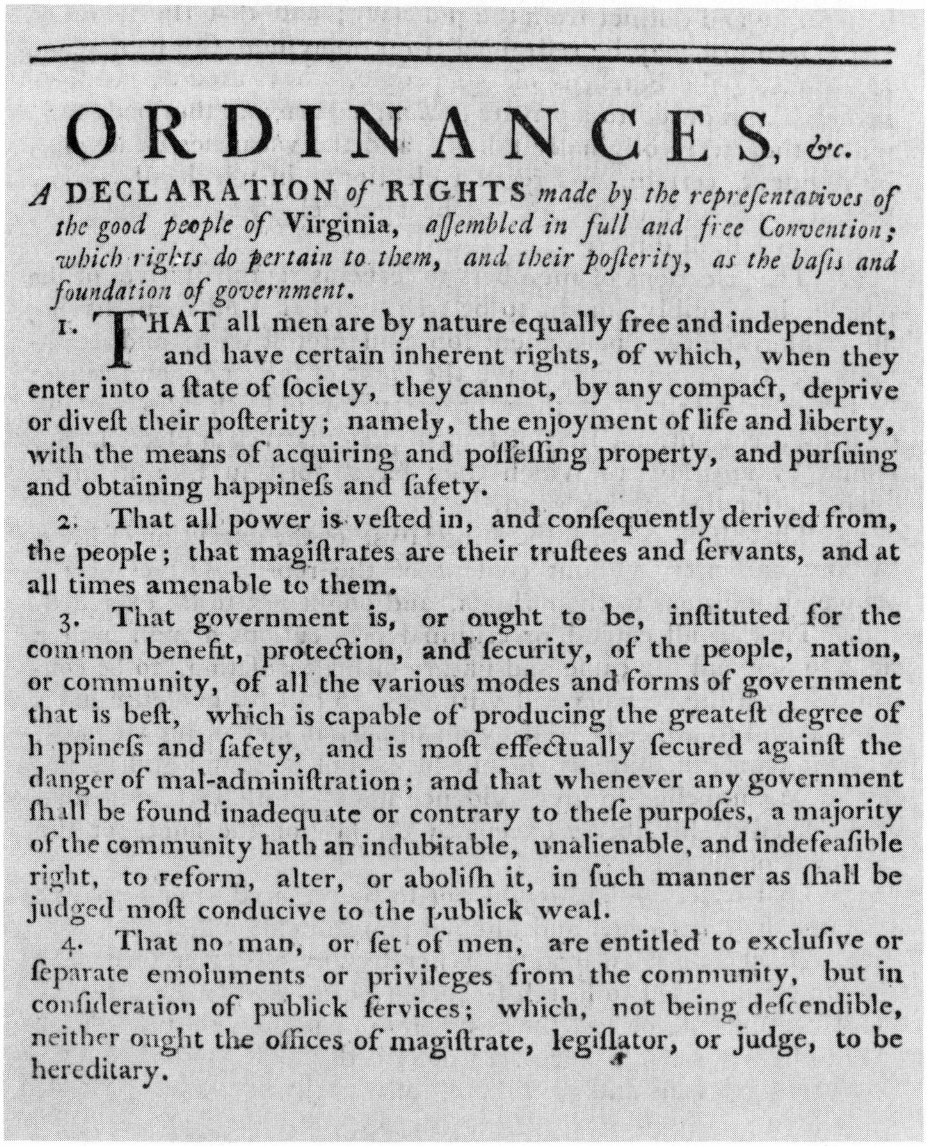

ORDINANCES, *&c.*

A **DECLARATION** *of* **RIGHTS** *made by the repreſentatives of the good people of* **Virginia,** *aſſembled in full and free Convention; which rights do pertain to them, and their poſterity, as the baſis and foundation of government.*

1. THAT all men are by nature equally free and independent, and have certain inherent rights, of which, when they enter into a ſtate of ſociety, they cannot, by any compact, deprive or diveſt their poſterity; namely, the enjoyment of life and liberty, with the means of acquiring and poſſeſſing property, and purſuing and obtaining happineſs and ſafety.

2. That all power is veſted in, and conſequently derived from, the people; that magiſtrates are their truſtees and ſervants, and at all times amenable to them.

3. That government is, or ought to be, inſtituted for the common benefit, protection, and ſecurity, of the people, nation, or community, of all the various modes and forms of government that is beſt, which is capable of producing the greateſt degree of h ppineſs and ſafety, and is moſt effectually ſecured againſt the danger of mal-adminiſtration; and that whenever any government ſhall be found inadequate or contrary to theſe purpoſes, a majority of the community hath an indubitable, unalienable, and indefeaſible right, to reform, alter, or aboliſh it, in ſuch manner as ſhall be judged moſt conducive to the publick weal.

4. That no man, or ſet of men, are entitled to excluſive or ſeparate emoluments or privileges from the community, but in conſideration of publick ſervices; which, not being deſcendible, neither ought the offices of magiſtrate, legiſlator, or judge, to be hereditary.

is the paragraph saying about the topic? What is the main idea of the paragraph? The main idea is that our country was born in the summer of 1787 with the writing of the Constitution. Where was that idea stated? The first sentence comes close to stating that main idea.

Incidentally, the paragraph is the first one in an article called "Summer of Destiny." Why was that a good title for an article that starts this way? How would thinking about that title help you in getting the main point of the article?

Practicing Finding the Main Idea of a Paragraph

Here are other paragraphs from Pryor's article. Read each paragraph. Identify the topic. Then write down the main idea.

1. Some of the 55 men who took part in the Constitutional Convention bore legendary names: George Washington, James Madison, Alexander Hamilton, Benjamin Franklin. But, except for Madison, their names are known more for other achievements than for what they did in Philadelphia. Others with names as legendary, including Thomas Jefferson and John Adams, were occupied with other duties so never attended. And a few with names not widely known, notably James Wilson and Gouverneur Morris of Pennsylvania, won their special place in history for the way they helped forge the framework for the nation we have been for the past 200 years.

The topic: _____

The main idea (what the author is saying about the topic) _____

_____

_____

2. Despite the glorious strike for freedom in 1776 and the victorious end of the War of Independence in 1781, the Articles of Confederation governing our land were "nothing more than a treaty of amity and alliance between independent and sovereign states." The words are those of James Madison. Working perhaps more than anyone else to bring the states together in the Constitutional Convention, he faced a land with no President, no national courts. The only central body was the Continental Congress, in which each state had one vote, which had no power to impose taxes or coerce states to raise an army.

Topic: _____

Main idea (what the author is saying about the topic): _____

_____

_____

3. By the 1780s, the lack of national purpose and direction had brought economic depression and even talk of war between states. There was no uniform currency, foreign trade was regulated by individual states, and trade barriers were being erected between states. By 1785, General Washington, looking sadly at the land he had led to freedom so recently, declared, "The wheels of government are clogged."

Topic: _____

Main idea (what the author is saying about the topic): _____

_____

_____

4. As Virginia delegate Washington arrived in Philadelphia on Sunday, May 13, 1787, from Mount Vernon, where he had retired, thousands of citizens turned out excitedly to meet him. When at last the convention met with a quorum present—11 days later than scheduled—the delegates unanimously paid him the honor due him as America's liberator by naming him to preside.

Topic: _____

Main idea (what the author is saying about the topic): _____

_____

_____

Special question (Check the glossary if you are not sure.):

What is the meaning of these words?

unanimously _____

preside _____

quorum _____

5. The choice contributed mightily to the ultimate success of the long, hot weeks and months that were to follow, often in perilous disagreement. And yet Washington spoke out only once—at the end. The General's commanding presence was such that all were simply awed into persisting in their work.

Topic: _____

Main idea (what the author is saying about the topic): _____

_____

_____

6. And so the gathering set to work, on track from the start thanks to Madison. The soft-spoken but brilliant young Virginian—he was 36—had outlined a proposed system of government in informal talks with other delegates during the days they were awaiting a quorum. His so-called Virginia Plan, presented by Virginia governor Edmund Randolph, called for a national government split three ways, with legislative, executive, and judicial branches.

Topic: _____

Main idea (what the author is saying about the topic): _____

_____

_____

Special questions (Check your dictionary for answers if you do not know them.):

What is the legislative branch of government? _____

_____

_____

What is the executive branch of government? _____

_____

_____

What is the judicial branch of government? _____

_____

_____

7. The [Virginia] plan envisioned a bicameral Congress with two houses whose members would be in proportion to the general electorate. A curious mechanism was proposed by which Senators would be elected by the House of Representatives "from persons nominated by the individual legislatures" of the states. And as a counterbalance to the Congress and the states, veto power would be given to a council formed by the executive branch and "a convenient number of the national judiciary."

Topic: _____

Main idea (what the author is saying about the topic): _____

_____

_____

Special questions:

Do we have a bicameral Congress today? _____
How are Senators elected today? _____

_____

8. After agreeing to two houses of congress, the delegates squared off on the issue of membership in the lower chamber, or House of Representatives. Delegates from smaller states wanted the states represented equally there. But delegates from the larger states pushed through representation in proportion to the population. They insisted on the same rule in the Senate and won their point—for the moment—by one vote.

Topic: _____

Main idea (what the author is saying about the topic): _____

_____

_____

Special question:

Today how is membership in the House of Representatives determined?

_____

9. A whole new debate followed on the make-up of the executive branch. It should consist, some said, of three men. Others wanted a council headed by one man. The idea of one man alone was finally adopted with a big "but": The executive should be chosen, not by the people, but by the national legislature. And he could serve only one term of seven years.

Topic: _____

Main idea (what the author is saying about the topic): _____

_____

_____

Special questions:

What name do we call the person who leads the executive branch? _____

Who elects the president today? _____

How long is the president's term of office? _____

Why does the article use the pronoun *he?* _____

A Reading Clue

When you read, it pays to keep relating what you are reading to what you already know. The special questions given with the last exercises are questions that a good reader would ask himself or herself while reading. Reading about the executive branch of government, the good reader thinks about what he or she knows about the American presidency. Reading about the legislature, the good reader thinks about what he or she knows about the American Congress. In reading these paragraphs, the good reader would be continuously comparing what exists today with what was proposed initially. In short, you should be thinking about what you are reading by relating the new information to what you know.

Vocabulary Review

Complete the following sentences.

1. A *bicameral* legislature has
   a. one house.
   b. two houses.
   c. three houses.

2. A *quorum* generally consists of
   a. one less than half.
   b. half.
   c. one more than half.

3. The *legislative branch* of government is responsible for
   a. running the courts.
   b. making the laws.
   c. administering the government.

4. The *electorate* are the people who
   a. are elected to office.
   b. have the franchise.
   c. have the franchise but who cannot run for office.
   d. do not have the franchise.

5. A *unanimous* vote is one in which
   a. a majority, or more than half, of voters agree.
   b. fewer than half the voters agree.
   c. all voters agree.

6. To *preside* over a meeting or convention is to
   a. chair it.
   b. attend it.
   c. speak at it.
   d. send a letter to it.

SELECTION 2: JAMES MICHENER

In this section of the chapter, you will have the opportunity to use your main idea strategy as you read an article.

Expanding Your Vocabulary for Reading

The underlined words in the following sentences are from the selection. Think about them before reading. Use both context and word structure clues to unlock their meanings. Check the glossary if you are unsure of a meaning. Record the meanings in the space provided. Select one or two to add to your personal vocabulary notebook.

1. The difference between the two versions of the story was practically imperceptible. I could hardly tell that any changes had been made. (Use word structure clues: *im-* means "not," *-ible* means "able.") _____

   _____

2. That writer eschews publicity. He avoids it at all costs. (Use a synonym clue.)

   _____

   _____

3. I try to be objective, but unfortunately I end up letting my own viewpoint take over. (Use a phrase of opposite meaning as a clue.) _____

   _____

4. The Pulitzer Prize is one of the most prestigious awards in this country. People look up to writers who receive this award for writing. (Use the meaning of the word *prestige* to help. Check the glossary.) _____

   _____

5. Michener's voice is resonant; his words roll through the room like organ notes in a cathedral. (Use context clues, especially the description.) _____

   _____

6. <u>Fortuitously,</u> I found my lost term paper one hour before it was due. ____

Getting Ready to Read

Preview the selection by reading the title and first paragraph.

- What is the topic? _____

- What do you already know about this topic? _____

  _____

  _____

- Michener is a writer. What would you like to find out about him through your reading? Write two questions you would like to answer. _____

  _____

  _____

Reading with Meaning

Now read the selection, keeping your two purpose-setting questions in mind. As you read each paragraph, write the topic and main idea in the outer margin. Review the main idea strategy before beginning.

JAMES MICHENER

William Ecenbarger

1. **Topic:** America's most popular serious novelist.

Main idea: America's most popular serious novelist is a very ordinary-looking man who acts in an ordinary way.

The lobby of the hotel just outside Washington, D.C., is teeming with purposeful, name-tagged men and women awaiting the beginning of the afternoon convention schedule. Outside, motorists are locking horns on the busy street, and a taxi breaks free and sprints to the hotel entrance. A man in a rumpled blue suit emerges, fumbles for the fare and steps through the door. He is bespectacled and looks like a college professor, which he once was. He carries a small overnight bag and is not wearing a name tag. He walks, with an almost imperceptible limp, to the registration desk and hands a piece of paper to the clerk, who advises him, "Your room is ready, Mr. 'Mikener.'" America's most popular serious novelist eschews an offer to carry his bag and walks to the elevator alone. None of the crowd in the lobby has noticed him.

2. **Topic:**

Main Idea:

Later, James Albert Michener (MITCH-ner) shrugs off his suit coat, squeaks into a leather chair, and responds to the first question: "No, I'm never noticed anywhere. I even did one of those American Express commercials because of it. I guess when you look at it objectively, there are at least 30 countries in which it is better to be a writer than the United States. The best are Russia, France, Germany and China. They revere their writers. America is still a frontier country that almost shudders at the idea of creative expression."

Michener has come to Washington for a meeting of a national commission studying the problems of UNESCO. It is one of three such groups of which he is now a member. Over the past decade he has served on the boards of a dozen prestigious organizations, including the advisory board of the National Aeronautics and Space Administration while he was writing his 1982 novel *Space.*

3. Topic:

Main idea:

"If you last into your 70s, you get a lot of breaks that you're not entitled to. Almost every week I'm invited to participate in something at a level at which young men just don't get asked. These meetings are very intense and real, and just being around a lot of brilliant people keeps me young. I should have to pay to attend them." Michener's voice is resonant, and his words roll through the room like organ notes through a cathedral. . . .

4. Topic:

Main idea:

Michener follows a seven-day-a-week routine, which he follows with the persistence of gravity. He rises at 7:30 A.M., drinks a glass of grapefruit juice, which he calls battery acid, and within five minutes is at his desk and typing with two fingers until 12:30, when he usually has completed six pages. He never works in the afternoon and works only two or three evenings a month.

5. Topic:

Main idea:

Michener was 40 years old before he settled on a literary career, but in the 37 years since then he has written 33 books that have sold 21 million copies, been translated into 52 languages, inspired 12 films and one smash Broadway musical. All but a few of his books are still in print and readily available. The popularity of such novels as *The Bridges at Tokori, Hawaii, The Source, Chesapeake* and *Centennial* have made him America's most popular serious novelist—a distinction he views with considerable humility. . . .

6. Topic:

Main idea:

While Michener, in keeping with a longstanding practice, will not discuss the

7. Topic:

Main idea:

content of his new novel, there are threads running through his previous fiction that are not likely to be absent here. His women are strong, resourceful, independent. There is a great deal of scholarly instruction for the reader. And nearly every Michener book deals at least once with interracial or intercultural marriage. The central theme of Michener's work is the destructiveness of injustice and prejudice—a subject that he, making a temple of his fingers, is willing to discuss.

8. Topic:

Main idea:

"When you grow up at the bottom of the totem pole, you see things in a different perspective, and with me there's the circumstance of my birth." His eyes crinkle sagely. "If I really don't know who I am, I can hardly look down on anyone. I seem to have a Germanic turn of mind, but I may be Jewish or Lithuanian or part black. With that uncertain background, one's attitude becomes quite tolerant very early."

9. Topic:

Main idea:

Michener is not the real name of the man who created Bali-ha'i and Bloody Mary—it's the name of the woman who found him on her doorstep in Doylestown, Pennsylvania, and adopted him.

10. Topic:

Main idea:

"I've been led to believe for various reasons that I was born somewhere near Mount Vernon, New York. There's never been any doubt that the year was 1907 because I turned up almost immediately in Pennsylvania. It was a matter of weeks." Two extensive investigations into Michener's origins—one by the State Department when he applied for a passport, the other by the U.S. Navy when he was commissioned—failed to solve the mystery of his biologic origins. He does not know for sure where or exactly when he was born, and he has no idea who his natural parents are.

11. Topic:

Main idea:

Mabel Michener was a widow when she took in the waif she named James Albert. She had one son of her own and raised five or six other children at various times. She scratched out a living as a laundress and seamstress, but when times were bad, as they often were, young Jim had to weather the storm in the Bucks County Poorhouse.

12. Topic:

Main idea:

"My mother did absolutely backbreaking, sweatshop labor, but there were times when we had nothing. Zero! Money was absolutely all-important to me when I was young, simply because I never had any. This tightens you inside. I've had one success after another, but don't forget that it came very late. I have a very hard inner consciousness. I'm tougher inside than people think.''

The chance adoption by Mabel Michener was fortuitous for a future writer because she loved literature, especially Dickens, and she read aloud from the classics to her children nearly every night. "It was an absolutely formative part of my life," Michener recalls. "I remember it most vividly today. We would all gather around and she would read from *Oliver Twist* or *David Copperfield*. From this I learned that there were certain conventions to use to make things happen and move the narrative along.''

13. Topic:

Main idea:

Michener began reading himself at an early age. At 14, he chanced upon an issue of *National Geographic*—and was instantly beset by a thirst for travel that he has never managed to slake. By the time he finished high school in 1925, young Michener had visited 45 of the then 48 states— mostly by hitchhiking.

14. Topic:

Main idea:

"I usually got a ride within 15 minutes. I was young and had a lot of blond hair and kept myself neat. I could always find someone to feed me and bed me down for the night, and I had no hesitation whatever about leaving for a month with 85 cents in my pocket. The whole experience left me very optimistic about the human race.''

15. Topic:

Main idea:

Today Michener is probably the most traveled writer in history. He estimates he has been to Singapore 50 times, Burma 20 times and Bora Bora eight times. He has lived and worked for extended periods in Afghanistan, Australia, Fiji, Hawaii, India, Israel, Japan, Mexico, Portugal, Samoa, Spain, Tahiti, Thailand and Vienna. . . .

16. Topic:

Main idea:

A dazzling academic high school record won Michener the first full four-year scholarship ever awarded by Swarthmore College, where he graduated summa cum laude in 1929. He spent the next decade traveling, teaching and studying at nine universities in the United States and Europe.

17. Topic:

Main idea:

He volunteered for the U.S. Navy in 1942 during World War II and was assigned to the South Pacific, where as an island-hopping aircraft maintenance officer he was given wide latitude, partly because it was sometimes assumed that he was related to an admiral named

18. Topic:

Main idea:

Mitscher—an impression he did nothing to clarify. He came to know the area intimately, and on lonely afternoons at a cacao plantation on the island of Espiritu Santo, he began plotting a novel. At night he battled mosquitoes and humidity in an abandoned building and typed his material. He completed *Tales of the South Pacific* after his discharge. It was not and never has been a bestseller, but it won the 1947 Pulitzer Prize and came to the attention of Richard Rodgers and Oscar Hammerstein, who transformed it into a Broadway musical with staggering success.

19. Topic:

Main idea:

Unfortunately, Mabel Michener never was able to enjoy James's literary rewards. She died on March 22, 1946, while he was still in the South Pacific, 11 months before publication of his first novel. . . .

Checking for Understanding

Place a T *(true) or* F *(false) on the line before each statement based on the main idea notes you jotted down in the margin during reading.*

___F___ 1. Michener is a brash and self-important man.

___F___ 2. Michener believes that Americans revere their writers.

___T___ 3. Michener serves on national boards and commissions.

___T___ 4. Michener enjoys his work on national commissions.

___T___ 5. Michener has a daily writing schedule that he sticks to.

___T___ 6. Michener is America's most popular serious novelist.

___F___ 7. The central theme of Michener's novels is the horror of war.

___T___ 8. Michener's background may have affected his attitude toward people.

___F___ 9. Michener was raised by a sister named Mary.

___T___ 10. Michener was born on June 8, 1907.

___F___ 11. His mother was a writer.

___F___ 12. Michener was raised in a well-to-do home.

___T___ 13. Literature was important to him in his youth.

___F___ 14. Michener began to travel when he was 40.

___F___ 15. He is very pessimistic, or negative, about the human race.

___F___ 16. Michener has not had much opportunity to travel, although he enjoys traveling.

___F___ 17. Michener was an average student.

___T___ 18. Michener plotted out his first novel while in the South Pacific during World War II.

___F___ 19. Michener's mother read all of his books.

Reviewing Basic Vocabulary

Underline the best response.

1. He was chairperson of the most *prestigious* committee.
   a. high-standing, or honored
   b. responsible
   c. hard-working
   d. productive

2. Try to be *objective*. Don't let your feelings color your decision.
   a. prestigious
   b. thoughtful
   c. impartial
   d. subjective

3. My friend had an almost *imperceptible* flaw in his character, but I recognized it after knowing him for two years.
   a. recognizable
   b. serious
   c. very slight
   d. terrible

4. His voice was *resonant*. I thought he was a singer.
   a. soft
   b. serious
   c. wonderful
   d. full and vibrant

5. That man *eschews* all offers to pay him for his work.
   a. avoids
   b. criticizes
   c. accepts
   d. rewards

6. My meeting him was *fortuitous*. He drove me home and I avoided a long bus ride home.
   a. sad
   b. happy
   c. lucky
   d. unpleasant

IDENTIFYING THE MAIN IDEA
OF AN EXTENDED SELECTION

You know now that when authors write a paragraph, they have an idea in mind that they are trying to communicate to their readers. The same is true when writers compose a longer piece. They generally have a major idea that is at the core of the piece.

Take, for example, the selection about James Michener that you just read. It expresses a major thought. What is it? Review the selection, studying the main ideas of the individual paragraphs as you recorded them in the margin. Think about the major thought the author is communicating. Here is a model of what you might say to yourself in your head in thinking about the main thought:

The article starts out by saying that Michener is America's most popular author, but one who goes unrecognized. The first part of the article tells me about his work on committees, his daily routine, and his many books. The next part tells about Michener's youth when he was adopted by a poor woman who loved books. It tells about his early interest in books, his early travels, and his service in the Navy. All of these experiences must have affected his writing. The major idea seems to be that Michener, America's most popular author who often goes unrecognized, had many varied experiences as a young man—experiences that made him the writer he is today.

The best way to get at the major thought of an entire selection is to think through the main idea of each paragraph as in the example just given, asking yourself the major idea question: What big thought is the author trying to tell me in this selection? What general point is he or she making about the topic?

In some instances, authors come right out and state the major point they are trying to make. They can do this anywhere in a selection. Sometimes authors state their main idea (or thesis, as it is called when referring to an extended selection) at the beginning to help guide your reading. In other instances, authors state the thesis at the end of the selection. Earlier paragraphs in the selection lead up to and into the main idea. In still other instances, authors express their main idea, or thesis, somewhere in the middle of the selection. And at times, they do not state their main point at all; they only imply, or suggest it indirectly. You, the reader, must figure out the general point being made; you must infer it from the paragraphs of the selection. In these cases, which occur more often than not, you must keep asking the major idea question as you read: What is the general idea this author is trying to tell me about the topic?

In the following section, you will have the opportunity to practice reading for the main ideas of paragraphs and the thesis of an entire selection.

SELECTION 3: THE SECRET OF AMERICA

Extending Your Vocabulary for Reading

The underlined words in the following sentences are from the selection. Think about them before reading. Use both context and word structure clues to figure out their meanings. Record the meanings in the space provided. Select one or two to add to your personal vocabulary notebook.

1. In the underlined years, from 1787 to now, the Constitution has served us well. (Note the prefix *inter-*.) _____

_____

2. The chairperson took measures to ensure that all members of the committee had equal opportunity to present their opinions. (Note the root *sure;* it is a clue to meaning.) _____

_____

3. The most salient feature of the building was a large wall projecting out in front. (Note the overall meaning of the sentence. Check the glossary.) _____

_____

4. The document is a <u>testament</u> to what free people can do. (Relate this word to the word *testify*. What does one do when one testifies?) _____

_____

5. A <u>stalwart</u> nation is one that is firm, steadfast, and uncompromising. (Here is a definition of the term given in context.) _____

_____

Getting Ready to Read

Preview the selection.

1. *Read the title of the next selection and the information about the author. Rapidly run your eyes over the article, looking for key words that give you a clue as to the topic of the article. Based on your preview, predict what the topic of the article is (what it is about).*

   - The topic is _____

   - Predict: What does Michener mean by "The Secret of America"?

   _____

   _____

2. What do you already know about the author? What do you already know about the topic? Having just read an article about the author and another article on the same topic, you should have considerable background to bring to your reading of the selection. Record what you already know about the Constitution on the following idea web. Note that the idea web includes *what, why, who, when,* and *where* questions, which is a good way to organize your thinking before reading.

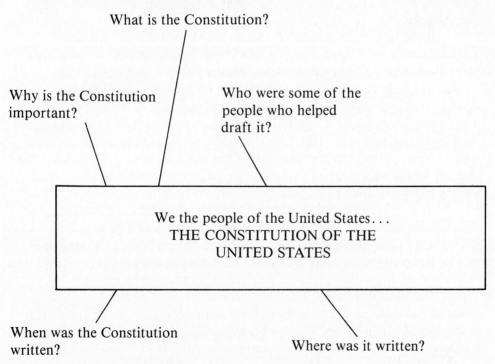

What is the Constitution?

Why is the Constitution important?

Who were some of the people who helped draft it?

We the people of the United States...
THE CONSTITUTION OF THE
UNITED STATES

When was the Constitution written?

Where was it written?

3. Set a purpose for reading.

Reading with Meaning

Now read the selection. As you read, keep your pen in hand. Record the main idea of each paragraph in the outer margin. As you read, also keep asking: What is Michener saying about the Constitution? What is the major point he is trying to make about it?

THE SECRET OF AMERICA

James A. Michener

Born in 1907, James Michener is an American novelist whose books include The Bridges at Tokori, Hawaii, Chesapeake, Texas, *and* Centennial. *The following article is by Michener. If you like stories with considerable historical detail, you will enjoy reading a novel by Michener.*

In the closing years of the 18th century the American colonies in North America won two stunning victories. In 1781 on the battlefield at Yorktown they sealed a military victory which ensured their freedom, and during the summer of 1787 in the debating halls of Philadelphia they won a political struggle which enabled them to survive triumphantly until today.

The writing of the Constitution of the United States is an act of such genius that philosophers still wonder at its accomplishment and envy its results. Fifty-five typical American citizens met and argued for 127 days during a ferociously hot Philadelphia summer and produced one of the magisterial documents of world history. Almost without being aware of their great achievement, they fashioned a nearly perfect instrument of government, and I have studied it for nearly 70 years with growing admiration for its utility and astonishment at its capacity to change with a changing world. It is a testament to what a collection of typical free men can achieve.

I think this is the salient fact about our Constitution. All other nations which were in existence in 1787 have had to alter their form of government in the intervening years. France, Russia and China have undergone momentous revolutions. Stable nations like Sweden and Switzerland have had to change their forms radically. Even Great Britain, most stalwart of nations, has limited sharply the power of its monarch and its House of Lords. Only the United States, adhering to the precepts of its Constitution, has continued with the same form of government. We are not of the younger nations of the world; we are the oldest when it comes to having found the government which suits it best.

It is instructive to remember the 55 men who framed this document. Elder statesmen like George Washington and Benjamin Franklin contributed little to the debate but greatly to the stability and inspiration of the convention. Thomas Jefferson, perhaps the most brilliant American of those days, missed the meetings entirely; he was on diplomatic duty in France. The hard central work of determining the form of government seems to have been done by a handful of truly great men: James Madison and George Mason of Virginia, Roger Sherman of Connecticut, James Wilson and Gouverneur Morris of Pennsylvania.

Alexander Hamilton of New York did not speak much but did exert considerable influence.

The 55 contained a college president, a banker, a merchant, a great teacher of law, a judge, a major, a clergyman, a state governor and a surgeon. One-sixth of the members were foreign born. Two were graduates of Oxford University, one of St. Andrews in Scotland. But the group also contained some real nonentities, including a military man who had been court-martialed for cowardice during the Revolution, some who contributed nothing to the debate, and some who were not quite able to follow what was being debated.

What this mix of men did was create a miracle in which every American should take pride. Their decision to divide the power of the government into three parts—Legislative, Executive, Judicial—was a master stroke, as was the clever way in which they protected the interests of small states by giving each state two Senators, regardless of population, and the interest of large states by apportioning the House of Representatives according to population.

But I think they should be praised mostly because they attended to those profound principles by which free men have through the centuries endeavored to govern themselves. The accumulated wisdom of mankind speaks in this Constitution. (641 words)

Checking for Understanding

1. Complete Figure 4.4 by recording the main idea of each of the paragraphs from the selection. You may look back at your margin notes. At this point, leave the box labeled "Thesis" blank.

2. What is the major point that Michener is making in the article?
   a. The Constitution was written by fifty-five men who worked during the summer of 1787.
   b. The Constitution, one of the great documents of the world, was written by fifty-five men of varying talents and backgrounds.
   c. The Constitution, written during the summer of 1787, owes its greatness to the fact that it has never changed in a changing world.
   d. The Constitution was written by many people working together cooperatively.
   e. The Constitution was written by many people, all of whom were thinkers of the highest order.

3. Record the main point you selected in the second question in the box labeled "Thesis" in question 1. That chart is a visual map of the ideas from the selection. The lines from the individual paragraphs to the thesis box indicate that the main ideas of the individual paragraphs build into and support the thesis of the entire selection.

4. The title, "The Secret of America" refers to
   a. the fifty-five men who framed the Constitution.
   b. the wisdom that speaks to us in our Constitution that made America what it is.
   c. the year 1787.

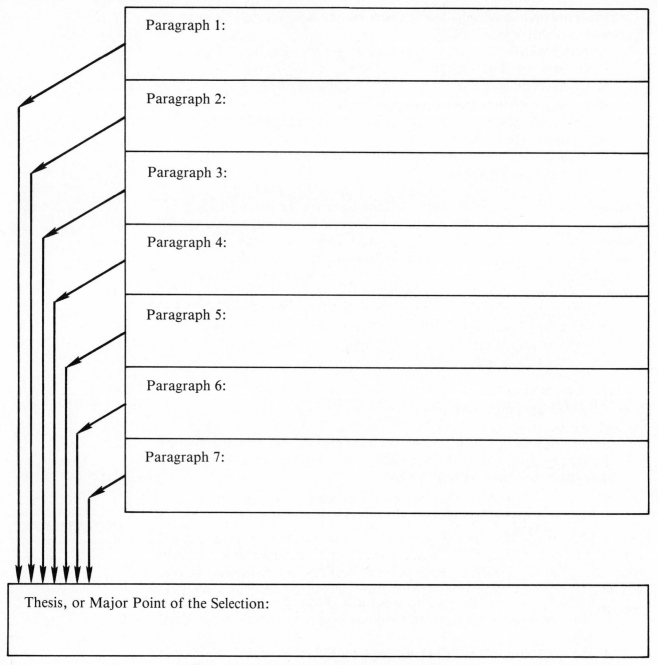

Paragraph 1:

Paragraph 2:

Paragraph 3:

Paragraph 4:

Paragraph 5:

Paragraph 6:

Paragraph 7:

Thesis, or Major Point of the Selection:

Figure 4.4 *Main Ideas and the Thesis of a Selection*

      d. Madison, Mason, Sherman, Wilson, Morris, and Hamilton—men who had considerable influence in the drafting of the Constitution.

      e. the fact that no women were among the drafters of the Constitution.

5. Michener calls the writing of the Constitution a
    a. revolution of the magnitude of the French Revolution.
    b. battle still to be won.
    c. victory of the eighteenth century.
    d. defeat for the forces of evil.
    e. tornado that whipped across the original colonies.

6. When we talk about *intervening* years, we are talking about the years that
   a. have gone by.
   b. will come.
   c. come between.
   d. have just ended.

7. If we *ensure* the freedom of all people, we
   a. make sure of.
   b. do away with.
   c. forget about.
   d. handle thoughtfully.

8. When we say of a person that he was our most *stalwart* supporter, we mean that he was
   a. forgiving.
   b. helpful.
   c. firm and steadfast.
   d. understanding.

9. Michener says that the Constitution is a *testament* to what free people can achieve. By this he means that it is a/an
   a. legal document.
   b. written report.
   c. essay.
   d. piece of evidence.

10. A *salient* feature is one that is
    a. unimportant.
    b. conspicuous.
    c. unhelpful.
    d. related.

Applying the Strategy to Your Reading

Find an article in a news magazine such as *Newsweek* or *Time*. Preview the article to identify the topic. Then think about what you know about the topic. Read the article to identify the main point the writer is making about the topic. Finally, on an index card, record the title of the article, the date when it was written, the topic as you identify it, and the major idea, or thesis, of the article.

EXTENDING WHAT YOU HAVE LEARNED

Reading for Main Ideas

In this chapter you have been learning a strategy for identifying main ideas as you read paragraphs. List the steps that you use to find the main idea of a paragraph.

1. _____

   _____

2. _____

   _____

3. _____

_____

Applying the Strategy to Textbook Reading

Read a two- or three-page section from a textbook you are using in another course. Use the main idea strategy to identify the main idea of each paragraph. Record the ideas in the margin as you read along. When you finish reading, review the ideas you have written down, and in the bottom margin, write the major point, or thesis, of the entire section. Then make a map of the ideas as you did on page 82. You may be asked to share your idea map with the class, so make it large.

Building a Knowledge Base for Future Reading

Geographic sites mentioned in this chapter include Washington, D.C.; Massachusetts; Virginia; and Philadelphia, Pennsylvania. Circle the names of these places on the map on page 11.

5

Thinking About Details

Before reading the chapter, read the title, the stated objective, and the headings and subheadings. Ask yourself: What is the topic of the chapter? In the space above and beside the chapter number, jot down what you already know about that topic. Then in the space below the chapter number, jot down at least two questions you hope to answer through reading the chapter.

OBJECTIVE

In this chapter, you will learn strategies for thinking about details as you read. Specifically, you will learn to

1. sort details to identify the more significant ones,
2. make inferences based on details, and
3. relate details in a passage to what you already know.

INTRODUCTION—THINKING ABOUT DETAILS

In developing the main idea of a paragraph, a writer generally includes considerable detail. Some details bear directly upon the main idea; these help substantiate, or support, the point the writer is making. Other details relate in some way to the main idea, but they are not essential to the point the writer is making. In a way, these details are icing on the cake; they add interest and flavor.

In the same way, some details require little or no interpretation by the reader. These details are relatively clear. In contrast, some details require the reader to go beyond surface meaning—beyond what is explicitly stated. They require the reader to read between the lines to tap meanings that the writer has only implied, or hinted at. In these cases, the reader must make an inference; he or she must figure out what the writer is getting at, or implying.

Identifying Significant Details

Let us look at a paragraph with these two thoughts in mind—that details differ in how essential they are to the main point and in how explicitly they are set forth. The paragraph is the first one in the selection about James Michener, which you read for the main idea in Chapter 4. Quickly reread it, recalling the main idea as you read.

> The lobby of the hotel just outside Washington, D.C., is teeming with purposeful, name-tagged men and women awaiting the beginning of the afternoon convention schedule. Outside, motorists are locking horns on the busy street, and a taxi breaks free and sprints to the hotel entrance. A man in a rumpled blue suit emerges, fumbles for the fare and steps through the door. He is bespectacled and looks like a college professor, which he once was. He carries a small overnight bag and is not wearing a name tag. He walks, with an almost imperceptible limp, to the registration desk and hands a piece of paper to the clerk, who advises him, "Your room is ready, Mr. 'Mikener.' " America's most popular serious novelist eschews an offer to carry his bag and walks to the elevator alone. None of the crowd in the lobby has noticed him.

The point about Michener that the writer is making is that he is not a man who puts on airs or thinks too much of himself. He is no egotist. What details from the paragraph support this picture of Michener? Before reading on, write down three details that help communicate this message.

1. _____

2. _____

3. _____

Supporting details include the fact that he carries his own bag, wears a rumpled suit, does not wear a name tag, and does not correct the clerk who mispronounces his name. These details are clear; they are explicitly set forth. And they support the idea of the paragraph—Michener, the humble man.

There are, however, other details that are less clearly set forth that support the main idea. What is the writer of the paragraph saying when he describes Michener's suit as blue? That takes a bit of thinking about, because the author is sending an implied message. The average businessperson checking into a prestigious Washington hotel typically does not wear a blue suit. The businessperson—dressed for success, as we say today—wears a three-piece dark gray or black suit. The fact that Michener does not adhere to the dressed-for-success model implies something about him: He does not put on airs.

To make meaning of the detail (and to recognize it as a significant detail rather than a minor one), you must know something about the way businesspeople tend to dress. You must bring that knowledge to bear in making an inference.

In the same way, the fact that Michener simply hands a piece of paper to the clerk supports the main idea—but only if you read between the lines to make an inference and bring your knowledge about hotels to bear upon your reading.

What was that paper? If you have checked into a big hotel, you know that the piece of paper was Michener's reservation form. What does he do with it? He simply gives it to the clerk. What could he have done? He could have announced—as many self-important people would have done—"I am James Michener," so that those in the lobby would have recognized him. He used the reservation form, instead. Therefore, you—the reader—perceive him as a humble man.

What about the less significant details? In the space below, write down at least one detail that has little bearing on the main idea.

One rather insignificant detail is the fact that motorists are locking horns. Another is that the street is busy. Even the fact that the lobby of the hotel is filled with people has little bearing on Michener's natural humility.

What function do these details have in the paragraph? They are the icing! They make for an interesting beginning and add style to the writing. In a way, they also provide a contrast. Here are all these purposeful, name-tagged men and women probably dressed for success. In contrast is this rumpled and fumbling man, America's most popular serious novelist.

Is it important to remember these lesser details? In most cases, no. The reader moves his or her eyes over them, getting the flavor of the writing and going on to other details that add to the main idea.

Interpreting Specific Details

Here is another paragraph from the Michener article. Reread it, asking yourself: Which details are significant? How shall I handle them?

> Michener was 40 years old before he settled on a literary career, but in the 37 years since then he has written 33 books that have sold 21 million copies, been translated into 52 languages, inspired 12 films and one smash Broadway musical. All but a few of his books are still in print and readily available. The popularity of such novels as *The Bridges at Tokori, Hawaii, The Source, Chesapeake,* and *Centennial* have made him America's most popular serious novelist—a distinction he views with considerable humility.

The main idea is that Michener is a prolific writer; he has produced many books. But how do you handle all those specific numbers that support the main point?

Unless you have a reading purpose in mind that makes you want to know these details, typically you generalize based on the numbers. In this case, you probably do not try to remember that Michener wrote thirty-three books but think in terms of *more than thirty books*. Notice that this is a "ballpark figure"—in other words, an approximation. Similarly, you come away with the generalized fact that the books have been translated into *many languages* and *some films* have been based on the books.

Now reread this paragraph from the Michener article. As you read a detail, do not try to remember it. Rather, try for a ballpark approximation:

> Today Michener is probably the most traveled writer in history. He estimates he has been to Singapore 50 times, Burma 20 times and Bora Bora eight times. He has lived and worked for extended periods in Afghanistan, Australia, Fiji, Hawaii, India, Israel, Japan, Mexico, Portugal, Samoa, Spain, Tahiti, Thailand and Vienna.

The main point of the paragraph is that Michener is widely traveled. Write two details from the paragraph—in ballpark terms—to support the point.

1. _____

2. _____

From the data, you may have generalized that Michener has visited some locations from eight to fifty times. You may have noted that he has traveled all over the world—from Spain to Tahiti. It probably is not important to remember the full list of places mentioned in the article, unless that list relates directly to the purpose for reading you initially set for yourself.

Bringing Your Prior Knowledge to Bear on Details Read

In writing the article about Michener, William Ecenbarger included a short, one-sentence paragraph that we left out in our reprinting of it. That paragraph is hard to comprehend because full understanding requires considerable prior knowledge about books and considerable ability to read between the lines. As you read it here, ask yourself the main-idea question: What point is Michener making? Notice that most of the paragraph is a quotation; the words are Michener's as he responds to the interviewer:

> "I am frequently approached by people who tell me that they enjoy 'my' books, especially *Mister Roberts* and *From Here to Eternity*," he says, his mouth forming a crescent of pleasure.

Details are especially important here. You must note them if you are to get Michener's point. Why does Michener put quotation marks around the word "my"? Why does Michener grin when he tells the anecdote? Do you know? Do you know anything about *Mister Roberts* and *From Here to Eternity?* Well, to fully understand Michener, you have either to get the message implied by the use of quotation marks around "my" and Michener's grin or know these books. Michener uses quotation marks because he is not the author of the two books mentioned! He grins because he is poking fun at readers who do not know who wrote what. The main idea of the paragraph is that people know little about authors of their books, even though they may pretend to. In this paragraph, there are many significant details; however, meanings are hidden within the details and you must think about those details in terms of what you already know about the topic.

Strategies for Working with Details

In sum, here is a strategy for sorting significant from less essential details in reading.

1. Ask yourself:
   - How does this detail relate to the main idea?
   - Does this detail support the main point, or is it icing on the cake?
2. Look at precise details and approximate a ballpark figure.

Do this as you read a paragraph. Do not wait until you get to the end. Sorting significant from less essential details in reading is a continuous process; you do it all the time as you read.

As you have learned, writers do not come out and state everything explicitly. You must make inferences about points and details. Here is a strategy for getting at implied meanings, for reading between the lines.

Ask yourself:

- How does this detail relate to other details in the selection?
- What do I already know about this detail? What ideas come to my mind in relation to this detail?

Being able to figure out meanings not explicitly stated in a text is dependent on what you already know. The less you know about a topic, the less likely it is that you will be able to pick up implied meanings. That is the reason you need to get into the reading habit. To be a good reader, you must read. Through reading, you build a knowledge base that helps you in the future as you read more involved selections. Remember that Michener was a reader. He grew up in a poor home, but it was a "wealthy"one. Fortuitously, for Michener, his mother loved literature and read the classics to him. That made him a good reader as well as a fine writer.

In the remainder of this chapter, you will have the opportunity to refine your ability to apply the strategies discussed in this introduction to the chapter.

PRACTICING THE STRATEGIES: SEEING THE SIGNIFICANCE OF DETAILS

To handle main ideas and details with any degree of proficiency, you must be able to identify whether details support a main idea. For example, read this statement of a main idea:

Main Idea: The Great Pyramids of Gizeh are the most famous of the pyramids of Egypt.

Now read these statements of detail, asking yourself: Which of the statements provides a detail that supports the main idea—the idea that the Gizeh Pyramids are the most famous? Which are about the pyramids but do not relate directly to the fame of the pyramids?

    a. The Step Pyramid is older than the Pyramids of Gizeh.

    b. The Great Pyramid at Gizeh is one of the Seven Wonders of the Ancient World.

    c. The Mayans also built pyramids.

    d. The Pyramids of Gizeh are located near the city of Cairo.

All of the details are true, but only one really supports the idea of the fame of the pyramids: that the Great Pyramid is one of the Seven Wonders of the Ancient World. The Gizeh Pyramids must have been outstanding and famous to be so designated. The other facts—that the Step Pyramid is older, that the Mayans built pyramids, and that the Pyramids of Gizeh are located near Cairo—are true, but they do not relate directly to or support the main idea, the fame of the Pyramids of Gizeh.

    Read the following main idea statements. For each, circle the detail that most strongly supports the main idea. All of the items deal with great constructions of the past.

1. Main Idea: The Great Sphinx is a colossal sculpture set like a guard near the Pyramid of Khafre in Egypt.
   a. The Great Sphinx has the head of a human and a body of a lion.
   b. Thousands of sphinxes were built in ancient Egypt.
   c. The sphinx is part of Greek mythology.
   d. In Greek mythology, the sphinx was a winged monster with the head of a woman and the body of a lion.

2. Main Idea: The Colossus of Rhodes was a large bronze statue that once stood in the harbor of Rhodes, an island in the eastern Mediterranean Sea.
   a. Legend says that the Colossus stood across the harbor and ships passed between its legs.
   b. A famous American colossus is the Statue of Liberty.
   c. People have always been intrigued by great statues.
   d. The Mediterranean Sea separates Europe from North Africa and has been important in the trade of this area.

3 Main Idea: Some astronomers theorize that the standing stones of Stonehenge in England were built by ancient peoples to measure solar and lunar movements.
   a. There are some similarities between Stonehenge and another ancient monument of stones near Avebury in England.
   b. So many visitors now come to Stonehenge that it is no longer possible to wander among the upright stones.
   c. The astronomer Gerald Hawkins used computers to test his hypothesis that the stones related to astronomical movements.
   d. Stonehenge is a short day trip from London.

4. Main Idea: The term *Romanesque* describes the style of architecture that

was seen in western Europe between the end of the ninth and the twelfth centuries.
a. Architects who worked during the ninth and twelfth centuries were considered of low social status.
b. The church was a dominant force during the ninth and twelfth centuries.
c. The Durham Cathedral, built in Durham, England, between 1093 and 1280, is considered one of the outstanding examples of Romanesque architecture.
d. Few Romanesque cathedrals remain today exactly as they were originally constructed.

5. Main Idea: The Gothic age that occurred between 1150 and 1300 was a period of great cathedral building in France.
a. The ribs on a Gothic vault are primarily for aesthetic purposes.
b. People harnessed themselves to carts to pull the limestone building blocks from the quarry to the cathedral site.
c. The people of the period felt that the cathedral belonged to them; they took pride in their gift to God.
d. French cathedrals built during this period included Notre Dame de Paris, Rheims, Chartres, Amiens, Le Mans, Beauvais, and many others that are lesser known.

6. Main Idea: The Suez Canal is an important navigational link that facilitates world trade.
a. The Suez Canal connects the Mediterranean Sea with the Gulf of Suez and then with the Red Sea.
b. The Suez Canal was constructed in the period between 1859 and 1869.
c. The modern-day Canal was planned by a French engineer; the British underwrote much of the cost of the Canal.
d. The Suez Canal is a sea-level canal that is more than 100 miles long; it is longer than the Panama Canal.

7. Main Idea: Mount Rushmore is a national shrine that honors great American presidents.
a. The same sculptor who worked on Stone Mountain in Georgia conceived of Mount Rushmore.
b. Mount Rushmore is located in the state of South Dakota in the Black Hills.
c. It took fourteen years to carve the faces in the stone; the sculptor, Gutzon Borglum, died before the carving was completed.
d. Carved in the rock of the mountain are the faces of four great presidents: Washington, Jefferson, Lincoln, and Theodore Roosevelt.

8. Main Idea: The Verrazano-Narrows Bridge is the longest suspension bridge in the United States.
a. The Verrazano-Narrows Bridge was designed by O. H. Ammann.
b. The Verrazano-Narrows Bridge is 4,260 feet long and spans the Narrows at the entrance to New York harbor.
c. The Verrazano-Narrows Bridge was named for Giovanni da Verrazano, an Italian explorer sailing in the service of France, who possibly was the first European to enter New York Bay.
d. The Verrazano-Narrows Bridge has two levels; each holds six lanes of traffic.

PRACTICING THE STRATEGIES: MAKING INFERENCES BASED ON DETAILS

At times you can go beyond the facts stated in a passage to identify other information. When you do that, you are making an inference, as described earlier in this chapter.

Read the following segments from a selection entitled "The Bridge They Said Couldn't Be Built," by Lee Sheridan. When you have read it, you will have to answer questions that require an inference based on details stated in the paragraphs.

THE BRIDGE THEY SAID COULDN'T BE BUILT
Lee Sheridan

New York in the Winter of 1866-1867

The winter of 1866-1867 was one of the worst ever recorded in the history of New York. Snow covered most of the area, and great blocks of ice clogged the East River between Manhattan and Brooklyn. Often the Fulton Street ferryboat was unable to cross the East River. So people trying to get to work in Manhattan or return home to Brooklyn were jammed up at each river bank. What's more, with no electricity and no telephones, there was no way of even communicating across the river except by boat.

What the East River needed was a bridge. Many people thought so, but most said building a bridge would be impossible: the river was too wide; the currents, winds, and ocean tides were too powerful.

Select the inference that is most probable based on what you know so far.

1. The Brooklyn Bridge that spans the East River was completed
   a. before the winter of 1866-1867.
   b. during the winter of 1866-1867.
   c. after the winter of 1866-1867.

2. The telephone was invented
   a. before the winter of 1866-1867.
   b. during the winter of 1866-1867.
   c. after the winter of 1866-1867.

3. Before the construction of the Brooklyn Bridge,
   a. many bridges had successfully been built across distances as great as the width of the East River.
   b. few bridges had successfully been built across distances as great as the width of the East River.
   c. no bridges had successfully been built across distances as great as the width of the East River.

John A. Roebling

One person who didn't think a bridge was impossible was an engineer named John A. Roebling. Roebling was known throughout the

Figure 5.1 *The Brooklyn Bridge*

world as the expert bridge builder of the day. Suspension bridges were his specialty. A suspension bridge is a bridge suspended by wire cables hung over towers and fastened on the land at both ends.

Roebling had founded his own Wire Rope Company to manufacture the cables for suspension bridges. In 1866 he had just completed the longest suspension bridge ever built—a bridge in Cincinnati over the Ohio River. If anyone could build a suspension bridge over the East River—a length of half a mile—John A. Roebling was the one to do it.

Several years earlier, Roebling had submitted a plan for a suspension bridge connecting Manhattan and Brooklyn. No other kind of bridge could be built across an area as wide as the East River and also allow ships to pass underneath. Still, the officials of both New York and Brooklyn had doubts. They rejected Roebling's first plan as impossible.

Select the inference that is most probable based on what you know so far.

4. Before designing the Brooklyn Bridge, Roebling had designed
    a. no other suspension bridges.
    b. one other suspension bridge.
    c. several suspension bridges.

5. The Cincinnati bridge over the Ohio River was probably
    a. less than a half-mile long.
    b. a half-mile long.
    c. greater than a half-mile long.

6. Shipping was of
    a. no importance to people living in this area.
    b. little importance to people living in this area.
    c. considerable importance to people living in this area.

Roebling's New Design

Roebling persisted in presenting his plan for a bridge across the East River. He assured people that he had added something new to suspension bridges to make them safer. He had designed a series of diagonal supports running downward from the top of the two towers to points on the suspenders. [Look at Figure 5.1.] With the added strength of these diagonal supports, he said, the bridge was guaranteed to withstand strong winds and last for generations.

Still, Roebling's design might never have been accepted if it hadn't been for the harsh winter of 1866–1867. By then, the people of Brooklyn and New York were willing to take any chance on a bridge, if it meant an easier way to get across the river. In the same year the bridge project was begun. John A. Roebling gladly took up his appointment as chief engineer of the project.

Select the inference that is most probable based on what you know so far.

7. What phrase best characterizes the way people in 1866–1867 viewed long suspension bridges?
    a. very, very safe

b. safe

c. not too safe

8. What word best characterizes the feelings of the people of Brooklyn and New York during the winter of 1866–1867?
   a. calm
   b. desperate
   c. unconcerned

Accident on the Ferryboat

Unfortunately, John Roebling, who had designed most of the details for the project, was not able to see his great bridge even begun. In the summer of 1869, he was riding on the Fulton ferry to locate the exact spot for the Brooklyn tower of the bridge. His foot was accidently crushed between some loose logs as the ferry slammed into the Brooklyn dock.

Such an injury alone is not enough to kill a person, but John Roebling would not rest as the doctors told him. He was so concerned about his bridge that he refused medicine and wouldn't even stay in bed. Within sixteen days of the accident, John A. Roebling, the master bridge builder, was dead.

Select the inference that is most probable based on what you know so far.

9. What kind of engineer was Roebling?
   a. a designer who got directly involved in bridge-building projects
   b. a designer who left the details to other, more practical engineers
   c. a designer who was primarily concerned with putting ideas together
10. If Roebling had obeyed the doctor's orders, he probably would have
    a. lived to see his bridge finished.
    b. died anyway, because medical science then was not what it is today.

(Note: The Brooklyn Bridge was completed in May 1883. Roebling's son, also an engineer, became the chief engineer on the project after the death of his father.)

SELECTION 1: THE DREAM AT PANAMA

Expanding Your Vocabulary Through Reading

Determine the meaning of the underlined terms by using context and word-structure clues. Where you are uncertain, check the glossary for a definition. Record the definition in the space provided. The underlined words are from the selection you will read shortly.

1. The isthmus, the narrow strip of land between the two islands, was visible only at low tide. _____

2. <u>Devastating</u> winds roared over the countryside, destroying everything in sight.

_____

_____

3. The situation that existed after World War II was <u>akin</u> to the situation after World War I. _____

_____

4. All the energy he could <u>muster</u> was not enough for him to move the boulder.

_____

_____

5. For Washington, the Battle of Long Island was a <u>debacle</u>. He was forced to retreat with his troops. _____

_____

6. The wagons became <u>mired</u> in the mud. We had no way to pull them out.

_____

_____

7. During the war, we had to endure <u>horrific</u> conditions—lack of food, medicine, adequate shelter, and even pure water. _____

_____

8. The <u>incumbent</u> judge—the one currently in office—will try the case. _____

_____

9. He was a <u>virtual</u> prisoner of the rebels for two months; there was a guard at his door, and he could not leave his home. _____

_____

10. At the end of the month we were <u>inundated</u> with bills. There were so many we could not pay them. _____

_____

11. The <u>Continental Divide</u> is a ridge of mountains that separates rivers flowing into one ocean from those flowing into another. In North America, the Continental Divide is the ridge of the Rocky Mountains, which separates westward-flowing streams from eastward-flowing ones. _____

_____

Getting Ready to Read

Preview the selection.

- Read the title, the italicized introductory section, and the first paragraph. Study Figure 5.2. What is the topic of the selection? Write the topic in the center of the idea web on page 97.
- What do you already know about the topic? Record what you know on this idea web.

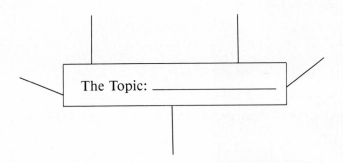

The Topic: _____

- What questions do you want to answer based on your preview of the selection? Write two questions here. _____

_____

_____

Reading with Meaning

Read the following selection, keeping your purpose-setting questions in mind. As you read, keep a pen in hand and record significant details that support, or substantiate, the main idea. The first two paragraphs are done as a model for you.

THE DREAM AT PANAMA

George Cruys

Perhaps there is only the moon to compare with it. Of all the achievements of American engineering, only the landing on the moon and the planting there of a wrinkled flag can rival the construction of the Panama Canal as an epoch-making accomplishment. The Suez Canal, the trans-Siberian Railroad and the Taj Mahal all pale beside it. The canal's construction is more closely akin to the pyramids of Egypt in its scope and difficulty of execution, but in the modern era, there is only the moon.

Like the landing on the moon, the construction of a canal across the narrow Isthmus of Panama was a dream long before it became reality. As early as 1534, Charles I of Spain proposed a canal at Panama, but it would take nearly 400 years for builders to catch up with his imagination.

When the canal finally was proposed, it required all the creativity the twentieth century

1. Main idea: The building of the Panama Canal is an accomplishment that equaled the landing of men on the moon.
Supporting detail: Building the canal is akin to building the pyramids.

2. Main idea: People had long dreamed of a canal in Panama.
Supporting detail: A Panama Canal was proposed as early as the 1500s.

Panama Canal Company

Figure 5.2   *Views of the Panama Canal Being Built*

Panama Canal Company   Panama Canal Company

could muster. It was the largest public work ever attempted. Its engineers had to control a wild river, cut the continental divide, construct the largest dam and man made lake known to that date and swing the largest locks ever constructed from the biggest cement structures ever poured. Along the way, two of the world's most devastating diseases had to be wiped out in one of their greatest strongholds. And all of this was to be done without the airplane or the automobile: Kitty Hawk rose into the headlines in 1903–the same year the U.S. signed a treaty with Panama—and there was no road across the isthmus until World War II.

If Panama has had an unusual role in bygone dreams, it most certainly has a startling relationship to the hard facts of geography. The country is farther east than most people imagine—the canal and about half of Panama actually lie east of Miami. Because of the country's shallow "S" shape and east-west orientation, it has places where the sun rises in the Pacific and sets in the Atlantic. More significantly, Panama is squeezed into the narrowest portion of Central America. At the canal, just 43 miles of land separate Atlantic and Pacific shores. Perhaps even more important, Panama offers the lowest point in the North American continental divide—originally 312 feet above sea level at the canal's Culebra Cut. By comparison, the lowest pass in the United States is nearly 5,000 feet.

Spanish & French Era

The first path across the isthmus was Las Cruces Trail. A winding, difficult tunnel through the jungle from Panama City to Portobelo, it was built by slaves to transport riches to the Spanish Main. At the edge of the narrow trail a tangled mass of strange plants issues threatening noises even today. "It's O.K. in the daytime," said guide José Turner during a recent visit, "but imagine it at night."

California's gold rush sent thousands of prospectors to Panama in search of a quick crossing to the Pacific. By 1855, a small railroad operated between coasts and some prospectors paid $25 in gold just to walk along its tracks. Today the train costs $1.75 to ride and takes about an hour and a half to cross the continent.

3. **Main idea:** The canal required great creativity.
Supporting detail:

4. **Main idea:** Geographic relationships are important at the canal.
Supporting detail:

5. **Main idea:** The first path across the isthmus was Las Cruces Trail.
Supporting detail:

6. **Main idea:** A railroad was built, which encouraged the French to try to build a sea-level canal.
Supporting detail:

7. Main idea: It is hard to imagine today what it was like then.
Supporting detail:

8. Main idea: Excessive rainfall was a major problem.
Supporting detail:

9. Main idea: Threatening vegetation and creatures were a problem.
Supporting detail:

10. Main idea: The worst problem was the mosquito.
Supporting detail:

11. Main idea: Many people lost their lives to diseases.
Supporting detail:

The new railroad encouraged engineers toward one of the greatest peacetime debacles in human experience: the ill-fated French attempt to build a sea level canal at Panama.

Crossing the canal today, it is hard to imagine the impossible challenge Panama presented just a century ago. Today's transit is so smooth and the surrounding grounds so park like, the stories of horror in the jungle sound like tropical exaggerations. But in 1881, when the first party of French engineers arrived to dig the canal, the Isthmus of Panama was—as an American senator would later put it—"death's nursery."

Panama is inundated by seventy inches of annual rainfall on the Pacific side, and an improbable 144 inches on the Atlantic side. Up to six inches can fall in a single day. Fed by this rain, the Chagres River, which empties into the Atlantic just west of modern Cristobal, could rise more than forty-five feet. During one storm it rose ten feet in just twenty-four hours.

The rain forest is a threatening wall of vegetation inhabited by all manner of equally threatening creatures. On Barro Colorado—a single island in modern Gatun Lake—there are twenty-two species of alligators, two species of crocodiles and thirty-seven species of serpents, while area mammals include the jaguar, puma and ocelot.

But the most formidable creature of Panama, when the French were deciding to build a canal there, was one of its smallest. The clean, soft skins of engineers and laborers were about to be welcomed by clouds of mosquitoes—and at the time that the French arrived, nobody knew that they carried disease.

Malaria and yellow fever were the worst diseases, but others included nearly all of the bad ones: cholera, typhoid, dysentary, tuberculosis, smallpox, and—for a frightening interlude during the American era—black plague. In the twenty years that the French would labor to build their hopeless canal, roughly 20,000 people would perish—most of them from disease. Jules Dingler, the director of the French excavations in 1883, lost his entire family in Panama to disease—wife, son, daughter and prospective son-in-law. After two crushing years, he went home to France.

The French canal, spearheaded by Suez builder Ferdinand de Lesseps, became mired in mud, jungle, disease, rising costs, corruption and controversy. Leaders of the private undertaking were sentenced to prison; 25,000 Jamaican laborers were stranded when the company went bankrupt. In 1904 the French sold their interest in the canal to the United States for $40 million—a sum considerably short of the $287 million they had invested and vastly less than it had cost them in lives and broken dreams.

12. Main idea: French canal builders faced problems that made them give up the project.
Supporting detail:

In spite of all their difficulties, the French had done excellent work. In 22 years of labor, they excavated 78 million cubic yards of earth under the most horrific conditions. Sadly, due to the different nature of the American canal, most of the French work was useless. Today, if you want to see what the French sacrificed so much to accomplish, you must watch carefully on the western bank, moving toward the Atlantic from Gatun Locks. There by a red buoy, number sixteen, there is a wide channel that disappears quickly into the jungle. It is the only section of the French canal that is left.

13. Main idea: The French had actually done fine work.
Supporting detail:

The American Era

In 1906, when the bespectacled Theodore Roosevelt came to Panama to see the "Big Ditch" for himself, the occasion marked the first visit of an incumbent president to a foreign country in the history of the United States. It was a clear sign of the importance Roosevelt would place on the canal's construction.

14. Main idea: President Roosevelt recognized the importance of building the Panama Canal.
Supporting detail:

At the turn of the century Panama was part of Colombia, ruled by Bogotá. When negotiations with Colombia for U.S. rights to build a canal came to a standstill, Panama proclaimed its independence in 1903 with key U.S. support. Less than a month later, a treaty with the Panamanian Republic established a Panama Canal Zone to be controlled by the U.S. "in perpetuity," extending five miles on either side of the proposed waterway.

15. Main Idea: U.S. signed a treaty with Panama in the early 1900s to establish a Canal Zone.
Supporting detail:

The Americans arrived in 1904 equipped with several advantages over their French predecessors. Larger steam shovels, bigger train cars, a huge national effort supported by a closer home country and an astonishingly corruption-free administration all favored the American attempt. The new engineers, it was

16. Main idea: The Americans had advantages that the French did not have.
Supporting detail:

17. Main idea: The key advantage was the virtual elimination of disease.
Supporting detail:

18. Main idea: Workers were brought into Panama.
Supporting detail:

19. Main idea: The solution to the construction problem was a series of locks that raised ships and the formation of a lake.
Supporting detail:

20. Topic: The Gatun Dam
Main idea:

Supporting detail:

21. Topic: Getting across the continental divide
Main idea:

Supporting detail:

noted, were particularly adept at using the rails to transport excavated material.

The key initial accomplishment was the virtual elimination of disease by Dr. William Gorgas, a U.S. Army physician who had already survived a yellow fever attack in Texas and one of malaria in Panama. With exacting and lifesaving thoroughness, Dr. Gorgas wiped out the breeding grounds of mosquitoes in the construction area. In an immense effort which at times included as many as 4,000 sanitation laborers, Gorgas eliminated yellow fever by the end of 1905 and radically reduced malaria.

With disease on the wane, engineers set to work. By 1907 some 30,000 men had arrived, primarily from Barbados, Jamaica and the U.S. Due to a shortage of available labor, Panama itself supplied just 357 workers for the canal.

The solution for the flooding Chagres River was to build an enormous dam that would create a lake over which ships could sail. Locks would raise ships to lake level, reducing the dig at Culebra on the continental divide to a conceivable scale. Ironically, both solutions had been previously suggested by Frenchmen.

The troublesome Chagres River was turned on itself. At the town of Gatun, engineers built what was, in its day, the largest earth dam ever constructed. One and a half miles long, half a mile wide at its base, Gatun Dam rose to 105 feet above sea level. Behind it gathered the waters of what was then the largest manmade lake in the world, 163-square-mile Gatun Lake. The massive waterway inundated several towns, rerouted the Panama Railroad, completely changed the geography of the canal area and furnished 23.5 navigable miles of the canal itself. The engineers had saved themselves a lot of digging, but there was still the question of the continental divide.

There are seventy hill formations along the canal route, but the cut across the continental divide at Culebra was the deepest and most difficult. The deeper the men dug, the more the mountains fell into the hole around them— sometimes burying steam shovels and railroad equipment. In 1912 alone, four and a half months were spent removing landslides from Culebra Cut. At one point, engineers discovered to their astonishment that the bottom of the excavation actually was rising under pressure from the surrounding mountains. In one place the ground rose six feet in five minutes.

The solution at Culebra was to keep removing dirt. Originally expected to require a 670-foot width, the final excavation grew to more than a quarter of a mile across and nine miles in length. Lt. Col. David Gaillard—the engineer in charge and the person who later would give his name to Culebra—would have been amused to note that the astronauts who returned from the moon brought with them just forty-seven pounds of lunar rocks.

22. Topic: The Culebra solution
Main idea:

Supporting detail:

The ditches at sea level and at eighty-five feet that crossed the continental divide were connected by the largest canal locks ever attempted. Radical in scale, they were reliable in operation. Seventy-two years after the opening of the canal, the same locks and seven-story, 700-ton lock gates are still in use, still activated by the same forty-horsepower motors. Nearly three quarters of a century after their construction, the tower control panels look almost exactly the same as the day they were built. It has proven to be a very workable design.

23. Topic: The canal locks
Main idea:

Supporting detail:

The Modern Era

The Panama Canal was completed under budget at $387 million. The *SS Ancon* made the first transit ahead of schedule on August 15, 1914, a landmark event overshadowed by the outbreak of World War I.

24. Topic: Completion of the canal
Main idea:

Supporting detail:

Since the canal's opening, work has continued at a surprising rate. In 1915 the channel was closed for eight months due to landslides, twenty-six of which fell into the canal in that year alone. The last major landslide occurred in 1970.

25. Topic: Landslides
Main idea:

Supporting detail:

In all, 262 million cubic yards of earth were removed from the canal—enough to fill a twelve-foot hole through the center of the earth. As a result, the sea route from New York to San Francisco is reduced by roughly 8,000 miles. Since its opening, more than 650,000 vessels have taken the shortcut, carrying everything from oil and grains to elephants, giraffes, and London Bridge. Admittedly a miracle of engineering, the canal also has proven to be a marvel of operational efficiency. Tolls have been raised just four times since the waterway was completed.

26. Topic: Results of the canal
Main idea:

Supporting detail:

27. Topic: Change to Panamanian control
Main idea:

Supporting detail:

28. Topic: Traveling the canal today
Main idea:

Supporting detail:

29. Topic: The dream at Panama
Main idea:

Supporting detail:

In 1977, the United States signed two new treaties with Panama which provided for the gradual transition of canal operations into Panamanian hands by the year 2000. With the tenth anniversary of the treaty's signing . . . , about eighty percent of today's canal workers are Panamanians, more than thirty of whom are canal pilots.

The transit of the canal today holds a special fascination for anyone who enjoyed the amusement park water slide as a kid. The ship is raised and lowered eighty-five feet via six pairs of chambers. Each lock chamber is 1,000 feet long and 110 feet wide. When the chambers fill with water there is no sensation of movement but you are readily aware that something amazing is underway. The passage through the Gaillard Cut is a narrow, steep-walled slot. In the two-hour crossing of Gatun Lake you are sailing over what were once the most feared jungles of the American coast. Average transit time for the entire canal is about nine hours.

When you are sailing through the Panama Canal there is ample time to stand at the ship's rail and reflect. The deep green hills still look rugged, the thick clot of the jungle has not changed. Admittedly, there are no more pirate treasure mules, the French left long ago with their sad story, and the astronauts have been to the moon and back. But the canal—the realization of so many dreams—is there and it is working. It is probably the most fascinating place you can go to revel in the genius of first rate engineering until that day, far in the future, when you can stand by the flag on that distant lunar plain and stir up the dust with your boot.

Checking for Understanding of Supporting Detail

Circle the best response.

1. In scope and difficulty, the canal's construction was most closely akin to that of the
   a. Suez Canal.
   b. trans-Siberian Railroad.
   c. Taj Mahal.
   d. pyramids of Egypt.

2. A canal in Panama was first proposed in the
   a. 1300s.
   b. 1500s.

    c. 1600s.

    d. 1700s.

3. The canal was built with the help of

    a. the airplane.

    b. the automobile.

    c. both the plane and the automobile.

    d. neither the plane nor the automobile.

4. Which of these statements is true?

    a. About half of Panama lies east of Miami.

    b. Panama is squeezed into the narrowest portion of Central America.

    c. Panama offers the lowest point in the North American continental divide.

    d. All of the above are true.

    e. Both "b" and "c" are true.

5. A small railroad was operating across the isthmus by the

    a. beginning of the 1700s.

    b. middle of the 1700s.

    c. beginning of the 1800s.

    d. middle of the 1800s.

6. Today's transit of the canal is

    a. scary.

    b. a challenge.

    c. smooth.

    d. horrific.

7. The annual rainfall on the Atlantic side is closest to

    a. 50 inches.

    b. 100 inches.

    c. 150 inches.

    d. 200 inches.

8. Which of these are found in Panama?

    a. crocodiles

    b. alligators

    c. serpents

    d. all of the above and more

9. The worst diseases in Panama during the building of the canal were

    a. malaria and yellow fever.

    b. cholera and typhoid.

    c. smallpox and black plague.

    d. smallpox and dysentary.

10. According to the treaty of the early 1900s, the Panama Canal Zone was to be controlled by

    a. Panama.

    b. Colombia.

    c. Bogotá.

    d. the United States.

11. Gorgas attacked malaria and yellow fever by

    a. changing the breeding patterns of mosquitoes in the area.

b. wiping out the breeding grounds of mosquitoes there.

c. interbreeding the mosquitoes to get a new breed.

d. All of the above are true.

12. The large Gatun Lake was formed by
   a. building locks.
   b. building a dam.
   c. rerouting the railway.
   d. building a roadway.

13. The major construction problem at Culebra Cut was
   a. landslides.
   b. lack of money.
   c. the flooding river.
   d. weak concrete.

14. The locks used today are
   a. the same ones built initially.
   b. the second set built.
   c. the third set built.

15. The first transit of the Panama Canal occurred at the time of
   a. the Spanish-American War.
   b. World War I.
   c. World War II.
   d. the Korean War.

16. The average transit time through the canal today is
   a. fifteen minutes.
   b. two hours.
   c. nine hours.
   d. two days.

Checking Your Word Power

Circle the best response.

1. The isthmus of Panama is a
   a. canal.
   b. narrow strip of land.
   c. kind of crocodile.
   d. man who once ruled Panama.

2. A devastating storm is one that
   a. brings destruction.
   b. comes and goes quickly.
   c. is accompanied by thunder.
   d. occurs only at night.

3. I felt something akin to love.
   a. actual
   b. foreign
   c. similar, or related
   d. funny about

4. The building of the canal required all the creativity its builders could muster.
   a. play with

   b. carry
   c. pull
   d. call forth

5. The French <u>debacle</u> occurred because they tried to build a sea-level canal.
   a. debate
   b. departure
   c. complete breakdown
   d. happening

6. Their plan became <u>mired</u> in red tape.
   a. stuck
   b. mixed with
   c. married
   d. manufactured

7. They plodded on despite <u>horrific</u> problems—floods, landslides, and disease.
   a. causing honor
   b. causing pleasure
   c. causing sadness
   d. causing horror

8. I will vote for the <u>incumbent</u> governor.
   a. one who is coming
   b. one holding office
   c. one who is running for office
   d. one who is living in the state

9. The key accomplishment of the period was the <u>virtual</u> elimination of malaria.
   a. nearly complete
   b. absolute
   c. partial
   d. parallel

10. The waters of the overflowing river <u>inundated</u> the surrounding countryside.
    a. flooded
    b. watered
    c. irrigated
    d. washed

11. The <u>Continental Divide</u> is a
    a. railroad that divides the continent.
    b. mountain range that divides the continent.
    c. river that divides the continent.
    d. canal that cuts across the isthmus.

Writing with Significant Details

   According to the selection you just read, the construction of the pyramids of Egypt was an engineering feat akin to the construction of the Panama Canal. Read a brief selection in an encyclopedia about the pyramids. Then decide on the main idea you want to express and some details you can use to support that idea. Map the main idea and the details on Figure 5.3. Using your idea map, write one paragraph about the pyramids. Start with a topic sentence that com-

Main Idea:
Supporting Detail:
Supporting Detail:
Supporting Detail:
Supporting Detail:

Figure 5.3   *A Guide for Plotting Main Idea and Supporting Details of a Paragraph Before Writing. Jot your thoughts directly on the guide before you begin to draft your paragraph.*

municates the main idea. Next write several sentences with details that support the main point you make in the topic sentence.

EXTENDING WHAT YOU HAVE LEARNED

Building Your Knowledge Base

Circle or plot these locations on the map in Figure 5.4.

Central America	Isthmus of Panama
South America	North America
Pacific Ocean	Atlantic Ocean

Building Your Personal Vocabulary

Select several words emphasized in this chapter to add to your personal vocabulary list. Record the chosen words as well as a model sentence using each word.

Reviewing Your Strategy for Working with Details

What two questions should you ask yourself to determine whether a detail is significant?

1. _____

   _____

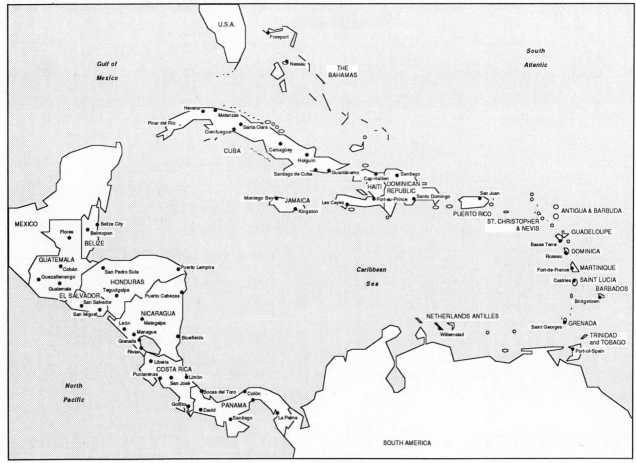

Figure 5.4 *Central America*

2. _____
_____

How do you generally handle dates and numbers as you meet them in reading?

_____
_____
_____

Practicing Your Strategy

Locate an article that describes an event, person, or place that interests you. Read the article. As you read, focus on the main idea and those details you need to remember to support that idea. On paper, record the title and author as well as the source; record the main idea and the details you feel are significant.

6

Using Clue Words to Anticipate an Author's Thoughts

Before reading the chapter, read the title, the stated objective, and the headings and subheadings. Ask yourself: What is the topic of the chapter? In the space above and beside the chapter number, jot down what you already know about that topic. Then in the space below the chapter number, jot down at least two questions you hope to answer through reading the chapter.

OBJECTIVE

In this chapter, you will learn a strategy for using clue words to perceive relationships among ideas so that you can anticipate what is going to happen next in a sentence or paragraph. You will learn to use clue words such as these:

1. *one, two,* and *three,* which indicate the number of items to be enumerated or discussed;
2. *for example* and *such as,* which indicate that an example is coming;
3. *also* and *furthermore,* which indicate that more on the same idea is coming and *but, however,* and *yet,* which indicate a change in direction;
4. *similarly* and *on the other hand,* which indicate that a comparison or contrast is on the way;
5. *if/then, hence,* and *consequently,* which indicate a conditional relationship (a condition followed by an outcome);
6. *because* and *for this reason,* which indicate that a reason is coming.

INTRODUCTION—USING CLUE WORDS

In previous chapters, you learned that writing has structure. For example, paragraphs may have a topic sentence followed by sentences that provide supporting details. Being able to perceive this kind of paragraph structure aids in comprehension; your perception gives you a framework for understanding the paragraph.

Writers also use clue words to give structure to their writing and to help you, the reader, predict, or anticipate, what will happen next in a sentence or paragraph. If you know the way clue words function in writing, you are better able to understand important sentence relationships.

Being able to predict what will happen next in a passage is important in reading. Good readers are not passive receivers; they are active "makers of meaning." Reading a sentence, they actively pick up clues about relationships among ideas and anticipate what kinds of thoughts are coming next.

Predicting: How Many Items Are to Be Discussed?

Preview the following selection by skimming the title, the first sentence, and the italicized words. Then read the selection. As you do, keep alert for number words that tell you how many items the writer is going to discuss. Circle the number words.

THE THREE CLASSES OF ROCKS
George Hennings

All the rocks in the earth's crust are grouped into three classes. When magma (the molten material beneath the earth's crust) and lava (the molten rock coming out on the earth's surface) cool, they harden and become *igneous rocks,* the first class. The word *igneous* comes from the Latin word for fire. As the molten mass loses heat, minerals harden into a crystalline igneous rock.

As rocks are exposed to a variety of forces (water, lower surface temperatures, lower surface pressures, and abrasion), the igneous rocks start to come apart both chemically and physically. The broken rock particles may be transported downgrade by wind and water and come eventually to rest as sediments. As time passes, sediments cover other sediments, layer on layer. Particles are compacted together; grains fit more tightly. Dissolved chemicals form cement, and particles turn into stone. Thus we have the formation of the second class of rock— *sedimentary rocks.*

Deeply buried sedimentary rocks are heated and squeezed together by enormous pressures. They change in form as grains rearrange themselves and minerals change their composition. The change in form is called metamorphism; the result is the third class of rock, the *metamorphic rocks.*

Did you circle the word *three* in the first paragraph? When you came to that word, did you predict and say to yourself, "This is going to be about three classes

Thesis of the Entire Passage:

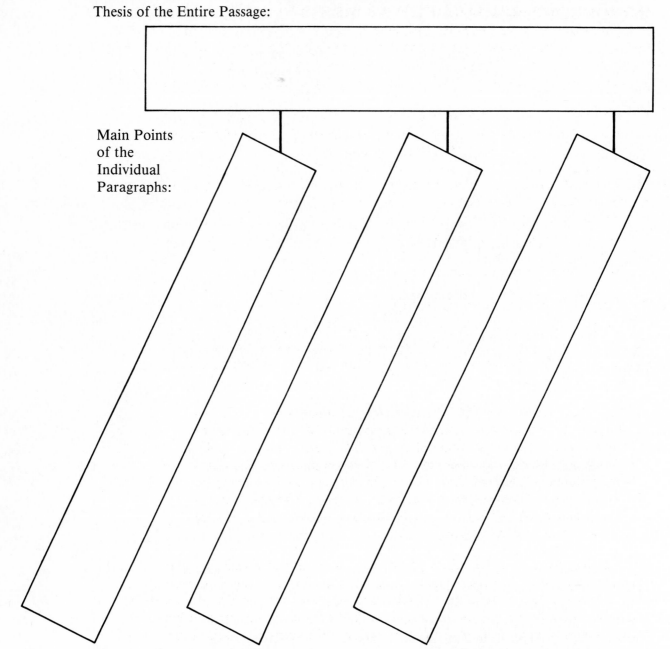

Main Points
of the
Individual
Paragraphs:

Figure 6.1   *An Idea Map of a Passage. Map the passage by recording the thesis, or main point, of the entire passage about rocks in the top box. Record the main ideas of the individual paragraphs in the connecting boxes.*

of rock. The author will probably start out by describing the first class, go on to the second, and finish with the third"? Did you circle the word *first* in the first paragraph, *second* in the second, and *third* in the third? Those words are clues to the framework the author is using to develop his ideas: The author is enumerating and discussing three items, one after the other.

History and science writers often use the pattern just described in organizing their writing. In the first sentence of their first paragraph, they tell the number of items they are going to discuss. In this respect, that first sentence serves as the topic sentence for the series of paragraphs to follow. In the first paragraph, they then discuss the first item—in this case igneous rocks. Completing that topic, they move to a discussion of the second item; completing that, they move to a discussion of the third. At each transition, the reader, who is wise to the ways of writers, says to himself or herself: "Now the author is going to move to the next point."

The writer of the geology paragraphs built a second organizing clue into the paragraphs. He italicized the names of the rock classes. A reader who realizes the importance of previewing before reading may pick up this clue during the preview. Learning in the first sentence that there are three classes of rocks, the reader scans the paragraphs that follow, noting the three italicized rock types. The reader then knows that the first paragraph is about igneous, the second about sedimentary, and the third about metamorphic—all before reading the passage in depth. Previewing pays dividends; it provides a framework for anticipating while reading.

Now reread the passage and complete the idea map in Figure 6.1.

Predicting: Is an Example Coming?

Read this short passage. As you read, look for any word or phrase that gives you a clue as to what is coming. Circle the clue word that allows you to predict while reading and provides a framework for your reading. Underline the main idea sentence.

> Cities have been completely destroyed by volcanic eruptions. An example of note is the destruction of Pompeii in Italy by the eruption of Mt. Vesuvius. On the morning of August 24, A.D. 79, horrific explosions broke the stillness of the day; columns of smoke, gases, and steam rose into the air; and a rain of ash and glowing debris fell on Pompeii. Within several hours of the first volcanic rumblings, Pompeii was inundated under twenty feet of volcanic ash; roofs collapsed; people were suffocated by poisonous gases.

Did you note the significance of the phrase "an example"? That phrase is a clue to the design of the paragraph. The first sentence obviously states the main idea. But then the writer shifts gears slightly. She supports the main idea with an example of one well-known volcanic eruption. Figure 6.2 shows the relationship among main and supporting ideas in the paragraph. Complete it by adding the main idea and the supporting example.

Phrases like "an example of note" in the paragraph on Pompeii are clues that you can use to predict what is coming. Reading it, you shift gears—just as the writer is going to do. You get ready to handle the example. You predict: "The author is going to give an example." Similar phrases that tell you that you can anticipate an example are "such as," "for example," and "for instance." Sometimes a writer provides more than one example and introduces it with the phrase "Another example . . . " or "Another instance . . . . "

Read the next paragraph and contrast it to the structure of the one about Vesuvius. Ask yourself as you read: How is it similar in design to the previous paragraph? How is it different? (Note that the word *pertinacious* used in the first [and topic] sentence means "extremely persistent, clinging tightly to a purpose.")

Main Idea:

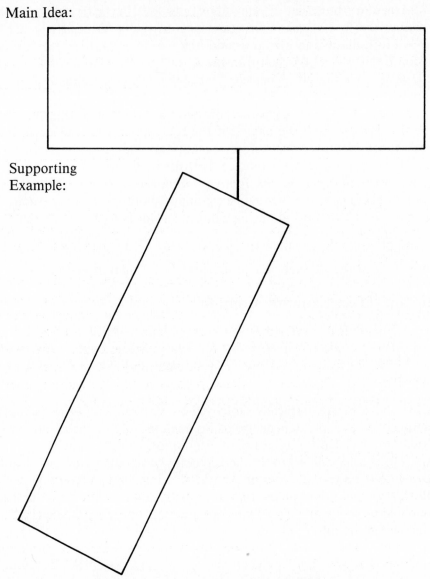

Supporting
Example:

Figure 6.2   *An Idea Map to Show Relationships in a Paragraph. Map the paragraph to show the relationship between the main idea and the supporting example. Record the main idea in the top box and the supporting example in the connecting box.*

The human race is extraordinarily pertinacious in continuing to live around volcanoes and even high up on their slopes. Vesuvius, "the pride and terror of Naples," is thickly surrounded by towns and villages and is covered with gardens, groves, and vineyards that extend far up toward its summit. Etna is cultivated up to an altitude of 4000 feet, intensively below an elevation of 1500 feet—orange and lemon groves, vineyards, and oleanders, all in vivid contrast to the black lava flows. Mount Rosso, 700 feet high, the largest cinder cone on Etna, built in 1669 during the most disastrous eruption in the history of Etna, is now green with vineyards half way to its summit.

1. What is the main idea? _____

   _____

2. How is the paragraph similar to the previous one about Vesuvius? _____

   _____

   _____

3. How is it different? _____

   _____

   _____

If you said that both paragraphs start with a topic sentence, you recognized a basic element in their design. If you said that the pattern was a topic sentence supported by examples, you recognized a second element in their design. Both paragraphs rely on examples to support the main idea.

Now consider the difference. The first paragraph provides a clue phrase that helps you predict during reading: "an example of note." The second paragraph does not. In the latter case, you must figure out as you read about the towns and villages surrounding Vesuvius that this is an example. When you get to the sentence on Etna, you must figure out that this is a second example. What helps you predict during reading, in this case, is your knowledge of the way paragraphs develop. Figure 6.3 shows the relationship between the main idea and the supporting examples. Complete the idea map by adding these points.

Predicting: A Continuation of the Same Topic or a Change of Direction?

Being able to predict whether an author is going to provide more information on the topic or instead is going to provide details about a different aspect of that topic can also guide your reading. Some words or phrases are clues to what the writer is going to do.

Words an author uses to tell you that he or she is going to provide more details about the same idea include

and	also
in addition	additionally
moreover	furthermore

Words an author uses that are clues that he or she is going to change direction and provide details on some other, perhaps opposing, aspect of the topic include

but	yet
however	on the other hand
nevertheless	instead

Main Idea:

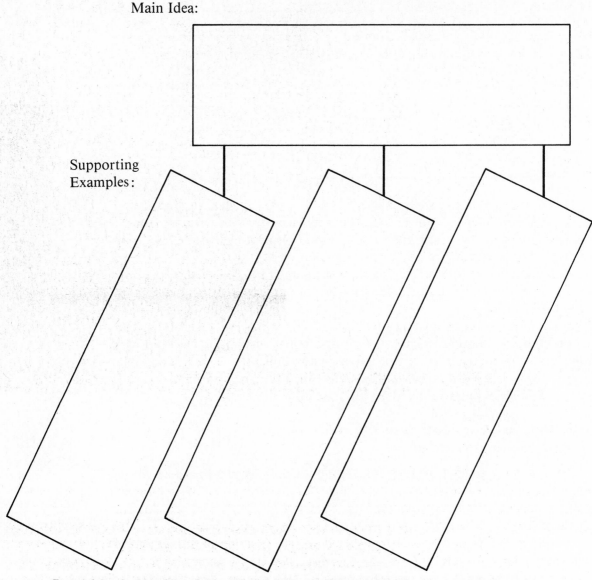

Figure 6.3 *An Idea Map to Show Relationships in a Paragraph. Map the paragraph to show the relationship between the main idea and the supporting examples. Record the main idea in the top box and the supporting examples in the connecting boxes.*

Read the following paragraphs. As you read, you will see how the authors use examples to support their main idea. You will also see how the authors use some of the transitional words listed above to either (1) maintain the same direction and add more details about the topic, or (2) change direction and add details on some other aspect of the topic. Some of the words have been underlined. In the balloons connected to these words, write what the authors are doing at that point—giving an opposite point or adding more information relative to the topic. The word eject in the first paragraph means "to throw out." Viscous means "sticky, or adhesive"; pancake syrup is viscous.

UPI Bettmann Newsphotos

Figure 6.4   *Mount St. Helens volcano in Washington State*

Why the Earth has yielded, <u>and</u> is still yielding, so great a variety of magmas is a highly interesting problem. Different volcanoes erupt lavas of different kinds. Vesuvius erupts one kind, Etna another. More remarkable still, neighboring volcanoes may erupt very unlike lavas. Stromboli and Vulcano are in the Lapari Islands north of Sicily, only 25 miles apart: Stromboli is ejecting basalt, <u>but</u> Vulcano in the recent past has ejected rhyolite—lavas about as far apart in composition as possible.

<u>Furthermore</u>, a volcano during the course of its life may erupt lavas of several kinds. As many as five kinds of lava were erupted from San Francisco Mountain, a large extinct volcano rising 5000 feet above the plateau of northern Arizona.

Very fluid lavas flow rapidly, especially on steep slopes. Some, like the great flow from Mauna Loa in 1850, average 10 miles an hour. <u>However</u>, speeds of more than 5 miles an hour

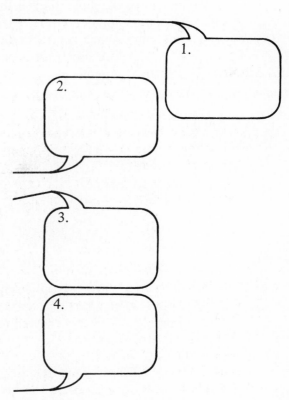

1.

2.

3.

4.

are exceptional. As the lava flows cool and become viscous, they move extremely slowly, creeping onward, possibly for several years.

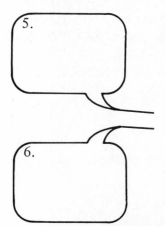

From the prevalence of volcanic islands in the sea, it is evident that vast outpourings of lava have occurred on the sea floor. The volcanic chain of the Hawaiian Islands is an example of this. Eruptions in progress beneath the sea have been recognized by the issuance of vapors and ash from the water.

Eruptions occur <u>also</u> on the floors of bodies of fresh water. <u>Moreover</u>, streams of lava flow from the land into the sea or into lakes. The resulting lava flow resembles a pile of pillows. Such lavas are expressively termed "pillow lavas."

As a review, underline the topic (or main idea) sentence and put a check by each example in the preceding paragraphs. Are you finding that main ideas and examples are beginning to stand out as you read? As you encounter a supporting example in reading, do you quickly recognize one for what it is?

Predicting: Is a Comparison or Contrast Coming?

Just as authors use word clues that tell you they are going to cite an example, provide more information on the topic, or provide information on a different aspect of the topic, they at times use words that tell you they are going to make a comparison or contrast. When comparing, writers tell how things or events are the same. When contrasting, writers tell how they differ.

Here are some words and phrases that hint that an author is comparing or contrasting items:

Comparisons	Contrasts
similarly	on the other hand
as in the case of	on the contrary
like the	unlike the
the same as	in contrast to
	whereas or whereas others

Read these two paragraphs. As you read, see whether you can find the transition point where the authors begin to make a comparison or contrast. Ask yourself: What are they comparing or contrasting? Are they giving similarities or differences?

When the lava first flows out, it is red or white hot and highly fluid. It soon cools on the surface, darkens, and crusts over. As it cools it becomes more and more viscous. When the flow becomes very viscous, the under part may still be moving while the upper part crusts over and breaks up into rough, angular, jagged blocks, which are borne as a tumbling, jostling mass on the surface of the slowly moving flow. When eventually the flow comes to rest and solidifies, the resulting lava sheet is extremely rough. Its top is a chaotic assemblage of blocks and fragments, bristling with innumerable sharp points. Such lava flows are termed *block lava.* In Hawaii they are called *aa* (a a).

In marked contrast to the block lava, other flows harden with smooth surfaces, which have curious ropy, curved, and billowy forms. "Corded" lava of this kind the Hawaiians term *pahoehoe* (pa-ho a-ho a).

1. In the two paragraphs, what are the authors comparing? _____

    _____

2. Are they telling how the items differ or are the same? _____

    _____

3. What phrase do the authors use as a clue to tell you that there is going to be a contrast? _____

4. How does the paragraphing help you make sense of the contrast? _____

    _____

The English language provides another clue that writers are developing a contrast in a paragraph—the use of the ending *-er* or the word *more.* For example, an author may begin one paragraph with the phrase "In older volcanoes . . ." and begin the follow-up paragraph with the phrase "In younger volcanoes . . . ." The use of the comparative *-er* lets you predict that the author is contrasting the two.

Read these paragraphs. Can you identify the clue words that tell you that a comparison or contrast is being developed? What is being compared or contrasted? Are similarities or differences being developed? The word *veritable* in the selection means "true," or "genuine."

That lavas, even after they have issued from the volcanic vent, still contain dissolved gases is amply shown not only by the clouds of steam that escape from them for weeks and months but also by the structures they assume as they solidify into rock. Viscous lava may become highly inflated by the expansion of innumerable bubbles of gas. Each bubble hole is a vesicle (like a sac), which is spherical if the lava was stationary and almond shaped if the lava was moving and drawing out the vesicle while the hole was forming. The upper portion of a flow, especially of a viscous lava, may contain so many holes that it has become a veritable froth. Rock froth is known as *pumice.*

In more fluid lava, the gas cavities, or vesicles, attain larger sizes. If the cavities are highly irregular in shape and size and are so abundant that there is at least as much empty space as solid matter, the resulting rock is *scoriaceous.* Loose pieces of such material are called *scoriae.*

1. What is being compared or contrasted? _____

_____

2. Are similarities or differences being stressed? _____

3. What word clues do the authors use to let you know that there is to be a contrast? _____

4. How does the design of the paragraphs help you understand the contrast?

_____

_____

_____

Predicting: Is a Conditional Relationship Being Set Up?

Conditional relationships are common in scientific writing, both in the natural and social sciences. When authors express conditional relationships, they state a condition and then tell what results when that condition is met. A common language pattern for doing this is an *if* clause followed by a *then* clause, as in this sentence map:

If this condition exists,   *then this results*

If the rocks are radioactive,   then heat will build up.

---

1. What happens if the rocks are radioactive? What then? Write the answer here.

_____

_____

Often the word *then* is left out; you must mentally add it in reading. You must think to yourself: If this happens, what then? Asking the "what then" question is a simple strategy for interpreting a conditional relationship.

If magma reaches the Earth's surface and is discharged from an opening,   it flows out on the surface where it cools rapidly and solidifies.

---

2. What happens if the magma is discharged from the volcano? If this happens (if the condition is met), what is the outcome, or effect? _____

_____

Read the following paragraph. Whenever you run into an "if" clause, ask the "what then" question to keep yourself on track. Ask: If this happens, what then? (Note: The word edifice in the paragraph means "a building, especially a large one.")

The shape and structure of the edifice built up around a volcanic vent depends on the material of which it is formed. If the edifice is made wholly of fragmental ejecta (materials thrown out), a steep cone is built. Slopes of 30 degrees, rarely 40 degrees, are attained before the accumulating mass begins to slide. Volcanic edifices of this kind are called *pyroclastic cones;* they are characteristic results of explosive eruptions. A pyroclastic cone built of huge angular blocks forms the summit of Etna. If a pyroclastic cone consists wholly of cinders, it is called a *cinder cone.* Cinder cones are relatively small.

3. If the cone is made totally of fragments, what then?

   What is the effect? _____

   _____

4. If the cone consists of cinders, what then? What is the effect? _____

   _____

Other phrases that are clues to a conditional relationship include *consequently, therefore, thus,* and *hence.* Here are some examples:

If this condition exists	Effect or result
At the time it is being extruded, a magma may be too viscous to flow readily.	Consequently the sluggish pasty mass piles up over the vent as a great dome.

5. What happens if the magma is too viscous to flow readily?

   _____

   _____

6. What word warns you that an effect may be coming?

   _____

7. Rewrite the two sentences, substituting another clue phrase for *consequently* so that you get the feel for how this kind of conditional writing operates.

   (Perhaps use *hence* or *thus* to express the conditional relationship.) _____

   _____

   _____

If this condition exists	Effect or result
In forming an intrusive body the magma cools under a thick jacket of rocks;	hence its dissolved gases can not escape easily.

8. What happens if the magma cools under a thick jacket of rocks? _____

_____

9. What word warns you that an effect may be coming? _____

10. Rewrite the sentence, substituting another clue phrase for *hence* so that you understand how this kind of conditional thinking operates.

_____

_____

_____

Predicting: Is a Reason Going to Be Given?

Just as writers of social and natural science content often set forth if-then relationships, they also give reasons for why things happen or are as they are. You can predict when writers are getting ready to provide reasons by looking out for these word clues:

because	for	as a result
for this reason		since

Here is an example:

Reason	What happens
Because rocks are exceedingly poor conductors of heat,	the magma loses heat slowly and solidifies slowly.

1. What clue word introduces the reason? _____

2. Why does the magma lose heat slowly? Complete this sentence in answering:

The magma loses heat slowly and solidifies slowly because _____

_____

Did you notice that in the model sentence the reason (because rocks are exceedingly poor conductors of heat) comes before what happened? In your sentence, the happening comes before the reason (the magma loses heat slowly and solidifies slowly). This indicates that reasons can come before or after the related event or happening, as shown in these two sentence maps:

Reason ⟶ What happens as a result
What happens ⟶ The reason for it

Now read this paragraph. Use the clue words that warn of "reason-giving" to figure out the points where the author is going to give reasons. Also ask yourself: Why does this happen? The why question is a key one to ask when handling reasons.

Because the Hawaiian volcano, Mauna Loa, is about sixty miles long and thirty miles wide and because it rises from a base 15,000 feet below sea level to 13,680 feet above sea level, it is known as the "Monarch of Mountains." Since Mauna Loa is the world's largest active volcano, each year many tourists visit the island of Hawaii to view it.

3. Why is Mauna Loa known as the Monarch of Mountains? _____

_____

_____

4. What word introduces the reason? _____

5. Why do tourists visit Mauna Loa? _____

_____

_____

6. What word introduces the reason? _____

7. Rewrite the first sentence, placing the reasons after the happening they explain. Start the sentence: "Mauna Loa is known as the Monarch of Mountains _____

_____

One caution before going on: Remember that when writers are giving reasons, they are really telling you why something is as it is or why something happened as it did. The key question to ask as you interpret reasons is: Why? In contrast, when writers are expressing an if-then relationship, they are telling you the conditions under which events occur. The key question to ask in handling if-then relationships as you read is: If that is true, then what?

RECOGNIZING SENTENCE RELATIONSHIPS

In this section you will read a selection entitled "Elements Known to Ancient Civilizations." The title gives you the topic of the selection. Before you begin, make a prediction: What elements were known to ancient people? Write your prediction here.

_____

_____

_____

Now read to see whether your prediction is correct and to see if you can recognize sentence relationships. As you read, you will find numbers inserted in the text. Ignore those for now. Later you will be asked to answer questions about the numbered sentences.

Paragraph A

1. Not many of the elements occur in nature as pure substances, lying around waiting for someone to pick them up. 2. A few do, and it is not surprising that these were known and collected for various uses in societies around the globe as far back as several thousand years B.C. 3. *Sulfur* is one of those elements. 4. It was known to burn with smelly results and have an odd appearance. 5. Its use was probably confined to religious ceremonies. 6. *Carbon* was also known since antiquity, because the charred bones of animals and portions of partially burned trees consist largely of carbon in the form of charcoal. 7. Although we don't know all the uses primitive peoples made of charcoal, we do know that it was the key to releasing many other elements from their chemical combination in rocks. For example, 8. if a copper-containing rock was heated in a hot fire with charcoal present, the carbon in the charcoal would combine with the other elements in the rock, leaving free metallic copper. 9. In ways like this people were able to discover the elements *copper, iron, lead, tin,* and *zinc,* although they didn't necessarily appreciate that these substances were elementary. 10. They just knew that they were useful.

1. What is the main idea of this paragraph?
   a. Not many elements occur in nature as pure substances.
   b. Ancient peoples found copper, iron, lead, tin, and zinc very useful, although they did not consider these to be elements.
   c. Ancient peoples discovered elements found free or lying around in their natural form and put them to use.
   d. Sulfur and carbon have been known to human beings for thousands of years.

2. What is the purpose of sentence 3?
   a. It states the main idea.
   b. It supports the main idea by providing a reason.
   c. It supports the main idea by providing an example.
   d. It states an idea that is in contrast to the main idea.

3. What is the purpose of sentence 6?
   a. It states the main idea.
   b. It supports the main idea by providing a reason.
   c. It supports the main idea by providing an example.
   d. It states an idea that is in contrast to the main idea.

4. What is the purpose of the group of words marked 8?
   a. It provides an example of carbon combining with other elements.
   b. It states the condition under which carbon combines with other elements.
   c. It contrasts carbon with other elements found free in nature.
   d. It states the main idea of the paragraph.

5. Which word or words in the selection introduce(s) a reason?
   a. and
   b. because
   c. also
   d. for example

6. The word *although* is used twice in the paragraph. In both cases, the word introduces a/an
   a. reason.
   b. example.
   c. opposite idea.
   d. condition.

Paragraph B

   1. Iron also arrived occasionally from the heavens in the form of iron-containing meterorites. 2. Because of this, one might think that iron would have been thought of as a "heavenly" element, a gift from the gods. 3. Instead, this honor has always fallen to the element *gold*. 4. Gold doesn't fall from the skies, but it is found in its pure state in some places. 5. It has the unusual property of never tarnishing like other metals do. 6. Gold objects don't rust, as iron does, nor do they turn green or black on the surface, as do many other metals.

1. What is the main idea of the paragraph?
   a. Iron arrived from the heavens, and for this reason ancient peoples considered it a heavenly gift.
   b. Ancient peoples did not consider iron a gift from the gods.
   c. Ancient peoples considered gold, not iron, as a gift from the gods because it never tarnishes or rusts.
   d. Gold objects are very valuable because they do not tarnish or rust.
2. What is the purpose of sentence 3?
   a. It states the main idea.
   b. It provides an example of the idea stated in the previous statement.
   c. It states an opposite point from that given in the previous statement.
   d. It develops the idea stated in the previous statement.
3. What is the purpose of sentence 5?
   a. It states the main idea.
   b. It provides an example of the idea stated in the previous statement.
   c. It states a point that is opposite from that given in the previous statement.
   d. It develops the idea stated in the previous statement.
4. What word or words set up a comparison in the paragraph?
   a. also
   b. because
   c. nor
   d. like
5. What kind of relationship does the word *but* establish in sentence 4?
   a. It indicates that more, but opposing, information is coming.
   b. It introduces an example.
   c. It indicates that more on the same thought is coming.
   d. It indicates that the writer is going to enumerate, or list, several points on the same topic.
6. What kind of relationship is established in sentence 6 by the last group of words, "as do many other metals"?
   a. example

b. reason
c. condition
d. comparison

Paragraph C

1. The ancient Egyptians used gold for jewelry and for coins. 2. Gold is still used for jewelry, although pure gold is too soft for this purpose. 3. Coins and jewelry, instead, are made of *alloys*. 4. These are metals made by melting two or more metals in a pot together in such a way that they dissolve in one another. 5. Gold coins are usually 90 per cent gold and 10 per cent copper. 6. An alloy of gold and silver is called *white gold.*

1. What is the main idea of the paragraph?
   a. Coins and jewelry are and have been made from alloys of gold.
   b. An alloy of gold and silver is white gold.
   c. An alloy is made by melting two or more metals in a pot together so that they dissolve in one another.
   d. The ancient Egyptians used gold for jewelry and for coins.

2. The word *instead* in the third sentence suggests
   a. an example.
   b. continuation of the thought.
   c. more information on a different aspect of the subject.
   d. a reason.

3. What is the purpose of sentence 4?
   a. It states the main idea.
   b. It gives a detail to support the idea in the previous sentence.
   c. It provides an example in support of the idea in the previous sentence.
   d. It lists, or enumerates, several points relative to the main idea.

Paragraph D

1. Silver was one of the first metals to be used by human beings; alloys of silver continue to be used today in a variety of products, including jewelry and coins. 2. Unlike gold, silver tarnishes to become blackish in color. 3. On the other hand, silver is like gold in that it is melted with other elements to form alloys. 4. One alloy is coin silver, consisting of 90% silver and 10% copper. 5. A second alloy is sterling silver, which contains 92.5% silver and 7.5% copper. 6. Other silver alloys today are used in dental fillings and for electrical contacts.

1. What is the main idea of the paragraph?
   a. Silver tarnishes to become blackish, so it is necessary to use silver alloys instead of pure silver.
   b. Alloys of silver continue to be used today in a variety of products.
   c. Silver alloys are formed by melting silver with other elements such as copper.
   d. Sterling silver has a larger percentage of silver than does coin silver.

2. The purpose of sentence 2 is to
   a. establish a contrast between gold and silver.
   b. give a reason for the tarnishing of silver.

c. show that gold is better than silver.
d. give the condition under which silver will tarnish.

3. The purpose of sentence 3 is to
   a. compare gold and silver.
   b. give an example of how an alloy is formed.
   c. give a reason for making alloys of silver.
   d. give a weakness of silver.

4. The purpose of sentence 4 is to provide a/an
   a. comparison.
   b. example.
   c. reason.
   d. condition.

5. The purpose of sentence 5 is to provide a/an
   a. comparison.
   b. example.
   c. reason.
   d. condition.

APPLYING WHAT YOU KNOW IN WRITING

In the previous sections, you have seen how writers structure their writing to express relationships and how they choose words and phrases that provide clues as to the relationships they are developing. Using those clue words in reading, you can predict where a particular writer is going next in a selection. Figure 6.5 on page 128 is a composite chart of clue words writers use.

To help you gain control over these words that provide clues to relationships being expressed, next you will write sentences and paragraphs using them.

Study the following chart of data:

The Three States of Matter

The State	Characteristics	Relation to Heat	Examples
Solid	Retains its volume (how much space it occupies) and shape		Ice below 0°C; gold and silver at room temperature
Liquid	Retains its volume but takes the shape of its container	May be formed by heating the solid form	Water above 0°C; mercury at room temperature
Gas	Takes the shape and volume of its container	May be formed by heating the liquid form	Water vapor above 100°C; oxygen and hydrogen at room temperature

Using the data in the chart, write a three-paragraph article in your notebook about the states of matter. Model your paragraph after the one about the three classes of rocks that opens this chapter. Use the idea map in Figure 6.1 as a guide.

What Is Going to Happen	Clue Words	Strategy for Handling the Clues
A. Writer is going to enumerate or discuss a number of items.	*three* kinds, *two* problems, *four* reasons, the *first*, the *second*, the *third* . . .	Ask: How many items is the author going to enumerate (list) or talk about?
B. Writer is going to enumerate or describe examples to support a point.	*An example* of this is, *For example, such as, For instance.*	Ask: Is this an example of the point?
C. Writer is going to provide more on the topic or change the direction.	More on the topic: *and, also, in addition, moreover, furthermore, additionally.*	Ask: Does this relate to what went before?
	Change of direction: *but, yet, however, on the other hand, nevertheless.*	Ask: Does this present the other side of the point?
D. Writer is going to compare or contrast.	Similarities are to be presented: *similarly, as in the case of, like the, the same as, like . . . .*	Ask: Is the author stating the way things are the same?
	Differences are to be presented: *on the other hand, on the contrary, unlike the, in contrast to, whereas, while.*	Ask: Is the author stating the way things differ?
E. Writer is going to set up a conditional relationship.	*If . . . then, consequently, hence, thus.*	Ask: If *x*, then what?
F. Writer is going to give reasons.	*Because, for, as a result, since, for this reason.*	Ask: Why?
G. Writer is going to indicate "in spite of the fact that . . . ."	*Although, even, though.*	Ask: In spite of what?

Figure 6.5 *Clue Words*

1. Start with a topic sentence that tells that there are three states of matter. Then, in the same paragraph, tell about solids and give some examples.
2. Shift to a new paragraph about liquids. Perhaps use the phrase "In contrast . . . " to make the transition. Again, include examples.
3. Shift to a third paragraph about gases. Include examples.
4. Take details from the chart on page 127 in constructing your paragraphs.
5. Remember to use clue words to show key relationships. In this case, number words may be useful in identifying the three kinds of matter. Phrases like "for example . . . " or "An example of . . . " may help when presenting examples. Phrases like "If-then" may be useful in talking about conditions under which matter exists as solid, liquid, or gas.

Go back and circle the key words you used to clarify relationships you are expressing in your paragraphs. Note in the margin the kind of relationship you are establishing in each case. Use Figure 6.5 as a guide in doing this. Share your paragraphs with another student. Have him or her help you edit the paragraphs so that they express your ideas as clearly as possible.

SELECTION 1: THE NATURE
OF SCIENTIFIC INVESTIGATION

Expanding Your Vocabulary for Reading

Use word structure and context clues to figure out the meanings of the underlined words, which are from the selection you will read next. If you are not sure of the meanings of the terms, check the glossary. Write the meaning of each underlined term in the space provided.

1. An example of predation is the chase and capture of antelopes by lions in the grasslands. _____

   _____

2. To retype a term paper on a typewriter for the fourth time proved to be a tedious job. _____

   _____

3. Do not speculate on the outcome; at this stage you have too little evidence to make a reasonable guess. _____

   _____

4. With so little evidence, the scientist could not give an unambiguous answer, even though she tried hard to be clear. _____

   _____

5. The cook inadvertently substituted salt for sugar in baking the cake; he realized what he had done only when he tasted a piece. _____

   _____

6. I was merely stating my opinion, not presenting facts on the case. _____

   _____

Getting Ready to Read

Preview the following selection, which is from a college biology text, by reading the title.

- Write the topic of the selection here. _____
- What do you already know about the topic before you read it? Jot some ideas here. _____

  _____

- Write at least one question that you hope to be able to answer after reading it. _____

  _____

Reading with Meaning

Read the selection. As you read, study the way the circled words are used to show relationships among ideas within the sentences. In the balloon connected to each of the circled words, indicate what that clue word tells you. For example, the clue word may tell you that the author is going to do one of the following:

1. write about a specific number of items,
2. provide an example,
3. add more information on the same aspect of the topic,
4. add more information, but on a different aspect of the topic,
5. make a comparison or contrast,
6. state a condition and the effect of that condition (if/then), or
7. give a reason.

You may refer to Figure 6.5 for help. The first word is done for you.

THE NATURE OF SCIENTIFIC INVESTIGATIONS
Pamela Camp and Karen Arms

Science and Society

1. introduces a reason
2.
3.
4.
5.
6.

Most of us decide to take a biology course (because) we feel that we should study at least one science (if) we are to be adequate members of a society in which science and its products are so important. Many decisions affecting our future depend on appropriate interpretations of scientific discoveries. Democratic government requires that everyone participate in decisions on such subjects as pollution standards, population control, protection of wildlife, and compulsory immunization. The body of scientific knowledge is already so vast that no one person can learn it all. As responsible citizens, (however,) we can follow some of the important studies that bear on public issues, (and) we can apply scientific reasoning to arrive at our own positions on these issues.

There is nothing mysterious about scientific reasoning or experiments. They are merely logical ways of trying to solve problems (such as) are used by business people, historians, and each of us in our everyday lives. We do not need specialized scientific training or knowledge to decide whether conclusions are justified from the data presented. We can request further tests of a theory that does not appear to be well supported by the evidence, (and) we can agree or disagree with predictions from a theory. We can improve the way we do these things ourselves if we first understand how a scientist arrives at conclusions about natural phenomena through the same kind of process.

Scientific Method

You may never have thought about how you solve problems, test theories, or decide upon a plan of action. Let us consider how a biologist attacks a problem so that we can examine the main types of thinking involved.

Science usually starts with observations of the natural world and makes a generalization from those observations. For instance, if you are collecting insects, you may notice that many have black and yellow stripes. As you catch them, you probably think they are all bees or wasps and handle them cautiously. However, if you examine them more carefully, you may find that some have features showing that they are flies and not bees.

Is it merely coincidence that these flies look unlike their drab housefly cousins and resemble unrelated bees? Modern biologists would doubt it, and would instead speculate that the flies' coloration evolved as a result of some advantage that comes from looking like a bee. What might that advantage be?

To answer this question, you need some ideas, or *hypotheses,* that will account for your observations. You may think of hypotheses such as "a fly's resemblance to bees protects it from being eaten by predators," or "the flies fool bees into accepting them as members of the hive, and sneak in and steal honey."

The next step is to design and perform *experiments* that will test such a hypothesis. Some hypotheses are of no use to science because they cannot be tested. For instance, the hypothesis "predators think harmless flies are dangerous bees" is untestable because you can never know what an animal thinks. Even a testable hypothesis cannot be tested directly; you must first develop a testable prediction from it.

Suppose you use your first hypothesis (that the fly's coloring protects it from predators) to make this prediction: if a predator has been stung by bees and has learned not to eat them, it

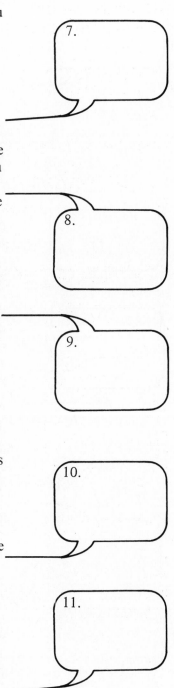

7.

8.

9.

10.

11.

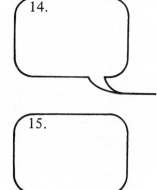

will not eat a fly that looks like a bee. This is a prediction you can test.

For this experiment, you need predators that eat insects. Toads will do. Toads eat by catching insects flying or crawling nearby. If you put bees into the cage of a naive toad (one not acquainted with bees), it will catch a few, learn that they sting, and refuse to catch any more. You next put a black-and-yellow striped fly into the cage and see if the toad also refuses the fly. If it does, the hypothesis that the fly's resemblance to a bee protects it from predation is supported.

But perhaps bees have nothing to do with it. Maybe toads just do not eat striped flies. To test this possibility, you must use a second naive toad. If this toad cheerfully devours black-and-yellow striped flies, you have gained additional support for the hypothesis that the fly's striped suit is advantageous because it resembles the bee's.

A valid experiment always includes a *control treatment* as well as an *experimental treatment;* the two treatments differ by one (*and only one*) factor. In this experiment, you should make sure that the two toads are as alike as possible; for example, both should be of the same species, sex, age, and size. You must also keep them in the same kind of cage, with the same conditions of light, temperature, humidity, and so forth. The only differences should be that you give one toad, but not the other, a chance to eat bees before you offer it flies. If you do not use the control treatment, the toad might refuse the flies because of some factor that you do not notice, such as not being hungry, and you might conclude, wrongly, that the resemblance to the bees was responsible. (In fact you can do a further control by offering the first toad a harmless housefly for dessert after it refused the striped fly; this will control for the possibility that it was no longer hungry.)

You have now conducted a good scientific experiment. What conclusions can you draw? Let's go back to the hypothesis, "A fly's resemblance to bees protects it from predation." Have you proved that? No; all you've shown is that one toad refused to eat a striped fly after learning to refuse bees, while another toad, which had never eaten bees, would eat striped flies.

Scientists hesitate to accept the results of an

experiment until they are sure of its repeatability. Repeating the experiment guards against (two) kinds of errors. First, you may have inadvertently made a mistake in your technique, such as switching the toads, or confusing the flies with the bees, or writing your results in the wrong column in your data notebook, or alarming the toad by dropping it or by making a loud noise (even in this simple experiment, the possibilities go on and on). Second, your experiment is subject to *sampling error;* you used a small sample—only two toads—and it is almost inevitable that they are in some ways inadequate to represent the toad population as a whole. You can be more confident of your results if you repeat your experiment, using more toads and following precisely the same procedure. How many toads do you need to use? The more the better, (but) it would be impractical (and tedious) to test all the toads in the world. In fact, there are statistical tests that can tell how "sure" you are of your results with a given sample size. (If) some of the toads do not behave as you expected, you can also use statistical tests to decide whether your results are so far from your prediction that you should discard your hypothesis.

After all this work, it is disappointing to realize that a hypothesis can never formally be proved, but can only be disproved. Why is this? As is shown in Figure 6.6, a correct hypothesis will generate predictions that will turn out to be true, but an incorrect hypothesis may also produce true predictions. (Therefore,) if the prediction turns out to be true, we are still not sure about the truth of the hypothesis. So, in the case above, you can never "prove" that the flies' stripes protect them from predation. (However,) you can disprove at least some of the hypotheses that you think of as alternative explanations for the resemblance, by showing that their predictions are false. You can also test your prediction that the flies' coloration will discourage "bee-wise" predators by doing more experiments, using frogs, birds, lizards, and other predators of insects in place of toads. The more alternative hypotheses you disprove, (and) the more kinds of predators refusing striped flies after a close encounter with bees, the more you will have strengthened your hypothesis.

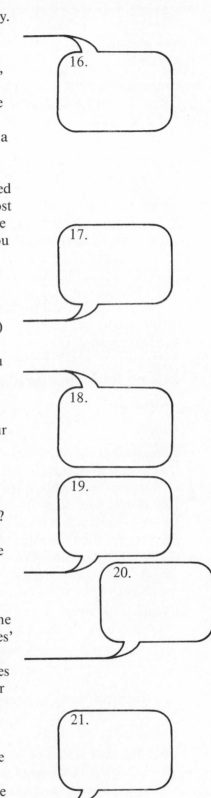

16.

17.

18.

19.

20.

21.

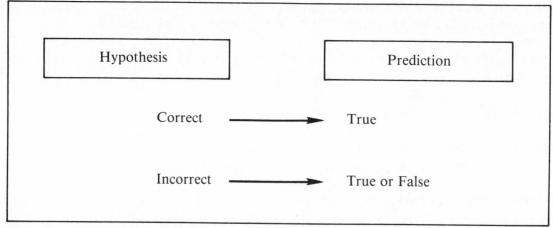

Figure 6.6   *Relationship Between a Hypothesis and a Prediction*

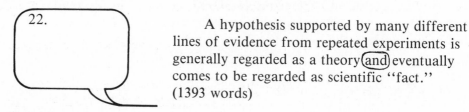

22. A hypothesis supported by many different lines of evidence from repeated experiments is generally regarded as a theory and eventually comes to be regarded as scientific "fact." (1393 words)

Checking for Understanding

Circle the best answer.

1. What is the relationship between science and society? (This question asks you to find the main idea of the first segment.)
   a. People must understand science to function adequately as members of a society in which science plays a role.
   b. People need scientific understanding to arrive at positions on public issues that have a scientific aspect.
   c. People need to know how scientists arrive at conclusions to decide whether conclusions are justified.
   d. All of the above are true.
   e. None of the above are true.

2. What is the order in which scientists generally pursue investigations? (This question asks for the steps in the scientific method, which is one of the big ideas stressed in the second segment.)
   a. observe, question, hypothesize, test predictions, conclude
   b. question, hypothesize, observe, test predictions, conclude
   c. test predictions, question, observe, hypothesize, conclude
   d. hypothesize, question, test predictions, observe, conclude
   e. observe, test predictions, hypothesize, question, conclude

3. What is the purpose of the control treatment in a scientific experiment?
   a. to avoid a sampling error
   b. to overcome any errors in technique that you may have made
   c. to absolutely prove your hypothesis
   d. to be sure that no other factor was the cause of the outcome
   e. All of the above are true.

4. What is the meaning of the term *theory*?

a. an idea that accounts for your observations

b. a hypothesis supported by many different lines of evidence from repeated experiments

c. events that are repeated in identical fashion or about which we have un-unambiguous records

d. the scientific method

e. a repeatable experiment

Reviewing New Vocabulary

Select from the list the word that best fits the meaning of each sentence.

a. inadvertently   c. predation   e. tedious

b. merely   d. speculate   f. unambiguous

1. The girl _____ stepped on her contact lens while she was looking for it.

2. We can only _____ as to what happened that night; we can never be certain.

3. When we dropped thousands of blue, green, and yellow chips on the floor, we were faced with the _____ task of re-sorting them.

4. The fence around their coop protected the chickens from _____ by wolves.

5. Because the teacher's statement was _____, everyone knew what she meant.

6. "Do not think I am snooping," she remarked. "I ask _____ to find out what I must do."

EXTENDING WHAT YOU HAVE LEARNED

Applying the Strategies as You Read

Review the word clues contained in Figure 6.5. Then read an article from a science magazine such as *Scientific American* or a section from a biology or earth science textbook. As you read, on a card write down some of the clue words that help you grasp what is happening in the article. On the card, next to each clue word, write what you learned from that clue word: the author is going to enumerate the number of items to be considered, change the direction of the thought, continue with the thought, present an example, compare/contrast, give an if-then relationship, or give a reason. Be ready to share your findings with classmates.

Extending Your Vocabulary

Select several words from those emphasized in the chapter to use in writing and speaking. Record these in your personal vocabulary list. Include a model sentence for each.

Building Your Knowledge Base

Locate the Hawaiian Islands on a globe. Locate the following sites on the map in Figure 13.1: Mt. Etna in Sicily, and Mt. Vesuvius in Italy.

7

Handling
Text Structure:
SQ3R Part One

Before reading the chapter, read the title, the stated objective, and the headings and subheadings. Ask yourself: What is the topic of the chapter? In the space above and beside the chapter number, jot down what you already know about that topic. Then in the space below the chapter number, jot down at least two questions you hope to answer through reading the chapter.

OBJECTIVE

In this chapter you will learn to use headings and subheadings, introductory segments, summaries, and specialized elements of a text to build a framework to guide your reading. You will learn to handle the first two steps of a study plan called SQ3R. Those steps are to survey the text and to raise questions before reading.

INTRODUCTION TO ELEMENTS OF TEXT STRUCTURE

In Chapter 1, you learned to preview a selection by reading the title and author, the introductory material, and concluding sections and by looking at the illustrations. You learned to use the information from your prereading survey to identify the topic of the selection, to relate what you already know on the topic to what you will read, and to set a purpose for reading.

When selections are more complex—as in advanced textbooks, your prereading survey must be more comprehensive. You must also preview to identify the way the text is organized; knowledge about how a selection is structured helps you organize your thoughts before and as you read.

In this chapter, you will first learn how texts are structured and how you can use that structure to guide your reading. Then you will have the opportunity to apply what you have learned in reading highly structured material.

Headings and Subheadings—Clues to Text Structure

Many authors of articles and textbooks organize their writing in a tight, logical way, much in the manner of an outline. One clue to that organization is found in the headings. The first-level headings are generally in large, bold, or italic type and set off from the ongoing text. These headings indicate main aspects of the topic, just as in an outline the main entries indicate major divisions of a topic. The second-level headings—the subheadings—are generally printed a little smaller than the main headings but larger than the text itself. They indicate lesser, or subordinate, aspects of the topic, just as in an outline the secondary entries indicate subdivisions of a topic.

Study this outline:

I. Introduction to elements of text structure
  A. Headings and subheadings
  B. Introductory segments
  C. Summaries
  D. Special text features
II. Strategies for working with text organization
  A. Studying introductory segments
  B. Using headings to build a framework for reading
    1. Building an outline directly into the text
    2. Writing questions based on the headings
    3. Making relational webs based on the headings
    4. Making data charts based on the headings
    5. Making time lines with the headings
  C. Making use of special text features
    1. Vocabulary lists and italicized words
    2. Focusing questions and objectives
    3. Summaries
    4. End-of-chapter questions

The two main entries in the outline,

I. Introduction to elements of text structure
II. Strategies for working with text organization,

are the same as the first two main headings in large, bold type in this chapter. The entries preceded by capital letters (A, B, C) are comparable to the second-level headings—the subheads—in the chapter. Notice that the manner in which the main headings are set into type is consistent throughout each chapter; each main heading within the chapter is in the same form and location on a line. The same is true of the second-level headings.

Some authors provide additional clues to the organization of ideas within a chapter. At times they list points within a section of text, setting off those points with numbers (1, 2, 3) or bullets (•). Look ahead to pages 139–141 of this chapter. There you will see that ideas are set off and numbered. Again this is similar to the way entries are set off in a formal outline.

Can you see how previewing, or surveying, the headings and subheadings before reading a selection can give you a framework for organizing your thinking while reading? The headings and subheadings become your reading outline. As a matter of fact, some textbook authors place an outline of main headings and subheadings at the beginning of each chapter to guide your reading.

Introductory Segments

At the beginning of a chapter or article, authors often include introductory paragraphs. These paragraphs serve two purposes: (1) they try to interest you in the topic by providing an overview of it; and (2) they describe the organization of the chapter.

To see an example of this, reread the introduction to this chapter—the paragraphs found under the main heading, "Introduction to Elements of Text Structure." In that section, I began by introducing the idea of text structure—that there is an organization to text. Next I described in sentence form the way the chapter is organized. I did this when I told you that in the chapter you would first learn how texts are structured and how you can use that structure in reading, that in the chapter you would then have the opportunity to apply what you have learned as you read well-structured selections. Can you see the relationship between the organization described in that paragraph and the organization shown in the outline on page 137? The paragraph and the outline are telling you the same thing—how the ideas have been structured in the selection.

Because the introductory section of a chapter is likely to contain overview material and may provide clues to the organization of the chapter, you should read the introduction as part of your prereading survey.

Summaries

In many instances, too, authors use final segments of a chapter or article to sum up major points made within the selection. Sometimes, authors even present a list of main ideas. When an author supplies an end-of-chapter summary, studying it before reading the chapter can provide a framework for reading.

Special Text Features

Other text features that can provide a framework for reading include focusing questions that precede a chapter or article, a statement of objectives that comes at the beginning, a list of important vocabulary words, and end-of-chapter questions.

STRATEGIES FOR WORKING WITH TEXT STRUCTURE

Your prereading survey of a chapter or article should include a study of the introductory and summary sections, the framework of headings and subheadings, and any special text features that the author has supplied.

Studying Introductory Segments

One of the first things you should do as you begin reading a chapter in a textbook or an article is to preview the introductory segments. As part of the preview survey, you should keep these questions in mind:

1. What big ideas will the author be developing in the chapter?
2. In what order or manner will the author develop those ideas?

Use words such as *first, then,* and *finally* as clues to the organization of the material to come. Also use phrases such as ''I will cover four points'' as indicators of structure.

Using Headings to Build a Framework for Reading

In well-written textbooks and articles, the system of headings and subheadings is probably your best clue to the overall organization of the material. Having surveyed the introductory segments, your next step in previewing should be to thumb through it, scanning the headings and subheadings to see how the author is going to structure the ideas and to get a mental framework for reading. As you scan, you might say to yourself such things as: ''First the author is going to talk about. . . . Topics under this that she is going to consider are. . . . She is going to go into detail about one of these topics. She has listed four points. Next the author is going to discuss. . . . Subtopics under that heading are. . . . The last major topic is. . . . Aspects of that topic that the author is going to explain are. . . . ''

When ideas are complex and you are being held responsible for them in a college course, your previewing should go beyond scanning the headings and talking to yourself in your head about the organization. You should develop a graphic scheme for reading. Here are some ideas for organizing your thinking before reading:

1. Build an outline directly into the text. As you survey the chapter or article, place Roman numerals in the margin in front of main headings, capital letters in the margin in front of second-level headings, and numbers in front of third-level headings if the author has not already used numbers and letters as part of the headings. Doing this can clarify the organization for you.

    Similarly, in a section where an author talks about the first reason (or point), then the second reason, then the third without indicating these divisions with subheads, you put numbers into the margin to highlight the development of the ideas.

2. Convert the headings and subheadings into questions that you will try to answer as you read. Write those questions in the margin or on paper, leaving room to write answers as you read. For example, these are questions that you could have written to guide your reading of this segment of this chapter: How can I use the system of headings and subheadings to build a framework for reading? What specific things can I do with the headings and subheadings before reading to improve my understanding?

3. Create an idea-cluster web as a framework for reading. Rather than writing questions based on the headings, in some cases you may find it helpful to create an idea-cluster web. To do this, you simply record the topic of the selection in the middle of a paper. In areas around this hub, you record the topics of the subsections. Having created the framework of an idea cluster, you now read with pencil in hand, recording the points from the selection in the appropriate segment of the idea-cluster web as you go along. You have already used an idea-cluster web on page 5 of this text. In that case, the book supplied the web. Reading independently, you create your own web as part of your preview survey and use it to take notes during reading.

4. Make a data chart for recording while reading. Use the headings of a selection as headings on a data chart. For example, if you were reading a selection that described the contribution of several inventors, you might construct a chart that looks like this:

Inventor	Where and When He Worked	Contribution	Why Important
Edison			
Marconi			
Bell			

Having organized yourself for reading, you now read the selection and add data to the chart as you go along. Notice that again reading requires a pencil.

5. Make a time line for recording while reading. A time line is simply a line on which dates and related events are labeled in chronological order. The strategy works well when there are chronological dates in a selection that give you a clue that the material is organized chronologically. Record those dates as a time line as part of your prereading survey. As you read the selection, record on the time line events as they occurred.

Making Use of Special Text Features

Here are ways to handle special text features:

1. Study the vocabulary list (if there is one) at the beginning of a chapter. Think about the meaning of the words before reading. Ask yourself: What do I

already know that relates to these words? Do the same with words set off in italics or bold type within the passage.

2. Try to answer the focusing questions that some authors set at the beginning of a section. Predict the answers. Keep the questions in mind as you read. As you find material relative to a question, revise your answer so that by the end of the chapter you know the answers to the focusing questions. If the author has provided a set of objectives, or things that you should be able to do by the end of the section, think about what you already know relative to the objectives or convert the objectives into questions to answer while reading.

3. Read the summary section that contains major ideas of the chapter. Ask yourself: What examples do I already know relative to these ideas? What specific facts?

4. Study the end-of-chapter questions before reading. Predict the answers. Keep the questions in mind as you read, answering them as you go along.

Obviously you do not apply *all* of these strategies as part of your preview survey of a particular selection. You apply those that seem relevant to the structure of the selection.

SELECTION 1: PHYSICAL GEOLOGY

Physical Geology, a college science textbook, introduces each chapter with a list of "Student Objectives." Here is the list of objectives for a chapter entitled "Glaciation and the Pleistocene":

Student Objectives

On completing this chapter, the student should:

1. understand the nature of the Pleistocene Epoch
2. be able to describe how glaciers form
3. understand how glaciers move
4. recognize erosional and depositional features of glaciers
5. know the difference between stratified and unstratified glacial drift
6. recognize depositional and erosional landforms produced by glaciers
7. be conversant with hypotheses relating to future ice ages

Convert each of the objectives into one or more questions that you would hope to be able to answer by completing the chapter. Write your questions in the space provided.

1. _____

   _____

2. _____

   _____

3. _____

   _____

4. _____

_____

5. _____

_____

6. _____

_____

7. _____

_____

The same text also prints an outline of the chapter at the beginning of it. The entries in the outline are the same as the main headings and subheadings in the text.

Glaciation and the Pleistocene

The Mystery of the Ice

Historical Background

Major Glacial Advances

How Do Glaciers Form?

   Movement of glacial ice

   Movement of debris by glaciers

Erosional Features of Continental Glaciers

Erosional Features of Valley Glaciers

Depositional Features of Glaciers

   Stratified deposits

   Unstratified deposits

Changes Produced by Glaciers

Will the Ice Ages Return?

Summary

---

1. Suppose you were previewing the chapter and decided that building an outline right into the text would help you grasp its structure. You could add a capital letter or number in the margin to the left of each heading and subheading to show the relationship of main and subordinate ideas. To the outline above, add capital letters before the headings and numbers before the subheadings to distinguish main and subordinate ideas the way you would if each entry were a heading or subheading in the ongoing text.

2. Working from the chapter outline, create an idea-cluster web that you could use for recording notes if you were to read the chapter on glaciation and the Pleistocene. Show relationships among ideas by organizing your web so that subordinate ideas are connected to main ones. Some ideas have been recorded to help you get started.

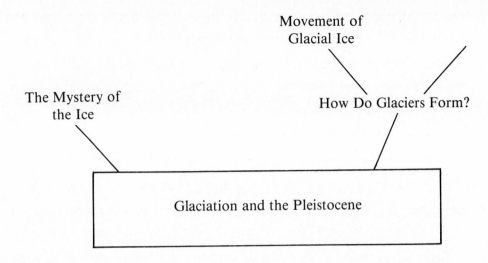

SELECTION 2: THE NORTHWEST ORDINANCE OF 1787

In this section of the chapter, you will read a well-structured article with headings and subheadings that you can use to guide your reading.

Expanding Your Vocabulary for Reading

Use word structure and context clues to determine the meaning of each underlined term. Write a definition for each featured word in the space provided.

1. The husband and wife held <u>coordinate</u> positions in the college: She was Dean of Science and Mathematics, and he was Dean of Humanities.

   _____

   _____

2. Important in selecting a marriage partner is finding someone with whom one is <u>compatible</u>.

   _____

   _____

3. After twenty-five years of marriage, the couple <u>reaffirmed</u> their marriage vows.

   _____

   _____

4. To establish a colony in the wilderness of North America was a <u>daunting</u> endeavor for the Pilgrims to undertake.

   _____

   _____

5. During the <u>era</u> of exploration the Spanish, the English, and the French sent many explorers across the Atlantic to stake claims.

   _____

   _____

6. Some people who came to the "new world" are known for their <u>exploitation</u> of native Americans.

   _____

   _____

7. Ruled by a <u>tyrant</u>, the people had no freedom at all.

   _____

   _____

8. Americans are heirs to a <u>legacy</u> of freedom left behind by the Founding Fathers.

   _____

   _____

9. Before coming ashore, the Pilgrims made a <u>compact</u> in which they agreed on basic principles of government. The document they wrote is known today as the Mayflower Compact.

   _____

   _____

10. The Magna Carta was the English people's attempt to <u>perpetuate</u> their ideas of freedom for generations to come.

    _____

    _____

11. The King <u>repudiated</u> his daughter; he cast her off, or disowned her. In doing this he perpetuated the belief that she was not really his.

    _____

    _____

12. The enterprise was <u>fraught</u> with hazards. But undaunted, the Pilgrims struggled on.

    _____

    _____

Getting Ready to Read

Preview the next selection. Read the title, author, and introductory two paragraphs.

• What is the topic of the selection? _____

• What do you already know about the topic? _____

   _____

   _____

Now study the headings that introduce the main sections of the article. For each, write a question that you hope to answer by reading that section.

1. _____

2. _____

3. _____

Finally, read the captions on the two figures that accompany the article. How do they relate to the main sections of the article? _____

_____

_____

Reading with Meaning

Now read the selection. After you finish reading each subsection, stop and tell yourself the answer to the question you prepared based on the heading.

THE NORTHWEST ORDINANCE OF 1787: PART OF THE AMERICAN HERITAGE

John Patrick

During the summer of 1787, the Federal Convention and the Confederation Congress responded to critical problems of constitutional government with coordinate solutions. The Founding Fathers in Philadelphia, faced with the daunting challenge of how to establish a workable republic in a large country, created novel principles of free government. Meanwhile, members of Congress in New York, confronted by the difficult decision of how to treat newly acquired lands north and west of the Ohio River, designed unique means for transforming dependent territories into self-governing and coequal states of an expanding federal union.

The Ordinance of 1787, enacted on July 13 by the Confederation Congress, was the world's most equitable policy for territorial administration; and the Constitution of 1787, signed on September 17 by delegates to the Federal Convention, provided the freest government in the world at that time. Both documents included compatible ideas about federalism, republicanism, civil liberties, and national development. Thus, the Federal Convention and Confederation Congress created interlocking parts in the foundation of American constitutional democracy.

Provisions for Governance in the Northwest Ordinance

The Ordinance of 1787, passed by Congress under the Articles of Confederation, was reaffirmed as federal law by the new U.S. Congress in 1789. The Ordinance provided for government north and west of the Ohio River, a vast area of more than 265,000 square miles. No less than three and no more than five states were to be made within the Old Northwest, and from 1803–1848, five states were created: Ohio (1803), Indiana (1816), Illinois (1818), Michigan (1837), and Wisconsin (1848). A portion of Minnesota, which became a state in 1858, had also been part of the Old Northwest Territory.

The Ordinance of 1787 provided a three-stage plan by which a territory could become a state on equal terms with all other states of the federal union. During stage one, a governor and other officials appointed by the federal government ruled the territory. During stage two, when the population surpassed 5000 adult males, eligible voters could elect representatives to the lower house of a territorial legislature, which would share power with the appointed executive and judicial officials and an appointed upper house of the legislature. A territory entered the third stage when its population reached 60,000. At this point, the territory was permitted to write a state constitution and petition the U.S. Congress for statehood. Thus, the Ordinance of 1787 bound western settlers to the United States with guarantees of citizenship and self-government—a remarkable development in an era when most people in the world were ruled by tyrants of one sort or another and when colonies were held by ruling powers only for exploitation.

Articles of Compact in the Northwest Ordinance

The Ordinance of 1787 included guarantees of civil liberties and rights in six Articles of Compact. Many of these civic values were not

Figure 7.1   *Stages of Government Under the Northwest Ordinance of 1787 (from J. Patrick)*

	Territorial Status	Elected & Appointed Officials	Lawmaking Body
First Stage	Population less than 5,000 adult males.	Territorial Governor Secretary Three Judges Officials appointed by U.S. Congress.	Governor and judges make laws.
Second Stage	Population between 5,000 and 60,000 adult males.	Territorial Governor Secretary Three Judges Territorial Delegate (nonvoting) to U.S. Congress—elected by territorial legislature.	Bicameral Legislature *Lower House* Voters elect representatives; one rep. for each 500 men. *Upper House* Five members appointed by U.S. Congress.
Third Stage	Population more than 60,000 inhabitants.	Voters elect delegates to write a state constitution. Submit petition for statehood to U.S. Congress. Receive approval of Congress to enter Federal Union on equal terms with other states. Elect and appoint state government officials according to the state constitution.	Legislature established in terms of state constitution.

It is hereby Ordained and declared . . . That the following Articles shall be considered as Articles of compact between the Original States and the people and States in the said territory, and forever remain unalterable unless by common consent, to wit.

Article the First. No person demeaning himself in a peaceable and orderly manner shall ever be molested on account of his mode of worship or religious sentiments in the said territory.

Article the Second. The Inhabitants of the said territory shall always be entitled to the benefits of the writ of habeas corpus, and of the trial by Jury; of a proportionate representation of the people in the legislature, and of judicial proceedings according to the course of the common law; all persons shall be bailable unless for capital offenses, where the proof shall be evident, or the presumption great; all fines shall be moderate, and no cruel or unusual punishments shall be inflicted; no man shall be deprived of his liberty or property but by the judgment of his peers, or the law of the land; and should the public exigencies make it necessary for the common preservation to take any person's property, or to demand his particular services, full compensation shall be made for the same; and in the just preservation of rights and property it is understood and declared; that no law ought ever to be made, or have force in the said territory, that shall in any manner whatever interfere with, or affect private contracts. . . .

Article the Third. Religion, Morality and knowledge being necessary to good government and the happiness of mankind, Schools and the means of education shall forever be encouraged. The utmost of good faith shall always be observed towards the Indians, their lands and property shall never be taken from them without their consent; and in their property, rights and liberty, they never shall be invaded or disturbed unless in just and lawful wars authorised by Congress. . . .

Article the Fourth. The said territory, and the States which may be formed therein shall forever remain a part of this Confederacy of the United States of America, subject to the Articles of Confederation, and to such alterations therein as shall be constitutionally made. . . .

Article the Fifth. There shall be formed in the said territory, not less than three nor more than five States. . . . [A]nd whenever any of the said States shall have sixty thousand free Inhabitants therein, such States shall be admitted . . . into . . . the United States, on an equal footing with the original states, in all respects whatever; and shall be at liberty to form a permanent constitution and State government, provided the constitution and government so to be formed, shall be republican, and in conformity to the principles contained in these Articles. . . .

Article the Sixth. There shall be neither slavery nor involuntary servitude in the said territory. . . .

Figure 7.2 *Articles of Compact of the Northwest Ordinance*

included in the U.S. Constitution until ratification of Amendments I-X (Bill of Rights) in 1791 and Amendments XIII and XIV in 1865 and 1866. Freedom of religion, due process in legal proceedings, the privilege of the writ of habeas corpus, trial by jury, protection against cruel and unusual punishments, protection of property, sanctity of contracts, and free public education were proclaimed as inviolable rights of territorial inhabitants. Furthermore, slavery was prohibited. Thus, the Northwest Ordinance guaranteed basic liberties and rights of citizenship in an era when these civic values were rarely practiced in Western civilization and were virtually nonexistent anywhere else in the world.

Historic Importance of the Northwest Ordinance of 1787

Throughout American history, the Northwest Ordinance has been viewed as one of the most important living legacies of the Founding Period. Long ago, in 1830, Senator Daniel Webster of Massachusetts said during his memorable debate with Robert Hayne: ". . . I doubt whether one single law of any lawgiver, ancient or modern, has produced effects of more distinct, marked, and lasting character than the Ordinance of 1787."

President Abraham Lincoln pointed to the importance of the Ordinance of 1787 in state-making beyond the boundaries of the Old Northwest Territory. He explained how "that Ordinance was constantly looked to whenever a new territory was to become a state. Congress always traced their course by the Ordinance of 1787." In Lincoln's time and afterwards, the Northwest Ordinance was used as a model to create states across the Great Plains to the Pacific Coast. In all, thirty-one of the fifty states of the federal union advanced to statehood under principles and values in the Northwest Ordinance.

At the turn of the twentieth century, President Theodore Roosevelt wrote about the place of the Northwest Ordinance in the American civic heritage: "In truth the Ordinance of 1787 was so wide reaching in its effect, was drawn in accordance with so lofty a morality and such far seeing statesmanship, and was fraught with such weal for the nation, that it will ever rank among the foremost of American State papers, coming in that little group which includes the Declaration of Independence, the Constitution, Washington's Farewell Address, and Lincoln's Emancipation Proclamation and Second Inaugural."

President Franklin D. Roosevelt noted the importance of the Ordinance of 1787 in national development, calling it "that third great charter (after the Declaration of Independence and the Constitution). The principles therein embodied served as the highway, broad and safe, over which poured the westward march of our civilization. On this plan was the United States built."

Leading historians have agreed that the Ordinance of 1787 had a significant effect on national development. Ray Allen Billington, for example, wrote that "the Ordinance of 1787 did more to perpetuate the Union than any document save the Constitution. Men could now leave the older states assured they were not surrendering their political privileges."

In his prize-winning work, *The Americans: The National Experience,* Daniel J. Boorstin commented that "the Ordinance of 1787, this scheme of progressive decolonization . . . (became) a glorious fixture among American institutions. . . . The successful application of this notion of a predictable, gradual step-by-step progress toward self-government and national involvement is one of the marvels of American history."

Samuel Eliot Morison, Henry Steel Commager, and William E. Leuchtenberg discussed the innovative and liberative qualities of the Ordinance of 1787 in their classic textbook, *The Growth of the American Republic:* "The time-honored doctrine that colonies existed for the benefit of the mother country and were politically subordinate and socially inferior was repudiated. In its stead was established the principle that colonies were but the extensions of the nation, entitled, not as a privilege but by right to equality. The Ordinance of 1787 is one of the great creative contributions of America."

Summary

The Northwest Ordinance is indisputably at the core of the American heritage, one of our most important civic legacies. (1131 words)

Checking Your Understanding

Select the best answer from the given options.

1. What documents were written in 1787?
   a. the Declaration of Independence and the Constitution
   b. the Declaration of Independence and the Northwest Ordinance
   c. the Constitution and the Northwest Ordinance
   d. the Emancipation Proclamation and the Northwest Ordinance
   e. the Declaration of Independence, the Constitution, and the Northwest Ordinance

2. Which of the following were provisions for governance in the Northwest Ordinance? (Note that this question is based on information under the first heading.)
   a. At first territories would be ruled by a governor and other officials appointed by the federal government.
   b. When the population of the territory became greater than 5,000, the residents of the territory would elect their own governor.
   c. Women were to be counted as members of the population in determining whether a territory was ready for statehood.
   d. When the population became greater than 5,000, the territory could apply for statehood by petitioning the national government.
   e. People living in the territories would never have the same rights of citizenship as people living in the original thirteen states.

3. Which state was part of the Old Northwest Territory?
   a. Maryland
   b. California
   c. Pennsylvania
   d. Iowa
   e. Michigan

4. What did the Articles of Compact of the Northwest Ordinance achieve? (Note that this question is based on the second heading.)
   a. The Articles guaranteed civil rights and liberties.
   b. The Articles explained when a territory could become a state.
   c. The Articles indicated who would govern a territory.
   d. The Articles provided for a three-stage for transition of a territory into a state.
   e. All of the above are true.

5. What was the historical significance of the Northwest Ordinance? (Note that this question is based on the third heading.)
   a. The Ordinance was a guide whenever a new territory became a state—even states beyond the Old Northwest Territory.

b. The Ordinance guaranteed political privileges to those who left the original thirteen states to move west.

c. The Ordinance established the principles that colonies were extensions of the nation.

d. The Ordinance repudiated the doctrine that colonies existed for the good of the mother country.

e. All of the above are true.

Reviewing New Vocabulary

Select the word from the following list that best fits the meaning of each sentence. Use each word only once.

a. compact	e. era	i. perpetuate
b. compatible	f. exploitation	j. reaffirmed
c. coordinate	g. fraught	k. repudiated
d. daunting	h. legacy	l. tyrant

1. The writers of the Northwest Ordinance believed that slavery was not _____ with their belief in freedom.

2. The writers also believed that _____ of a colony by a mother country was wrong.

3. The statesman stood up on the floor of the Senate and _____ his belief in human rights.

4. If you continue to speak in that way, you will only _____ the rumor, rather than stopping it.

5. The man who did not believe in human rights for all was a _____ in his own home.

6. During the _____ in which slavery existed in this country, many people were treated in a harsh and unjust manner.

7. The man _____ his debt; he refused to acknowledge that he owed the money to his friend.

8. We played _____ roles in developing that committee; I was in charge of financial arrangements, while he was in charge of social arrangements.

9. The pioneers who went west were faced with a _____ trip across mountains and plains.

10. Their trip was _____ with hazards; they met a new problem at each step of the way.

11. Those pioneers left us a _____ of courage and fortitude, which we would do well to draw upon.

12. Each citizen should make a _____ with himself, promising to uphold the principles of democracy.

Writing from Reading

Suppose you were writing a report on problems you see at your college or university. You would probably start with an introduction in which you talk about the problems in a general way. Then you would use a heading to introduce the section in which you discuss in detail the first problem, followed by headings to introduce each of the problems in turn.

In your notebook, write the introductory paragraph of this report. Then list the headings you would use to introduce each of the problems. Make sure your headings clearly identify the nature of each problem.

EXTENDING WHAT YOU HAVE LEARNED

Applying What You Have Learned to Other Reading

Pick a chapter from a college textbook and use it to practice your study reading skills. As you have learned, start your reading by previewing the chapter: Read the title and the author and the introductory segments; study the headings and write questions based on them; read the summary section, if there is one, and any questions found at the end of the chapter. Also read the focusing questions at the start of the chapter and the objectives if they are listed. Finding the answers to the questions you have written is your reading purpose.

Using this approach, read the chapter you have chosen. At the end of each section, tell yourself the answer to the question you prepared based on the headings. When you have finished reading, answer any questions at the end of the chapter.

On an index card, record the questions you prepared based on the headings and your answers. Be ready to share your information with class members.

Expanding Your Knowledge Base for Reading

Label the following states on the map in Figure 7.3: Ohio, Indiana, Illinois, Michigan, Wisconsin, a part of Minnesota.

Figure 7.3 *Area of the Northwest Territories*

Making Words Your Own

Select at least seven words from those you studied in this chapter. Record those in your vocabulary notebook with a sample sentence and the definition for each. Try to use them in your writing.

8

Remembering Through Reciting and Reviewing: SQ3R Part Two

Before reading the chapter, read the title, the stated objective, and the headings and subheadings. Ask yourself: What is the topic of the chapter? In the space above and beside the chapter number, jot down what you already know about that topic. Then in the space below the chapter number, jot down at least two questions you hope to answer through reading the chapter.

OBJECTIVE

In this lesson you will learn to use a study plan called SQ3R to help you remember what you read. Specifically, you will learn to recite and review as part of study reading. You will also learn some strategies for studying for and taking tests.

INTRODUCTION—REMEMBERING WHAT YOU HAVE READ

What steps should you take as you get ready to read a textbook chapter? As you learned in Chapters 1 and 7, Step 1 is to survey, or preview, the chapter. This is the first step in the study plan, SQ3R. The *S* stands for *survey*. As part of your survey, you

- read the title, author, and any introductory and summary paragraphs, including focusing questions, statements of objectives, and review questions. You identify the topic, think about what you already know about that topic, and set your general purpose for reading the selection.
- check the introduction to see if it provides clues to the main point of the chapter and the organization of it (for example, does it say, "In this section you will read about two ways . . . ." or "In this section, we will consider four events . . ."?).
- survey the subheadings, using them to predict what each subsection is about. As you do this, scan related illustrations and boldface terms.

Step 2 is to organize yourself for reading the selection based on the information you picked up during your survey. One way to do this is to convert the major subheadings into questions to answer while reading. This is the second step in SQ3R. The *Q* stands for *question*. A related strategy is to insert capital letters and numbers into the text to show main and lesser sections as in an outline or to create a logically organized data web, chart, or time line for recording while reading.

Step 3 is to begin to read the chapter, keeping your questions in mind. That is the first *R* in SQ3R.

Step 4 is to recite—the second *R* in SQ3R. After reading each major subdivision of a chapter, you stop to go over the main points and terms in your mind.

Step 5 is to review—the third *R* in SQ3R. This you do when you finish reading a chapter and on several occasions thereafter as you prepare for a test on the material.

In sum, SQ3R is a five-step study plan that includes these components:

> **Survey Question Read Recite Review**

Chapter 7 explained how to proceed with Steps 1, 2, and 3. In this chapter are a discussion of strategies for Steps 4 and 5 and selections that provide opportunities for you to practice those strategies.

Reciting by Talking to Yourself in Your Head

As you read a subsection, keep in mind the question or questions that you wrote based on the subheadings during your prereading survey. Also as you read, keep sifting through details to get the main idea of the section and keep alert for clues to the structure of the piece. Clues, as you remember, include organizing words such as *first, second,* and *finally.*

Having read the subsection, stop to recite—or to talk to yourself in your head. Tell yourself

1. the main idea, or point, of that part of the text,
2. the important points the author made to support the main idea,
3. the points explained in the graphs, charts, or other visuals that accompany that part of the text,
4. the answers to the questions you prepared during your prereading survey, and
5. the meanings of key terms defined in that subsection.

If you have trouble talking to yourself about what you have just read, reread. As you recite, you may find it helpful to make the following kinds of notes directly in your book:

1. If there is a main idea, or topic, sentence, after reading a paragraph, underline that sentence with a pen. Do the same with definitions you will need to remember. Or in the margin write the definition of a key term in abbreviated form to use in future study of the text (or in a special vocabulary section of your notebook). Using a pen for making in-text notes generally takes less time than using a highlighting marker.
2. If the author makes a series of related points within a paragraph, insert numbers in front of the points to keep track of them. This is helpful if the author talks about "first," "second," and so on. Insert directly into the text a number 1, a number 2, and so forth at such sites. Or you may want to list main points in the margin, listing a key word for each point to remind you of it. That is another advantage of using a pen rather than a colored highlighting marker. You can write clear notes with the pen.

    Generally you will want to underline points and make notes *after* rather than while reading a paragraph. In that way you know what is important in the section and avoid marking sentence after sentence. There is not much sense in marking almost every line of text, as many students do while reading. And marking too many lines wastes your time.

Here is a paragraph from a college business text, with in-text notes made by a reader. Study the notes to decide why that reader underlined and made notes in the margin as she did.

Purpose and Objectives of Business

Why do businesses exist? A business has one <u>main purpose: to serve the public.</u> Any business that does not serve the public will not exist too long. However, if a business is striving to operate at maximum production and efficiency, serving the public is often not enough. Generally, a business owner will strive to accomplish two major objectives. First, the owner will try to <u>provide a specific service and/or good that will satisfy human needs and wants.</u> For example, your local clothing store provides a service by selling consumer goods such as coats, shoes, pants, and other

A. main purpose

B. Objectives

related clothing articles. These are products that you need and want for everyday use. Second, the owner will strive to operate at a profit. In other words, an important objective of business is to generate income that exceeds the expenditures it incurs for such things as salaries, rent, and the cost of goods, and at a rate that will satisfy the risk.

Reviewing

If you are to remember what you have read and noted, you must review the material several times. The first point at which to review is upon finishing the reading of a chapter. (Remember that you have already recited at the end of each subsection.) End-of-chapter reviewing means reciting again—telling yourself main ideas, rereading key details, reciting definitions of terms, going over your own margin notes, telling yourself about charts, graphs, and other visuals that are part of the text.

You also should review at spaced-out periods between your initial reading of a chapter and a test on the material. These reviews consist of talking to yourself in your head, telling yourself about the material. Specific things to do during review sessions include the following:

1. Tell yourself the answers to the focusing and end-of-chapter questions where provided.

2. Tell yourself the answers to the questions you prepared based on the major headings.

3. Review your in-text notes, rereading main ideas and definitions you high-lighted after reading. Paraphrase these ideas and definitions, putting them in your own words as you repeat them in your head.

4. Check where you inserted numbers to keep track of main points within para-graphs. Repeat those points, one by one, to yourself in your own words.

5. When you have trouble repeating the points, reread them. Having reread, again try to repeat the points. If you still have trouble, write out a list of the points in abbreviated form. Then try reciting again.

6. Write your own summary of main ideas from the selection. Research indi-cates that writing summaries of content is the best way to learn it. Compare your summary paragraph with the one supplied in the text. To your sum-mary, add points made in the book summary that you forgot to include in your own.

   In writing a summary, start with a sentence that states the main point, or thesis, of the entire selection. Chapter 4 explains how to identify the the-sis. Then using the subheadings as a guide, write some sentences providing details that support the main point. Here is a model summary based on the selection about the Northwest Ordinance of 1787 in Chapter 7.

The Northwest Ordinance of 1787

The Northwest Ordinance of 1787 provided for the governance of the Northwest Territories (the area north and west of the Ohio River) and provided articles of compact that guaranteed the civil rights of people living or moving there. The ordinance established a three-stage plan by which a territory could become a state; Ohio, Indiana, Illinois, Michigan, Wisconsin, and a part of Minnesota became states following this plan. The ordinance also contained a "Bill of Rights" before the American Constitution contained such a statement. For these reasons, the ordinance is of historic importance.

Go back and study the selection in Chapter 7. See how the summary follows the organization of the selection. The selection starts by stating the thesis. The next section of the selection talks about the governance of the territories, the next addresses the Articles of Compact, or Bill of Rights, and the last talks about the historic importance. The summary does the same. See Figure 8.1 on page 158 for a map showing the design of the summary. You can use this design for writing your own summary.

7. Hypothesize test questions that your instructor may ask on the material. This is difficult to do if the test is the first in the semester. However, once you have taken one test, you should have a good idea of the kinds of things the instructor typically asks. Write out answers to possible test questions.

You should repeat these steps during several study sessions preceding a test until you can tell yourself main points, supporting detail, and key definitions with ease. You may think that this is a time-consuming process. Studying does take time. You generally cannot remember complex and new material without in-depth study. In the next selection, taken from a college text in music, you will have an opportunity to apply these strategies.

SELECTION 1: BLACK FOLK MUSIC

Expanding Your Vocabulary Through Reading

As you read, watch for words that are new to you. Circle them. Use word-structure and context clues to figure out their meaning. Write definitions of new words in the margin.

Getting Ready to Read

1. *Preview the selection by reading the title, author, first paragraph, and headings.*

   • What is the topic of the selection? _____

   • What do you already know about this topic? Write some phrases that come to your mind on the topic here. _____

   _____

2. In the margin of the selection next to each heading, write a question that you will answer through your reading. Answering these questions will be your reading purpose.

Reading with Meaning

As you read the selection, answer the questions you have written in the margin. Since this text does not provide any end-of-chapter summary or questions, you must provide your own questions for study and ultimately your own summary. After each section of text, stop and tell yourself the answer to your ques-

Main Point, or Thesis:

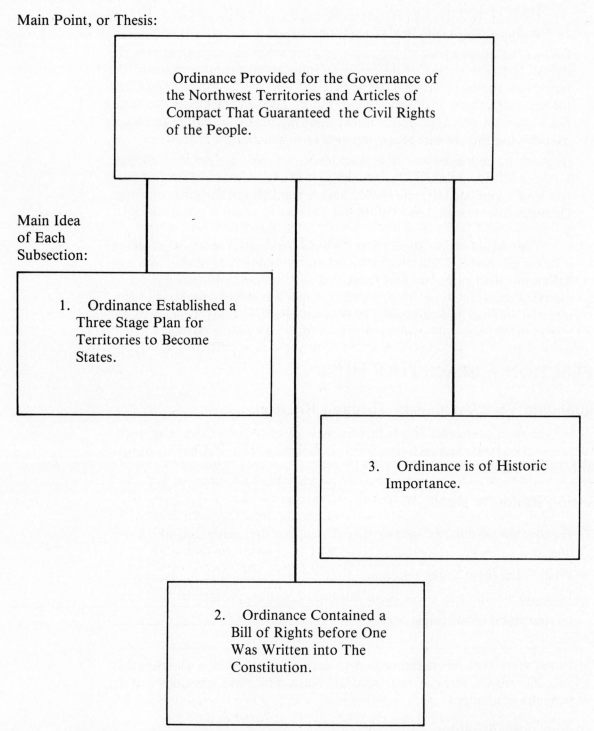

Main Idea
of Each
Subsection:

Ordinance Provided for the Governance of
the Northwest Territories and Articles of
Compact That Guaranteed the Civil Rights
of the People.

1. Ordinance Established a
Three Stage Plan for
Territories to Become
States.

3. Ordinance is of Historic
Importance.

2. Ordinance Contained a
Bill of Rights before One
Was Written into The
Constitution.

Figure 8.1   *An Idea Map to Plot Relationships for a Summary Before Writing One.*

tion based on that heading. Also review in your head the meaning of any italicized terms.

BLACK FOLK MUSIC, THE BLUES, AND BLACK SPIRITUALS

Daniel Politoske

Black Folk Music

Of all the ethnic influences that have gone into the creation of popular music in America, probably the most important has been that of black Africa. West African music, though very different from European music, shared with it certain basic characteristics of harmony. Thus, when the two traditions were brought together in America by slavery, it was possible for them to blend. Black folk music was just the first of many important and widely influential results.

Generally pressed into slavery by European adventurers on the west coast of Africa, the hundreds of thousands of blacks who began arriving in America in 1619 brought with them a highly developed musical tradition and a habit of incorporating music into virtually every activity of life. Religion, dance, and work were some of the main functions it served. Much of their music came to America intact. Once here it was gradually altered to meet new needs. The banjo, unique to America, is thought to have African roots. The use of drums, the most important instrument of West Africa, was continued in the New World.

Field Holler

American blacks developed a wide repertory of songs, both secular and religious. One early type of secular song, perhaps the closest of all to African prototypes, was the *field holler* that slaves often sang while working. A field holler was the yearning cry of a slave working alone, a sound midway between a yell and a song, whose words determined the tone. It began with a high, long-drawn-out shout and then glided down to the lowest note the singer could reach. Such songs were characterized by falsetto tones, swoops and slides from note to note, complicated and unexpected changes of rhythm, and an occasional line of melody from Anglo-American ballads or hymns. They were heard not only in the fields but wherever a black man or woman worked at hard, lonely tasks. When slavery ended, the songs were taken onto the docks, into the railroad camps, and onto the Mississippi River.

Group Work Song

Related to the field holler was the *group work song*. This, too, was close to African sources, for whenever Africans worked together at a task they found it natural to pace their labor with a song. Field hands sang as they hoed or picked the cotton. Rowing songs were used to time the strokes on the flat-bottomed boats of the South. Later on, work songs were chanted by chain gangs and by railroad workers, whose backbreaking, dangerous labor was regulated by the rhythmic chanting of the song leader. The leader played a very important part in the group work song, choosing the song to be sung, setting the pace, adjusting it to the feel of the work being done, and improvising catchy lyrics and musical byplay to fire the energies of the other workers. A good song made the work go faster and better and relieved the weary monotony of it.

Although there was great variety in their lyrics and uses, the earliest work songs were almost entirely African in sound and structure. They made use of the African call-and-response pattern, expressive African vocal techniques such as those used in the field holler, and occasional syncopated African rhythms built around a steady meter. Most work songs were sung with the leader and chorus responding to each other, but some were performed almost in unison, with incidental improvised variants.

Ring Shout

Another musical style that closely resembled its African counterparts was the *ring shout,* a shuffling dance with chanting and handclapping. To an African, dancing was a natural part of worship, but as the Bible was thought to prohibit dancing in church, slaves had to be content with a short shuffling step executed counterclockwise in a ring. This circular movement was accompanied by excited clapping and a kind of *shout song* that provided more rhythm than melody. Biblical stories supplied the words for the shout songs, which were changed in the customary leader-chorus fashion. Starting slowly, the music gathered speed and intensity with the hypnotic repetition of body movements and musical phrases.

Song Sermons

In many black religious services, the sermon also took on some of the qualities of song, generally with a driving, hypnotic rhythm. Delivering such a *song sermon,* the preacher would at different times speak, chant, or sing, steadily increasing speed and passion as the song proceeded. The congregation, caught up in the pulse of the rhythm, would interject rhythmic cries or abbreviated lines of melody, using words such as "Amen!" or "Yes, my Lord!"

Lining Out

Lining out was a technique borrowed from white colonial churches. In many of these churches hymn books were in short supply; in others many of the people of the congregation were illiterate. Thus, it was common practice for the preacher to sing each line of a hymn or psalm and then wait for the congregation to repeat it. This technique adapted itself perfectly to the African call-and-response pattern.

The Blues

The invention of the *blues* represents a major contribution of black folk music. Its influence on popular music has been notable, even since 1960. The blues style is characterized by distinctive *blue notes* produced by slightly bending the pitch of certain tones of the major scale. The style was somehow right for plaintive songs of sadness. A whole repertory of such songs grew up, created by unrequited lovers, prisoners, lonely people far from home, and thousands of others who needed to ease their pain by expressing it.

Black Spirituals

In many respects, the religious counterpart of the blues was the *spiritual*. Developed largely in rural areas in the mid-nineteenth century, spirituals did not receive much public attention until they were made popular after the Civil War by groups who performed harmonized arrangements such as the Fisk University Jubilee Singers. *Nobody Knows the Trouble I've Seen* and *Steal Away* are among the most familiar examples. The black spiritual was superficially similar to spirituals written early in the nineteenth century. However, it is the black spiritual that has remained important to the present day. The music of the black spiritual was in effect an extremely successful mixture of church melodies and harmonies and West African rhythms and styles of performance. (1046 words)

Checking Your Understanding

When you have read the entire selection, go back and tell yourself again the answers to the questions you composed based on the headings. You should be able to answer questions that not only begin with *what* but also with *why* and *how*. Tell yourself the definitions of terms italicized in the text. Write a summary with a first sentence that states the thesis of the selection, and with supporting sentences based on the subsections. Use Figure 8.2 to map your ideas before writing. Be ready to take a test on what you have read. Before studying for and taking that test, read the section of this chapter (pp. 164–167) that deals with test-taking strategies.

SELECTION 2: THE EDUCATION OF RICHARD RODRIGUEZ

Expanding Your Vocabulary Through Reading

As you read, circle words that are new to you. Using word-structure and context clues, figure out the meanings of the circled words. Write their definitions in the margins.

Getting Ready to Read

1. *Preview the selection by reading the title, author, and introductory note. Skim the first paragraph as part of your prereading survey.*

   • What is the topic of the selection? _____

   • What thoughts come to your mind as you begin to read? _____

   _____

2. Write two or three general questions you hope to answer through reading. This selection, as you see, does not come from a text. It is from an autobiography of a type you may well have to read in a college humanities course.

   _____

   _____

   _____

Main Point, or Thesis:

```
┌─────────────────────────────────────────────────────┐
│                                                       │
│                                                       │
│                                                       │
│                                                       │
└───────────────────┬─────────────┬────────────────────┘
                    │             │
Main Idea of Each   │             │
Subsection:         │             │
┌───────────────────┴─┬───────────┴────────────────────┐
│ Black Folk Music     │ Field Holler                   │
│                      │                                │
│                      │                                │
├──────────────────────┼────────────────────────────────┤
│ Group Work Song      │ Ring Shout                     │
│                      │                                │
│                      │                                │
├──────────────────────┼────────────────────────────────┤
│ Song Sermons         │ Lining Out                     │
│                      │                                │
│                      │                                │
├──────────────────────┼────────────────────────────────┤
│ The Blues            │ Black Spirituals               │
│                      │                                │
│                      │                                │
└──────────────────────┴────────────────────────────────┘
```

Figure 8.2 *An Idea Map to Plot Relationships for a Summary Before Writing One. Record the thesis in the top box and the main ideas of the subsections in the connecting boxes. Then use your idea map to write a summary paragraph that includes those points.*

Reading with Meaning

As you read this section, stop at the end of each paragraph. Ask yourself: What is the main idea Rodriguez is trying to get across? What points does he use to support that idea? Recite the answers to yourself at the end of each paragraph.

THE ACHIEVEMENT OF DESIRE

Richard Rodriguez

Richard Rodriguez is the son of working-class Mexican immigrant parents. He spoke Spanish as a child. He graduated from Stanford and Columbia Universities, did graduate work at the Warburg Institute in London and the University of California at Berkeley, and today works as a writer and lecturer.

OPEN THE DOORS OF YOUR MIND WITH BOOKS, read the red and white poster over the nun's desk in early September. It soon was apparent to me that reading was the classroom's central activity. Each course had its own book. And the information gathered from a book was unquestioned. READ TO LEARN, the sign on the wall advised in December. I privately wondered: What was the connection between reading and learning? Did one learn something only by reading it? Was an idea only an idea if it could be written down? In June, CONSIDER BOOKS YOUR BEST FRIENDS. Friends? Reading was, at best, only a chore. I needed to look up whole paragraphs of words in a dictionary. Lines of type were dizzying, the eye having to move slowly across the page, then down, and across. . . . The sentences of the first books I read were coolly impersonal. Toned hard. What most bothered me, however, was the isolation reading required. To console myself for the loneliness I'd feel when I read, I tried reading in a very soft voice. Until: 'Who is doing all that talking to his neighbor?' Shortly after, remedial reading classes were arranged for me with a very old nun.

At the end of each school day, for nearly six months, I would meet with her in the tiny room that served as the school's library but was actually only a storeroom for used textbooks and a vast collection of *National Geographics*. Everything about our sessions pleased me: the smallness of the room; the noise of the janitor's broom hitting the edge of the long hallway outside the door; the green of the sun, lighting the wall; and the old woman's face blurred white with a beard. Most of the time we took turns. I began with my elementary text. Sentences of astonishing simplicity seemed to me lifeless and drab: "The boys ran from the rain . . . She wanted to sing . . . the kite rose in the blue." Then the old nun would read from her favorite books, usually biographies of early American presidents. Playfully she ran through complex sentences, calling the words alive with her voice, making it seem that the author somehow was speaking directly to me. I smiled just to listen to her. I sat there and sensed for the first time some possibility of fellowship between a reader and a writer, a communication, never *intimate* like that I heard spoken words at home convey, but one nonetheless *personal*.

One day the nun concluded a session by asking me why I was so reluctant to read by myself. I tried to explain; said something about the way written words made me feel all alone—almost, I wanted to add but didn't, as when I spoke to myself in a room just emptied of furniture. She studied my face as I spoke; she seemed to be watching more than listening. In an uneventful voice she replied that I had nothing to fear. Didn't I realize that reading would open up whole new worlds? A book could open doors for me. It could introduce me to people and show me places I never imagined existed. She gestured toward the bookshelves. (Bare-breasted African women danced, and the shiny hubcaps of automobiles on the back covers of the *Geographic* gleamed in my mind.) I listened with respect. But her words were not very influential. I was thinking then of another consequence of literacy, one I was too shy to admit but nonetheless trusted. Books were going to make me 'educated.' *That* confidence enabled me, several months later to overcome my fear of silence.

In fourth grade I embarked upon a grandiose reading program. 'Give me the names of important books,' I would say to startled teachers. They soon found out that I had in mind 'adult books.' I ignored their suggestion of anything I suspected was written for children. (Not until I was in college, as a result, did I read *Huckleberry Finn* or *Alice's Adventures in Wonderland*.) Instead, I read *The Scarlet Letter* and Franklin's *Autobiography*. And whatever I read I read for extra credit. Each time I finished a book, I reported the achievement to a teacher and basked in praise my effort earned. Despite my best efforts, however, there seemed to be more and more books I needed to read. At the library I would literally tremble as I came upon whole shelves of books I hadn't read. So I read and I read and I read. . . . Librarians who initially frowned when I checked out the maximum ten books at a time started saving books they thought I might like. Teachers would say to the rest of the class, 'I only wish the rest of you took reading as seriously as Richard does.'

Checking Your Understanding

Review on your own until you can tell yourself the main points and some supporting details from the selection. Then write a summary that includes those points and details. Your instructor will give you a short quiz later to check your understanding, just as an English instructor might quiz you on your reading. Before studying for and taking that quiz, read the next section of this chapter that deals with test-taking strategies.

TAKING AN EXAMINATION ON WHAT YOU HAVE READ

Having read a selection such as those in this chapter, you may be tested on what you have learned from it. In some instances, your instructor may give you an essay examination to which you must respond by writing out your answers. In other instances, your instructor may give you a short-answer examination.

Generally it pays to ask the instructor what kind of examination he or she plans to give.

Preparing for and Taking Essay Examinations

The best way to prepare for an essay examination is to review your textbook and your class notes by systematically reciting main ideas and supporting details to yourself as described in the preceding section. Do not simply reread the text or your notes. Test yourself by asking yourself: What is the main idea? What are the important facts? What is the significance of these ideas and facts? Follow your "explaining-to-yourself" study with writing. Compose questions that you believe the instructor may ask. Write out possible answers.

Instructors tend to ask questions that can be categorized as follows:

- Definition questions, which ask you to give the precise meaning of a term. (Example: Define the word *theory*. To answer this kind of question, start with the term and state, "A theory is . . . .")

- Give-an-example questions, which ask you to provide an example, or a specific instance. (Example: Give an example of a theory that made a radical difference in the way scientists viewed the earth. To answer this kind of question, begin: "An example of a theory that made a radical difference in the way scientists viewed the earth is . . . .")

- Enumeration or listing questions, which ask you to give a series of items. (Example: List the names of four scientists who contributed to that discovery. To answer this kind of question, do not give an extended explanation. Make a *(1), (2), (3), (4)* list of the names, or whatever the question asks for.)

- Explanation questions, which ask you to explain how or why. (Example: Explain why the Puritans left England to come to America. To answer an explain-why question, start: "The Puritans left England to come to America because . . . ." If you want to give more than one reason, continue: "A second reason the Puritans came to America . . . ." The words *because* and *reason* are useful in writing an answer to an explain-why question. To answer an explain-how question—(Explain how iron ore is made into steel)—give the steps in the process. Start: "There are four steps in the process in which iron ore is transformed into steel. The first is . . . . The second is. . . . "It helps to use number words—"four steps", "the first", "the second"—to answer explain-how questions.)

- Evaluation questions, which ask you to judge something. (Example: Give your opinion of the Treaty of Versailles. To answer this kind of question, state what you think. Then give some facts to support your opinion.)

- Discussion questions, which ask you to talk about a particular topic. (Example: Discuss the causes of the Civil War. These are generally the most difficult questions to answer because they are vague. Do not answer by simply listing. You must include an analysis in your answer, suggesting why events happened as they did and how they happened.)

- Description questions, which ask you to tell about the main characteristics of an event or item. (Example: Describe a plant cell. To answer this kind of question, talk about the key aspects of the plant cell. Sometimes you can use a diagram to clarify your written description.)

- Comparison/contrast questions, which ask you to tell how two things are the same and different. (Example: Compare a plant cell to an animal cell. In this case, first describe the animal cell; then talk about the plant cell, telling how it is the same and different from the animal cell.)

- Summarization questions, which ask you to give the main points. (Example: Summarize the important points about natural selection. This is another vague kind of question. To answer a summarization question, think in terms of main ideas, or big points.)

Interpreting Essay Questions

The following are examples of essay questions. Circle the word that tells you the task you must do. Then explain what kind of answer you would give in each case. (Note: Do not answer the questions as stated.)

1. List the three branches of the federal government.

   _____

   _____

2. Explain how a bill becomes a law.

   _____

   _____

3. Compare the process of osmosis to the process of diffusion.

   _____

   _____

4. Discuss the events leading up to the American Civil War.

   _____

   _____

5. Define the word *protoplasm*.

   _____

   _____

Preparing for and Taking Short-Answer Examinations

In preparing for a short-answer examination—multiple choice, fill-in-the-blanks, matching—you should rely on your talking-to-yourself-in-your-head strategy. As with essay exams, tell yourself the main points. Go over significant facts: names, dates, definitions, items in a sequence. Keep telling yourself this information until you can remember it without looking at your notes or your textbook.

Here are some clues for taking an examination:

- Place your answer sheet near the hand with which you write so that you do not waste time by crossing that hand over the examination paper.

- Put your name on your paper immediately.

- Read the directions carefully. Ask: How am I supposed to respond to the questions—by circling, underlining?

- Preview the entire examination before beginning, to get a general sense of what is being asked and of how long the exam is.
- Read each question carefully. Ask yourself: What is the question asking?
- Pace yourself while taking the test. Do not spend too much time on any one question. If you find a question that is difficult for you, put a check on the test paper at that point, continue with the next question, and go back to the difficult question after finishing the others.

You will have the opportunity to practice these strategies when your instructor gives you an examination on the selections in this chapter.

EXTENDING WHAT YOU HAVE LEARNED

Applying SQ3R to Your College Reading

Select a chapter from another textbook—perhaps one that you are reading in a course you are currently taking. On a piece of paper, record the name of the text and its author. Then survey a chapter and on the paper write a series of questions to be answered through reading. Base your questions on the major headings. Read the chapter, stopping at the end of each subsection to make in-text notes and to recite the answers to the questions you posed before reading. When you have read the entire chapter, go back and review what you have read to the extent that you will be able to share orally your new understandings with classmates.

Making Vocabulary Your Own

Select several words from those you circled in the two selections of the chapter to make your own. Record them and a sample sentence or two in your personal vocabulary list.

9

Increasing Your Reading Rate

Before reading the chapter, read the title, the stated objective, and the headings and subheadings. Ask yourself: What is the topic of the chapter? In the space above and beside the chapter number, jot down what you already know about that topic. Then in the space below the chapter number, jot down at least two questions you hope to answer through reading the chapter.

OBJECTIVE

In this chapter you will practice a strategy for increasing your reading rate. Specifically, you will learn to

1. concentrate on getting the gist, or main point, as you go along,
2. block out unrelated thoughts,
3. move your eyes quickly across the lines, pausing two or three times on each line to pick up an "eyeful" of words at each pause, and
4. read in chunks of meaning.

You will also learn to calculate your reading rate.

INTRODUCTION—INCREASING YOUR READING RATE

Faced with extended reading assignments, some college students complain that they read too slowly. They recognize that it takes them far longer to complete reading assignments than it takes their friends. Here are some ideas for increasing the rate at which you read.

Developing Your Powers of Concentration

You must concentrate on the task at hand if you are to read rapidly with a high level of comprehension. For rapid reading, you must block out external distractions—movements of other students in the room, the noise of people talking, the noise of cars in the distance. You must block out thoughts that do not relate to the reading task—fears of not doing well, thoughts about other events, thoughts about how other people are doing. How do you do this?

Some of the strategies you have already learned in this book are designed to help you concentrate. Especially with longer selections, one of those strategies is previewing the selection by running your eye over it quickly before beginning, particularly noting the title, introductory and concluding words, and headings and italicized words, if there are any. Based on your preview, you make predictions of what is to come and phrase questions you will answer through reading. As you learned in the first chapter of this book, having a purpose in mind helps you to understand what you are reading. It also helps you to concentrate.

With longer selections, too, it pays to stop after reading sections of text to recite to yourself what you have read. At first you may think this slows you down. It does not. It makes you think about what you are reading. It forces you to concentrate.

With some selections that are followed by questions you must answer after reading, it may help you to skim those questions before reading the selection. Previews of this kind should be rapid, but research indicates that your ability to answer those questions is increased if you know them ahead of time. That makes sense, doesn't it? So where it is allowed, before reading, quickly skim the questions you must answer after reading.

Reading in Chunks of Meaning

It is important to read in "chunks of meaning" rather than to focus on every word. Reading in chunks, or "chunking," not only helps you understand what you read but also increases your reading speed.

Practice Exercise 1. Rapid Reading. *Preview the following selection by reading the title and predicting what you will learn through reading it. Based on the title, devise a purpose-setting question. Notice that the selection is set on the page in a narrow column to help you fixate on chunks that have meaning. Record in this fashion the time when you start reading:*

9 o'clock   10 minutes   10 seconds

For this purpose you will need a watch with a second hand. Before reading the selection that follows, record your starting time here:

_____ o'clock _____ minutes _____ seconds

Next read the selection. Be prepared to record your ending time as soon as you finish the selection and before you answer the follow-up questions.

WHAT'S INVOLVED IN RAPID READING

Nila Smith and H. Alan Robinson

Investigations of eye movements have shown
that the rapid reader's eyes
move fleetingly across the lines,
pausing briefly two or three times on each line,
picking up an "eyeful" of words at each pause,
while the eyes of the poor reader
pause on every word
or on small word units.

It is the mind, of course,
that controls the eye movements.

The great value
of eye-movement investigations
is that they furnish us
a picture of the different ways
in which the mind works
in perceiving reading symbols.

They tell us
that the mind of the poor reader loafs along,
picking up very small units at a time,
while the eyes of the excellent reader
race over the lines,
gathering an entire, meaningful idea at a glance.

Cultivating the habit of reading for *ideas* not only increases speed;
but also increases understanding.

A person who reads one word at a time
thinks in terms of the meanings
of these separate words
and thus 'can't see the woods for the trees.'

The first and most important instruction is,
'Read for Ideas!'
If you can cultivate the habit
of rapidly picking up one complete thought unit
after another,
the eye movements
will take care of themselves. (216 words)

Record the time when you stopped reading here:

_____ o'clock _____ min _____ sec

Now, based on your reading of the passage, select the best answer.

1. Most important in rapid reading is
   a. keeping the eyes moving.
   b. reading for ideas.
   c. keeping the lips still.
   d. keeping the head still.

2. How do rapid readers move their eyes in reading?
   a. They pause two or three times per line.
   b. They never pause while reading.
   c. They look primarily at the first words on a line.
   d. They look primarily at the last words on a line.

3. What controls eye movements?
   a. the body
   b. the eyes themselves
   c. the hand
   d. the mind

4. What is the meaning of the phrase "can't see the woods for the trees" in this selection?
   a. There are many woods in a forest.
   b. The trees get in the way of seeing the forest.
   c. In reading, it is important to focus on the big ideas rather than on the individual words.
   d. In reading, it is important to focus on individual words rather than on the big ideas.

5. The author of the selection believes that eye-movement investigations are
   a. worthless because they tell us little about how expert readers function.
   b. worthless because eye movements have nothing to do with skillful reading.
   c. valuable because they provide a picture of the ways the mind works in perceiving word symbols.
   d. valuable because they tell us much about the way the eye is put together.

Next determine your reading rate by first subtracting your starting time from your ending time.

Ending time: _____ o'clock   _____ min   _____ sec
Starting time: _____ o'clock   _____ min   _____ sec

_____

Reading time: _____ min   _____ sec

Use the directions in the appendix to determine your reading rate on this practice passage. The number of words in it is 216.

Reading rate is measured in words per minute—for example, 110 words per minute, or 320 words per minute. Most readers vary their reading rate depending on the topic of the selection, on what they know about that topic, and on the complexity of the sentences.

Practicing Reading in Chunks of Meaning

Efficient reading requires that you *not* dwell on individual words. Pointing your finger at or fixating your eyes on each word slows down your reading. So does moving your lips to say each word as you read and moving your head from left to right as you read lines.

Here is a summary of "Don'ts" to help you read more rapidly:

- Do not point at each word as you read.
- Do not move your head or lips while reading. Reading is thinking, not mouthing individual words.
- Do not fixate on, or focus on, individual words. Rather keep your eyes moving across lines and down the page, and focus on meaningful chunks.

Practice Exercise 2: The Microscope and Microorganisms.   *Preview the following very short selection by reading the title, predicting what you will learn through the passage, and devising a purpose-setting question. Before reading it, recall that the prefix* micro- *means "small." The selection has been set on the page in phrasal units to help you read in chunks of meaning. Record the time when you start reading here:*

_____ o'clock _____ min _____ sec

THE MICROSCOPE AND MICROORGANISMS

Thomas Brock, David Smith, and Michael Madigan

Although the existence of creatures too small to be seen with the eye
had long been suspected,
their discovery was linked to the discovery of the microscope.

Robert Hooke described the fruiting structures of molds in 1664,
but the first person to see microorganisms in any detail
was the Dutch amateur microscope builder Antony van Leeuwenhoek,
who used simple microscopes of his own construction.

Leeuwenhoek's microscopes were extremely crude by today's standards,
but by careful manipulation and focusing
he was able to see organisms as small as bacteria.

He reported his observations in a series of letters
to the Royal Society of London,
which published them in English translation.

His observations were confirmed by other workers,
but progress in understanding the nature of these tiny organisms
came slowly.

Only in the nineteenth century
did improved microscopes become available
and widely distributed. (152 words)

Record the time when you stopped reading here:

_____ o'clock _____ min _____ sec

Based on your reading of the passage, select the best answer. Mark items either T (true) or F (false).

New York Academy of Medicine

Figure 9.1 *An Old Microscope from Hooke's Micrographia*

_____ 1. Robert Hooke was the first person to see microorganisms in any detail.

_____ 2. By today's standards, Leeuwenhoek's microscope was very fine.

_____ 3. Improved microscopes became available in the seventeenth century.

_____ 4. Leeuwenhoek was able to see organisms as small as bacteria.

_____ 5. The discovery of microorganisms was linked to the invention of the microscope.

Determine your reading rate by first subtracting your starting time from your ending time:

Ending time: _____ o'clock _____ min _____ sec

Starting time: _____ o'clock _____ min _____ sec

_____

_____ min _____ sec

Use the directions in the appendix to determine your reading rate on this practice passage. The number of words in it is 152.

Practice Exercise 3: The Germ Theory of Disease. *Read the following paragraphs. Try to read the words in meaningful clusters as you did in the prior practice passages. Try not to fixate on individual words.*

Before reading the selection, read the title. Think about what you already know about the germ theory of disease. Then set a purpose for your reading. Keep that purpose in mind as you read. Recall the meaning of the prefix micro-. Micro- *means "small." Microscopy is the use of the microscope to study small organisms. Record the time at which you begin to read:*

Starting time: _____ o'clock _____ min _____ sec

THE GERM THEORY OF DISEASE

Thomas Brock, David Smith, and Michael Madigan

Proof that microorganisms could cause disease provided one of the greatest forces leading to the development of the science of microbiology. Indeed, even in the sixteenth century it was thought that something could be transmitted from a diseased person to a well person to induce in the latter the disease of the former. Many diseases seemed to spread through populations and were called *contagious;* the unknown thing that did the spreading was called the *contagion.* After the discovery of microorganisms, it was more or less widely felt that these organisms might be responsible for contagious diseases, but proof was lacking.

In 1845, M. J. Berkeley provided the first clear demonstration that microorganisms caused diseases by showing that a mold was responsible for potato blight. Discoveries by Ignaz Semmelweis and Joseph Lister provided some evidence for the importance of microorganisms in causing human diseases, but it was not until the work of Koch, a physician, that the germ theory of disease was placed on a firm footing.

In his early work, published in 1876, Koch studied *anthrax,* a disease of cattle, which sometimes also occurs in man. Anthrax is caused by a spore-forming bacterium now called *Bacillus anthracis,* and the blood of an animal infected with anthrax teems with cells of this large bacterium. Koch established by careful microscopy that the bacteria were always present in the blood of an animal that had the disease.

Figure 9.2   *Spirilla Bacteria as Seen Under a Microscope*

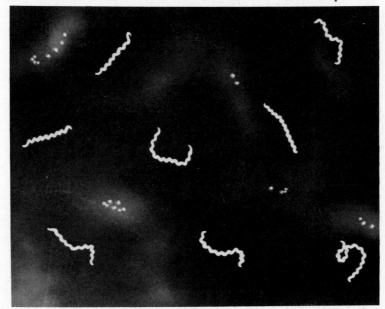

However, he knew that the mere association of the bacterium with the disease did not prove that it caused the disease; it might instead be a result of the disease. Therefore, Koch demonstrated that it was possible to take a small amount of blood from a diseased animal and inject it into another animal, which in turn became diseased and died. He could then take blood from this second animal, inject it into another, and again obtain the characteristic disease symptoms. By repeating this process as often as 20 times, successively transferring small amounts of blood containing bacteria from one animal to another, he proved that the bacteria did indeed cause anthrax: the twentieth animal died just as rapidly as the first; and in each case Koch could demonstrate by microscopy that the blood of the dying animal contained large numbers of the bacterium.

Koch carried this experiment further. He found that the bacteria could also be cultivated in nutrient fluids outside the animal body, and even after many transfers in culture the bacteria could still cause the disease when reinoculated into an animal. Bacteria from a diseased animal and bacteria in culture both brought about the same disease symptoms upon injection. On the basis of these and other experiments Koch formulated the following criteria, now called *Koch's postulates,* for proving that a specific type of bacterium causes a specific disease:

1. The organism should always be found in animals suffering from the disease and should not be present in healthy individuals.

2. The organism must be cultivated in pure culture away from the animal body.

3. Such a culture, when inoculated into susceptible animals, should initiate the characteristic disease symptoms.

4. The organism should be reisolated from these experimental animals and cultured again in the laboratory, after which it still should be the same as the original organism.

Koch's postulates not only supplied a means of demonstrating that specific organisms cause specific diseases but also provided a tremendous impetus for the development of the science of microbiology by stressing the use of laboratory culture. (591 words)

Record the time when you finished reading the selection.

_____ o'clock _____ min _____ sec

Answer the questions by marking them T (true) or F (false).

_____ 1. By the sixteenth century, it was thought that something could be transmitted from a diseased person to a well person to make the latter sick.

_____ 2. Diseases that spread through populations were said to be contagious.

_____ 3. Koch was a microbiologist by profession.

_____ 4. Koch studied anthrax, a disease that infected rats.

_____ 5. Koch proved that infected animals had the anthrax bacterium in their mouths.

_____ 6. Koch showed that when blood from infected animals was transferred to well animals, the bacteria did not show up in the blood after the fifteenth transfer.

_____ 7. Koch cultivated the bacteria in nutrient fluids outside the body of the host animal.

_____ 8. Lister's work was more important to the development of microbiology than was Koch's.

_____ 9. Koch's postulates are important in that they supply a means of proving that a specific type of bacterium causes a specific disease.

_____ 10. Koch published his work in the second half of the nineteenth century.

Subtract your starting time from your ending time.

Ending time: _____ o'clock _____ min _____ sec

Starting time: _____ o'clock _____ min _____ sec

_____

Reading time: _____ min _____ sec

Determine your reading rate for the selection by referring to the table in the appendix. There are 591 words in the selection.

In the next section are four selections. One is from an autobiography of a writer (Eudora Welty), the second from a computer magazine, the third from a professional booklet, and the fourth from a college microbiology text. Comparing your reading rate on these selections will give you a general idea of how fast you read different kinds of materials.

SELECTION 1: ONE WRITER'S BEGINNINGS

Getting Ready to Read

Before beginning to read, read the title. From it, predict what the selection will be about—given the fact that you know it is autobiographical. Ask yourself: What will I learn through reading this selection? Record your starting time here:

_____ o'clock _____ min _____ sec

Reading with Meaning

ONE WRITER'S BEGINNINGS
Eudora Welty

Jackson Carnegie Library was on the same street where our house was, on the other side of the State Capitol. "Through the Capitol" was the way to go to the Library. You could glide through it on your bicycle or even coast through on roller skates, though without family permission.

I never knew any one who'd grown up in Jackson without being afraid of Mrs. Calloway, our librarian. She ran the Library absolutely by herself, from the desk where she sat with her back to the books and facing the stairs, her dragon eye on the front door, where who knew what kind of person might come in from the public? SILENCE in big black letters was on signs tacked up everywhere. She herself spoke in her normally commanding voice; every word could be heard all over the Library above a steady seething sound coming from her electric fan; it was the only fan in the Library and stood on her desk, turned directly onto her streaming face.

As you came in from the bright outside, if you were a girl, she sent her strong eyes down the stairway to test you; if she could see through your skirt she sent you straight back home: you could just put on another petticoat if you wanted a book that badly from the public library. I was willing; I would do anything to read.

My mother was not afraid of Mrs. Calloway. She wished me to have my own library card to check out books for myself. She took me in to introduce me and I saw I had met a witch. "Eudora is nine years old and has my permission to read any book she wants from the shelves, children or adult," Mother said. . . .

Mrs. Calloway made her own rules about books. You could not take back a book to the Library on the same day you'd taken it out; it made no difference to her that you'd read every word in it and needed another to start. You could take out two books at a time and two only; this applied as long as you were a child and also for the rest of your life, to my mother as severely as to me. So two by two, I read library books as fast as I could go, rushing them home in the basket of my bicycle. From the minute I reached our house, I started to read. Every book I seized on, from *Bunny Brown and His Sister Sue at Camp Rest-a-While* to *Twenty Thousand Leagues under the Sea,* stood for the devouring wish to read being instantly granted. I knew this was bliss, knew it at the time. Taste isn't nearly so important; it comes in its own time. I wanted to read immediately. The only fear was that of books coming to an end.

My mother was very sharing of this feeling of insatiability. Now, I think of her as reading so much of the time while doing something else. In my mind's eye *The Origin of Species* is lying on the shelf in the pantry under a light dusting of flour—my mother was a bread maker; she'd pick it up, sit by the kitchen window and find her place, with one eye on the oven. I remember her picking up *The Man in Lower Ten,* while my hair got dry enough to unroll from a load of kid curlers trying to make me like my idol, Mary Pickford. A generation later, when my brother Walter was away in the Navy and his two little girls often spent the day in our house, I remember Mother reading the new issue of *Time* magazine while taking the part of the Wolf in a game of "Little Red Riding Hood" with the children. She'd just look up at the right time, long enough to answer—in character—"The better to eat you with, my dear," and go back to her place in the war news. (671 words)

Record your ending time here:

_____ o'clock _____ min _____ sec

Checking for Understanding

Select the best answer without looking back at the selection.

1. As a child, Eudora Welty felt that reading was
   a. a wonderful thing to do.
   b. a very difficult task, especially for herself.
   c. something best left to librarians like Mrs. Calloway.
   d. a weekend pastime.

2. What description best fits Mrs. Calloway, as Eudora Welty perceived her?
   a. warmhearted person
   b. dragon
   c. mother-substitute
   d. fellow reader

3. How did Mrs. Calloway "test" the girls coming into the library?
   a. She checked that they did not coast through the Capitol building on roller skates.
   b. She checked that they had their own library cards.
   c. She checked that they were over nine years of age.
   d. She checked that they wore enough petticoats so that she could not see through their skirts.

4. Which statement best describes Eudora Welty as a reader?
   a. She read everything she could get her hands on.
   b. She had a high degree of literary taste, even as a child.
   c. She followed the dictates of the librarian as to which books to read.
   d. She read very few books—only the best.

5. Which of the following was a rule in Mrs. Calloway's library?
   a. Children could check out only two books at a time, but adults could take four books.
   b. Children and adults could check out only four books at a time.
   c. Children and adults could check out only two books at a time.
   d. Children could check out books only when accompanied by an adult.

6. Eudora Welty remembered seeing *The Origin of Species* under a light dusting of flour. This came about because
   a. Eudora's mother was a poor housekeeper.
   b. Eudora's mother would read as she baked bread.
   c. Eudora read the book as her mother baked bread.
   d. Eudora read the book as she herself baked bread.

7. How did Eudora get to the library?
   a. by walking
   b. by bus
   c. by bicycle
   d. by a car driven by her mother

8. Eudora Welty's attitude toward reading was probably influenced most strongly by the fact that
   a. her mother loved to read.
   b. her house was located near the library.
   c. she liked going to the library.
   d. she liked the librarian.

Checking Your Reading Rate

Subtract your beginning time from your ending time.

Ending time: _____ o'clock _____ min _____ sec

Starting time: _____ o'clock _____ min _____ sec

_____ min _____ sec

Determine your reading rate for the selection by referring to the table in Appendix A. There are 671 words in the selection.

SELECTION 2: BIG BROTHER IS WATCHING YOU

Getting Ready to Read

*This selection is from a computer magazine (*MacUser*). Before reading, read the title. Predict what the article is about. What do you hope to learn from the article? Record your starting time here:*

_____ o'clock _____ minutes _____ seconds

Reading with Meaning

BIG BROTHER IS WATCHING YOU

Robert Wiggins

In his book *1984*, George Orwell envisioned a future society where every aspect of a person's life was watched and controlled by the evil Big Brother. We are now several years past that infamous year, and have avoided the dismal fate Orwell had in store for us. Or have we?

When you walk into a store and purchase a product with a credit card, most of the time the credit card company is immediately informed of the purchase (and makes the decision to accept or deny the charge) via telecommunications. As point-of-sale terminals become more sophisticated, you may not even know it is happening.

When you apply for a loan, a credit card or try to rent an apartment, a computerized credit check is usually run on you, and almost every aspect of your financial life is scrutinized. Thanks to federal legislation, there are now ways to see your credit report and offer rebuttals for inaccuracies that may have gotten into your report. Prior to these laws, there were many horror stories about false and even malicious information that had been carried in some credit reports and widely circulated. TRW, the largest credit reporting service, in a brilliant marketing move, is even selling a service to allow you to periodically review and update your credit history (something you can do for free if you are denied credit based on a TRW report).

When you have a brush with the law, no matter how minor, they can tap into the FBI's National Crime Information Center (NCIC) computer and instantly find out if you've ever been arrested or otherwise managed to get into any law enforcement files. The FBI Advisory Policy Board last year approved proposals to link NCIC to IRS, INS, Social Security, SEC and several other data bases and to create a system to track anyone *suspected* of a crime. More and more organizations, including private companies, are pushing to gain access to this system and, in the absence of legislation, the same excesses that used to be possible in credit reporting will be extended to law enforcement. Orwell may not have been so far off. (363 words)

Record your ending time here:

_____ o'clock _____ min _____ sec

Checking for Understanding

Mark the following items T (true) or F (false) based on the information from the article. Do not reread or look back.

_____ 1. George Orwell envisioned a world in which people's lives were watched by an evil power.

_____ 2. The article suggests that some aspects of the world envisioned by Orwell have come to be.

_____ 3. Federal legislation prevents your seeing your credit report if you have been denied credit.

_____ 4. Usually when you try to rent an apartment, a credit check is run on you.

_____ 5. You can see your credit report only by paying for the service.

_____ 6. The National Crime Information Center is under the control of TRW.

_____ 7. Today there are federal laws that determine who can tap into NCIC data banks.

_____ 8. Private companies are pressing to gain access to the data in the National Crime Information Center.

_____ 9. George Orwell's prediction was for the world in 2001.

_____ 10. Every time you buy anything with a credit card, the credit card company is immediately informed before credit is granted.

Determining Your Reading Rate

Subtract your starting time from your ending time.

Ending time: _____ o'clock _____ min _____ sec
Starting time: _____ o'clock _____ min _____ sec

_____

Reading time: _____ min _____ sec

Now use the table in the appendix to find your reading rate on this selection. There are 363 words in the selection. Record your rate here. _____

SELECTION 3: LANGUAGE AND COMMUNICATION

Getting Ready to Read

This selection is from a booklet published by a professional organization. Before reading, read the title. Predict what the article is about. What do you hope to learn by reading the article? Record your starting time here:

_____ o'clock _____ min _____ sec

Reading for Meaning

LANGUAGE AND COMMUNICATION
Alan Mandell

One of the characteristics that distinguishes human beings from the other animals is their highly developed ability to communicate—that is, to transfer ideas from one individual to another through abstract visual or oral symbols and, especially to record these symbols so that they can communicate with individuals far away in place or time. Many of the other animals also communicate with each other in a less complex but nevertheless interesting fashion. Some birds have a repertoire of calls, each of which appears to have a significant meaning to other birds. Worker bees have a sign system, by which they inform other bees in the hive of the direction and distance to a food supply. Some animals communicate by using a chemical language; the odors they produce may attract or repel other animals. Still others project messages by gestures, facial expressions, or body attitudes. Communication by use of a language composed of abstract symbols—particularly recorded symbols— appears, however, to be confined to the human animal. (168 words)

Record your ending time here:

_____ o'clock _____ min _____ sec

Checking for Understanding

Select the best answer.

1. The main idea of this selection is that
   a. although other animals can communicate, only human beings have a language composed of abstract symbols that they can record.
   b. all animals have a system of communication.
   c. worker bees communicate with one another.
   d. to be abstract is to be better.

2. According to the selection, bird calls
   a. are simply pleasurable sounds that enrich the environment.
   b. have a meaning to other birds.
   c. have no meaning.
   d. are part of the chemical language birds use to communicate.

3. Which is an example of chemical language?
   a. body attitudes
   b. gestures that animals use to communicate
   c. facial expressions
   d. odors animals produce that attract or repel other animals

4. When the article talks about "recorded symbols," it is talking about
   a. speech.
   b. sounds.
   c. writing.
   d. computer activity.

5. Worker bees use their sign system to tell other bees of
   a. impending danger.
   b. the direction and distance to food.
   c. changes in the weather.
   d. ways to improve the structure and design of the hive.

Determining Your Reading Rate

Calculate your reading time by subtracting your starting time from your ending time.

Ending time: _____ o'clock _____ min _____ sec
Starting time: _____ o'clock _____ min _____ sec

_____

_____ min _____ sec

Use the chart in the appendix to find your reading rate for college textbook material in science. There are 168 words in the selection. Write your reading rate here. _____

SELECTION 4: THE MICROBIAL ENVIRONMENT

Getting Ready to Read

The next selection is from a college microbiology text. Before reading, remember again the meaning of the prefix micro-. Micro- *means "small." A* microbial environment *is an environment in which microorganisms—very small living things—are found. Another name for microorganism is* microbe. *Record your starting time here:*

_____ o'clock _____ min _____ sec

THE MICROBIAL ENVIRONMENT

Thomas Brock, David Smith, and Michael Madigan

Whether life as we know it is unique to the planet earth is an unsolved question. That the earth is an excellent environment on which life has evolved and developed, however, is clear from the diversity of living organisms it now supports. Of all living organisms, none are more versatile than the microorganisms. In no environment where higher organisms are present are microorganisms absent, and in many environments devoid of, or hostile to, higher organisms, microorganisms exist and even flourish. Because microorganisms are usually invisible to the naked eye, their existence in an environment is often unsuspected. Yet, microorganisms carry out a number of functions vital for the life of higher organisms, so that without microbes higher organisms would quickly disappear from the earth.

The geologist divides the earth into three zones, the lithosphere, the hydrosphere, and the atmosphere; to these zones we add the biosphere. The lithosphere is the solid portion of earth, composed of solid and molten rocks and soil. Microbes make up an important part of the soil. The hydrosphere represents the aqueous environments of the earth, such as the oceans, lakes, and rivers. Microorganisms are found throughout the oceans as well as in freshwater habitats from the tropics to the poles. The atmosphere is the gaseous region that surrounds the earth, relatively dense near the surface but thinning to nothing in its upper reaches. Although microbes are carried around the world on winds and other air currents, they do not actually reproduce in the atmosphere. The biosphere represents the mass of living organisms found in a thin belt at the earth's surface. Living organisms have had a profound influence on the earth itself, being responsible for almost all of the oxygen found in the atmosphere as well as for the enormous deposits of oil, coal, and sulfur found underground. Higher organisms and their corpses provide excellent microbial environments, and thus we find large populations of microbes associated with higher plants and animals.

Although the earth provides suitable environments for microbial growth, we do not find the same organisms everywhere. In fact, virtually every environment, no matter how slightly it differs from others, probably has its own particular complement of microorganisms that differ in major or minor ways from organisms of other environments. Because microorganisms are small, their environments are also small. Within a single handful of soil many microenvironments exist, each providing conditions suitable for the growth of a restricted range of microorganisms. When we think of microorganisms living in nature, we must learn to "think small."

New environments for microorganisms are continually being created. Some of these result from natural processes, such as the formation of a new volcanic island or the creation of a new lake after an earthquake. Most are artificial, however. Pollution of streams and lakes, clearing of forests, planting of exotic crops, introduction of new pesticides and fertilizers, and sewage treatment on a large scale all create new microbial environments. These new conditions sometimes make possible a further step in evolution and the development of a new organism.

Thus the great diversity of microbial life on planet earth should not surprise us: it only reflects the great diversity of habitats within which microbes can grow and evolve. Microorganisms are not passive inhabitants, however, and their activities affect their environments in many ways. Some organisms cause diseases, effects far more harmful than we would have predicted from their small sizes. Other deleterious changes, such as food spoilage, souring of milk, deterioration of clothing and dwellings, and corrosion of metal pipes, also occur primarily through microbial action. But microorganisms play many beneficial roles in nature. They are responsible for most of the decomposition of dead animal and plant bodies, thus returning important plant nutrients to the soil. Many microorganisms that live in the intestinal tracts of animals synthesize certain vitamins, thus freeing their hosts of the need to obtain these in their diets. Without microorganisms, animals such as cows, sheep, and goats would be unable to digest the cellulose of grass and hay and hence would be unable to survive on earth. On the whole, the beneficial effects of microorganisms far outweigh their harmful ones. (702 words)

Record your ending time here: _____ o'clock _____ min _____ sec

Checking for Understanding

Answer the questions by placing T *(true) or* F *(false) on the line.*

_____   1. Higher organisms are more versatile than microorganisms.

_____   2. Higher organisms can live where microorganisms cannot.

_____   3. Microorganisms carry out functions vital to higher organisms.

_____   4. The biosphere represents the aqueous environments of the earth.

_____   5. The same microorganisms are found everywhere.

_____   6. The environments of microorganisms are small in size.

_____   7. New environments for microorganisms are continually being created.

_____   8. Microorganisms are passive inhabitants of their environments.

_____   9. Some microorganisms cause diseases.

_____   10. The harmful effects of microorganisms outweigh the beneficial effects.

Determining Your Reading Rate

Calculate your reading time by subtracting your starting time from your ending time.

Ending time: _____ o'clock _____ min _____ sec

Starting time: _____ o'clock _____ min _____ sec

_____

_____ min _____ sec

Use the chart in the appendix to find your reading rate for college material in science. There are 702 words in the selection. Write your reading rate here.

_____

THINKING ABOUT YOUR READING RATE

Think about your reading rates on the last four selections. Do they vary? They should. Most people slow down when they read a technical selection in a science or economics text. They read more quickly when faced with general articles in magazines and newspapers. Expert readers also vary their reading rate depending on their familiarity with the content they are reading. They read quickly on topics with which they are familiar; they read slowly when faced with material that is rather new to them. Try to vary your rate based on these factors.

This chapter has proposed a number of strategies for increasing your rate of reading. Perhaps the best single way of improving your reading efficiency, however, is practice. You must read to become a better reader. Spending spare time reading rather than viewing television is essential. To this end, make a visit to a library to select a book for recreational reading. Make your selection a book on a topic that really interests you. Carry it with you. Whenever you have a spare moment, read that book. Set a time limit for finishing it. Then return to the library for another book. You should try to read at least one book as recreation during every three-week period. If you do that and vary the kinds of books you choose to read, you will find your reading speed increasing.

KEEPING A READING LOG

Buy yourself a stenographer's notebook. As you read, write in your notebook brief summaries and reactions to what you read. Periodically go back and read what you have written. Writing summaries is one of the best ways to increase your reading comprehension.

10

Critical Thinking: Comparing, Inferring, Concluding, Judging

Before reading the chapter, read the title, the stated objective, and the headings and subheadings. Ask yourself: What is the topic of the chapter? In the space above and beside the chapter number, jot down what you already know about that topic. Then in the space below the chapter number, jot down at least two questions you hope to answer through reading the chapter.

OBJECTIVE

In this chapter, you will refine your strategies for thinking critically as you read; specifically, you will refine your ability to

1. compare,
2. infer,
3. conclude, and
4. judge.

INTRODUCTION—COMPARING, INFERRING, CONCLUDING, AND JUDGING

As you learned in Chapter 1, reading is an active process in which you think about and expand upon ideas from a selection. Of course, to get actively involved while reading, you must be able to find the main idea, sort significant from less significant details, and follow the author's train of thought. But to read with full understanding, you must leap beyond the text. You must analyze relationships and come up with your own ideas.

Comparing

One way that you can get actively involved while reading is to make comparisons. In *comparing,* you consider two or more items and determine how those items are similar and how they are different. The items can be people, events, ideas—almost anything, for that matter.

Your strategy for comparing is to

- Identify the significant features of each item you are comparing;
- Ask: What features do the items share, or have in common?
- Ask: How do the items differ?

Sometimes in reading a selection, you find a description or explanation of one item. You still can and should make comparisons. You compare the item described or explained in a passage to items with which you are already familiar.

- Ask: What does this remind me of? How is it like what I already know? How does it differ?

Read the following two paragraphs. Of course, start by previewing. Your purpose for reading is to compare the two experiments. How are they the same? How are they different? To this end, complete the data chart in Figure 10.1 as you read.

CAN CHIMPANZEES LEARN TO SPEAK?

Jean Berko Gleason

In 1931 Professor and Mrs. W. N. Kellogg became the first American family to raise a chimpanzee and a child together. The Kelloggs brought into their home Gua, a seven-month old chimpanzee, who stayed with them and their infant son Donald for nine months. No special effort was made to teach Gua to talk; like the human baby she was simply exposed to a speaking household. During this period, Gua came to use some of her natural chimpanzee cries rather consistently; for instance she used her food bark not just for food but for anything else she wanted. Although Gua was rather better than Donald in most physical accomplishments, unlike Donald she did not babble and did not learn to say any English words.

In the 1940s psychologists Catherine and Keith Hayes set out to improve upon the Kelloggs' experiment by raising a chimpanzee named

	Gua	Viki
When was the experiment done?		
Who did the experiment?		
What procedure did the investigator use?		
What was the outcome?		
What did the investigation seem to prove?		

Figure 10.1   *Chart for Gathering Data*

Viki as if she were their own child. They took her home when she was six weeks old, and she remained with them for several years. The Hayeses made every effort to teach Viki to talk; they had assumed that chimpanzees were rather like retarded institutionalized children and that love and patient instruction would afford Viki the opportunity for optimal language development. After six years of training, Viki was able to say four words: "mamma," "pappa," "cup," and "up." She was never able to say more, and the words she did say were very difficult to understand: in order to pronounce a *p,* she had to hold her lips together with her fingers. (267 words)

Review the data you have organized in Figure 10.1. In what ways were the two experiments similar? In what ways were they different? Complete Figure 10.2.

Before reading the next section, study the two charts you just completed based on the Gua/Viki passage. You can use them as models for your own charts to collect and analyze data while reading.

Inferring

A second way that you can get actively involved while reading is to read between the lines and infer relationships not stated directly by the author. In

How the experiments were similar:
How the experiments differed:

Figure 10.2   *Chart for Making Comparisons*

inferring, you pick up hints or clues from the passage. You relate those clues to things you already know and come up with an idea that the author has only alluded to, or suggested indirectly.

The key strategy question in this case is this:

• What is the author suggesting (or hinting at) through the facts he or she is giving? What can you "read into" what he or she is saying?

Here is an example: What inference do you make when you read the line "When she saw him, her lips tightened"? Having seen people tighten their lips when they are angry (or when they are "uptight" about something), you may infer that the person was not pleased at all; she was angry. That is an inference because the writer does not come right out and state "She was angry." You must figure that out from the clues given.

What inferences do you draw from the statements in Figure 10.3? Complete the chart by filling in the empty cells.

Having completed the chart, you can draw a conclusion about kinds of inferences you can make. You can make inferences about the age of a person, the kind of person he or she is, the kind of relationship that exists between people, a person's feelings, the season of the year, the time of day, the place where a story is set, the date when an event took place.

Concluding

A third kind of thinking that you should do as you read is *concluding*—developing conclusions based on information given. A conclusion is a generalization about a topic. It is a big idea that you put together based on the facts. Very often your conclusions flow out of the comparisons you have made and the inferences you have drawn. Reread the last paragraph of the preceding section. That paragraph states a conclusion about kinds of inferences. The examples in the chart support the generalization. Can you see how?

In formulating conclusions, the main question to ask yourself is this:

• What big idea or ideas can I put together based on the facts given in the selection?

Statement	Question	Inference	Clue in the Sentence That Helps You Infer
His face was lined with wrinkles.	How old was he? What else might you infer?		
He had a scowl on his face as he passed me without speaking.	How did he feel about me? What else might you infer?		
The fellow and girl were holding hands as they strolled through the mall.	What can you infer about their relationship?		
It was snowing heavily and the light had almost disappeared from the heavens.	What season of the year was it? What else can you infer?		
The car was swerving from one side of the road to the other.	What can you infer was wrong here?		
A man remarks, "I do not believe a woman should serve on the Supreme Court."	What kind of man is he?		
She had straight black hair done up in a bun.	What kind of woman was she?		
There were tears running down his face.	What can you infer?		
I gave the grocer a quarter for the quart of milk.	What can you infer?		

Figure 10.3 *Chart for Making Inferences*

Reread the selection about Gua and Viki. What conclusion can you draw about whether chimpanzees are capable of humanlike speech? Write your conclusion here. _____

_____

_____

Did you conclude that chimpanzees cannot learn to speak as humans do, even when given explicit instruction? That would be an acceptable conclusion based on the facts given. What details from the selection support that conclusion? Write some supporting facts here.

_____

_____

_____

In drawing conclusions, you are really getting at the ultimate meaning of things—what is important, why it is important, how one event influenced another, how one happening led into another. To simply get the facts in reading is not enough. You must think about what those facts mean.

Judging

A fourth kind of thinking to do while reading is *judging*—developing judgments of your own about the content you are reading and reasons to support that judgment. In making a judgment, you decide whether an act is right or wrong, good or bad, fair or unfair.

A strategy for rendering a judgment includes asking these questions:

- Do I agree with the point of view expressed in the selection? Why? Why not?
- Do I believe the action described in the selection is right or wrong? Good or evil? Fair or unfair?
- Are the facts in the selection accurate?
- Is the selection clearly written? Or is the phrasing awkward and the organization illogical?

Again go back to the selection about Gua and Viki. Do you believe that it is right to experiment with animals in the way described in the passage? In your notebook, write a topic sentence that states your opinion. Then write a sentence or two with points that support your opinion.

Thinking and Reading

What the introduction to this chapter has been saying is that you should continuously be thinking about ideas as you read. Generally you do this by asking and answering questions as you go along. These questions include:

- Comparing: What does this (person, place, event, etc.) remind me of? How are these two things similar? Different? How does this event, person, or place relate to other events?

- Inferring: What does this clue—hidden between the lines—tell me? What does it hint as to the feelings involved, the age of the person, the kind of person he or she is, the kind of relationship that exists between people, the season of the year, the time of day, the place where the story is set, the date when the event took place?
- Concluding: Why is this important or significant? Why did this happen? What is the ultimate meaning of these events?
- Judging: Do I agree or disagree? Why? Is this accurate? Is this good or bad? Why?

In the selections you will read next, you will have opportunity to think in these terms.

SELECTION 1: AMERICAN INDIAN MYTHS AND LEGENDS

Expanding Your Vocabulary for Reading

Determine the meaning of the underlined words by using word structure and context clues. Use the glossary to check your prediction. Write the meaning in the space provided.

1. His achievements became legendary; they have been celebrated and described over and over again. _____

   _____

2. The general rallied the army after the defeat and later led the army to victory. _____

   _____

3. The keening of the women for the dead general filled the air; their wailing could be heard through the village. _____

   _____

4. The construction workers erected a scaffold to display the golden ornaments so all could see them. _____

   _____

5. His first name is Grant and his last name is Evans, or vice versa.

   _____

   _____

6. In the United States, a ring on the third finger of the left hand signifies that the wearer is married. _____

   _____

7. She aspires to be a lawyer. She aims at this vocation because her mother is a lawyer. _____

   _____

8. My <u>coup</u> for the year is winning the contract to build the shopping center. I count it as one of my greatest accomplishments. _____

_____

9. A peace-loving person, my grandmother <u>abhorred</u> war. She regarded it with extreme loathing. _____

_____

10. No one knows the real reason for the <u>extinction</u> of the dinosaur; we only know that dinosaurs ceased to be. _____

_____

Getting Ready to Read

Survey the selection by reading the title, author, headings, and introductory section.

- What is the topic of the selection? _____
- What kind of selection is it? _____
- What do you know about the topic and this kind of selection? _____

_____

- As you read, complete the data chart in Figure 10.4 and keep in mind the following questions:

1. How are the two stories similar? Different? (comparison)
2. What do the stories tell you about the White River Sioux and the Cheyenne? (inference)
3. What conclusions can you develop about the Sioux and the Cheyenne and the way they view courage? (conclusion)
4. Do you view courage in the same way? If not, why not? (judgment)

Reading with Meaning

AMERICAN INDIAN MYTHS AND LEGENDS: THE WHITE RIVER SIOUX AND THE CHEYENNE

*Richard Erdoes, as Told by Jenny Leading Cloud
at White River, Rosebud Indian Reservation,
South Dakota, 1967*

War for many Indians was an exciting but dangerous sport. In a way it resembled a medieval tournament, governed by strict rules of conduct. The battlefield became an arena for an intensely personal competition of honor in which a young man might make a name for himself and earn the eagle feathers which signified adulthood. One could be killed in this game, but killing enemies was not the reason why men went to war. Total war resulting in the extinction of a tribe was almost unknown and generally abhorred. . . .

A. *Read about:* As you read, record data in the blocks of the data chart. Use the design of this chart to make similar grids for recording while reading and comparing stories.

	Main Characters	
	Chief Roman Nose	**Brave Woman**
Setting: time/place		
Tribe to which he/she belonged		
Personal qualities of the character		
The problem—the core of the legend		
Beginning event of the legend		
Central event in the legend		
Concluding event in the legend		
Meaning of the legend		

B. *Think about:*

1. In what ways are the two legends similar? Use your chart to make comparisons.

2. In what ways are the two legends different? Use your chart to decide.

3. Which legend appeals to you more? Give reasons to support your judgment.

Figure 10.4 *Data-gathering Chart—Comparing Stories*

The conduct of war was a ceremonial affair, full of magic and ritual. Men rode to war with protective medicine bundles, miracle-working pebbles, or medicine shields, their horses covered with sacred gopher dust or painted with lightning designs—all intended to make the wearer arrow- or bullet-proof, and to give his horse supernatural speed.

The main object in any battle—and the only way to gain honors— was to "count coup," to reckon one's brave deeds. Killing a man from an ambush with a gun was no coup because it was easy—even a coward could do it. But riding up on an unwounded and fully armed enemy and touching him with the hand or with one's coupstick, was a great feat. Stealing horses right under the enemy's nose was also a fine coup. Coups were proudly boasted of around campfires, their stories and details told and retold. In some tribes a young man could not aspire to marry unless he had counted coup. . . .

(*Here are two stories that show how the White River Sioux viewed war.*)

Chief Roman Nose Loses His Medicine

The Lakota and the Shahiyela—the Sioux and the Cheyenne—have been good friends for a long time. Often they have fought shoulder to shoulder. They fought the white soldiers on the Bozeman Road, which we Indians called the Thieves' Road because it was built to steal our land. They fought together on the Rosebud River, and the two tribes united to defeat Custer in the big battle of the Little Bighorn. Even now in a barroom brawl, a Sioux will always come to the aid of a Cheyenne and vice versa. We Sioux will never forget what brave fighters the Cheyenne used to be.

Over a hundred years ago the Cheyenne had a famous war chief whom the whites called Roman Nose. He had the fierce, proud face of a hawk, and his deeds were legendary. He always rode into battle with a long warbonnet trailing behind him. It was thick with eagle feathers, and each stood for a brave deed, a coup counted on the enemy.

Roman Nose had a powerful war medicine, a magic stone he carried tied to his hair on the back of his head. Before a fight he sprinkled his

Figure 10.5 *Map of the Little Big Horn Region*

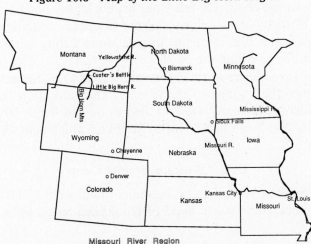

Missouri River Region

war shirt with sacred gopher dust and painted his horse with hailstone patterns. All these things, especially the magic stone, made him bulletproof. Of course he could be slain by a lance, a knife, or a tomahawk, but not with a gun. And nobody ever got the better of Roman Nose in hand-to-hand combat.

There was one thing about Roman Nose's medicine: he was not allowed to touch anything made of metal when eating. He had to use horn or wooden spoons and eat from wooden or earthenware bowls. His meat had to be cooked in a buffalo's pouch or in a clay pot, not in a white man's iron kettle.

One day Roman Nose received word of a battle going on between white soldiers and Cheyenne warriors. The fight had been swaying back and forth for over a day. "Come and help us; we need you" was the message. Roman Nose called his warriors together. They had a hasty meal, and Roman Nose forgot about the laws of his medicine. Using a metal spoon and a white man's steel knife, he ate buffalo meat cooked in an iron kettle.

The white soldiers had made a fort on a sandspit island in the middle of a river. They were shooting from behind and they had a new type of rifle which was better and could shoot faster and farther than the Indians' arrows and old muzzle-loaders.

The Cheyenne were hurling themselves against the soldiers in attack after attack, but the water in some spots came up to the saddles of their horses and the river bottom was slippery. They could not ride up quickly on the enemy, and they faced murderous fire. Their attacks were repulsed, their losses heavy.

Roman Nose prepared for the fight by putting on his finest clothes, war shirt, and leggings. He painted his best horse, with hailstone designs, and he tied the pebble which made him bulletproof into his hair at the back of his head. But an old warrior stepped up to him and said: "You have eaten from an iron kettle with a metal spoon and a steel knife. Your medicine is powerless; you must not fight today. Purify yourself for four days so that your medicine will be good again."

"But the fight is today, not in four days," said Roman Nose. "I must lead my warriors. I will die, but only the mountains and the rocks are forever." He put on his great warbonnet, sang his death song, and then charged. As he rode up to the whites' cottonwood breastwork, a bullet hit him in the chest. He fell from his horse; his body was immediately lifted by his warriors, and the Cheyenne retreated with their dead chief. To honor him in death, to give him a fitting burial, was more important than to continue the battle.

All night the soldiers in their fort could hear the Cheyennes' mourning songs, the keening of the women. They too knew that the great chief Roman Nose was dead. He had died as he had lived. He had shown that sometimes it is more important to act like a chief than to live to a great old age.

Brave Woman Counts Coup

Over a hundred years ago, when many Sioux were still living in what now is Minnesota, there was a band of Hunkpapa Sioux at Spirit Lake under a chief called Tawa Makoce, meaning His Country. It was his country, too—Indian country, until the white soldiers with their cannon finally drove the Lakota tribes across the Mni Shoshay: The Big Muddy, the Missouri.

In his youth the chief had been one of the greatest warriors. Later when his fighting days were over, he was known as a wise leader, invaluable in council, and as a great giver of feasts, a provider for the poor. The chief had three sons and one daughter. The sons tried to be warriors as mighty as their father, but that was a hard thing to do. Again and again they battled the Crow Indians with reckless bravery, exposing themselves in the front rank, fighting hand to hand, until one by one they were all killed. Now only his daughter was left to the sad old chief. Some say her name was Makhta. Others call her Winyan Ohitika, Brave Woman.

The girl was beautiful and proud. Many young men sent their fathers to the old chief with gifts of fine horses that were preliminary to marriage proposals. Among those who desired her for a wife was a young warrior named Red Horn, himself the son of a chief, who sent his father again and again to ask for her hand. But Brave Woman would not marry. "I will not take a husband," she said, "until I have counted coup on the Crows to avenge my dead brothers." Another young man who loved Brave Woman was Wanblee Cikala, or Little Eagle. He was too shy to declare his love, because he was a poor boy who had never been able to distinguish himself.

At this time the Kangi Oyate, the Crow nation, made a great effort to establish themselves along the banks of the upper Missouri in country which the Sioux considered their own. The Sioux decided to send out a strong war party to chase them back, and among the young men riding out were Red Horn and Little Eagle. "I shall ride with you," Brave Woman said. She put on her best dress of white buckskin richly decorated with beads and porcupine quills, and around her neck she wore a choker of dentalium shells. She went to the old chief. "Father," she said, "I must go to the place where my brothers died. I must count coup for them. Tell me that I can go."

The old chief wept with pride and sorrow. "You are my last child," he said, "and I fear for you and for a lonely old age without children to comfort me. But your mind has long been made up. I see that you must go; do it quickly. Wear my warbonnet into battle. Go and do not look back."

And so his daughter, taking her brothers' weapons and her father's warbonnet and best war pony, rode out with the warriors. They found an enemy village so huge that it seemed to contain the whole Crow nation— hundreds of men and thousands of horses. There were many more Crows than Sioux, but the Sioux attacked nevertheless. Brave Woman was a sight to stir the warriors to great deeds. To Red Horn she gave her oldest brother's lance and shield. "Count coup for my dead brother," she said. To Little Eagle she gave her second brother's bow and arrows. "Count coup for him who owned these," she told him. To another young warrior she gave her youngest brother's war club. She herself carried only her father's old, curved coupstick wrapped in otter fur.

At first Brave Woman held back from the fight. She supported the Sioux by singing brave-heart songs and by making the shrill, trembling war cry with which Indian women encourage their men. But when the Sioux, including her own warriors from the Hunkpapa band, were driven back by overwhelming numbers, she rode into the midst of the battle. She did not try to kill her enemies, but counted coup left and right, touching them with her coupstick. With a woman fighting so bravely among them, what Sioux warrior could think of retreat?

Still, the press of the Crows and their horses drove the Sioux back a second time. Brave Woman's horse was hit by a musket bullet and went down. She was on foot, defenseless, when Red Horn passed her on his speckled pony. She was too proud to call out for help, and he pretended not to see her. Then Little Eagle came riding toward her out of the dust of battle. He dismounted and told her to get on his horse. She did, expecting him to climb up behind her, but he would not. "This horse is wounded and too weak to carry us both," he said.

"I won't leave you to be killed," she told him. He took her brother's bow and struck the horse sharply with it across the rump. The horse bolted, as he intended, and Little Eagle went back into battle on foot. Brave Woman herself rallied the warriors for a final charge, which they made with such fury that the Crows had to give way at last.

This was the battle in which the Crow nation was driven away from the Missouri for good. It was a great victory, but many brave young men died. Among them was Little Eagle, struck down with his face to the enemy. The Sioux warriors broke Red Horn's bow, took his eagle feathers from him, and sent him home. But they placed the body of Little Eagle on a high scaffold on the spot where the enemy camp had been. They killed his horse to serve him in the land of many lodges. "Go willingly," they told the horse. "Your master has need of you in the spirit world."

Brave Woman gashed her arms and legs with a sharp knife. She cut her hair short and tore her white buckskin dress. Thus she mourned for Little Eagle. They had not been man and wife; in fact he had hardly dared speak to her or look at her, but now she asked everybody to treat her as if she were the young warrior's widow. Brave Woman never took a husband, and she never ceased to mourn for Little Eagle. "I am his widow," she told everyone. She died of old age. She had done a great thing, and her fame endures. (2122 words)

Checking for Understanding

Use data from your chart to answer these questions.

1. What was the most significant difference between Little Eagle and Red Horn? _____

_____

2. Why did Brave Woman give her oldest brother's lance to Red Horn and her second brother's bow to Little Eagle, and not vice versa? _____

_____

3. Why did Red Horn pretend not to see Brave Woman? _____

_____

4. Why did Little Eagle give his horse to Brave Woman? _____

_____

5. Do you think Little Eagle realized that by giving away his horse he was also giving away his life? Tell why. _____

_____

6. Why did the Sioux warriors break Red Horn's bow and take his feathers away? _____

_____

7. Today the deeds of Brave Woman are legendary. Do you believe she did the right thing when she went into battle with the warriors? Why? Why not? Would you have done what she did? Explain. _____

_____

_____

_____

8. Do you believe that the Sioux were right in killing Little Eagle's horse? Explain. _____

_____

9. In what ways were Little Eagle and Roman Nose similar? Different?

_____

_____

10. Why do you think the whites gave Roman Nose that name? _____

_____

11. Why do you think Roman Nose forgot about the laws of medicine and ate with metal tools? _____

_____

12. Why did Roman Nose sing his death song before going into battle? What does this say about the kind of man he was? _____

_____

13. What does honor mean to a Cheyenne or a Sioux? _____

_____

14. What is the relationship between coup and bravery to a Cheyenne or a Sioux?

_____

_____

15. How do the Sioux feel about the white man? How do you know? _____

_____

Reviewing Vocabulary

Select the word from this list that best fits the context of the sentence.

a. abhorred   f. rallied

b. aspires   g. repulsed

c. extinction   h. scaffold

d. keening   i. signifies

e. legendary   j. vice versa

1. After her death, she became a _____ figure; people told and re-told stories of what she had done.

2. They fought until the _____ of their enemies; by the end of the battle, none of the enemy was left alive.

3. That woman _____ cigarette smoking. It was something she hated more than anything else.

4. The Indians _____ the attackers who were trying to take their land; the attackers withdrew in disorder.

5. I will always help my brother, and _____ .

6. They erected a _____ to hold all their equipment.

7. His signature on the contract _____ his acceptance of it.

8. During the battle, the troops _____ around their leader and continued to fight.

9. We heard the _____ of the women as they mourned their dead; the noise of it filled the air.

10. She _____ to become a Supreme Court justice; this is her greatest ambition.

Extending Your Understanding Through Writing

What is the most honorable or brave deed that you have read about or seen someone perform? In your notebook, write a paragraph in which you tell about that deed, much in the manner that Jenny Leading Cloud recounted the stories of Brave Woman and Roman Nose to her interviewer.

SELECTION 2: HAYDN AND MOZART

Expanding Your Vocabulary for Reading

Use context and word-structure clues to figure out the meanings of the underlined terms. Check your predictions in the glossary. Write the meanings in the space provided.

1. The return of the soldiers proved to be a <u>festive</u> occasion; flowers and streamers were everywhere and people danced in the streets. _____

_____

2. In times gone by, artists had <u>patrons</u>, wealthy people who supported them so that they could pursue their artistic endeavors. _____

   _____

3. Just before the exam, there was a <u>frenzy</u> of last-minute study by the students in the class. _____

   _____

4. He had an <u>aristocratic</u> way about him; he held himself as if he were somebody of wealth and position. _____

   _____

5. After her campaign for president, she was left with <u>staggering</u> debts—debts so large that no one believed she could ever be free of carrying their weight.

   _____

   _____

6. It is <u>degrading</u> to have to get down on one's knees and beg for support.

   _____

   _____

7. There were <u>ominous</u> rumblings in the earth just before the volcano erupted.

   _____

   _____

8. By the time he left the presidency, his popularity had <u>dwindled</u> to lower than a 25 percent acceptance rate. _____

   _____

9. She was in the <u>elite</u> group that was invited to the White House to meet the Prime Minister of England. _____

   _____

10. He was a child <u>prodigy</u>; at age 7, he was writing music and performing it before large audiences. _____

    _____

11. The widow fell into the hands of an <u>unscrupulous</u> financial adviser who used every trick to get her money for himself. _____

    _____

12. He received a <u>commission</u> from a wealthy patron to write a comic opera.

    _____

    _____

13. There is <u>irony</u> in the fact that he regained popularity just before he died.

    _____

    _____

Getting Ready to Read

Preview the selection by reading the title, headings, and introduction.

- What is the topic of the selection? _____
- What do you already know about these two men? _____

_____

- What purpose are you setting for yourself as you read? _____

_____

As you read, complete the data chart (Figure 10.6). Make comparisons and contrasts between the two men and their music. Try to read between the lines. Think in terms of the meaning, or significance, of the events recounted, and formulate judgments about the rightness and wrongness of acts described.

Reading with Meaning

JOSEPH HAYDN
AND WOLFGANG AMADEUS MOZART

Roger Kamien

The classical period in music extended from 1750 to 1820. Master composers of this period were Joseph Haydn, Wolfgang Amadeus Mozart, and Ludwig van Beethoven. In this selection, you will read about Haydn and Mozart.

Joseph Haydn (1732-1809)

Joseph Haydn was born in a tiny Austrian village called Rohrau. His father made wagon wheels, and until the age of six, Haydn's musical background consisted of folksongs his father loved to sing and the peasant dances that whirled around him on festive occasions. (This early contact with folk music later had an influence on his style.) Haydn's eager response to music was recognized, and he was sent to live with a relative who gave him basic music lessons for two years. At eight, he went to Vienna to serve as a choirboy in the Cathedral of St. Stephen. There, though his good voice was appreciated, he had no chance for composition lessons or for perfecting an instrumental technique. And when his voice changed, Haydn was dismissed from St. Stephen's and turned out on the street without a penny. "I barely managed to stay alive by giving music lessons to children for about eight years," he wrote. Throughout those years he struggled to teach himself composition and also took odd jobs, including playing violin in the popular Viennese street bands that offered evening entertainment.

Gradually, aristocratic patrons of music began to notice Haydn's talent. For a brief time he was music director at the court of a Bohemian count, but the orchestra was dissolved because of his patron's financial problems. At the age of twenty-nine, Haydn's life changed for the better, forever.

A. *Read about:* As you read, record data in the blocks of the data chart. Use the design of this chart to make similar grids for recording while reading and for composing life histories.

Composers		
	Haydn	Mozart
Time and place of birth		
Father's background		
Personal qualities		
How he got started in music		
Major events in his musical career 1. 2. 3. 4.		
Concluding events in his life		

B. *Think about:*

1. In what ways were the lives of the two composers similar? Use your chart to make comparisons.

_____

2. In what ways were the lives of the two composers different? Use your chart to decide.

_____

3. Which composer led the more successful life? Give reasons to support your judgment.

_____

Figure 10.6 *Data-gathering Chart—Comparing Life Histories*

In 1761, Haydn entered the service of the Esterhazys, the richest and most powerful of the noble Hungarian families. For almost thirty years, from 1761 to 1790, most of his music was composed for performance in the palaces of the family. Haydn spent much of his time at Esterhaz, a magnificent but isolated palace in Hungary that contained an opera house, a theater, two concert halls, and 126 guest rooms.

As a highly skilled servant, Haydn was to compose all the music requested by his patron, conduct the orchestra of about twenty-five players, coach singers, and oversee the condition of instruments and the operation of the music library. He also was required to "appear daily in the antechamber before and after midday and inquire whether His Highness is pleased to order a performance of the orchestra." The amount of work demanded of Haydn as assistant music director and later as music director was staggering; there were usually two concerts and two opera performances weekly, as well as daily chamber music in the prince's apartment. Since Nicholas Esterhazy played the baryton (a complicated stringed instrument now obsolete), Haydn wrote over 150 pieces with a baryton part.

Though today it seems degrading for a genius to be dependent on the will of a prince, in the eighteenth century patronage was taken for granted. Composers had definite advantages in that they received a steady income and their works were performed. And though Haydn felt restricted by his job from time to time, he later wisely said, "Not only did I have the encouragement of constant approval, but as conductor of an orchestra I could make experiments, observe what produced an effect and what weakened it, and was thus in a position to improve, alter, make additions or omissions, and be as bold as I pleased. I was cut off from the world; there was no one to confuse or torment me, and I was forced to become original."

Despite an unhappy marriage, Haydn was good-humored and unselfish. He was conscientious about professional duties, and he cared about the personal interests of his musicians. Prince Nicholas loved Esterhaz and once stayed at the palace longer than usual. The orchestra members came to Haydn and asked to return to Vienna; they tired of being isolated in the country, away so long from their wives and children. Haydn obliged by composing a symphony in F-sharp minor, now known as the "Farewell." At its first performance for the prince, the musicians followed the indications in the score: During the last movement, one after another stopped playing, put out his candle, and quietly left the hall. By the time that only Haydn and the first violinist remained, Nicholas took the hint; the next day he ordered the household to return to Vienna.

Haydn met the younger Mozart in the early 1780s and they became close friends. To someone finding fault with one of Mozart's operas, Haydn replied, "I cannot settle this dispute, but this I know: Mozart is the greatest composer the world possesses now."

Over a period of twenty years, word spread about the Esterhazys' composer, and Haydn's music became immensely popular all over Europe. Publishers and concert organizations sent commissions for new works. After the death of Prince Nicholas Esterhazy in 1790, Haydn was free to go to London where a concert series was planned around his compositions. He'd been asked by concert manager Johann Peter Salomon to write and conduct new symphonies for performance at public concerts. Six were composed for a first visit in 1791-1792 and six more for a second visit in 1794-1795. These twelve became known as the "Salomon Symphonies" or "London Symphonies."

Reports of the time say that Haydn's appearances were triumphs. By the end of the eighteenth century, London was the largest and richest city in the world. Its concert life was unusually active and attracted many foreign musicians. Acclaim at Haydn's concerts was so overwhelming that some symphony movements had to be repeated. One listener noted that there was "an electrical effect on all present and such a degree of enthusiasm as almost amounted to a frenzy."

And so, a servant had become a celebrity. Haydn was wined and dined by the aristocracy, given an honorary degree at Oxford, and received by members of the royal family. And, as though to balance out earlier personal unhappiness, he had a love affair with a rich English widow. After thirty years of service to the Esterhazys, Haydn's reception by the English moved him to write, "How sweet is some degree of liberty. The consciousness of no longer being a bond servant sweetens all my toil."

Rich and honored, Haydn returned to Vienna in 1795 and maintained good relations with Esterhaz. The new prince, Nicholas II, did not have his father's wide musical interests and liked only religious music. Haydn's agreement specified that he would compose a Mass a year. There are six, and all reflect the mature, brilliant writing of the London Symphonies. In this period of his late sixties, Haydn composed two oratorios, *The Creation* (1798) and *The Seasons* (1801). They were so popular that choruses and orchestras were formed at the beginning of the nineteenth century for the sole purpose of performing them.

Haydn died in 1809, at the age of seventy-seven, while Napoleon's army occupied Vienna. A memorial service indicated the wide recognition of Haydn's greatness: Joining the Viennese were French generals and an honor guard of French soldiers.

Wolfgang Amadeus Mozart (1756-1791)

One of the most amazing child prodigies in history, Wolfgang Amadeus Mozart was born in Salzburg, Austria, the son of a court musician. By the age of six, he could play the harpsichord and violin, improvise fugues, write minuets, and read music perfectly at first sight. At eight, he wrote a symphony; at eleven, an oratorio; and at twelve, an opera. By his early teens, Mozart had behind him many works that would have brought credit to a composer three times his age.

Mozart's father, Leopold, was understandably eager to show him off and went to great lengths to do so. Between the ages of six and fifteen, Mozart spent almost half his life on tour in Europe and England. He played for Empress Maria Theresa in Vienna, for Louis XV at Versailles, for George III in London and for innumerable aristocrats along the way. On his trips to Italy he was able to study and master the operatic style which he later put to superb use. At fourteen, Mozart was in Rome during Holy Week, and he went to the Sistine Chapel to hear the famous

Library of Congress

Figure 10.7   *Joseph Haydn and Wolfgang Amadeus Mozart*

choir performing a work that was its treasured property. Anyone caught copying this choral piece was to be punished by excommunication. Mozart heard it once, wrote it out afterward almost completely, returned with his manuscript to make a few additions—and was discovered. That anyone should copy the music was a crime; that Mozart should hear and remember it accurately was incredible. He not only escaped punishment but was knighted by the Pope for his musical accomplishments.

At fifteen, Mozart returned to Salzburg, which was ruled by a new Prince—Archbishop, Hieronymus Colloredo. The Archbishop was a tyrant who did not appreciate Mozart's genius, and he refused to grant him more than a subordinate seat in the court orchestra. With his father's help, Mozart tried repeatedly over the next decade to find a suitable position, but there were never any vacancies.

The tragic irony of Mozart's life was that he won more acclaim as a boy wonder than as an adult musician. His upbringing and personality were partly to blame. As a child, his complete dependence on his father gave little opportunity to develop initiative. Even when Mozart was twenty-two, his mother tagged along when he went to Paris to seek recognition and establish himself. A Parisian observed that Mozart was "too good-natured, not active enough, too easily taken in, too little concerned with the means that may lead him to good fortune."

Unlike Haydn, Mozart began life as an international celebrity, pampered by kings. He could not tolerate being treated like a servant and eating with valets and cooks, and his relations with his patron went from bad to worse. Mozart became totally insubordinate when the Prince-Archbishop forbade him to give concerts or perform at the houses of the aristocracy. Mozart wrote: "He lied to my face that my salary was five hundred *gulden,* called me a scoundrel, a rascal, a vagabond. At last my blood began to boil, I could no longer contain myself, and I said, 'So Your Grace is not satisfied with me?'" He was answered with, "What, you dare to threaten me—you scoundrel? There is the door!" On his third attempt to request dismissal, Mozart was thrown out of the room by a court official and given a kick.

By 1781, when he was twenty-five, Mozart could stand it no longer. He broke free of provincial Salzburg and traveled to Vienna, intending to be a free-lance musician. To reassure his father, he wrote, "I have the best and the most useful acquaintances in the world. I am liked and respected in the best houses, and all possible honors are given me, and moreover I get paid for it. I guarantee you, I'll be successful."

Indeed, Mozart's first few years in Vienna were successful. His German opera *The Abduction from the Seraglio* (1782) was acclaimed. Concerts of his own music were attended by the Emperor and nobility. Pupils paid him high fees, his compositions were published, and his playing was heard in palace drawing rooms. He even went against his father's wishes by marrying Constance Weber, who had no money and was as impractical as he. Contributing to the brightness of these years was Mozart's friendship with Haydn, who told his father, "Your son is the greatest composer that I know, either personally or by reputation. . . ."

Then, in 1786, came his opera *The Marriage of Figaro*. Vienna loved it, and Prague was even more enthusiastic. "They talk about nothing but *Figaro*. Nothing is played, sung, or whistled but *Figaro*," Mozart joyfully wrote. This success led a Prague opera company to commission *Don Giovanni* the following year. *Don Giovanni* was a triumph in Prague, but it pushed the Viennese too far. The Emperor Joseph II acknowledged that it was a masterwork, but not appropriate for his pleasure-loving subjects. . . .

Mozart's popularity in Vienna began to decline. It was a fickle city: one was society's darling for a few seasons, then suddenly ignored. And Mozart's music was considered complicated and hard to follow. . . . A publisher warned him: "Write in a more popular style, or else I can neither print nor pay for any more of your music!" His pupils dwindled, and the elite snubbed his concerts. In desperate financial straits, he wrote to friends, "Great god, I would not wish my worst enemy to be in this position. . . . I am coming to you not with thanks but with fresh entreaties."

Many of Mozart's letters have been published. These span his life, and it is sad to move from the colorful, witty, and keenly observant notes of a prodigy on tour through his initial optimism about Vienna to the despair of "I cannot describe what I have been feeling. . . . A kind of longing that is never satisfied."

The events of Mozart's last year would have been good material for a grim opera plot. Though his health was failing in 1791, Mozart was delighted to receive a commission from a Viennese theater for a German comic opera, *The Magic Flute*. While hard at work, Mozart was visited by a stranger dressed entirely in gray who carried an anonymous letter commissioning a Requiem, a Mass for the Dead. Unknown to Mozart, the stranger was a servant of an unscrupulous nobleman who meant to claim the Requiem as his own composition. Mozart's health grew worse, and the Requiem took on ominous implications; he believed it to be for himself and rushed to finish it while on his deathbed. A final bit of happiness came to him two months before his death. *The Magic Flute* was premiered to resounding praise in Vienna. Its success probably would have brought large financial rewards, but it came too late. Mozart died shortly before his thirty-sixth birthday, and the final sections of the Requiem were not his. The work was completed from sketches by Sussmayr, his favorite pupil.

Mozart's funeral was the poorest possible. His body was laid in a common grave assigned to paupers. (2366 words)

Checking for Understanding

1. In what ways were the lives of Haydn and Mozart similar? In what ways were they different? _____

_____

_____

2. Of the two composers, which one do you believe had the better life? Why?

_____

_____

_____

3. Why do you think that Haydn could better accept being dependent on the will of a patron than did Mozart? _____

_____

_____

4. Haydn called Mozart the greatest composer the world then possessed. What does that tell you about the kind of person Haydn was? _____

_____

_____

5. The selection states: "The tragic irony of Mozart's life was that he won more acclaim as a boy wonder than as an adult musician." *Irony* in this context means "an outcome contrary to what might have been expected." Why is Mozart's life an example of tragic irony? _____

_____

_____

6. Why was it significant that Mozart married against his father's wishes?

_____

_____

7. As a boy, Mozart played for major rulers of Europe and was knighted by the Pope. How do you think this affected him and influenced his later life?

_____

_____

_____

8. Ludwig van Beethoven (1770–1827), who perhaps was the greatest composer of the classical period, came after Mozart. He, too, was a child prodigy, but he was never in the service of the Viennese aristocracy. He succeeded as a free-lance musician, despite deafness that struck him at 29. Based on what you have read about Mozart, hypothesize why Beethoven succeeded as a free-lancer, whereas Mozart had a hard time working without a patron.

_____

_____

9. It is interesting that the three great composers of the classical period—Haydn, Mozart, and Beethoven—lived in central Europe. Do you think this happened by chance? What reasons come to your mind to account for this?

_____

_____

_____

Reviewing Key Vocabulary

Select the word from the list that best fits the context of each sentence. Check the glossary if you need to review the meaning of a word.

a. aristocratic	e. elite	i. ominous
b. commission	f. festive	j. patron
c. degrading	g. frenzy	k. prodigy
d. dwindled	h. irony	l. staggering
		m. unscrupulous

1. The corporation became a _____ of the arts; it gave millions away to support artistic projects.

2. There was a _____ of activity at the end of the year as people did lots of last-minute tasks.

3. His friends _____ away until he had none at all.

4. The amount of work required of the man was _____ ; he could never get it done in a twelve-hour workday.

5. We heard an _____ rumble of thunder as we started our picnic.

6. The artist accepted a _____ to paint a portrait of the Queen.

7. Some people think it is _____ for women to parade in bathing suits during a beauty contest.

8. There is _____ in the fact that she got what she wanted only after she no longer had use for it.

9. Mozart was a _____ ; he could compose and play music even as a child.

10. The lords and ladies looked upon themselves as being among the _____ , or the privileged.

11. The members of the royal family acted in an _____ way during the coronation.

12. The _____ man lied and cheated on every occasion.

13. The New Year's celebration was a _____ time.

Writing About What You Know

In this selection, you learned about the patronage system as it existed during the classical period. In your notebook, write a paragraph in which you state your opinion of the system between patron and musician as it operated at the end of the 1700s. Support your opinion with details. Before writing, jot down your opinion and the details you will use to support it. In short, create a map of the ideas as demonstrated earlier in Chapter 5, in Figure 5.3.

EXTENDING WHAT YOU HAVE LEARNED

Reviewing Your Reading Strategies

List here a series of questions you should keep in mind as you read beyond the facts given in a selection.

_____

_____

_____

_____

_____

_____

Applying the Strategies to Your Reading

Locate a book of short stories, Greek myths, fables, or legends in the library. Read two stories from the book, and create a data chart for compiling information while reading. Then write a short paragraph in which you compare the two stories and draw a conclusion about them.

Building a Knowledge Base for Reading

Locate the following places on the maps in Figures 10.5 and 10.8:

Minnesota	Vienna and Salzburg in Austria	Rome, Italy
the Missouri River	Prague, Czechoslovakia	London, England
	Hungary	Paris, France
the Little Bighorn River		

Figure 10.8 *Map of Europe*

Gaining Ownership of Words

Select several of the words featured in this chapter. Record them in your personal vocabulary list. Try to use them in speaking and writing.

11

Interpreting Style, Tone, and Mood

Before reading the chapter, read the title, the stated objective, and the headings and subheadings. Ask yourself: What is the topic of the chapter? In the space above and beside the chapter number, jot down what you already know about that topic. Then in the space below the chapter number, jot down at least two questions you hope to answer through reading the chapter.

OBJECTIVE

In this chapter you will develop strategies for interpreting

1. style—the author's overall manner of writing,
2. tone—the way in which an author expresses feelings, and
3. mood—the feeling in a piece.

INTRODUCTION—STYLE, MOOD, AND TONE

The term *style* means the way in which an author expresses himself or herself—the way he or she chooses and uses words, punctuation, sentences, and paragraphs to communicate meaning. Writing can be bare-bones, matter-of-fact, and unembellished: The author uses words sparingly and comes directly to the point without elaboration. On the other hand, writing can be flowery and dramatic: The author uses colorful and melodious expressions, painting pictures with descriptive words and providing considerable elaboration. Of course, writing style can be somewhere between the plain and the dramatic. And it can be overly matter-of-fact or overly dramatic.

Elements of Style

In *Writer's Guide and Index to English,* Porter Perrin identifies elements to consider in thinking about an author's style.

1. *Development of ideas:* the way the author develops a thought
   a. Does the writer start with specific information and then develop generalizations based on the specifics? Or does he or she begin with a generalization and then provide details or examples?
   b. Does the writer lay it all out "in black and white"? Or do you, the reader, have to infer meanings, or put them together based on the data stated?
   c. Is the writer systematic in the way he or she presents ideas?
   d. Does the writer pack a lot of details into a short space? Does the writer provide considerable visual detail and elaboration?

2. *Qualities of sound:* the way the words would sound if read aloud
   a. Is there a melodious sound to the words, whether the piece is poetry or prose? Or is there an awkwardness in the way words flow?
   b. Has the writer effectively used alliteration (the repetition of beginning sounds as in "the forest's ferny floor") or rhyme (the repetition of end sounds, as in

   > Listen, my children, and you shall hear
   > Of the midnight ride of Paul Revere,
   > On the eighteenth of April, in Seventy five;
   > Hardly a man is now alive
   > Who remembers that famous day and year)?

   c. Does the writer purposefully repeat words, phrases, and sentences to heighten the message?
   d. How has the writer used punctuation to emphasize sound—for example, the dash to make you pause longer in reading; the exclamation mark to communicate excitement?

3. *Visual elements:* the way the author uses space and shape to communicate the message
   a. Does the piece have the appearance of poetry on the page—laid out in lines and verses?
   b. Does the author use italic type or punctuation to heighten the message?

4. *Sentences:* the way the author constructs sentences

     a. Does the author use short sentences? Long ones? A mix of sentence lengths?

     b. Does the author use complicated sentence patterns? Simple sentences that are easy to read?

5. *Words:* the words the author chooses
     a. Does the author rely on short words? Long words?
     b. Does the author rely on familiar words? Unfamiliar words?

6. *Imagery:* the pictures the author paints with words
     a. Does the author paint pictures that you can see in your mind's eye?
     b. Does the author work with abstractions that are difficult for you to picture?

7. *Figures of speech:* metaphors, similes, unique ways of handling language and turns of a phrase that an author uses
     a. Does the author build unusual relationships through metaphor or simile?

       (1.) A simile is a creative comparison that relies on the word *like* or *as* to make a connection between two things. Example: "The branches of the trees stretched heavenward like hands reaching for space."

                branches = hands

       (2.) A metaphor is a creative comparison without the word *like* or *as*. Example: "The wind proved to be a deadly dragon, ripping up the world with its tail."

                wind = deadly dragon

     b. Does the author use language in unique ways? Does he or she turn a phrase with style?

8. *Literary allusions:* references to other pieces of literature
     a. Does the author use words, phrases, sentences from the works of other authors without quoting directly or telling you their source?
     b. Does the author refer in some way to events from other pieces of literature?
     c. Does the author quote directly (with quotation marks) from the works of other authors?

Reading for Style

Now read aloud this poem by Nikki Giovanni, a modern-day poet of considerable repute. As you read, listen for sounds and rhythm and consider the creative relationship she has put together:

the drum

Nikki Giovanni

daddy says the world is
a drum tight and hard
and i told him
i'm gonna beat
out my own rhythm

Writing about the world, Giovanni could have spoken in literal terms and described the earth as a spinning sphere. But she did not. Ms. Giovanni relied on figurative language—in this case a metaphor—to establish a unique relationship that stretches your thinking as you read:

the world = a drum.

Reading her poem, you must ask yourself, "How is the world similar to a drum?" You play on a drum; you play on the world. You beat a drum; you beat the world. With a drum, you can make rhythm; with the world, you can make rhythm.

Now go back and reread the poem. How does Giovanni use capitalization and punctuation? She does not bother with them, does she? That is a part of her style. What kinds of words does she use? Short, familiar, mostly one syllable words. She also uses "gonna" rather than the standard "going to." These, too, are elements of the Giovanni style. What kinds of sentences does she use? One compound sentence comprises the entire piece. That is another aspect of her style. What sounds does she build into her poem? The hard sounds of the *b* and *t* in *beat* and *told*—sounds that are almost those of a drum.

One student reader wrote a poem modeled after Giovanni's. It, too, includes a creative comparison, a metaphor that stretches your thinking. It, too, relies on short words and repeating sounds of the *t* as in *tough, told,* and *top.* And it dispenses with punctuation and capitalization in the style of Giovanni.

the mountain

daddy says the world is
a mountain that is tough to climb
and i told him
i'd climb it
to the very top

- To what does this student compare the world? _____
- In what ways are the world and a mountain similar? _____

Style, Tone, and Mood

Tone is the manner in which a writer communicates feelings; it is closely related to writing style and is a part of it, really. It is comparable to tone of voice in speaking. The tone of a piece can be sharp and probing, antagonistic and critical, sarcastic, ironic, or warm and caring. Both in writing and speaking, tone reflects the attitude of the author toward his or her subject. An author's choice of words often determines the tone.

Mood is the feeling communicated in the piece. Both tone and style set the mood, which can be happy or sad, positive or negative, calm or excited, or at times just neutral.

What are the tone and mood of the Giovanni poem, "the drum"? Giovanni comes across with a determined tone of voice. Reading it aloud, you sense that. The mood is upbeat, isn't it? There is no sadness, calmness, or even anger to it. In this respect, both the tone and mood are part of the message. That message is "I am determined to make it!" Although Giovanni does not use an exclamation at the end, the exclamation is there—in the determined tone and upbeat mood.

SELECTION 1: THE GETTYSBURG ADDRESS

Expanding Vocabulary for Reading

Use word structure and context clues to determine the meanings of the underlined words. Check the glossary if you are not certain of the meanings. Record the definition of each underlined term in the space provided.

1. A score of years is twice as long as a decade. _____
   _____

2. He put this proposition to me: Every person must do his or her fair share of the work. _____
   _____

3. The priest consecrated the site by declaring it to be a sacred place. _____
   _____

4. "We cannot hallow this battlefield; we cannot make it a sacred, or holy, place," the president said. _____
   _____

5. Wearing a long skirt does not detract from your appearance. It may actually make you look better. _____
   _____

Getting Ready to Read

Read the title, author, and introduction to the selection.

• What do you already know about this selection and its author? _____
   _____

• Setting your Purpose for Reading: As you read the selection, pretend you are at Gettysburg and are hearing Lincoln deliver the address. How would it have made you feel? What elements of Lincoln's writing style would have led you to feel that way?

Reading for Meaning

ADDRESS AT THE DEDICATION OF THE GETTYSBURG NATIONAL CEMETARY

Abraham Lincoln

Lincoln delivered this address on November 19, 1863, at Gettysburg, Pennsylvania. The prior speaker, Edward Everett, had just presented a very formal, two-hour speech to an audience comprised of a hundred thousand people. Lincoln had made a rough outline of his own address, wrote it out on paper only shortly before, and scribbled the final sentence in pencil after arriving in Gettysburg. The Gettysburg Address, as we know it today, is one of the best known speeches of all times.

Fourscore and seven years ago our fathers brought forth on this continent a new nation, conceived in liberty, and dedicated to the proposition that all men are created equal.

Now we are engaged in a great civil war, testing whether that nation, or any nation so conceived and so dedicated, can long endure. We are met on a great battlefield of that war. We have come to dedicate a portion of that field as a final resting-place for those who here gave their lives that this nation might live. It is altogether fitting and proper that we should do this.

But, in a larger sense, we cannot dedicate—we cannot consecrate—we cannot hallow—this ground. The brave men, living and dead, who struggled here, have consecrated it far above our poor power to add or detract. The world will little note nor long remember what we say here, but it can never forget what they did here. It is for us, the living, rather to be dedicated here to the unfinished work which they who fought here have thus far so nobly advanced. It is rather for us to be here dedicated to the great task remaining before us—that from these honored dead we take increased devotion to that cause for which they gave the last full measure of devotion; that we here highly resolve that these dead shall not have died in vain; that this nation, under God, shall have a new birth of freedom; and that government of the people, by the people, for the people, shall not perish from the earth. (353 words)

Checking for Understanding

1. How did Lincoln's speech make you feel? _____

_____

2. What lines do you particularly like? Write them here and tell why you like

    the way he "turned" that particular phrase. _____

    _____

    _____

3. What words or phrases did Lincoln repeat? Write them here and tell why

    you think he repeated them. _____

    _____

    _____

4. How long is "fourscore and seven years"? Why did Lincoln not come right

    out and give the number of years? _____

    _____

5. Lincoln used the phrase "gave the last full measure of devotion." What did

    he mean by that phrase? Why didn't he come out and say it more clearly?

    _____

    _____

6. What is the tone of Lincoln's address?
    a. sarcastic
    b. serious

        c. humorous
        d. light

    7. Why do you think that Lincoln's address has become a classic piece of literature, whereas no one remembers the address of the prior speaker, Mr. Everett?

        _____

        _____

        _____

Reviewing Key Vocabulary

    1. How many years are two *score* and five?
        a. fifteen
        b. twenty-five
        c. thirty-five
        d. forty-five

    2. We are dedicated to the *proposition* that all people have a right to a free education through the twelfth grade. What is the meaning of *proposition* in that sentence?
        a. evil plan
        b. statement of basic belief
        c. dishonorable proposal
        d. way of doing something

    3. *Hallowed* ground is ground that has been
        a. made sacred.
        b. dug up.
        c. talked about.
        d. used at Halloween for ghostly purposes.

    4. When wine has been *consecrated,* it has been
        a. purified chemically.
        b. consumed.
        c. made impure.
        d. made holy.

    5. Behaving that way will *detract* from your reputation. What is the meaning of *detract* in that sentence?
        a. take away from
        b. increase
        c. inhibit
        d. clear

SELECTION 2: I HAVE A DREAM

Expanding Vocabulary for Reading

Use word-structure and context clues to get the meaning of the underlined words. Check the glossary when you are not sure. Write the definition of the key words in the space provided.

1. After surgery, he <u>languished</u> in bed; he got so weak that he could not stand up. _____

   _____

2. When Harry got the loan at the bank, he had to sign a <u>promissory</u> note.

   _____

   _____

3. Because of illness, Harry did not have the money to pay back the loan; he had to <u>default</u> on it. _____

   _____

4. The prince was the <u>heir</u> to a great fortune. At the death of his mother, the Queen, he would inherit much money and lands. _____

   _____

5. Having lived amid the hustle and bustle of the city, I was struck by the great <u>tranquility</u> of the countryside. _____

   _____

6. His mental health <u>degenerated</u> until he no longer could function on his own.

   _____

   _____

7. Determination and success are <u>inextricably</u> bound together. You cannot have one without the other. _____

   _____

8. Arriving at the <u>oasis</u> in the desert, we drank from the water there and cooled off under the trees. _____

   _____

9. In her <u>quest</u> for fame and fortune, the movie star trampled over the feelings of many others. _____

   _____

10. Do not <u>wallow</u> in self-pity even as a hippopotamus wallows in the mud. Get up and take action. _____

    _____

Getting Ready to Read

Read the title, author, and the first two paragraphs of the next selection.

- What is the topic of the selection? _____
- What do you know about this topic? About the selection? About its author?

_____

_____

- Setting Your Purpose for Reading: As you read, pretend you are in the audience on that day in 1963. How do King's words make you feel? What elements of his writing style do you find particularly effective? What words and phrases do you like?

Reading for Meaning

I HAVE A DREAM

Martin Luther King, Jr.

Five score years ago, a great American, in whose symbolic shadow we stand today, signed the Emancipation Proclamation. This momentous decree came as a great beacon of light and hope to millions of Negro slaves who had been seared in the flames of withering injustice. It came as a joyous daybreak to end the long night of their captivity.

But one hundred years later, the Negro is still not free. One hundred

Figure 11.1   *Dr. Martin Luther King*

UPI/Bettmann Newsphotos

years later, the life of the Negro is still sadly crippled by the manacles of segregation and the chains of discrimination.

One hundred years later, the Negro lives on a lonely island of poverty in the midst of a vast ocean of material prosperity. One hundred years later, the Negro is still languished in the corners of American society and finds himself an exile in his own land. So we have come here today to dramatize a shameful condition.

In a sense we have come to our nation's capital to cash a check. When the architects of our republic wrote the magnificent words of the constitution and the Declaration of Independence, they were signing a promissory note to which every American was to fall heir. This note was a promise that all men, yes, black men as well as white men, would be guaranteed the unalienable rights of life, liberty, and the pursuit of happiness.

It is obvious today that America has defaulted on this promissory note insofar as her citizens of color are concerned. Instead of honoring this sacred obligation, America has given the Negro people a bad check, which has come back marked "insufficient funds."

But we refuse to believe that the bank of justice is bankrupt. We refuse to believe that there are insufficient funds in the great vaults of opportunity of this nation. So we have come to cash this check—a check that will give us upon demand the riches of freedom and the security of justice.

We have also come to this hallowed spot to remind America of the fierce urgency of now. This is no time to engage in the luxury of cooling off or to take the tranquilizing drug of gradualism. Now is the time to make real the promises of democracy. Now is the time to rise from the dark and desolate valley of segregation to the sunlit path of racial justice. Now is the time to lift our nation from the quicksands of racial injustice to the solid rock of brotherhood. Now is the time to make justice a reality for all of God's children.

It would be fatal for the nation to overlook the urgency of the movement and to underestimate the determination of the Negro. This sweltering summer of the Negro's legitimate discontent will not pass until there is an invigorating autumn of freedom and equality. 1963 is not an end but a beginning. Those who hope that the Negro needed to blow off steam and will now be content will have a rude awakening if the nation returns to business as usual.

There will be neither rest nor tranquility in America until the Negro is granted his citizenship rights. The whirlwinds of revolt will continue to shake the foundations of our nation until the bright day of justice emerges.

But there is something that I must say to my people who stand on the warm threshold which leads into the palace of justice. In the process of gaining our rightful place we must not be guilty of wrongful deeds.

Let us not seek to satisfy our thirst for freedom by drinking from the cup of bitterness and hatred. We must forever conduct our struggle on the high plane of dignity and discipline. We must not allow our creative protest to degenerate into physical violence. Again and again we must rise to the majestic heights of meeting physical force with soul force.

The marvelous new militancy which has engulfed the Negro community must not lead us to a distrust of all white people, for many of our white brothers, as evidenced by their presence here today, have come to realize that their destiny is tied up with our destiny and they have come to realize that their freedom is inextricably bound to our freedom. This offense we share mounted to storm the battlements of injustice must be carried forth by a biracial army. We cannot walk alone.

And as we walk, we must make the pledge that we shall always march ahead. We cannot turn back. There are those who are asking the devotees of civil rights, "When will you be satisfied?" We can never be satisfied as long as the Negro is the victim of the unspeakable horrors of police brutality.

We can never be satisfied as long as our bodies, heavy with fatigue of travel, cannot gain lodging in the motels of the highways and the hotels of the cities. We cannot be satisfied as long as the Negro's basic mobility is from a smaller ghetto to a larger one.

We can never be satisfied as long as our children are stripped of their selfhood and robbed of their dignity by signs stating "for whites only." We cannot be satisfied as long as a Negro in Mississippi cannot vote and a Negro in New York believes he has nothing for which to vote. No, we are not satisfied, and we will not be satisfied until justice rolls down like waters and righteousness like a mighty stream.

I am not unmindful that some of you have come here out of excessive trials and tribulation. Some of you have come from areas where your quest for freedom left you battered by the storms of persecution and staggered by the winds of police brutality. You have been the veterans of creative suffering. Continue to work with the faith that unearned suffering is redemptive.

Go back to Mississippi; go back to Alabama; go back to South Carolina; go back to Georgia; go back to Louisiana; go back to the slums and ghettos of the Northern cities, knowing that somehow this situation can, and will be changed. Let us not wallow in the valley of despair.

So I say to you, my friends, that even though we must face the difficulties of today and tomorrow, I still have a dream. It is a dream deeply rooted in the American dream that one day this nation will rise up and live out the true meaning of its creed—we hold these truths to be self-evident, that all men are created equal.

I have a dream that one day on the red hills of Georgia, sons of former slaves and sons of former slave-owners will be able to sit together at the table of brotherhood.

I have a dream that one day, even the state of Mississippi, a state sweltering with the heat of injustice, sweltering with the heat of oppression, will be transformed into an oasis of freedom and justice.

I have a dream my four little children will one day live in a nation where they will not be judged by the color of their skin but by the content of their character. I have a dream today!

I have a dream that one day, down in Alabama, with its vicious racists, with its governor having his lips dripping with the words of interposition and nullification, that one day, right there in Alabama, little black boys and black girls will be able to join hands with little white boys and white girls as sisters and brothers. I have a dream today!

I have a dream that one day every valley shall be exalted, every hill and mountain shall be made low, the rough places shall be made plain, and the crooked places shall be made straight and the glory of the Lord will be revealed and all flesh shall see it together.

This is our hope. This is the faith that I go back to the south with.

With this faith we will be able to hew out of the mountain of despair a stone of hope. With this faith we will be able to transform the jangling discords of our nation into a beautiful symphony of brotherhood.

With this faith we will be able to work together, to pray together, to struggle together, knowing that we will be free one day. This will be the day when all of God's children will be able to sing with new meaning—"my country 'tis of thee, sweet land of liberty, of thee I sing; land where my fathers died, land of the pilgrim's pride; from every mountainside, let freedom ring"—and if America is to be a great nation, this must become true.

And so let freedom ring from the prodigious hilltops of New Hampshire.

Let freedom ring from the mighty mountains of New York.

Let freedom ring from the heightening Alleghenies of Pennsylvania.

Let freedom ring from the snow-capped Rockies of Colorado.

Let freedom ring from the curvaceous slopes of California.

But not only that.

Let freedom ring from Stone Mountain of Georgia.

Let freedom ring from Lookout Mountain of Tennessee.

Let freedom ring from every hill and molehill of Mississippi, from every mountainside, let freedom ring.

And when this happens, and when we allow freedom to ring, when we let it ring from every village and hamlet, from every state and city, we will be able to speed up that day when all of God's children—black men and white men, Jews and Gentiles, Catholics and Protestants—will be able to join hands and to sing in the words of the old Negro spiritual, "Free at last, free at last; thank God Almighty, we are free at last."

(1624 words)

Checking for Understanding

1. King's purpose for writing is to
   a. give members of his audience hope to continue the fight.
   b. make members of his audience feel bad about their plight.
   c. make members of his audience feel good about themselves.
   d. criticize the past.
2. Why do you think King began with the phrase "five score years"? To what

   other speech was he alluding, or referring? _____

   _____
3. Part of King's style is using contrasts. For example, he contrasts "a joyous

daybreak'' with ''the long night.'' Find at least two other contrasts he makes in his speech and record them here. _____

_____

4. Part of King's style is using sound-filled repetitions. List words and phrases that he repeats and you particularly like. _____

_____

5. King uses figurative language (metaphors and similes). For example, he speaks of the ''storms'' of persecution and the ''winds'' of police brutality. By doing this he is building creative comparisons. Go back and find at least two other examples of figurative language. For each explain the relationship King is pointing out.

_____

_____

_____

6. King's speech is filled with striking lines. Reread and locate one line that is particularly striking to you. Write it here and tell why you find it effective.

_____

_____

7. Do you recognize the phrase ''unalienable rights of life, liberty, and the pursuit of happiness''? Do you know the source? If so, write the name of the document here. _____

8. Do you recognize the phrase ''We hold these truths to be self-evident, that all men are created equal''? Do you know the document where these words are found? If so, write its name here. _____

9. Why do you think King used lines from the great documents of America's past?

_____

_____

10. What is the source of the lines ''my country 'tis of thee, sweet land of liberty . . . ''? Why do you think King used those familiar lines in his address? _____

_____

_____

Writing from Reading

What mood did King's speech create? How did it make you feel? Why did the speech make you feel that way? In your notebook, write a paragraph in which you describe your reaction to the address and why you reacted in the way you did.

Reviewing Key Vocabulary

a. defaulted   d. inextricably   g. promissory   i. tranquility

b. degenerated   e. languished   h. quest   j. wallowed

c. heir   f. oasis

From the list, select the word that best fits the context of each sentence. Write it in the blank.

1. The discussion _____ into a barroom brawl. At first the people talked calmly, but at the end they used their fists to make points.

2. The fate of his children was _____ tied to his fate.

3. Her home was an _____ to her at the end of a trouble-filled day.

4. The animals _____ in the heat of the drought, waiting for water.

5. The _____ of the summer evening was disturbed by a thunderstorm.

6. The daughter was named the only _____ under the terms of her mother's will.

7. The business owner signed a _____ note for $50,000.

8. When the business owner _____ on the loan, the bank took away the property that secured it.

9. The prospector panned for gold; his _____ was rewarded when he found a large nugget.

10. The woman who lost her son in the war _____ in despair for many months.

SELECTION 3: DREAM POEMS BY LANGSTON HUGHES

Expanding Your Vocabulary for Reading

In this selection, comprised of three poems, you will find the word *melody,* as in the sentence "She played the melody on the piano." Write the meaning of *melody* in the space provided below. Write its plural form, as well. _____

Getting Ready to Read

The following three poems were written by the twentieth-century black poet Langston Hughes. They are all about dreams. Before beginning to read, write down in the web given below any words that come to mind as you think about dreams. This is a good strategy to use as part of your prereading activity, especially when you are reading poetry. Simply brainstorm words and phrases on the topic.

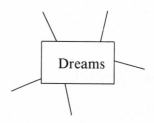

Reading for Meaning

Now read Langston Hughes's poems. Ask yourself: What is he saying about dreams? What mood is he creating? How does he use words to create that mood?

DREAMS

Langston Hughes

Hold fast to dreams
For if dreams die
Life is a broken-winged bird
That cannot fly.

Hold fast to dreams
For when dreams go
Life is a barren field
Frozen with snow.

THE DREAM KEEPER

Langston Hughes

Bring me all of your dreams
You dreamers,
Bring me all of your heart melodies
That I may wrap them
In a blue cloud cloth
Away from the too-rough fingers
Of the world.

DREAM DUST
Langston Hughes

Gather out of star-dust
Earth-dust
Cloud-dust
Storm-dust
And splinters of hail,
One handful of dream-dust
Not for sale.

Checking Your Understanding

1. What words and phrases from the poems did you particularly like? Record them here. For each, tell why it appeals to you. _____

   _____

   _____

2. What words or word patterns did Langston Hughes repeat? Write examples of repetitive usage here. _____

   _____

   _____

3. Why do you think Langston Hughes repeated words in this way? Did his repetitions help you to enjoy the poems? Explain. _____

   _____

   _____

4. Hughes built a creative metaphor (a creative comparison):

   life without dreams = a broken-winged bird

   In what way are life without dreams and a broken-winged bird the same?

   _____

   _____

5. Hughes built a second metaphor in the same poem. Record the parts of it here:

   _____

   In what way are the two parts of the metaphor the same?

   _____

   _____

6. Hughes likes to play with opposite meanings. That is part of his style. For example, he contrasts a "blue cloud cloth" to the "too-rough fingers of the world." In what ways are these two things different?

   _____

   _____

7. What mood does Hughes build in his three poems?
   a. despairing
   b. compassionate
   c. impassioned
   d. languishing

8. How are Langston Hughes's poems similar to King's speech? What message do they share? What similar elements of style do you find in both?

   _____

   _____

   _____

   _____

   _____

   _____

9. Which of the three Hughes poems do you like best? In your notebook, write a short paragraph telling why you like that one. In your topic sentence, name the poem you have chosen. In the following sentences, give your reasons. Give specific words and lines from the poems to support your judgment.

Figure 11.2   *The United States of America*

EXTENDING WHAT YOU HAVE LEARNED

Building a Knowledge Base for Reading

Circle or plot the following places on the map in Figure 11.2.

Washington, D.C.

The states of New York, Pennsylvania, Colorado, and California

The states of Mississippi, Tennessee, Georgia, and Alabama

Gettysburg, Pennsylvania

Gaining Ownership of Words

Select several words you have studied in this chapter to record in your personal vocabulary list. Try to use those words in speaking and writing.

Applying the Strategies in Independent Reading

Find a piece you feel you would enjoy reading. It can be anything that appeals to you. Think about the way the author is expressing himself or herself as you read. When you finish, write on a card the name of the author and the title of the selection. Then write down several words, phrases, or sentences that you think are typical of the writer's style, or manner of writing.

Reviewing Elements of Style

When you think of writing style, what elements come to your mind? Record at least three elements of style that particularly affect your enjoyment in reading. Next to each, write an example.

1. _____

_____

2. _____

_____

3. _____

_____

12

Understanding Definitions and Explanations

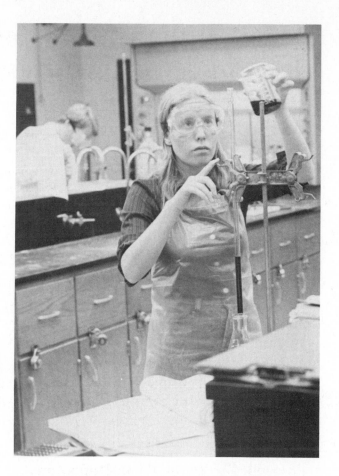

Before reading the chapter, read the title, the stated objective, and the headings and subheadings. Ask yourself: What is the topic of the chapter? In the space above and beside the chapter number, jot down what you already know about that topic. Then in the space below the chapter number, jot down at least two questions you hope to answer through reading the chapter.

OBJECTIVE

Through this chapter you will develop strategies for reading different kinds of writing, specifically,

1. writing that has as its purpose to define, and
2. writing that has as its purpose to explain.

INTRODUCTION—READING DEFINITIONS AND EXPLANATIONS

Not all writing communicates the same kinds of meanings. Some sentences within a selection are essentially definitions. In these sentences, an author states the meaning of a word or phrase by giving the fundamental qualities associated with it. In contrast, some sentences go beyond basic definitions to provide an explanation, describe something, give an account of what happened, or express an opinion.

Reading different kinds of sentences (definitions, explanations, narrations, descriptions, or opinions), you must shift your purpose and your reading strategies. This chapter focuses on strategies for dealing with the first two kinds of writing—definition and explanation. Later chapters deal with the other three kinds.

DEFINITIONS

Authors may build clues into their writing that tell you they are introducing an important term and are going to define it. Authors may print important words in boldface or italics. Or they may rely on sentence-pattern clues to provide hints that their purpose is to define.

A Strategy for Recognizing Definitions

Study the following sentences from *Human Anatomy and Physiology* by John W. Hole, Jr., and identify the clue words that indicate a term is being defined.

1. "*Plasma* is the straw-colored, liquid portion of the blood in which the various solids are suspended."
   - What is the simple clue word that links the term *plasma* with its definition?

   _____

2. "The term *hemostasis* refers to the stoppage of bleeding, which is vitally important when blood vessels are damaged."
   - What is the clue phrase that links the term *hemostasis* with its definition?

   _____

3. "If a blood clot forms in a vessel abnormally, it is termed a *thrombus*. If the clot becomes dislodged or if a fragment of it breaks loose and is carried away by the blood flow, it is called an *embolus*."
   - What is the clue phrase that ties the term *thrombus* to its definition?

   _____

   - What is the clue phrase that ties the term *embolus* to its definition?

   _____

A Strategy for Reading Definitions

Because definitions, especially in the natural sciences, tend to be technical, a useful strategy is to reread a definition when you encounter one and then try to picture what is being described in your mind's eye. We call the process of mental picturing, visualizing. Visualizing is particularly helpful in grasping definitions when you are dealing with concrete objects. In cases where definitions are really complex, you may find it helpful to sketch your mental image on paper.

Another useful strategy is to paraphrase the definition. By paraphrasing, we mean saying it to yourself in your own words. A related strategy is to devise an equation that puts together the term and its definition. A good check is to compare your equation to the definition in the glossary of the book.

How do these strategies work? Here is an example. Reading the definition of *plasma* given above, you might picture in your mind's eye the straw-colored liquid without its suspended solids. You might paraphrase by saying to yourself: *Plasma* is the liquid part of the blood without the solids. You then might build an equation:

Plasma = liquid part of blood without suspended solids

If you are studying a textbook section on which you will be tested, you might record that equation in your notebook or in the margin of the text. Finally you compare your equation to the glossary definition.

In sum, your strategy for working with a definition includes these steps:

* Reread the definition and try to picture what is being defined in your mind's eye.
* Paraphrase the definition in your own words.
* Devise an equation that includes the term and its definition.
* Record the equation in a vocabulary section of your notebook or in the margin of the text. This strategy is useful if you are studying a textbook for a college course in which you will be tested later on what you are learning.
* Verify your equation by comparing it to the definition in the glossary of the book.

Now reread the definitions given above, state them in your own words, and then write them in equation form in the space below.

1. Hemostasis = _____

2. Thrombus = _____

3. Embolus = _____

Practicing the Strategy

Preview each short section before reading it by noting the heading and the words in italics. Your purpose in reading is to find out the meaning of the highlighted terms.

1. ANATOMY AND PHYSIOLOGY
John W. Hole, Jr.

Anatomy is the branch of science that deals with the structure of body parts, their forms and arrangements. Anatomists observe body parts grossly and microscopically and describe them as accurately and in as much detail as possible. *Physiology,* on the other hand, is concerned with the functions of body parts—what they do and how they do it. Physiologists are interested in finding out how such parts carry on life processes. In addition to using the same observational techniques as the anatomists, physiologists are likely to conduct experiments and make use of complex laboratory equipment. (101 words)

a. Reread the definition of *anatomy,* tell it to yourself in your own words, and then write an equation with the term and the definition.

Anatomy = _____

b. Reread the definition of *physiology,* paraphrase it, and then write an equation with the term and definition.

Physiology = _____

2. A HYPOTHETICAL CELL

John W. Hole, Jr.

Because cells vary so greatly in size, shape, and function, it is not possible to describe a "typical" cell. However, for purposes of discussion, it is convenient to imagine that one exists. Such a hypothetical cell would contain parts observed in many kinds of cells, even though some of these cells in fact lack parts included in the imagined structure.

Commonly a cell consists of two major parts, one within the other and each surrounded by a thin membrane. The inner portion is called the *cell nucleus,* and it is enclosed by a *nuclear membrane.* A mass of fluid called *cytoplasm* surrounds the nucleus and is, in turn, encircled by a *cell membrane.* (119 words)

a. Reread the sentence that begins "Such a hypothetical cell . . . ." What is a hypothetical cell? Now write an equation that defines one.

Hypothetical cell = a cell that _____

b. Picture, or visualize, a hypothetical cell with its two parts and two membranes. Sketch your mental image here. Label the parts.

c. Reread the sentence that includes the term *cell nucleus.* Put together a definition and record it here in equation form:

Cell nucleus = _____

d. Reread the sentence that includes the term *cytoplasm.* Put together a definition and record it here in equation form:

Cytoplasm = _____

e. Reread the sentence that includes *cell membrane.* Tell yourself a definition of the term and record it here in equation form:

Cell membrane = _____

f. Now reread the sentence that includes *nuclear membrane.* Tell yourself a definition of the term and record it here in equation form:

Nuclear membrane = _____

g. Finally, based on your equations, revisualize the cell. Make any changes in your sketch you believe to be necessary.

3. THE CELL MEMBRANE
John W. Hole, Jr.

The *cell membrane* is the outermost limit of the living material within a cell. It is extremely thin—visible only with the aid of an electron microscope—but is flexible and somewhat elastic. Although this membrane can seal off minute breaks and heal itself, if it is damaged too greatly the cell contents are likely to escape and the cell will die.

In addition, to its function of maintaining the wholeness of the cell, the membrane serves as a gateway through which chemicals enter and leave. However, this "gate" acts in a special way: it allows some substances to pass and excludes others. When a membrane functions in this way, it is said to be *selectively permeable.* A *permeable* membrane, on the other hand, is one that allows all materials to pass through freely. (140 words)

a. Picture in your mind's eye a selectively permeable membrane. Then paraphrase the definition and write an equation:

Selectively permeable membrane = a membrane that _____

b. Picture in your mind's eye a permeable membrane. Then paraphrase the definition and write an equation:

Permeable membrane = a membrane that _____

SELECTION 1: DIFFUSION AND OSMOSIS

Expanding Your Vocabulary for Reading

The word *concentration* in the next selection you will read applies to the amount of matter in a particular area. For example, where there is a high concentration of people, there are many people in a particular area; where there is a low concentration of people, there are relatively few in a particular area. An *ion* is an electrically charged particle. See if you can figure out the meaning of *haphazard,* using context clues as you read.

Getting Ready to Read

Preview the next selection by reading the title and words highlighted by the author.

- What is the topic of the selection? _____
- What do you already know about that topic? _____

_____

Your purpose in reading is to understand the definition of the italicized words.

Reading with Meaning

As you read, apply your reading-for-definition strategy: Record in the outer margin a sketch of your mental picture of what is going on, an equation that clarifies the definition given at that point in the text, or both. Do not do this after reading the entire passage. Do it as you go along. Read a definition. Stop to visualize, sketch, paraphrase, and write an equation.

DIFFUSION AND OSMOSIS

John W. Hole, Jr.

Sketch your mental images here. Jot down definition equations as you read.

Diffusion is the process by which molecules or ions scatter or spread from regions where they are in higher concentrations toward regions where they are in lower concentrations. As a rule, this phenomenon involves the movement of molecules or ions in gases or liquids.

Actually, molecules in gases and molecules and ions in body fluids are constantly moving at high speeds. Each of these particles travels in a separate path along a straight line until it collides and bounces off some other particle. Then it moves in another direction, only to collide again and change direction once more. Such motion is haphazard, but it accounts for the mixing of molecules that commonly occurs when different kinds of substances are put together.

For example, if you put some sugar into a glass of water, the sugar will seem to remain at the bottom for a while. Then slowly it disappears into solution. As this happens, the moving water and sugar molecules are colliding haphazardly with one another, and in time the sugar and water molecules will be evenly mixed. This mixing occurs by diffusion—the sugar molecules spread where they are in higher concentration toward the regions where they are less concentrated. Eventually the sugar becomes uniformly distributed in the water. This condition is called *equilibrium.*

Osmosis is a special kind of diffusion. It occurs whenever water molecules diffuse from a region of higher concentration through a selectively permeable membrane, such as a cell membrane. (259 words)

Checking for Understanding

Select the best response. You may refer back to the selection.

1. The concentration of a material in an area refers to the
   a. area in which a material is found.
   b. amount of that material found in a particular area.
   c. kind of material it is.
   d. name of the material.

2. The phrase *haphazard motion* as used in this selection means motion that is
   a. orderly.
   b. careful.
   c. without a pattern or design.
   d. continuous.

3. The process by which molecules or ions move from regions of higher concentrations to regions of lower concentrations is termed
   a. diffusion.
   b. equilibrium.
   c. osmosis.

4. The process by which water molecules move from regions of higher concentrations to regions of lower concentrations across a selectively permeable membrane is called
   a. diffusion.
   b. equilibrium.
   c. osmosis.

5. The state when a material that is dissolved in another substance becomes uniformly distributed in that substance is known as
   a. diffusion.
   b. equilibrium.
   c. osmosis.

6. In questions 1 through 5, five different clue words or phrases were used to let you know that you were dealing with definitions. What are they? Write them here.

a. _____

b. _____

c. _____

d. _____

e. _____

7. What is the purpose of the first sentence in the first paragraph?
   a. to define diffusion
   b. to explain diffusion
   c. to give an opinion of diffusion
   d. to provide an example of diffusion

8. What is the purpose of the second sentence in the first paragraph?
   a. to elaborate on, or extend, the definition
   b. to give a specific example
   c. to state the main idea
   d. to give a conclusion

Before leaving this section, go back and check your answers against the definitions given in the text. This is the same thing you would do when encountering rather difficult terms and definitions in a college text. Remember to make a mental picture for each definition.

SELECTION 2: ENERGY VALUE OF FOOD

Expanding Your Vocabulary for Reading

The word *ignited* that you will find in the selection means "set on fire." "To oxidize" means "to combine with oxygen." When things burn, they are oxidized.

Getting Ready to Read

Preview the following selection by reading the title and italicized terms.

- What is the topic of the selection? _____

- What do you already know about that topic? _____

  _____

- What is your purpose in reading? _____

  _____

Reading with Meaning

As you read, note the italicized words. Visualize these concepts where possible and sketch your mental image in the outer margin. As you encounter a definition, paraphrase it and write an equation in the margin. Do this while reading, not when you finish the selection.

ENERGY VALUES OF FOOD
John W. Hole, Jr.

Jot equations and mental images here.

The amount of potential energy contained in a food can be expressed as *calories,* which are units of heat.

Although a *calorie* is commonly defined by a chemist as the amount of heat needed to raise the temperature of a gram of water by one degree Celsius (°C), the calorie used in the measurements of food energy is in fact 1,000 times greater. This *large calorie* is equal to the amount of heat needed to raise the temperature of a kilogram (1,000 g.) of water by one degree Celsius (actually from 15°C to 16°C). This unit is properly called a *kilocalorie,* but it is customary in nutritional studies to refer to it simply as a "calorie."

The caloric contents of various foods can be determined by using an instrument called a *bomb calorimeter,* which consists of a metal chamber submerged in a known volume of water. The food sample being studied is dried, weighed, and placed inside the metal chamber. The chamber is filled with oxygen gas and is submerged in the water. Then, the food inside is ignited and allowed to oxidize completely. As heat is released from the food, it causes the temperature of the surrounding water to rise, and the change in temperature is noted. Since the volume of the water is known, the amount of heat released from the food sample can be calculated in calories. (249 words)

Checking for Understanding

Select the best response. You may refer back to the passage in making your choice.

1. A chemist defines a *calorie* as the amount of heat needed to raise the temperature of one
   a. kilogram of water by 1 degree Celsius.
   b. kilogram of water by 1,000 degrees Celsius.
   c. gram of water by 1 degree Celsius.
   d. gram of water by 1,000 degrees Celsius.

2. A *large calorie* is the amount of heat needed to raise the temperature of one
   a. kilogram of water by 1 degree Celsius.
   b. kilogram of water by 1,000 degrees Celsius.
   c. gram of water by 1 degree Celsius.
   d. gram of water by 1,000 degrees Celsius.

3. A *kilocalorie* is the amount of heat needed to raise the temperature of one
   a. kilogram of water by 1 degree Celsius.
   b. kilogram of water by 1,000 degrees Celsius.
   c. gram of water by 1 degree Celsius.
   d. gram of water by 1,000 degrees Celsius.

4. A *bomb calorimeter* is an instrument for determining the
   a. ignition temperature of various foods.
   b. oxidation temperature of various foods.
   c. rise in temperature of foods when burned.
   d. caloric contents of various foods.

5. If you *ignite* a bundle of leaves, you would
   a. determine their caloric value.
   b. gather them up.
   c. set them on fire.
   d. put them in a bomb calorimeter.

EXPLANATIONS

As you may have perceived from the selections you just read, definition and explanation go hand in hand; having defined a term, the author moves on to explain something about it. This happens in the selection on diffusion and osmosis when Hole defines *diffusion* and then goes on to explain what happens when the molecules and ions in body fluids travel, collide, and bounce off one another. As Hole explains, haphazard molecular motion of this kind "accounts for the mixing of molecules that commonly occurs when different kinds of substances are put together."

What Is Involved in Reading Explanations

In explaining, an author tells why or how, illustrates with an example, states the conditions under which something happens, clarifies relationships, compares, contrasts, and generalizes. Clues that help you figure out that an author is explaining are words such as the following:

- *one, two,* and *three,* which indicate the number of items to be discussed or the steps in a sequence of events;
- *for example* and *such as,* which indicate an example;
- *also* and *furthermore,* which indicate a continuation of the idea and *but* and *however,* which indicate a change in direction;
- *similarly* and *on the other hand,* which indicate a comparison or contrast;
- *if-then* and *consequently,* which indicate a condition-effect relationship;
- *because* and *for this reason,* which indicate a cause-effect relationship.

See Chapter 6 for a full discussion of how to use these clue words to anticipate the direction in which an author is taking you.

The first component of a strategy for reading to understand explanations is to attend to these clue words through which authors signal what they are doing. Take a moment to reread Selections 1 and 2 above. As you do, circle the clue words that help you follow the author's explanation, and think about what those words are telling you.

A second component is visualizing, or picturing in your mind's eye, what the author is explaining, which is useful when the explanation is about something very concrete. For example, if a passage is explaining how food passes through the digestive tract, as you read, you might visualize that tract: mouth, esophagus, stomach, small and large intestines, rectum, and associated organs. You hold that picture in your mind, relating what the passage is saying at any one point to the appropriate part of your visual image. Or, if there is a diagram in the text, you keep referring to it, following the diagram as you read the text.

A third component of a strategy for reading explanations is talking to yourself in your head or (when the passage presents tough ideas) talking to yourself out loud. We call this "thinking along" or "thinking aloud." Here is a passage by John W. Hole, Jr., followed by a "think-along." The think-along demonstrates the kinds of thoughts that might come to the mind of a reader who is encountering the material for the first time.

To illustrate how diffusion accounts for the movement of various molecules through a cell membrane, let us imagine a container of water that is separated into two compartments by a permeable membrane (Figure 12.1). This membrane has numerous pores that are large enough for water and sugar molecules to pass through. Sugar molecules are placed in one compartment (A) but not in the other (B). As a result of diffusion, we can predict that although the sugar molecules are moving in all directions, more will spread from compartment A (where they are in greater concentration) through the pores in the membrane and into compartment B (where they are in lesser concentration) than will move in the other direction. At the same time, water molecules will tend to diffuse from compartment B (where they are in greater concentration) through the pores into compartment A (where they are in lesser concentration). Eventually, equilibrium will be achieved when there are equal numbers of water and sugar molecules in each compartment.

The Think Along—What Might Go On in Your Head as You Read

"To illustrate" . . . oh, the author is going to give an example . . . this example shows how different molecules move through a membrane . . . there is this beaker divided into two parts . . . with a permeable

Figure 12.1   *Diffusion of Molecules Through a Membrane*

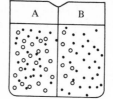 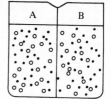

membrane between . . . I remember about permeable membranes . . . they let anything through . . . "This membrane has pores" . . . there are pores . . . tiny holes . . . like in the skin . . . These are big ones . . . let both water and sugar go through to the other side . . . From the diagram I can see that they put water and sugar in compartment A but only water in compartment B . . . "As a result of diffusion" . . . what is going to happen? . . . let's see, there are no sugar molecules in compartment B . . . there are more water molecules in compartment B than in compartment A. What will happen? I bet the sugar will move from A to B . . . the water will go from B to A . . . through the pores . . . from areas of high concentration to areas of low concentration . . . through diffusion . . . I can see it moving . . . sketch it . . . equilibrium at the end . . . eventually . . . takes time . . . equilibrium . . . same number of water molecules in both compartments . . . same number of sugar molecules in both compartments . . . this is an example of diffusion. . . .

Reading requires active thought. Reading a complicated passage such as this one, you do not just read the words. You must verbalize and visualize the ideas, expressing them again in your own words and perhaps even in a diagram of your own making. You must relate what is in the passage to what you already know about the topic. Especially helpful is to make analogies, or compare what is stated to something similar; say to yourself, "This is like . . . " (as in the reference to the skin in the think-along given above). And you must constantly predict based on what you already know on the topic and what you already have read. You say to yourself, "I bet . . . ."

In talking to yourself in your head or out loud, you should avoid using vague phrases. Do not just use "this stuff" or "that part." Instead, use the terms you are learning—in this case, *diffusion, concentration, equilibrium*. Using the terms as you think about the selection reinforces your understanding of them.

In thinking about a passage as you read, you should also raise questions. Examples from the think-along given above are the questions "What is going to happen?" and "What will happen?"

Strategies for Reading Explanations

In summary, here are strategies to employ when you read explanations. They are not steps to be applied in sequence. They are strategies to be applied in the order that best serves your reading purpose.

1. Use clue words (such as *for example, if/then*) to predict where the writer is going and what he or she is going to do.
2. Visualize in your mind's eye what is being explained; make a sketch if you believe that will clarify the explanation; refer to the visuals in the text while reading a related explanation.
3. Think aloud or along (or talk to yourself aloud or in your head):
   a. Paraphrase the explanation, drawing on what you already know and using any technical vocabulary you know.
   b. Make comparisons between things being explained and similar things you already know about.

   c. Predict as you read, saying to yourself, "I bet . . . ." Try to keep ahead of the writer and anticipate what he or she is saying.
   d. Ask yourself questions as you read.
   e. Answer your own questions or ones that the author raises in the text. Do this as you read.
4. Reread to clarify points.

In the following sections of this lesson, you will have opportunity to practice these strategies.

SELECTION 3: EVOLUTION BY MEANS OF NATURAL SELECTION

Expanding Your Vocabulary for Reading

In this selection, you will find some technical words you will need to know if you are to understand the authors' explanation.

Genetic material is "an organism's store of information; it contains the blueprints for the organism's development, body structure, chemical functions, and reproduction. During reproduction, copies of the genetic material pass on to the next generation of offspring.

The units of genetic material are the *genes*. Genes dictate features of organisms, such as eye color, blood type, or development of teeth. An organism has hundreds to thousands of different genes.

An *embryo* is the early developmental stage of an organism, a young organism before it emerges from its mother's body. A *larva* is an immature animal that looks different from the adult animal of that species.

To *evolve* means "to change slowly over time."

A *species* is a group of organisms that can interbreed in nature.

Getting Ready to Read

Preview the selection by reading the title, the introduction in italics, and the conclusion.

• What is the topic of the selection? _____

• What do you already know about this topic? _____

_____

• What question will you try to answer through your reading? _____

_____

Reading with Meaning

As you read this selection, record the thoughts that come into your head in the outer margin. Your think-along can include rephrasing ideas in your own words, relating a point to something you already know, asking and answering questions, predicting before the authors make a point, visualizing by sketching. The first paragraph—the introduction—is done as a model for you. If you prefer, you may work with a friend and tell him or her your thoughts even as you read the selection aloud.

EVOLUTION BY MEANS
OF NATURAL SELECTION
Pamela Camp and Karen Arms

For hundreds of years, farmers have selected and bred plants and animals to favor, or bring out, characteristics they desired. For example, cows that produced large amounts of milk were selected for breeding, while poor milk producers were not allowed to reproduce. In like manner, horses were bred for speed and strength. Those having these desired characteristics were selected for breeding. Over time, these preferred breeds became more common than earlier, less desired types. This selective breeding is called artificial selection.

In this passage, Camp and Arms explain how this same process occurs naturally.

The theory of evolution by natural selection was put forward in a joint presentation of the views of Charles Darwin and Alfred Russell Wallace before the Linnaean Society of London in 1858. Darwin and Wallace were not the first to suggest that evolution occurred; but their names are linked with the idea of evolution because they proposed the theory of natural selection as the mechanism by which evolution occurs. We are always more likely to believe in a process when people explain how it happens than if they merely assert that it does.

The theory of evolution by means of natural selection is based on three observations. First, as we can see by comparing one cat or human being with another, the members of a species differ from one another; that is, there is variation among individuals of the same species. Second, some (though not all) of the differences between individuals are inherited. (Other differences are not inherited, but are caused by different environments. For instance, two plants with identical genes may grow to different sizes if one of them is planted in poor soil.) Third, more organisms are born than live to grow up and reproduce: many organisms die as embryos or seeds, as saplings, nestlings, or larvae.

The logical conclusion from these three

"Bred" must mean mated.

That way farmers got more milk — more money. Another example is the way producers bred blueberries to get a bigger berry.

observations is that certain genetic characteristics of an organism will increase its chances of living to grow up and reproduce, over the chances of organisms with other characteristics. To take an extreme example, if you have inherited a severe genetic disease of the liver, you have much less chance of living to grow up and reproduce than someone born without this disease.

Inherited characteristics that improve an organism's chances of living and reproducing will be more common in the next generation and those that decrease its chances of reproducing will be less common. Various genes or combinations of genes will be naturally selected for or against, from one generation to the next, depending on how they affect reproductive potential. For natural selection to cause a change in a population from one generation to the next (that is, to cause evolution), it is not necessary that all genes affect survival and reproduction; the same result occurs if just some genes make an individual more likely to grow up and reproduce.

To summarize:

1. Individuals in a population vary in each generation.

2. Some of these variations are genetic.

3. More individuals are produced than live to grow up and reproduce.

4. Individuals with some genes are more likely to survive and reproduce than those with other genes.

Conclusion: From the above four premises it follows that those genetic traits that make their owners more likely to grow up and reproduce will become increasingly common in the population from one generation to the next. (573 words)

Checking for Understanding

Reread the selection. Jot in the margin any more thoughts that come to your mind as you reread. Or listen to a friend do a "think aloud." As you listen to him or her read and verbalize aloud, write any new thoughts in the margin. Remember to keep paraphrasing as you read.

Now answer these questions.

1. The main difference between natural and artificial selection is that human beings

    a. control the direction of artificial selection.
    b. control the direction of natural selection.
    c. make new genes in artificial selection.
    d. make new genes in natural selection.

2. Which of the following is *not* an example of artificial selection?
    a. the selection by a farmer of the best milk-producing cows for breeding
    b. a breeder's allowing only the fastest horses to reproduce
    c. the selection for reproduction of the best egg-laying chickens by the farmer
    d. an increase in the number of giraffes with long necks because of a decline in the number of low-lying plants used for feeding

3. Which statement is false?
    a. Members of a species differ from one another.
    b. All differences between individuals are inherited.
    c. Two organisms with identical genes may grow to different sizes.
    d. More organisms are born than live to reproduce.

4. Which two statements are true? (Before answering this question, paraphrase each option in your own words.)
    a. Inherited characteristics that decrease an organism's chances of living and reproducing will be more common in the next generation.
    b. Inherited characteristics that increase an organism's chances of living and reproducing will be less common in the next generation.
    c. Inherited characteristics that increase an organism's chances of living and reproducing will be more common in the next generation.
    d. Inherited characteristics that decrease an organism's chances of living and producing will be less common in the next generation.

5. Why are Darwin and Wallace linked to the idea of evolution?
    a. They were the first to suggest that evolution occurs.
    b. They clearly asserted a theory of evolution.
    c. They proposed natural selection as the mechanism by which evolution occurs.
    d. They proposed artificial selection as the mechanism by which evolution occurs.

6. A change in a population from one generation to the next is called
    a. a species.
    b. evolution.
    c. artificial selection.
    d. natural selection.

7. What feature do embryos, larvae, seeds, and saplings share?
    a. They all are very young forms of organisms.
    b. They all are the result of artificial selection.
    c. They all are members of the same species.
    d. They all are variations of the same species.

Reread the introductory paragraph set in italics. Answer questions 8–10 based on that paragraph.

8. What is the main idea of that introductory paragraph?
    a. For years, farmers have practiced selective breeding.

b. Cows that produced large amounts of milk were selected for breeding.

c. As time passed, the preferred breeds became more common because of selective breeding.

d. Selective breeding is called artificial selection.

9. The purpose of the second sentence in the introductory paragraph is to
a. state the main idea of the paragraph.
b. provide a reason or cause in support of the first sentence of the paragraph.
c. give an example to support the idea in the first sentence of the paragraph.
d. define a key term.

10. The purpose of the sentence "This selective breeding is called artificial selection" is to
a. state the main idea.
b. provide a reason.
c. give an example.
d. define a key term.

Reread the first paragraph after the ones in italics. Answer questions 11 and 12 based on it.

11. The main idea of the first paragraph is that
a. Darwin and Russell jointly proposed the theory of evolution in 1858.
b. The names of Darwin and Russell are linked with evolution because they explained how it happened.
c. The Linnaean Society of London in 1858 was a prestigious scientific society that honored scientists.
d. People tend to believe in a process when someone explains how it happens.

12. What is the purpose of the last sentence in the first paragraph?
a. to define
b. to explain
c. to give an example
d. to state the main idea

Summarizing to Increase Comprehension

Research suggests that writing a summary of a passage you have read increases your understanding of what you have read. In your notebook, write a short paragraph in which you sum up how natural selection operates in nature. The best way to write a summary is to start with a sentence that gives the main idea of the complete passage. Then write several sentences that give key details. Use the idea map in Figure 12.2 to plot the main ideas and supporting details before writing.

SELECTION 4: NATURAL SELECTION— THE PEPPERED MOTH

Expanding Your Vocabulary for Reading

Using context and structural clues, figure out the meanings of the underlined words, which are from the selection, and write down what you think those words mean. If you have trouble, check the glossary.

Main Point, or Thesis:

Supporting Ideas

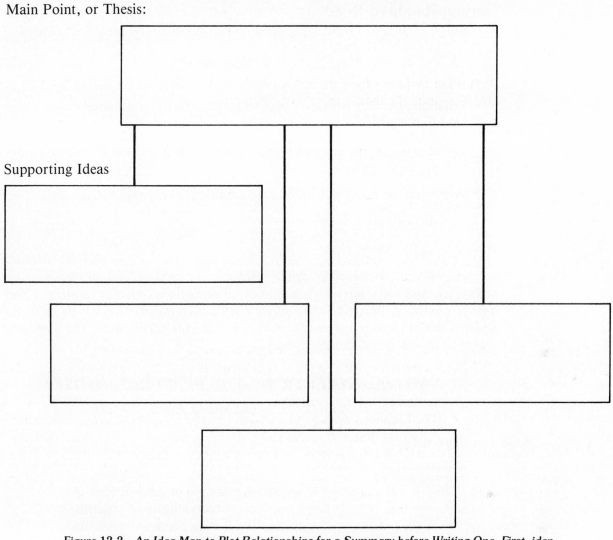

Figure 12.2 *An Idea Map to Plot Relationships for a Summary before Writing One. First, identify the thesis of the entire selection. Next, identify the supporting ideas. Record the thesis in the top box and the supporting ideas in the connecting boxes. Then use your idea map to write a summary paragraph that includes those points.*

1. He was an <u>avid</u> collector of rare moths; he would eagerly join any party that was looking for moths. _____

   _____

2. The marine's brown and green uniform <u>camouflaged</u> him. The enemy could not see him in the forest. _____

   _____

3. Birds are natural <u>predators</u> of moths; birds live by killing and eating moths. They prey on the moths. _____

   _____

4. If black moths became <u>rarer</u>, there would be fewer of them. _____

   _____

Getting Ready to Read

Preview the selection by reading the title, the first paragraph, and the last paragraph.

- What is the topic of the selection? _____
- What do you already know about this topic? (Tell things based on what you read in the previous selection.)

_____

_____

- What questions will you answer by reading the selection? _____

_____

Reading with Meaning

As you read, think aloud about what you are reading. Relate what you are reading to what you already know, make comparisons, predict, and raise and answer questions. Jot your think-along thoughts in the margin, or ask a friend to listen to you as you read and think aloud. Ask your friend to ask you questions as you read and think aloud.

NATURAL SELECTION—THE PEPPERED MOTH
Pamela Camp and Karen Arms

Write your think-along thoughts here.

A classic example of natural selection, documented by observation and experiment, is the case of the British peppered moth. In nineteenth century England, many people collected moths as eagerly as some people today collect stamps or coins, and collectors avidly sought rare specimens of the peppered moth that were black rather than the usual gray. By looking at collections made from about 1850 to 1950, biologists found that the black form of the moth became more and more common during the century, and the gray form scarcer, particularly near industrial cities.

Why had this change occurred? The biologists noted that the moths rest during the day, usually camouflaged on tree trunks covered with pale grayish lichens. Perhaps the increase in the proportion of black moths resulted from the industrial revolution: the large-scale burning of coal produced soot, which killed lichens and blackened the tree trunks. Against this darker background the gray form of the peppered moth was more visible to birds, the moths' chief predators, and so the gray moths were easier to catch. Now black moths were better camouflaged from hungry birds.

Bernard Kettlewell recognized that this was an excellent opportunity to study natural selection experimentally. He raised large numbers of both black and gray forms of the moth in the laboratory, marked them, and released them in two places: one an unpolluted rural area where the black form was more visible to a human observer, the other a polluted industrial area where the gray form was easier to see against the blackened trunks. Kettlewell then recaptured as many of the marked moths as he could. The percentage of black moths recovered was twice that of gray moths in the industrial area, but only half that of gray moths in the unpolluted countryside. This agreed with the prediction that the gray moths were more likely to survive (and so to be recaptured) in the country, and the black moths were more likely to survive near the town.

This experiment was done with a human "predator" (the person catching the moths), but human collectors are not normally much of a threat to the survival of either form of the peppered moth. Does the differential camouflage work against the moths' real predators? To find out, Kettlewell hid in a blind and watched the moths on tree trunks. On one occasion, he watched equal numbers of gray and black moths in an unpolluted area. Birds caught 164 of the black form and only 26 gray ones.

It is clear that, in a polluted area, a larger proportion of the black than of the gray moths will live long enough to reproduce. Since the color of the moths is inherited, the next generation will contain proportionally more black moths than the last. In other words, the frequency of the gene for black color increases in the population with time—and that is evolution.

The natural selective force that brings about this evolution is clear: in polluted areas birds kill a higher percentage of moths with the gene for gray color than of moths with the gene for black color. Natural selection has produced populations of the moth that are well adapted to survive in their environments, populations whose characteristics change as the environment changes.

On the basis of this evidence, we would predict that if pollution were reduced in industrial areas, black moths would become rarer and gray forms more common in these areas. In fact, the Clean Air Act of 1952 has reduced air pollution in England. Collections of the peppered moth from industrial Manchester in the years since 1952 reveal a dramatic increase in the ratio of gray to black individuals in the moth population. The ability to predict future events in this way is the most impressive evidence that can be produced for a scientific theory. (657 words)

Checking for Understanding

Reread the selection. Jot in the margin any other thoughts that come to mind during rereading. Or listen to a friend read the selection aloud while he or she tells the thoughts that come to mind during reading. Then recite aloud to yourself the main points of the selection. It generally pays to paraphrase a selection to yourself either in your head or aloud before going on.

Select the best response from those given here.

1. You collect moths in a highly industrialized area. Predict what you will find.
   a. There will be more gray moths than black moths.
   b. There will be more black moths than gray moths.
   c. There will be about the same number of black moths and gray moths.

2. You collect moths far out in the country. Predict what you will find.
   a. There will be more gray moths than black moths.
   b. There will be more black moths than gray moths.
   c. There will be about the same number of black moths and gray moths.

3. The work of Kettlewell with peppered moths
   a. supports the theory of natural selection.
   b. disproves the theory of natural selection.
   c. neither supports nor disproves the theory of natural selection.

4. If we were to clean up the air in a polluted area, what do you predict would happen then?
   a. increase in black moths; decrease in gray moths
   b. increase in black and gray moths
   c. increase in gray moths; decrease in black moths
   d. decrease in black and gray moths

5. The reason why black moths are found in greater numbers in polluted areas is that
   a. gray moths turn black from the pollution.
   b. gray moths get sick and die from the pollution.
   c. gray moths are easier for the predator to see in polluted areas.
   d. All of the above are true.

6. The city of Manchester mentioned in the selection is found in
   a. New Hampshire.
   b. Massachusetts.

c. Great Britain.
d. Galapagos Islands in the Pacific.

Writing to Learn

Writing a summary after reading helps comprehension. In your notebook, write a brief paragraph in which you summarize the major findings of Kettlewell's experiments. Remember to include a topic sentence that states your main idea and follow with sentences that support that idea. Make an idea map, as in Figure 12.2, before writing.

EXTENDING WHAT YOU HAVE LEARNED

Building a Knowledge Base for Reading

Darwin's theories were based on data collected on a trip to the Galapagos Islands in the Pacific Ocean. The Galapagos are located off the coast of Ecuador, almost on the equator. Plot the location of the Galapagos Islands, and circle the Pacific Ocean, Equador, and the equator on the map in Figure 12.3.

Reviewing Strategies for Reading Explanations

List here at least four things you can do as you read explanations to increase your comprehension.

1. _____
2. _____
3. _____
4. _____

Applying the Strategies for Reading Explanations

Read an explanation of some phenomenon in a natural or social science textbook. As you read, apply the strategies for reading explanations as outlined on pages 241–242 of this book. Jot the name of the book and the pages you read on an index card. On the card, list some of the thoughts that came to your mind as you read. Be ready in class to explain orally the phenomenon you read about.

Reviewing the Chapter Vocabulary

Reread the chapter words and the brief definitions given with them. Then select the word from the list that best fits the context of each of the sentences. Add several of these words to your personal vocabulary list.

a. anatomy — study of the structure of body parts

b. avid — eager

c. calorie — a unit of heat often used to indicate the energy value of foods

d. camouflaged — protected by blending with the environment

e. concentration — amount of material in an area

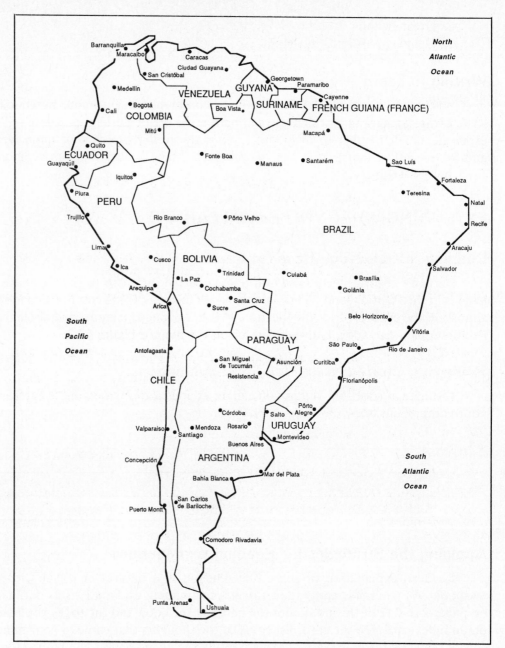

Figure 12.3   *Map of South America*

f. diffusion	movement of material from areas of high concentration to areas of low concentration
g. embryo	the young form of an organism before birth
h. evolved	changed slowly over time
i. haphazard	random, or by chance
j. ignited	set on fire
k. nucleus	inner portion of the cell, or the core of something
l. oxidize	combine with oxygen
m. physiology	study of the way the body functions

    n. plasma   liquid portion of the blood

    o. predators   ones who live by killing and eating others, or preying on others

1. He held a match to the twigs and _____ them.

2. When matter combines with oxygen, it is said to _____ .

3. The tiny _____ already resembled its adult parent in many respects.

4. The animal panicked when it realized it was surrounded by _____ , _____ which were intent on making a kill.

5. The bird was _____ by its feathers, which allowed it to blend with its surroundings.

6. He was an _____ physiologist. He worked twelve hours a day in his laboratory, conducting experiments on cell functioning.

7. There was such a high _____ of moths in that area that there was not enough food for them.

8. His activity was _____ ; it was without order or pattern.

9. Chemists define a _____ differently from the way dieters do.

10. Clark is interested in studying the structure of body parts, or what is known as _____ . In contrast, Karin is interested in studying the functioning of the body, or _____ .

11. The core part of the cell is the _____ .

12. His idea slowly _____ over time; by the time he announced it to the world, it was far different than when he began.

13. During the Renaissance, there was a general _____ of ideas—a movement of those ideas from where they originated across most of Europe.

13

Understanding Descriptions and Narratives

Before reading the chapter, read the title, the stated objective, and the headings and subheadings. Ask yourself: What is the topic of the chapter? In the space above and beside the chapter number, jot down what you already know about that topic. Then in the space below the chapter number, jot down at least two questions you hope to answer through reading the chapter.

OBJECTIVE

In this chapter, you will develop strategies for reading selections in which the author's purpose is to describe, to provide a narrative, or both.

INTRODUCTION—READING DESCRIPTIONS AND NARRATIVES

Authors write with different purposes in mind. As discussed in Chapter 12, authors may write with the intent to define or explain. In any one paragraph, an author may include statements of definition and explanation, moving smoothly from one to the other as the topic demands.

At other times and within the same selection, authors may write with the intent to describe or to give an account of something. The first kind of writing is *description,* the second *narrative.* This chapter focuses on reading as it relates to these two kinds of writings.

DESCRIPTION

In a description, a writer uses words to paint a picture of something. That something may be a person, a scene, or even a feeling. Typically in composing a description, the writer tells the most significant features, or attributes, of the thing he or she is describing.

Descriptions range from the very precise to the very creative. In science writing, descriptions tend to be exact, as when an author describes an apparatus or a particular organism. Descriptions in poetry are far more imaginative. In general, descriptions do not occur alone; they blend with definitions and explanations.

Reading Descriptions

Read the following description of Walden Pond by Henry David Thoreau, written in the 1800s. The word *exclusively* as Thoreau uses it means not including anything else. The *circumference* is the distance around. As you read, visualize, or picture, the pond in your mind. At the same time, in the right margin, write phrases that help you paint a picture in your mind.

WALDEN POND

Henry David Thoreau

Write phrases that help you visualize here.

[Walden Pond] is a clear and deep green well, half a mile long and a mile and three quarters in circumference, and contains about sixty-one acres; a perennial spring in the midst of pine and oak woods, without any visible inlet or outlet except by the clouds and evaporation. The surrounding hills rise abruptly from the water to the height of forty to eighty feet, though on the southeast and east they attain to about one hundred and one hundred and fifty feet respectively, within a quarter and a third of a mile. They are exclusively woodland.

The shore is composed of a belt of smooth rounded white stones like paving stones, excepting one or two short sand beaches, and is so steep that in many places a single leap will carry you into water over your head. . . . The stones extend a rod or two into the water, and then the bottom is pure sand.

Reading this, were you able to picture the pond with its green color, its ring of stones, its woodland surroundings? Did you visualize the pine and oak trees and the abrupt rise of the hills? Visualizing, or creating a picture in your mind's eye, is a first component of a strategy for reading description.

A second component is relating what is being described to something you already know. Sometimes the author of a text helps you to do this by providing an analogy, or creative comparison. For example, Thoreau called the pond a well. Picture a well with its steep sides in your mind's eye. Does visualizing a well help you picture how Walden Pond looks?

When Thoreau called Walden Pond a well, he was using a *metaphor.* A metaphor is an expressed comparison between two essentially different things. A metaphor differs from a *simile,* which is an expressed comparison between two different things that relies on the word *as* or *like* to make the comparison. Here is Thoreau's metaphor set in diagram form:

```
┌─────────────────────────────────────┐
│  Walden Pond with                    │
│  its steep banks is ──────▶ a well   │
│                         with its steep sides. │
└─────────────────────────────────────┘
```

At times, creating a metaphor or simile of your own when a writer does not supply one can help you visualize. For example, visualizing a rice field on a windy day, you might say to yourself: "The rice field in the wind looked like an ocean with waves moving to and fro." In doing that, you would have created a simile that paints a clearer picture in your mind.

```
┌─────────────────────────────────────┐
│  The rice field                      │
│  in the wind is ──▶ like ──▶ an ocean │
│                         with waves.   │
└─────────────────────────────────────┘
```

Now read this description of an eagle by the nineteenth-century English poet Alfred Lord Tennyson. As you read, apply these strategies: (1) Visualize the scene, and in the margin write phrases that help you picture it; (2) Create a comparison between what is being described and something you know, or identify the creative comparisons the author has used. The word *azure* means blue. A *crag* is a projecting outcrop of rock.

THE EAGLE

Alfred Tennyson

Write phrases that help you visualize here.

He clasps the crag with crooked hands:
Close to the sun in lonely lands,
Ringed with the azure world, he stands.

The wrinkled sea beneath him crawls;
He watches from his mountain walls,
And like a thunderbolt he falls.

Close your eyes for a minute. Visualize the scene in your mind—an eagle up on a projecting point of rock high above the sea, the big yellow sun in the background, the azure blue sky behind, the sea with its ripples below. Then the eagle falls, diving down from his craggy perch.

A key word that helps you paint a picture of the action part of the poem in your mind's eye is *thunderbolt*. Did you think of a thunderbolt, coming loudly and sharply—as you visualized the eagle? The word *thunderbolt* in this context is a simile, for here the word *like* makes the connection between two different things—the downward dive of the eagle and the clap of a thunderbolt.

> The eagle falls→like→a thunderbolt.

Practicing Visualizing

Here are a few descriptions that make use of metaphor and simile. Reading them, picture in your mind's eye the object being described, using the metaphor or simile to help you visualize. In the margin at the right as you read, jot down the particular words that help you see the picture in your mind:

Practice Exercise 1

Write phrases that help you visualize here.

The lands along the Missouri-Kansas border are a green patchwork of lush creek bottoms and rolling pastures, where eastern forests begin their retreat to western prairies. Farms, small towns and cities pulse with the strength of the American heartland.

Spring here brings thunderstorms to soak the earth and renew the cycle of life. As dusk comes, cottonwoods stir in the warm breeze,

robins pull worms from damp lawns and
lightning bugs flash their Morse messages against
darkening skies. In overgrown hollows, deer and
quail move through groves of hawthorn, oak and
walnut, and water moccasins hunt frogs in
pristine lotus ponds. The meadows are fringed
with daisies, clover and wild rose.

1. What is a patchwork quilt? _____

   _____

2. What picture does the author paint by calling the lands here "a green patchwork"? _____

   _____

3. What things do you know of that pulse? _____

   _____

4. How do farms, towns, and cities pulse? _____

   _____

5. What is Morse code? How does it work? _____

   _____

6. What picture does the author paint by saying that "lightning bugs flash their
   Morse messages against darkening skies"? _____

   _____

Practice Exercise 2

Write phrases that help
you visualize here.

MOON

Emily Dickinson

The moon was but a chin of gold
A night or two ago,
And now she turns her perfect face
Upon the world below.

7. Draw a picture of the moon when it was "but a chin of gold."

8. What phase of the moon was Dickinson describing with this first metaphor?
   (A metaphor is a creative comparison between two things.) _____

   _____

9. Draw a picture of the moon when it has a "perfect face."

10. What phase of the moon was Dickinson describing with the second metaphor? _____

_____

11. Why didn't Dickinson simply tell the names of the phases of the moon that she was describing? Why did she use the creative comparison of a metaphor?

_____

_____

SELECTION 1: FLORENCE THE MAGNIFICENT

Expanding Your Vocabulary for Reading

Using context and word-structure clues, figure out the meaning of each underlined word. Jot the meaning in the space provided. Check your definition in the glossary. In the selection, also you will meet the words palazzi *and* basilicas. *A basilica is a great church. A palazzi is a large dwelling place on the order of a palace.*

1. The crowd was so unruly that a dozen police officers were needed to keep order. _____

_____

2. When the cornerstone of the skyscraper was laid, a ceremony was held celebrating the event. _____

_____

3. She was a petulant child, inclined to be irritable whenever she did not get her way. _____

_____

4. The faces of the gargoyles on the cathedral stared down like avenging demons. _____

_____

5. After many unsuccessful forays into the country to raid, the bandits gave up their plundering. _____

_____

6. Michelangelo painted the frescoes that are on the ceiling of the Sistine Chapel in Rome. _____

_____

7. The sidewalks were so crowded that I was jostled with each step I took, and I felt like a puppet on a string. _____

_____

8. The books were stacked in such a higgledy-piggledy way that when I touched them, they came falling down like Humpty Dumpty. _____

_____

9. We stood in front of the building, looking at the highly decorated <u>façade</u> that had survived many wars. _____

_____

Getting Ready to Read

Preview the selection by reading the title and the headings and scanning the first paragraph.

- What is the topic of the selection? _____
- Write here what you know about that topic. _____

_____

- Write two questions you hope to answer through reading the selection.

_____

_____

Reading with Meaning

Read the following selection. As you read, try to visualize what the author is describing. In the margin, write words from the selection that paint pictures for you. Also record "equations" for the metaphors and similes. The first two items are completed for you. Remember that the Renaissance was the great period of learning in Europe during the fourteenth, fifteenth, and sixteenth centuries. The period marked the transition from the medieval to the modern world.

FLORENCE THE MAGNIFICENT: THE CITY OF DANTE AND DAVID, MICHELANGELO AND MACHIAVELLI, THE MEDICIS, GUCCIS AND PUCCIS

Anne Zwack

Write phrases that help you visualize and equations for metaphors and similes.

1. Metaphor:

Ring of hills =
palm of a giant

2. Metaphor:

orange roofs and domes =
bunch of marigolds

"The God who made the hills of Florence was an artist," wrote Anatole France as he looked down at the city, ringed by hills as though cupped in the palm of a giant hand, its orange roofs and domes jumbled like an unruly bunch of marigolds. Not just God, but centuries of Florentines have been artists. The Florentines invented the Renaissance, which is the same as saying they invented the modern world. For nearly three centuries, from Giotto's time to Michelangelo's, Florence was the hub of the universe, not only producing palazzi, basilicas

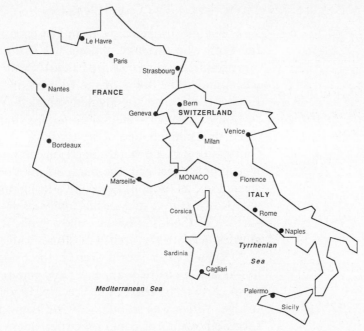

Figure 13.1 *Map of Italy*

and countless art treasures, but also generating ideas that form the cornerstone of 20th century thought.

Five centuries after the Renaissance, despite neon lights in the storefronts and swarms of mopeds and Fiats honking petulantly where horses and carts once rumbled past, Florence remains a Renaissance city. The streets in the center are still paved with uneven flagstones, and away from the main throughfares they're so narrow that the jutting eaves on opposite sides almost touch, keeping you dry on a rainy day if you hug the ochre-yellow walls. As it is, there is a war of wills every time you meet someone coming toward you on a sidewalk no wider than a ledge, and your umbrellas tend to get into a clinch. On a sunny day, look up at the skyline, at the leafy terraces, the square towers, the odd gargoyle or coat of arms worn smooth by time. The forbidding palazzi, built of massive blocks of brown stone, still seem to bristle as though in expectation of forays by bands of Guelfs or Ghibellines, the two warring factions that divided Florence in the Middle Ages. And the faces of today's townspeople come straight out of the frescoes painted centuries ago, when their ancestors were busy building the biggest dome in Christendom.

3. Metaphor:

ideas = cornerstone of the 20ᵗʰ century

4. Good descriptive phrase:

swarms of mopeds

5. Good descriptive phrase

The City's Pleasures

6. Good descriptive
phrase:

The most magical walk in Florence is down the Lungarno (literally, "along the Arno," as the streets skirting the river are called). Swallows wheel above the dome of the Church of San Frediano and over the higgledy-piggledy rooftops of houses. Some of the buildings, jostling each other in a hodgepodge of styles, have foundations in the water. The iron lampposts, whose lion's feet grip the parapets all along the river, look as though they were still lighted by gas. Rowers in kayaks occasionally skim over the surface of the fast-flowing yellow river, which gurgles beneath the arches of stone bridges.

7. Good descriptive
phrase:

Rebuilt after World War II, the bridges are not as ageless as they appear. Only one remains from early days: the Ponte Vecchio, or Old Bridge, which was so quaint, with its goldsmiths' shops elbowing for room on either side, that Hitler ordered his troops to leave it standing. The present structure dates from 1345, and the

8. Good descriptive
phrase:

tiny jewelers' boutiques that seem stuck to the sides of the bridge like limpets to a rock were once butcher shops. In the distance, atop one of the hills whose green flanks, crested with cypress trees, thrust their way into the city, sits that most harmonious of Florentine churches, San Miniato, with sun glinting on the gold in its perfectly proportioned Romanesque façade.

Art and Architecture

9. Good descriptive
phrase:

Whether you spend a lifetime seeing Florence or a few days, there are a number of things you must not miss. One, in the Academia, is Michelangelo's *David* (of which there are two copies, one in the Piazza Signoria and one in the Piazzale Michelangelo). Frowning down from his pedestal, his sling over his shoulder and every vein and sinew bursting out of the white marble, David makes the rest of us feel very small. One wonders how Michelangelo would have portrayed Goliath. There's more marble and more Michelangelo in the Medici Chapels behind the Basilica of San Lorenzo: the 16th century genius was responsible for both the architecture and the sculpture of the reclining figures of *Night and Day* and of *Dawn and Dusk* . . . .

In the days when justice was rough and rudimentary, the building that is now the Bargello Museum was Florence's courthouse, and condemned men were strung out of the windows of its tower. Today the museum houses Renaissance statues. . . . There is also another David, this one by Donatello, and it is said to be the first nude statue of the Renaissance.

The Pitti Palace crouches like an enormous yellow crab around Pitti Square, one of the few parking areas in Florence. The palace was built by a Renaissance nobleman, Luca Pitti, who wanted his mansion to be bigger and better than anyone else's. It is now divided into five museums. . . .

Like most Florentine basilicas, the Duomo, or cathedral is striped in a geometric patchwork of different colored marble. It looks huge even by today's standards, let alone those of 1296, when the cornerstone was laid. No one had succeeded in hoisting aloft a massive dome since the building of the Pantheon in Rome. But Brunelleschi, the great Renaissance architect, solved the problem in the early 15th century by building two separate domes, one on top of the other, like two salad bowls of different sizes. If you can face the 463 steps that lead to the very top, you actually can walk between the two layers of the dome. Or you can climb Biotto's bell tower, which Longfellow called "the lily of Florence blossoming in stone."

Another church of striped marble, Santa Croce, could be called Florence's hall of fame, as it contains tombs and monuments that constitute a *Who's Who* of Italy's glorious past. Among the greats memorialized there are Michelangelo, Galileo, Machiavelli and Dante. . . . You should visit Santa Maria Novella on a sunny day when shafts of light streaming through the windows pierce the gloom of the otherwise badly lit church. The splendid frescoes by Ghirlandaio and Filippino Lippi are sometimes swallowed up in the darkness of the chapels, which were built by leading Florentine families in gratitude for having survived the Black Death of 1348.

The Right and Left Banks

In the Middle Ages, when Florence flourished as the center of the world's wool trade, the fleeces were washed in the River Arno, which divides the city in two. The Oltrarno, or Left Bank, is my favorite half, with a little maze

10. Good descriptive phrase:

11. Simile:

12. Good descriptive phrase:

13. Simile:

14. Metaphor:

15. Good descriptive phrases:

16. Good descriptive phrase:

17. Metaphor:

of streets spreading out from the Pitti Palace and around the Church of Santo Spirito and its neighborhood square, where housewives shop at the morning market, old men doze on benches, and children and dogs tumble over the fountain. Since the times of the Medicis, this has been the city's artisan quarter, a hive of activity where craftsmen in sand-colored overalls bend over their workbenches surrounded by clouds of sawdust and pungent smells of glue. As you wend your way down the little streets, you can peer into the workshops and watch giant picture frames being gilded, antique furniture being restored, metals being forged. Artisans pedal past on their bicycles, the tools of their trade strapped on behind, and it is not unusual to see them stopping traffic as they carry a brass bedstead or an antique commode across the street.

18. Good descriptive phrase:

The other (right) side of the Arno is Florence's more pompous monumental half, site of most of the museums and churches, banks and offices. Here on wide streets like Via Tornabuoni and Via della Vigna Nuova, chic shoppers flit in and out of designer boutiques. All the big names in Italian fashion are lined up shoulder to shoulder: Gucci, Ferragamo, Armani . . . . You'll also find fun fashion stores and the plushest jewelers in Florence.

Perhaps my greatest Florentine pleasure is watching the sun set from Pizzale Michelangelo, with the entire city at my feet. The lights hover

19. Simile:

like fireflies over the slowly darkening town, and the arches of the bridges show black against the fierce red of a sun that sets twice, once in the waters of the Arno and once in the Tuscan heavens. At this time the light takes on the

20. Good descriptive phrase

gossamer texture of a down powder puff, dusting the roofs and domes a hazy apricot, and I find myself sharing with D. H. Lawrence the "feeling of having arrived, of having reached the perfect centre of man's universe." (1415 words)

Checking for Understanding

1. Florence has been described as "a feast for the eyes." Based on your reading of the article, explain the meaning of the metaphor. In what way is Florence a feast? What things do Florence and a feast have in common? _____

_____

2. Explain the meaning of this simile: Florence is ringed by hills "as though

cupped in the palm of a giant.'' A simile is a creative comparison between two things, the comparison includes the word *like* or *as*. _____

_____

3. The author writes that Florence's orange roofs and domes are "jumbled like an unruly bunch of marigolds." What two essentially different things is the author comparing through this simile? _____

   What qualities do these things share? _____

4. A limpet is a small-shelled organism that clings to a rock. The author writes, "The tiny jeweler's boutiques that seem stuck to the sides of the bridge like limpets to a rock were once butcher shops." What two essentially different

   things is the author comparing through this simile? _____

   What qualities do these things share? _____

5. The author writes, "The Pitti Palace crouches like an enormous yellow crab around Pitti Square." What two essentially different things is the author

   comparing in this simile? _____

   What qualities do these two things share? _____

6. Describing the domes, the author tells us that they are actually two separate domes, "one on top of the other like two salad bowls of different sizes." What two essentially different things is the author comparing in this simile?

   _____

   What qualities do these two things share? _____

7. When the author described the artisan section of the city as "a hive of ac-

   tivity," what picture came to your mind? _____

   _____

8. The author writes, "The lights hover like fireflies over the slowly darkening

   town." What two things is the author comparing in this simile? _____

   What qualities do these two things share? _____

9. The author describes the dusk through a metaphor: "At this time the light takes on the gossamer texture of a down powder puff, dusting the roofs and domes a hazy apricot." What two essentially different things is the author

   comparing metaphorically? _____

   What qualities do these two things share? _____

10. Longfellow called the bell tower "the lily of Florence blossoming in stone." What two essentially different things is the author comparing through met-

    aphor? _____

    What qualities do these two things share? _____

Making the Writing Connection

Create a metaphor or simile to complete each of the following:

1. The rocket, posed on the launching pad, looked like a _____
2. In the winter, the bare branches of the trees looked like _____

3. Blown by the wind, her hair became _____

4. The islands of Hawaii are _____

5. The great Rocky Mountain ridge is _____

Playing with Words

Here are the featured words from the selection. Draw a very rough picture, or sketch, to go along with each one to show the meaning that word has for you. The first ones will be relatively easy to do; as you progress, use your imagination in picturing meanings. Check the glossary if you are unsure of the meanings of the words.

1. cornerstone

2. façade

3. gargoyle

4. fresco

5. higgledy-piggledy

6. unruly

7. jostled

8. petulant

9. foray

NARRATION

A narrative is an account of an event or series of events. It can be fictional (not true) or nonfictional (true). Stories, poems that tell a story, some newspaper reports, history, biography, and autobiography are narrations.

There are four elements in a strategy for successful reading of nonfictional narratives: (1) grasping the chronology of the events, (2) perceiving cause-and-effect relationships within the events, (3) conceiving of the significance of the events, and (4) relating the events to other similar or different events. Let us talk about each of these elements.

Understanding Time Relationships in Reading

An ability to understand time relationships, or chronology, is important in reading narratives, especially **biographies** (passages that tell about the life of a person), **autobiographies** (passages that tell about the life of a person written by that person), and **historical accounts** (passages that tell about sequences of events). To help you comprehend sequence, authors provide two aids: dates and words that indicate sequence.

First, let us consider how to interpret dates. Start by previewing the following paragraph by circling the dates.

> Phyllis Wheatley, the first major African-American poet, was 1753 born about 1753. She was taken by slavers from Africa to Boston in 1761 and sold there as a slave to John Wheatley, a merchant. Wheatley and his wife recognized Phyllis's quickness of mind and ready wit and provided her with an education far beyond what was typically given to black slaves in America. She learned to read and write, began to read the poetry of English writers, and wrote poems of her own. When freed, she traveled to England, where she was recognized for her poetry and had a collection of poems published in 1773. The volume was titled *Poems on Various Subjects.*
>
> Returning to America, Phyllis Wheatley sent a copy of one of her poems to George Washington during the American Revolution. It expressed her feelings about the war and made reference to the general. This led to the publishing of one of her poems in *Pennsylvania Magazine* and gradual recognition of her as the Poet of the American Revolution. Despite this recognition, Wheatley died in virtual poverty in 1784.   1784

In your preview did you note that the selection is organized chronologically in the order in which events occurred? The first event was the birth of Ms. Wheatley in 1753. The last event was her death in 1784. The intervening events are presented as they happened, in chronological order. Biographies and historical accounts are often structured chronologically. The writers of such selections typically include some dates to give a framework to the account.

Having previewed a selection and discovered a sequence of dates in it, you will find it helpful to visualize a time line in your mind as you read. A time line is simply a line on which dates and related events are labeled in chronological order. Reading, you plot each event on your mental time line.

Reading, you also relate the dates mentioned in the selection to significant dates from the past that function as reference points. You say to yourself: This happened just after the Civil War. Or this happened before Columbus made his epic journey. Although you should develop your own series of historical reference points that have meaning to you, here are some "markers from the past" that you may want to use if you have some knowledge of these events:

Reference Points from History

1066	The conquest of Britain by William the Conqueror
1400s to 1700s	The Renaissance in Europe
1492	Columbus's voyage
1620	Landing of the Pilgrims in Massachusetts
1776	Declaration of Independence
1787	Constitution
1803	Louisiana Purchase, which doubled the country's size
1849	Gold Rush
1861 to 1865	American Civil War
1914 to 1918	World War I
1939 to 1945	World War II

Now go back and read the passage about Phyllis Wheatley. On the vertical time line in the right margin of the selection, plot the events of her life as well as two key reference points of history—the Declaration of Independence and the Constitution, 1776 and 1787. In other words, locate each date from the selection on the line and label that date with the event from Wheatley's life that happened at that time. Do the same for the historical reference points.

Based on your time line (which is what you have just constructed in the right-hand margin), answer these questions:

- How old was Phyllis Wheatley when she was enslaved? _____
- How old was she when she died? _____
- Was Ms. Wheatley alive when the Constitution was written? _____

Often active readers make simple calculations based on dates in a selection. They ask themselves questions similar to the three above; in so doing, they are monitoring their own comprehension.

The strategy you have been applying here has four elements:

1. In previewing the selection, check dates given to see whether the selection is organized chronologically.
2. In reading a chronologically organized selection, plot items on a mental time line. At times, plot dates sequentially on a time line in the margin.
3. Relate dates to key reference points in history that you know.
4. Make simple calculations based on the dates.

Dates are not the only way a writer expresses time relationships. A writer may use words that specify or signal the passage of time. Sequence words include these:

- first, second, third . . . sixth
- for one year . . . for ten years
- first, next, after that . . . finally
- yesterday, today, tomorrow
- before, while, as, when, after
- then, now
- meanwhile
- soon
- not long after
- later
- in (in the spring), on (on his birthday), during (during her early years)
- childhood, youth, middle years, old age
- pre- and post-, as in prewar and postwar periods.

Preview the following short selection by skimming it and circling words other than dates that communicate time relationships.

Emily Dickinson, considered by many to be one of the greatest 1830 American poets, was born in 1830 in Amherst, Massachusetts. Her childhood was a typical one of that day, filled with friends and parties, church and home activities. For about six years, she attended Amherst Academy. Then she attended Mt. Holyoke Female Seminary for a year. "Valentine Extravaganza," her first poem to appear in print, was published in the *Springfield Republican* when she was 22.

Before she was 30, however, Emily withdrew from Amherst society and increasingly applied herself to the writing of poetry. She would not see friends; and with the death of her father in 1874, she became a virtual recluse. During her life time, she had only two other poems published, "The Snake," in 1866, and "Success" in 1878. At her death in 1886, her sister dis- 1886 covered more than a thousand poems that Emily Dickinson had written throughout her life. The poems exhibit a directness of expression and a clarity of image that is apparent even to one who has read little poetry:

> To make a prairie it takes a clover and one
> bee,—
> One clover, and a bee,
> And revery.
> The revery alone will do
> If bees are few.

In this selection, sequence-giving words include *childhood, for about six years, then, for a year, when, before, during, at her death.*

Now reread the article. As you read, keep a pen in hand and record key events from Dickinson's life in the right-hand margin as a time line. Include a key reference point from history on the line so that you have a general idea of the period in which she lived. Ask yourself as you read: What do the time-sequencing words tell me about the life of Dickinson?

After reading, record your answers to these questions:

• What are the two major periods in Dickinson's life? _____

_____

• How does the organization of the selection and the key sequencing words help you identify those periods in her life? _____

_____

Did you identify the two periods? The first is Dickinson's childhood; it is discussed in the first paragraph. The second is the period characterized by her reclusive behavior; it is discussed in the second paragraph. Sometimes in reading chronological material about people and events, you may find it helpful to group events into periods or categories: youth, middle years, later years; pre-Darwin, post-Darwin; pre-Reformation, Reformation, post-Reformation. Sometimes, as in this case, the way the writer has organized the material into paragraphs helps you to identify patterns in the events.

You now have two more steps to add to your reading-for-sequence strategy.

5. Keep alert for sequencing words such as *first, then, finally,* and *before, during,* and *after* that are clues to the passage of time and the sequence of events. Use these words to add events to the time line you visualize, or picture in your mind, during reading.
6. Wherever possible, try to group events into periods or categories, such as childhood, youth, midlife . . . or prewar and postwar . . . or pre-Constitution and post-Constitution.

In sum, when working with sequence do not just skim over dates and words that suggest time relationships. Think about those dates. Make use of words that give time-relational clues to organize events into some framework that helps you remember what and when things happened. It is easier to remember that X happened during a person's childhood than to remember that X happened on May 4, 1862.

Analyzing Relationships Within Narratives

A second aspect of reading nonfictional narratives is delving beneath the facts of the account to think about why things came to pass, why they happened. Doing this, you are thinking in terms of cause and effect. For example, reading a biography, you must ask: What were the influences upon this person that made him or her do what he or she did? What were the influences that made him or her become the kind of person he or she was? Reading history, you must ask: What were the events leading up to this? What were the causes? This diagram shows one way to think about causes and effects:

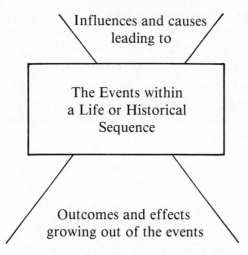

Practice asking these questions about the lives of Wheatley and Dickinson. What influenced both of these women to become poets? Write down a few points from each life that you think were important in making them the women they became.

Key Events in Their Lives
Wheatley
Dickinson

Determining the Significance of Events

A third aspect of a strategy for reading historical accounts and biographies is to consider the significance of the events. In thinking about the ultimate meaning of a person's life as you read biography, you ask: What influence did this person have on other persons and events? In thinking about the meaning of a series of events or a period of time in history, you ask: What changes did these events trigger? What were the effects of these events on people and events that were to come? These are fundamental questions to raise and answer as you read biographic and historical content.

Relating Events to Events in Your Own Life

A fourth element of a strategy for reading historical accounts and biographies is to relate events and lives to other events and lives with which you are already familiar. Reading, you say to yourself: This reminds me of X, Y, and Z that happened several years ago. Or this person's life resembles that of Mr. A.

Or this is just the opposite of what happened when. . . . Or this person's life started out the same as Ms. B's, but then took a different turn. In essence, what you are doing is to make comparisons and contrasts with things you already know: You are saying "This is like . . . . This is different from . . . ."

Practice asking these questions about Wheatley and Dickinson. Does the life of either of these women remind you of the life of someone you know? If so, in what way? In what way are the lives of Wheatley and Dickinson similar? In what way are their lives different?

Reviewing the Strategy for Reading Narratives

In sum, a strategy for reading nonfictional narrative has these components:

1. asking questions that help you grasp the sequence of events;
2. asking questions that help you identify causes of events and factors that influenced people's lives;
3. asking questions that help you think about the ultimate meaning, or significance, of events and people's lives;
4. asking questions that help you compare and contrast events and lives to other events and lives.

SELECTION 2: MUHAMMAD THE PROPHET

Expanding Your Vocabulary for Reading

The selection you will read contains a number of interesting words. Knowing them will help you understand the selection. Read the following sentences and study the underlined terms. Using context and word-structure clues, hypothesize a meaning for each term and record it in the space given. Check your hypotheses in the glossary.

1. In those days the king was <u>preeminent</u>; he was far above anyone else in authority. (Note: An eminent person is high in rank or is distinguished. How are the words *eminent* and *preeminent* related?) _____

   _____

2. The convict was <u>consigned</u> to the warden to begin his prison sentence. ___

   _____

3. "I appreciate your <u>forbearance</u>," said the man. "You have been very patient and understanding as you waited for me to pay my debt." _____

   _____

4. "You promised not to <u>divulge</u> the secret to anyone," remarked the lawyer. "Yet as soon as you learned it, you told everyone." _____

   _____

5. The <u>revelation</u> that he was a member of the CIA surprised us all. We had not known until then that he was working for the government. _____

   _____

6. In that society the king was <u>paramount</u>. His preeminence came as a right of birth. _____

7. To me that situation was <u>unique</u>. I had never seen anything like it before.

8. I had a sense of <u>impending</u> trouble as I entered the office and saw the principal behind the desk. Something was about to happen. _____

9. The <u>Koran</u> (or Quaran), the sacred scriptures of the Islamic religion, affirms the oneness of God. (Note: See also how the word <u>Koran</u> is defined within the sentence by a phrase coming right after it and set off by commas. You will find this technique for supplying basic information used a number of times in the selection.) _____

10. The pagans, who lived in Mecca, believed in many Gods. This belief is called <u>polytheism</u>. (Remember the meaning of the prefix *poly-*.) _____

11. and 12. Muhammad and his <u>adherents</u>, or supporters, <u>migrated</u> from Medina; they left together because it was unsafe for them there. _____

13. The leader of the neighboring country tried to <u>mediate</u> between the warring parties, but he could do nothing to help them end their struggles. _____

14. During the <u>siege</u> of the city by the enemy, many people were killed. _____

15. The siege lasted many weeks; yet the results were <u>inconclusive</u>. They proved nothing, for nobody came out the victor. (Remember the meaning of the prefix *in-*.) _____

16. After many hours of work we looked at what we had done and saw that we had made <u>negligible</u> progress. We could hardly see what we had done. _____

17. Only the most eminent persons were allowed <u>access</u> to the party; the rest of us were not allowed to enter. _____

18. The pagans that Muhammad fought worshipped <u>idols</u>, graven images that they held in high regard. _____

19. The Supreme Court generally adheres to the <u>precedents</u> set down in previous decisions. What has been decided in the past is a major factor in present cases. _____

_____

20. Muhammad made an <u>alliance</u> with other tribes—an agreement that bound them together as allies. _____

_____

21. The queen sent an <u>envoy</u> with a message to the emperor. The envoy served as the queen's agent and represented her in official talks. _____

_____

Getting Ready to Read

Preview the selection by studying the title, the first and last paragraphs, the headings, and the map.

- What is the main topic of the selection? _____

- Write what you already know about that topic. _____

_____

- Write two or three questions you hope to answer by reading the selection.

_____

_____

Reading with Meaning

As you read the selection, record a time line of events in the inner margin. Answer the questions in the outer margin as you go along. Keep thinking: What were the causes of this? What is the significance of this? Of what does this remind me?

MUHAMMAD THE PROPHET

Paul Lunde and John Sabini

1. Into what kind of family and society was Muhammad born?

In or about the year 570 the child who would be named Muhammad and who would become the Prophet of one of the world's great religions, Islam, was born into a family belonging to a clan of Quraysh, the ruling tribe of Mecca, a city in the Hijaz region of northwestern Arabia.

2. How might this have affected him?

Originally the site of the Ka'bah, a shrine of ancient origins, Mecca had with the decline of southern Arabia become an important center of sixth-century trade with such powers as the Sassanians, Byzantines, and Ethiopians. As a result the city was dominated by powerful

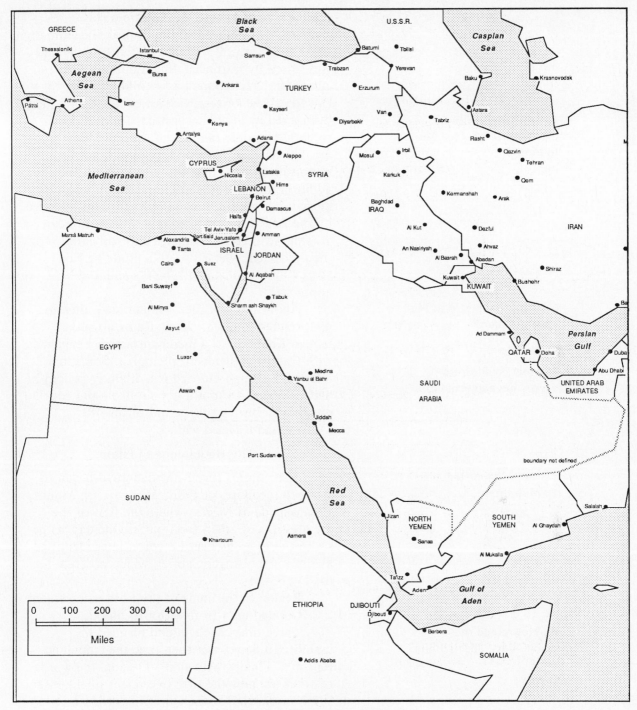

Figure 13.2 *Map of The Middle East*

merchant families among whom the men of Quraysh were preeminent.

Muhammad's Early Life

Muhammad's father, 'Abd Allah ibn 'Abd al-Muttalib, died before the boy was born; his mother, Aminah, died when he was six. The

3. What were key events in Muhammad's early life?

4. How might these events have affected Muhammad?

5. What happened to Muhammad next?

6. How could these events have affected him?

7. What happened next to Muhammad?

8. How could these events have affected him?

9. At first how did Muhammad react?

10. Based on your own experiences, suggest why Muhammad reacted in this way.

orphan was consigned to the care of his grandfather, the head of the clan of Hashim. After the death of his grandfather, Muhammad was raised by his uncle, Abu Talib. As was customary, Muhammad as a child was sent to live for a year or two with a Bedouin family that lived a desert life. This custom, followed until recently by noble families of Mecca, Medina, Tayif, and other towns of the Hijaz, had important implications for Muhammad. In addition to enduring the hardships of desert life, he acquired a taste for the rich language so loved by the Arabs, whose speech was their proudest art, and learned the patience and forbearance of the herdsmen, whose life of solitude he first shared and then came to understand and appreciate.

About the year 590, Muhammad, then in his twenties, entered the service of a widow named Khadijah as a merchant actively engaged with trading caravans to the north. Sometime later Muhammad married Khadijah, by whom he had two sons—who did not survive—and four daughters. During this period of his life Muhammad traveled widely.

The Beginnings of Islam

Then, in his forties, Muhammad began to retire to meditate, or think, in a cave on Mount Hira outside of Mecca, where the first of the great events of Islam took place. One day, as he sat in the cave, he heard a voice, later identified as that of the Angel Gabriel, which ordered him to:

Recite: In the name of thy Lord who created, Created man from a clot of blood.

Three times Muhammad pleaded his inability to do so, but each time the command repeated. Finally, Muhammad recited the words of what are now the first five verses of the 96th surah or chapter of the Quran—words which proclaim God the Creator of man and the Source of all knowledge.

At first Muhammad divulged his experience only to his wife and immediate circle. But as more revelations directed him to proclaim the oneness of God universally, his following grew, at first among the poor and the slaves, but later also among the most eminent men of Mecca. The revelations he received at this time and those he did so later are all incorporated in the Quran, the Scripture of Islam.

Not everyone accepted God's message transmitted through Muhammad. Even in his own clan there were those who rejected his teachings, and many merchants actively opposed the message. The opposition, however, merely served to sharpen Muhammad's sense of mission and his understanding of exactly how Islam differed from paganism. The belief in the unity of God was paramount in Islam; from this all else followed. The verses of the Quaran stress God's uniqueness, warn those who deny it of impending punishment, and proclaim His unbounded compassion to those who submit to His will. Because the Quaran rejected polytheism and emphasized man's moral responsibility, it presented a grave challenge to the worldly Meccans.

11. Based on your own experiences, suggest why opposition sharpened his determination—made him more determined.

12. Based on your own experiences, predict how the Meccans would react.

The Hijrah

After Muhammad had preached for more than a decade, the opposition to him reached such a high pitch that, fearful for their safety, he sent some of his adherents to Ethiopia, where the Christian ruler extended protection to them, the memory of which has been cherished by Muslims ever since. But in Mecca the persecution worsened. Muhammad's followers were abused and even tortured. At last, therefore, Muhammad sent seventy of his followers off to the northern town of Yathrib, which was later to be renamed Medina ("The City"). Later, in the early fall of 622, he learned of a plot to murder him and, with his closest friend, Abu Bakr al-Siddiq, set off to join the emigrants.

13. Of what historical event does this persecution remind you?

In Mecca the plotters arrived at Muhammad's home to find that his cousin, 'Ali, had taken his place in bed. Enraged, the Meccans set a price on Muhammad's head and set off in pursuit. Muhammad and Abu Bakr, however, had taken refuge in a cave where, as they hid from their pursuers, a spider spun its web across the cave's mouth. When they saw that the web was unbroken, the Meccans passed by and Muhammad and Abu Bakr went on to Medina, where they were joyously welcomed by the Medinans as well as the Meccans who had gone ahead to prepare the way.

14. Why did the Meccans not investigate the cave?

15. What is the significance of the Hegira?

This was the *Hijrah*—or in English the *Hegira*—usually, but inaccurately translated as "Flight"—from which the Muslim era is dated. In fact, the Hijrah was not a flight but a carefully planned migration which marks not only a break in history—the beginning of the Islamic era—but also, for Muhammad and the Muslims, a new way of life. Henceforth, the organizational principle of the community was not to be mere blood kinship, but the greater brotherhood of all Muslims. The men who accompanied Muhammad on the Hijrah were called the *Muhajirun*—"those that made the Hijrah" or the "Emigrants"—while those in Medina who became Muslims were called the *Ansar* or "Helpers."

16. Why was Muhammad well acquainted with the situation in Medina?

Muhammad was well acquainted with the situation in Medina. Earlier, before the Hijrah, the city had sent envoys to Mecca asking Muhammad to mediate a dispute between two powerful tribes. What the envoys saw and heard had impressed them and they had invited Muhammad to settle in Medina. After the Hijrah, Muhammad's exceptional qualities so impressed the Medinans that the rival tribes and their allies temporarily closed ranks as, on March 15, 624, Muhammad and his supporters moved against the pagans of Mecca.

Fighting for Islam

17. What was the significance of the Battle of Badr?

The first battle, which took place near Badr, now a small town southwest of Medina, had several important effects. In the first place, the Muslim forces, outnumbered three to one, defeated the Meccans. Secondly, the discipline displayed by the Muslims brought home to the Meccans, perhaps for the first time, the abilities of the man they had driven from their city. Thirdly, one of the allied tribes which had pledged support to the Muslims in the Battle of Badr, but had then proved lukewarm when the fighting started, was expelled from Medina one month after the battle. Those who claimed to be allies of the Muslims, but really opposed them, were thus served warning: membership in the community imposed the obligation of total support.

A year later the Meccans struck back. Assembling an army of three thousand men, they met the Muslims at Uhud, a ridge outside

Medina. After an initial success the Muslims were driven back and the Prophet himself was wounded. As the Muslims were not completely defeated, the Meccans, with an army of ten thousand, attacked Medina again two years later but with quite different results. At the Battle of the Trench, the Muslims scored a signal victory by introducing a new defense. On the side of Medina from which attack was expected they dug a trench too deep for the Meccan cavalry to clear without exposing itself to the archers posted behind earthworks on the Medina side. After an inconclusive siege, the Meccans were forced to retire. Thereafter, Medina was entirely in the hands of the Muslims.

The Growth of Islam

The Constitution of Medina—under which the clans accepting Muhammad as the Prophet of God formed an alliance, or federation—dates from this period. It showed that the political consciousness of the Muslim community had reached an important point; its members defined themselves as a community separate from all others. The Constitution also defined the role of non-Muslims in the community. Jews, for example, were part of the community; they were *dhimmis,* that is, protected people, as long as they conformed to its laws. This established a precedent for the treatment of subject peoples during the later conquests. Christians and Jews, upon a payment of a yearly tax, were allowed religious freedom and, while maintaining their status as non-Muslims, were associate members of the Muslim state. This status did not apply to polytheists, who could not be tolerated within a community that worshipped the One God.

Ibn Ishaq, one of the earliest biographers of the Prophet, says it was at about this time that Muhammad sent letters to the rulers of the earth—the King of Persia, the Emperor of Byzantium, the Negus of Abyssinia, and the Governor of Egypt among others—inviting them to submit to Islam. Nothing more fully illustrates the confidence of the small community, as its military power, despite the Battle of the Trench, was still negligible. But its confidence was not misplaced. Muhammad so effectively built up a series of alliances among the tribes—his early years with the Bedouins must have stood him in

18. Of what other events do these events remind you?

19. What was the significance of the Constitution of Medina?

20. What do these events tell you about Muhammad's strength at this point?

good stead here—that by 628 he and fifteen hundred followers were able to demand access to the Ka'bah during negotiations with the Meccans.

21. In 629, Muhammad reentered Mecca. Why was this significant?

This was a milestone in the history of the Muslims. Just a short time before, Muhammad had had to leave the city of his birth in fear of his life. Now he was being treated by his former enemies as a leader in his own right. A year later, in 629, he reentered and, in effect, conquered Mecca without bloodshed and in a spirit of tolerance which established an ideal for future conquests. He also destroyed the idols in the Ka'bah, to put an end forever to pagan practices there. At the same time Muhammad won the allegiance of 'Amr ibn al-'As, the future conqueror of Egypt, and Khalid ibn al-Walid, the future "Sword of God," both of whom embraced Islam and joined Muhammad. Their conversion was especially noteworthy because these men had been among Muhammad's bitterest opponents only a short time before.

22. What do you believe was Muhammad's contribution to world history?

In one sense Muhammad's return to Mecca was the climax of his mission. In 632, just three years later, he was suddenly taken ill, and on June 8 of that year, with his third wife 'Aishah in attendance, the Messenger of God "died with the heat of noon." (1791 words)

Checking on Understanding

1. How old was Muhammad when he died?
   a. 20
   b. 50
   c. 62
   d. 72

2. Young Muhammad lost his mother and father at a young age, then his grandfather. Propose what influence this might have had in making him the man he became. _____

   _____

3. Muhammad spent a year or two with a Bedouin family in the desert. Propose how this may have influenced him as a person. _____

   _____

4. What were two important effects of the Battle of Badr?

   a. _____

   b. _____

5. Why was the Hegira significant, or important? _____

_____

6. Why was the Constitution of Medina significant, or important? _____

_____

7. What do you believe was Muhammad's most significant contribution to the world? Give reasons to support your belief. _____

_____

Writing from Reading

As you read the selection, did you relate the content to other people, places, or times about which you know? Of what other events in history does this account remind you? How are the events similar? How are they different? In your notebook, write a short paragraph or two in which you identify a similar event in history and tell the similarities and then the differences. Use Figure 13.3 (page 282) to organize your ideas before writing. Be ready to talk about relationships.

Playing with Words

Here are the featured words from the selection. Match them with their definitions. Place the correct letter on the line at the left.

Adjectives

_____ 1. impending   a. standing out above others

_____ 2. inconclusive   b. chief in importance

_____ 3. negligible   c. one of a kind

_____ 4. paramount   d. about to occur, threatening

_____ 5. preeminent   e. so insignificant that it can be disregarded

_____ 6. unique   f. not decisive, without a definite outcome

Verbs

_____ 7. consign   g. hand over, deliver

_____ 8. divulge   h. serve as go-between, act to bring agreement between groups

_____ 9. mediate   i. move from one place to settle in another

_____ 10. migrate   j. make known to others, tell something

Nouns

_____ 11. access   k. messenger, diplomatic agent

_____ 12. adherents   l. union formed by agreement

_____ 13. alliance   m. patience, self-control

_____ 14. envoy   n. something made known

_____ 15. forbearance   o. the scriptures of Islam

_____ 16. Koran   p. belief in many gods

_____ 17. idols   q. objects or images worshipped as gods

The Event — Where, When, Who, What Happened:

Similarities between This Event and Another:

Differences between This Event and Another:

Figure 13.3   *An Idea Map for Plotting Similarities and Differences Before Writing. (Note: Decide on the event you want to compare to the event in the article. Write words and ideas about that event—time, place, people involved, what happened—in the event box. Then think of the ways in which that event is similar to the event in the article. Write similarities in the second box. Next think of ways the event you have chosen is different from the one in the article. Write differences in the third box. Then begin to draft your paragraphs. First draft a paragraph telling about the event you have chosen. Then draft a paragraph giving the similarities between it and the one in the article. Finally draft a paragraph giving differences. Use your idea map as a writing outline.)*

_____ 18. polytheism	r. long effort to overcome resistance
_____ 19. precedent	s. entrance, admission
_____ 20. revelation	t. case that serves as a reason for a later case
_____ 21. siege	u. followers, supporters

Using Words in Context

Select from the words just given, and place one in each sentence slot. Place an adjective in each sentence slot. Do not use a word more than once.

1. Graduating from college is of _____ importance to him; all other things are of lesser importance.

2. As a student, his income was _____ ; he barely had enough money for the basics.

3. The evidence against the prisoner was _____ so they had to release him.

4. He felt a sense of _____ trouble as the test date came closer and closer.

5. The thing that made the house _____ was the way it floated on water.

6. His family held a _____ position in society; they were leaders.

Place a verb in each sentence slot. Do not use a word more than once.

7. During the drought, the Bedouins would _____ across the desert in search of a new home.

8. He decided to _____ the information to the police when he heard of the seriousness of the crime.

9. The lawyer tried to _____ between the two angry men.

10. As a child, he was _____ to the care of a nurse and never saw his parents.

Place a noun in each sentence slot. Do not use a word more than once.

11. The two nations signed an _____ in which they agreed to assist each other in times of war.

12. The president sent an _____ to talk to the prime minister of that country.

13. It was a _____ to learn that the man she had married was a billionaire.

14. As a child, he read the _____ ; in that way he learned the important principles of Islam.

15. After a lengthy _____ , the city surrendered, for it had been without food for many days.

16. _____ is the belief in many Gods.

17. They denied him _____ into the city because he did not believe as they did.

18. Muhammad had many _____ who followed him when he left the city.

19. "I ask your _____ in this case," the hotel manager said. "There will be a long wait before a room is available for you."

20. They worshipped _____ , golden eagles studded with diamonds.

21. Because there is no _____ that we can follow, we must make up our own minds.

EXTENDING WHAT YOU HAVE LEARNED

Reviewing Reading Strategies

Write down the strategies you would apply as you read each of these forms of prose:

Description	Narration

Applying Strategies in Independent Reading

1. Read a section from a history book that recounts a sequence of events or tells about the events in a person's life. On a card write down:
   - the significant events in the order in which they occurred;
   - the factors that brought these events into being;
   - the significance of the events;
   - another event that you believe to be similar.

2. Read an article from the travel section of the Sunday newspaper or a travel magazine that describes a place you would like to visit. As you read, visualize what is being described. On an index card, record a few notes about the place. Be ready to tell about the place you have read about.

Building a Knowledge Base for Reading

Circle Florence, Italy, on the map in Figure 13.1. Locate Medina and Mecca in Saudi Arabia on the map in Figure 13.2.

Gaining Ownership of Words

Select several words from those featured in this chapter to record in your personal vocabulary list. Include a model sentence for each. Try to use the words you have selected in speaking and writing.

14

Understanding Opinions and Persuasive Writing

Before reading the chapter, read the title, the stated objective, and the headings and subheadings. Ask yourself: What is the topic of the chapter? In the space above and beside the chapter number, jot down what you already know about that topic. Then in the space below the chapter number, jot down at least two questions you hope to answer through reading the chapter.

OBJECTIVE

Through this lesson, you will develop strategies for understanding writing in which one of the author's purposes is to express his or her opinions.

INTRODUCTION—READING OPINIONS

At times authors write with the intent to state their opinions or judgments and perhaps to persuade you, the reader, to accept their point of view. Newspaper editorials, syndicated columns, political and social cartoons, and letters to the editor are forums for judgmental and persuasive writing. So are film and book reviews. Reading these pieces, in most cases you know you are dealing with opinion even though the authors may include explanations, narrations, and descriptions to support their opinions.

Opinions and judgments are found in a variety of other writing. Authors may have as their primary intent to explain or give an account. However, they color the explanation or account with their feelings about the subject. Those feelings give a point of view, or a *bias,* to their writing. Actually it is very difficult for writers to avoid bias and be completely impartial in writing. Writers' personal experiences serve as sieves through which they filter information as they write.

Reading to Detect Opinion and Bias

From what you have just read, you know that a writer can communicate opinions as well as facts and that his or her feelings toward the subject can color his or her interpretation of the facts. What strategies can you, the reader, use to detect that the author is presenting opinion rather than fact? What strategies can you use to detect an author's personal bias toward the subject, especially when that point of view is not explicitly set forth?

A first strategy is to identify the kind of piece you are reading. Ask: Is this an editorial? A column from the opinion page? A book or film review? A letter-to-the-editor? If the answer to this question is yes, you are probably working with opinion in some form or other. A related strategy is to identify who the publisher and writer are. Ask: Is the publisher of this an organization or group with a known point of view? Is the author of the piece known for supporting a particular view? Is he or she a well-known authority in that field? What background does the author bring to the writing of the piece? For example, a selection published by an antiwar group and written by a leading pacifist is likely to contain opinion and reflect an antiwar point of view, either explicitly or implicitly.

A second strategy is to look for words that indicate that an author is dealing with opinion rather than fact. Some of these clue words are rather obvious signals of opinion-giving. An author states:

> I believe   I feel   I like   I think

Other words tell that the author is advocating a particular course of action:

> We should   You ought to
> You should have   It would have been better to

Other words communicate an explicit evaluative message similar to the message carried by the grades A, B, C, D, and F assigned by professors:

unacceptable	acceptable	more acceptable
good	better	best
invalid	least valid	valid more valid
valuable	very valuable	invaluable
worthy	worthless	worthwhile
well done	poorly done	
unique	marvelous	terrible outrageous

There are hundreds of words like these that writers use in expressing judgments.

A third strategy is to think about an author's choice of words and what message he or she is communicating through the specific words chosen. Words often communicate an implied, or associated, meaning that goes beyond a strict dictionary definition. The implied meaning that a word carries is called *connotation*. The literal dictionary meaning (without the feelings and personal associations that people bring to a word) is *denotation*.

Some words communicate a positive connotation, others communicate a negative connotation, and others have no particular connotation. Actually it is a rare word that does not carry some positive or negative message to someone. A person's past experiences with words affect his or her personal view of a word—whether that word carries a positive or negative connotation or whether it is relatively neutral in the feelings it communicates.

Consider these three common words: *thin, slim,* and *skinny.* Of them, which communicates the most positive view, or carries a positive connotation? Which communicates the most negative view? Which is rather neutral in the feeling communicated? On the lines below, write the three words from most negative to most positive:

Most Negative Word **Neutral Word** **Most Positive Word**

1. _____ 2. _____ 3. _____

If an author decides to use the word *slim* in describing a person, what message is he or she sending? In contrast, if he or she selects the word *skinny,* what is the message?

Consider these pairs of words. In each case, circle the one that carries the more positive message.

egghead	genius
He-man's Shop	Fat-man's Shop
hard worker	grind
changed his mind	waffled on the issues

Consider these sets of words. In each case, circle the one that carries the most positive message. In these cases, there is really no right answer.

beautiful	gorgeous	pretty
pushy	persistent	dedicated
delicious	tasty	scrumptious
steaming	hot	scalding

As you read, you should keep alert for words such as these that carry particularly positive or negative connotations. They are clear clues to an author's point of view, or bias.

A fourth strategy is to ask: Is there another way to view the facts? Is there another side to the question? How would someone on the other side have described the situation, place, or person in question? How would someone on the other side have told the story?

Reading to Assess the Validity of a Judgment

Once you have identified a selection as one containing an opinion or judgment, your next step is to clarify in your own mind what the author is saying and how he or she is supporting the position he or she is taking. Generally a well-formulated judgment includes both the author's opinion and some kind of support for that opinion. In assessing the validity of a judgment, therefore, you must consider the quality and extent of that argument—the facts the author musters in support of his or her point of view.

In this context, you must ask as you read: What is this writer advocating? Answering this question helps you identify the main idea of the selection as well as the writer's basic opinion on the topic.

You must also ask: What facts (if any) does the author use to support his or her judgment? Does he or she organize those facts in a clear fashion? Does he or she present a logical argument?

And finally you must ask yourself: How do I feel about this topic? Do I agree with the writer? Disagree? Do I "buy" his or her argument? Why? Why not? Should I reserve judgment on this issue because the argument is insufficient to convince me either way? In reading opinion and judgment, you should at some point assess your own feelings on the topic. To help you grasp a writer's opinion and the facts he or she is using to support it and to arrive at your own opinion, you may find it useful to record on a guide such as the one in Figure 14.1.

Strategies for Understanding Opinions and Judgments

In the selections you read next, keep asking yourself the questions identified in the section above. Apply these strategies:

- Consider the kind of piece you are reading, the background the author brings to his or her topic, and the orientation of the publisher.
- Identify words that indicate judgment or opinion.
- Note words that communicate positive or negative connotations.
- Ask yourself if there is another way to view the facts.
- State to yourself the author's position relative to the topic.
- Assess the argument (if any) that the author presents in support of his or her position.
- Identify your own feelings on the topic.

In short, as you read, you carry out a conversation with yourself in your head, asking and answering questions as you go along. Do this as you read the next three selections.

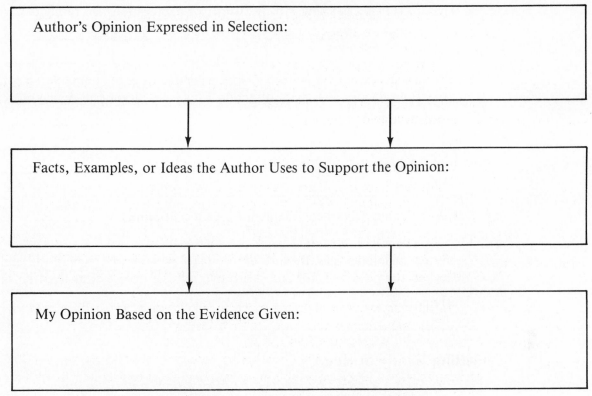

Figure 14.1 *A Guide for Recording Opinions*

SELECTION 1: THE EIGHT BEST PRESIDENTS— AND WHY

Expanding Your Vocabulary for Reading

Using context and word-structure clues, figure out the meaning of the underlined words. Check your ideas in the glossary. Record the meaning of the terms in the spaces given.

1. By limiting himself to two terms, Washington set a <u>precedent</u> that other presidents followed and was not broken for many years. _____

   _____

2. After years of peace and prosperity, people got <u>complacent</u> and began to believe that good times would last forever. _____

   _____

3. The rebels were <u>roundly</u> beaten by the well-trained troops. Few escaped injury or death. _____

   _____

4. The student took the job out of <u>economic</u> necessity; her financial condition required it. _____

   _____

5. That executive was known for his words of <u>deprecation</u>. He rarely offered praise to his employees. _____

_____

6. The business executives formed a <u>trust</u>, a combination of companies to control the production and price of <u>goods</u>. This is an illegal economic practice in this country. _____

_____

7. The Romans built a <u>pantheon</u> to honor their gods. _____

_____

8. I do not want a <u>synthetic</u> diamond; I want a genuine one. _____

_____

9. During the middle ages, the lord of the manor was the <u>sovereign</u> of the land. He had the power of life and death over all the people who lived on his estate. _____

_____

Getting Ready to Read

Preview the selection by reading the title, author, and subheadings.

• What is the topic of the article? _____
• What do you know about the author of the selection?

_____

_____

• What hint does the title give you as to the nature of the selection? Is it going to be mostly fact or opinion? How do you know? _____

_____

• Write one question that you would hope to answer through reading the selection by Truman. _____

_____

Reading with Meaning

Read each section of the selection. Keep asking yourself: What is Truman's judgment of this United States president? What words does Truman use that tell me he is presenting his opinion? What facts does he give to support his opinion? Answer the questions in the outer margin after reading each subsection.

THE EIGHT BEST PRESIDENTS—AND WHY
Harry S. Truman

George Washington

There isn't any question about Washington's greatness. If his Administration had been a failure, there would have been no United States. He had all the background that caused him to know how to make it work, because he had worked under the Continental Congress. Some Presidents have limited their roles to being administrators of the laws without being leaders. But Washington was both a great administrator and a great leader.

I guess, in fact, that the only anti-Washington thing I can say is that he made a mistake when he established the precedent of the two-term Presidency, and even there he had a good personal reason for wanting that, at least for himself. He was attacked viciously by the press of his day; he was called so many terrible things that he told friends even during his first term that he wasn't going to run again. But Thomas Jefferson and James Madison and Alexander Hamilton persuaded him to go ahead and serve a second term and finally he did. After he'd gotten through his second term, though, he made up his mind that he just wouldn't take it anymore, and he quit. That established the precedent. . . . (210 words)

Thomas Jefferson

Jefferson also had his share of press criticism and people who didn't like him, and I wonder how many people remember our history and realize how close Jefferson came to losing the election in 1800, and how close Aaron Burr came to being our third President. . . .

Jefferson was called a runaway President because he pushed through our purchase of Louisiana over a lot of opposition. I think Jefferson's purchase of Louisiana was one of the best decisions ever made because, if we hadn't taken over Louisiana, then either Britain, France or Spain would have owned it and our country would have ended at the Mississippi River, whereas the greatest part of our development has been by our ability to expand beyond the Mississippi. I don't like this talk about runaway Presidents, because the truth is that a President just does what he has to do. (149 words)

Andrew Jackson

Jackson was elected after a period of what they called in James Monroe's time "the era of good feeling." Well, when the era of good feeling got to feeling too good, meaning that the

1. Truman's opinion of Washington:

2. Clue words that tell you are dealing with opinion:

3. Reasons Truman gives to support his opinion:

4. Truman's opinion of the Louisiana Purchase:

5. Clue words that tell you are dealing with opinion:

6. Reasons Truman gives to support his opinion:

7. Truman's opinion of Jackson:

8. Clue words that tell you are dealing with opinion:

9. Reasons Truman gives to support his opinion:

10. Truman's opinion of Polk:

11. Clue words that tell you are dealing with opinion:

12. Reasons Truman gives to support his opinion:

13. Truman's opinion of Lincoln:

people and the government became too complacent and too lazy, why, the country went to the dogs, as it has always done. You have got to have opposition if you're going to keep a republic going. Old Jackson remedied that, and he did it in a way that was perfectly satisfactory to all concerned. The economic royalists, the favored few, had control of the government by controlling the finances of the country. A man named Nicholas Biddle and his Bank of the United States had all the government's money, and Jackson took the money away from him and in effect put all the dollar bills back into the Treasury of the United States, where they ought to be, by spreading the funds into various state banks. And, of course, he was roundly abused for doing things of that sort. (177 words)

James Knox Polk

This choice may surprise some people. Polk isn't much thought about these days. First, he exercised his powers of the Presidency as I think they should be exercised. He was President during the Mexican War, in an age when the terrible burden of making decisions in a war was entirely in the hands of the President. And when that came about, he decided that that was much more important than going to parties and shaking hands with people.

Second, he bought the Southwest part of the country for just about the same price that Jefferson paid for Louisiana; and third, he did something that most of the rest of us who were Presidents weren't able to do: He decided when he went in there that he would only serve one term, and that's what he did. He knew exactly what he wanted to do in a specified period of time and did it, and when he got through with it he went home. He said a moving thing on his retirement: "I now retire as a servant and regain my position as a sovereign." He was right, absolutely right. I've been through it, and I know. (201 words)

Abraham Lincoln

Lincoln was a strong executive who saved the government, saved the United States. He was a President who understood people, and, when it came time to make decisions, he was willing to take the responsibility and make those decisions, no matter how difficult they were. He knew how to treat people and how to make a decision stick, and that's why his is regarded as such a great Administration.

Carl Sandburg and a lot of others have tried to make something out of Lincoln that he wasn't. He was a decent man, a good politician, and a great President, and they've tried to build up things that he never even thought about. I'll bet a dollar and a half that if you read Sandburg's biography of Lincoln, you'll find things put into Lincoln's mouth and mind that never even occurred to him. He was a good man who was in the place where he ought to have been at the time important events were taking place, but when they write about him as though he belongs in the pantheon of the gods, that's not the man he really was. He was the best kind of ordinary man, and when I say that he was an ordinary man, I mean that as high praise, not deprecation. That's the highest praise you can give a man, that he's one of the people and becomes distinguished in the service that he gives other people. He was one of the people, and he wanted to stay that way. And he was that way until the day he died. One of the reasons he was assassinated was because he didn't feel important enough to have the proper guards around him at Ford's Theatre. (292 words)

Grover Cleveland

At least Cleveland was a great President in his first term; in his second term, he wasn't the same Grover Cleveland he was to begin with. Cleveland reestablished the Presidency by being not only a Chief Executive but also a leader. Cleveland spent most of his time in his first term working on bills that came from the Congress, and he vetoed a tremendous pile of bills that were passed strictly for the purpose of helping out people who had voted for the Republican ticket. He also saw to it that a lot of laws passed, if he felt those laws were needed for the good of the general public, even if the laws weren't popular with some members of the Congress.

For the most part, however, Cleveland was a considerably less impressive man in his second term. He had a terrible time with strikes, and he called out the soldiers, and they fired on the strikers. It was also during Cleveland's second

14. Clue words that tell you are dealing with opinion:

15. Reasons Truman gives to support his opinion:

16. Truman's opinion of Cleveland:

17. Clue words that tell you are dealing with opinion:

18. Reasons Truman gives to support his opinion:

term that a number of smaller companies got together and formed great big companies for the suppression of competition. That's why I say Cleveland was a great President only in his first term. (200 words)

Woodrow Wilson

19. Truman's opinion of Wilson:

I've been asked which Presidents served as models for me when I was President myself, and the answer is that there were three of them. Two were Jefferson and Jackson, and the third was Woodrow Wilson. In many ways Wilson was the greatest of the greats. He established the Federal Reserve Board. He established the Federal Trade Commission. He didn't make a great publicity stunt of being a trustbuster, the way Teddy Roosevelt did, but the trust situation was never really met until Wilson became President. Wilson also established the League of Nations, which didn't succeed but which served as a blueprint for the United Nations, which might succeed yet, despite its problems.

20. Clue words that tell you are dealing with opinion:

21. Reasons Truman gives to support his opinion:

All a good President tries to do is accomplish things for the good of the people, and if you want to call that liberal, then I'm with you. I guess the best way to describe Wilson, if I've got to use a label, is to say that he was a common-sense liberal. He wasn't one of these synthetic liberals who aren't very liberal to people who think differently from the way they do. He was a genuine liberal who used his heart and his brain. (202 words)

Franklin Delano Roosevelt

22. Truman's opinion of Roosevelt:

It goes without saying that I was highly impressed by him for a thousand reasons, but a main reason is that he inherited a situation that was almost as bad as the one Lincoln had, and he dealt with it. And he was always able to make decisions. Presidents have to make decisions if they're going to get anywhere, and those Presidents who couldn't make decisions are the ones who caused all the trouble.

23. Clue words that tell you are dealing with opinion:

It took a President who understood the United States and the world, like Roosevelt, to come along and start to get the country back on its feet again in the Depression, and also to make Americans remember that we're a world power and have to act like a world power.

We also, of course, got the United Nations as a result of Roosevelt's Administration and mine, which is exactly what the League of Nations was supposed to be in the first place. I'm not saying that the United Nations is a perfect organization, or ever will be. It's far from flawless, and it's weak in many ways. But at least it's a start. (193 words)

24. Reasons Truman gives to support his opinion:

Checking for Understanding

Place an F *before statements of fact, an* O *before statements of opinion.*

_____ 1. George Washington was the first president of the United States.

_____ 2. Thomas Jefferson was elected president in 1800.

_____ 3. Washington was both a great administrator and a great leader.

_____ 4. You have got to have opposition if you're going to keep a republic going.

_____ 5. A good president is going to get criticized.

_____ 6. Jackson remedied the situation in a way that was satisfactory to everyone.

_____ 7. When Polk said, "I now retire as a servant and regain my position as a sovereign," he was right, absolutely right.

_____ 8. The Louisiana Purchase occurred during Jefferson's administration.

_____ 9. Lincoln was a strong executive.

_____ 10. Lincoln was an ordinary man.

_____ 11. Cleveland was a great president during his first term, but a poor one in his second term.

_____ 12. Cleveland spent a great deal of time working on bills that came from Congress.

_____ 13. Wilson helped establish the League of Nations.

_____ 14. Wilson was a genuine liberal who used his heart and his brain.

_____ 15. Franklin Roosevelt was a great president because he was always able to make decisions.

_____ 16. The United Nations is far from flawless and is weak in many ways.

_____ 17. Truman believed that Woodrow Wilson was a great president.

_____ 18. Truman believed that big companies were not good for the country.

_____ 19. Big companies are not good for the country.

_____ 20. Wilson was the greatest of the greats.

Reviewing Vocabulary

Select several words from the selection vocabulary to include in your personal vocabulary list to use in reading and writing. Then place the words from this list in the sentence slots. Use each word only once.

a. complacent	d. pantheon	g. sovereign
b. deprecatory	e. precedent	h. synthetic
c. economic	f. roundly	i. trusts

1. Before the exam, the student was far from _____ ; he had not studied and he feared he would fail.

2. The _____ situation in the country was questionable; interest rates and unemployment were high.

3. I buy only genuine articles. Do not try to sell me something that is _____ .

4. The _____ had many servants to do her bidding.

5. That teacher is not known for praising his students. Rather he has a reputation for making _____ remarks.

6. The tennis star was _____ beaten in the championship match. Right from the beginning, he didn't have a chance.

7. Going into the basilica in Florence, I felt as though I was entering the _____ of the gods.

8. During Cleveland's administration, smaller companies got together to form _____ to suppress competition.

9. That court case set the _____ for the cases to follow. Future judges referred to that case in making their decisions.

Writing from Reading

Of the eight presidents selected by Truman as great, which one do you believe was the greatest? Write a paragraph in which you present your opinion and support that opinion with facts.

Truman is very explicit in the way he expresses his opinions. He also writes in a very clear, straightforward way. You could say that he is "up front," which is an opinion and not a fact. You will have to read the next selection more closely, for the author uses a more technical way of writing and you may not be as aware that he is dealing with opinion.

SELECTION 2: SOVIET REFORM REFLECTS TRAGEDY OF THE REVOLUTION

Expanding Your Vocabulary for Reading

Using context clues and word-structure clues, figure out the meaning of each underlined word. Check your ideas in the glossary and record the meaning of the term in the space given.

1. The situation became intolerable; there was just no way that I could take it any longer. _____

_____

2. During their teens, many adolescents experience a sense of alienation from their parents. _____

_____

3. There was a discrepancy between the amount the bank said was in my account and the amount I calculated to be there. _____

_____

4. The idea that he suggested was <u>sterile</u>; it had no life to it at all and would have gotten us nowhere. _____

_____

5. Her <u>orthodox</u> position on the issue was narrow and conventional; she would tolerate no change. _____

_____

6. The way he acted toward his friend was marked by <u>aberrations</u> from the normal way of behaving. _____

_____

7. The woman joined the group under the <u>guise</u> of friendship when she was really out to undermine the organization. _____

_____

8. A <u>literate</u> person can read and write; an illiterate one cannot. _____

_____

9. A <u>rational</u> person is both sensible and reasonable; an irrational person acts without reason or sound judgment. _____

_____

10. Don't <u>mutilate</u> the computer card by bending, folding, or marking on it.

_____

_____

In the article you will also encounter a few words that are more technical. The word *emancipate* means "to free." Do you remember that Lincoln signed the Emancipation Proclamation that freed the slaves? A *serf* is a person who must serve another. During medieval times, serfs belonged with the land and had to serve the lord of the land. The *intelligentsia* are intellectuals of the society. *Doctrinaire* means holding to a group of principles in a narrow, unyielding way.

Getting Ready to Read

The article you will read here is from the "Viewpoint" page of a newspaper. It is written by William Pfaff, a well-known political commentator. Preview it by reading the title and the first and last paragraphs.

- What is the topic of the article? _____
- What do you predict will be Pfaff's view of Soviet reform? _____

_____

- What do you know about the topic? _____

_____

- What purpose will you keep in mind as you read it? What question will you try to answer? _____

_____

Reading with Meaning

Read the selection. Keep asking yourself: What is Pfaff's judgment about the Russian Revolution? What words does he use that tell he is dealing with opinion? What facts does he cite to support his judgment? Answer the questions in the outer margin as you finish the related paragraph.

SOVIET REFORM REFLECTS TRAGEDY OF THE REVOLUTION

William Pfaff

1. What is Pfaff's view of the Russian Revolution?

2. Circle the words that give Pfaff's opinion.

3. Circle the words in this paragraph that communicate a negative view of Russia.

4. How does Pfaff view the outcomes of the Russian Revolution?

5. Circle sentences that support that view.

6. Circle two words that carry a very negative connotation, or message.

7. How does Pfaff view the "life of the mind" in Russia during the last seventy years?

The Soviet Union has been celebrating the 70th anniversary of the Russian Revolution—but what is there to celebrate? The revolution cruelly failed Russia.

The leader of the Soviet Union, Mikhail Gorbachev, draws world attention today not because he presides over a society of brilliance, accomplishment and popular well being, but because of his determination to rescue his country from what he describes as "a pre-crisis situation" marked by aberrations . . . in the social, spiritual and moral spheres," "alienation and immorality" and a discrepancy between socialist principles and everyday reality that is "becoming intolerable."

The measures of reform Gorbachev urges represent, he says, "the biggest step in developing socialist democracy since the October Revolution." Yet what is the balance sheet of the October Revolution? It worsened the lot of most ordinary Russians, at least for the period from 1918 to the 1950s. It led to the murder or exile of the country's elites, stifling its creative powers and ruining an intelligentsia whose 19th and early 20th century accomplishments in the novel, music, the dance, theater, chemistry, mathematics and medicine had been as imposing as anything any nation has ever achieved.

The successors to those Russians, during the decades after the revolution, were imprisoned, exiled to Siberia or murdered. A stupid and sterile political orthodoxy was imposed, worse than anything that existed under the czars. Even today original and gifted people in the Soviet Union are cautious when they express themselves in public.

For 70 years, the life of the mind has had to be conducted in secret in the Soviet Union, in unpublished and unpublishable novels and essays, unproduced plays, unscreened or mutilated films, unexhibited paintings. All of this is well known to Russians themselves. If they do not say so, this is not only because to do so still may be dangerous, but because it seems intolerable to confront the waste of it all.

Russian industry and the economy were in progress the years before the war. Russia was the most rapidly developing nation in Europe. The subsequent crippling of the economy resulted from the world war and the civil war and destructive Western interventions that followed the revolution, but it also followed from the ignorance and doctrinaire arrogance of Vladimir Lenin and his associates. They knew little of how a society and economy really functioned.

Lenin wrote that "the great majority" of modern industrial and administrative functions "have become enormously simplified and reduced, in practice, to very simple operations such as registration, filing and checking. Hence they will be quite within the reach of every literate person. . . . " Any worker could run a power station.

In practice, this belief created a centrally planned command economy which, in the guise of rationality, produced a system without rationality, where today it is all but impossible to discover real costs, real margins, real demand, real markets. It produced the disaster of agricultural collectivization, which cripples Soviet farm production to the present day.

Russia in 1914 was badly and oppressively governed. The middle classes were largely excluded from power. The serfs had been emancipated but still lived in medieval conditions. The way the country worked was only painfully changing.

It was changing, though, and if there had been no world war and no October Revolution, and the evolutionary forces at work in the society had not been suddenly cut off, it is reasonable to think that Russia—and Russians— would today be far better off than they actually are.

It didn't happen that way. Instead there was world war, revolution, collectivization, Stalinism, and then another war. And then the Cold war.

Max Beloff, the British historian of Soviet Russia, wrote more than 20 years ago that little remains there "to attest to the fact that one is present at the building of what once was heralded as 'a new civilization.'"

8. What is Pfaff's opinion of Russia before World War II?

9. Circle the sentence that tells you.

10. What is Pfaff's opinion of Lenin and his associates?

11. Circle the words that clearly express the writer's opinion of the Soviet economy.

12. What was wrong in Russia in 1914?

13. Is this fact or opinion?

14. What is Pfaff's judgment of the Russian Revolution?

Nothing has happened in the last two decades to cause one to change that judgment. Today even if Gorbachev succeeds in every single one of the reforms he wants to carry out, he merely will bring his country a little closer to the levels of social, political and material well-being which are taken for granted in Western Europe, Japan and the United States.

What, then, was it all about? The October Revolution was a tragedy—a tragedy because it did begin in noble purpose and an intention to make men better. It is a tragedy which, as Gorbachev demonstrates, despite himself, is not over yet.

15. Circle the words that sum up Pfaff's judgment of the Russian October Revolution.

Checking for Understanding

1. In about what year did the Russian Revolution occur? In what month?

_____

2. What is William Pfaff's point of view on the Russian Revolution? Write a complete sentence or two summarizing it. _____

_____

_____

Figure 14.2   *A Guide for Recording Opinions from the Pfaff Article*

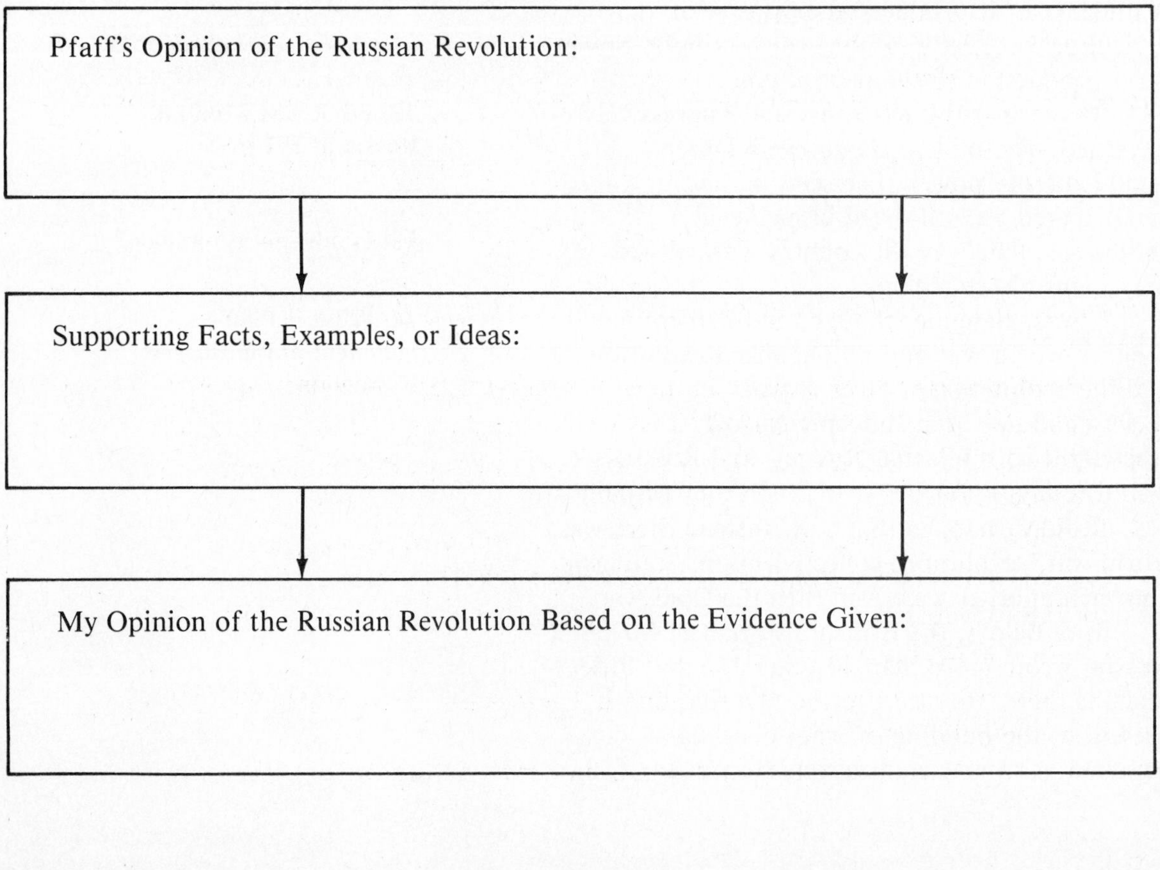

Pfaff's Opinion of the Russian Revolution:

Supporting Facts, Examples, or Ideas:

My Opinion of the Russian Revolution Based on the Evidence Given:

3. What words that carry a negative connotation does Pfaff use that help you see his point of view? _____

4. What argument does Pfaff make to support his viewpoint? Summarize here.

_____

_____

_____

5. According to Pfaff, would Russia have been better today for the people if the Revolution had not occurred? Underline a sentence or two from the selection that supports your answer.

6. Do you agree with Pfaff? Explain why or why not. _____

_____

_____

7. Use your understanding to complete Figure 14.2. Remember to go back and review in this fashion when you study.

8. On the map on page 302 locate the Soviet Union. Is the Soviet Union in Asia? Europe? Both Asia and Europe? Is the land mass of the Soviet Union larger than that of the United States? Of China? Of Saudi Arabia?

Reviewing Important Vocabulary

Fill in the blanks with words from this list. Use context clues to help you.

a. aberrations	e. intolerable	i. rational
b. alienation	f. literate	j. sterile
c. discrepancy	g. mutilate	
d. guise	h. orthodox	

1. The bandages must be kept _____ if you are to prevent bacteria from entering the wound.

2. In a democracy it is important for citizens to be_____ ; they must know how to read and write.

3. In a democracy, citizens must also function in a _____ , or logical, way.

4. Today many people feel a sense of _____ ; they do not feel they belong anywhere.

5. Conditions became almost _____ during the siege. There was not enough food or water for everyone in the city.

6. There was a _____ between what he said happened and what actually happened.

7. After suffering a concussion to the head, he suffered from mental _____ . He thought he saw things that did not exist.

8. She tended to behave in an _____ manner; there was never anything unusual about what she did.

9. He wormed his way into the group under the _____ of friendship; actually he was a spy.

10. Do not _____ the façade of the building with graffiti.

Figure 14.3   *A Map of the USSR, East and Southeast Asia*

SELECTION 3: MAYA ANGELOU'S SCHOOL THOUGHTS

Expanding Vocabulary for Reading

Use context and word-structure clues to figure out the meaning of each underlined term. Check the glossary if you are unsure. Write the meaning in the space provided.

1. The prime minister had an <u>aura</u> of authority that made her stand out from the others in the room. _____

_____

2. The people were so convinced of their <u>invincibility</u> that when they lost the war, they could hardly accept it. _____

_____

3. Until his mother called a halt, the older boy <u>intimidated</u> his younger brother, making him fearful and timid. _____

_____

4. The shopper was struck by the <u>rarefied</u>, or very refined, atmosphere in the elite store. _____

_____

5. I experienced severe <u>trauma</u> each time I recalled the appalling accident.

_____

_____

6. His <u>florid</u> complexion indicated to me that the man had been drinking.

_____

_____

7. The teacher told me to <u>elaborate</u> on what I had said, but I could not think of anything more on the topic. _____

_____

8. The student's interest <u>diminished</u> as the time went on; soon she was asleep.

_____

_____

9. The dollar is the major unit of <u>currency</u> in the United States, whereas the pound is the major unit of currency in England. _____

_____

10. Her behavior was often a bit <u>frivolous</u>; as a result, she got a reputation for not being a serious person. _____

_____

Getting Ready to Read

Preview the name of the title and of the author and the introductory matter before reading.

- What is the selection about? _____
- Do you know anything about the author? If so, note it here.

_____

_____

Reading with Meaning

Read the selection to see how Maya Angelou felt about George Washington High School and her teacher there. As you read, think about similar experiences you had in high school.

SCHOOL THOUGHTS FROM
I KNOW WHY THE CAGED BIRD SINGS

Maya Angelou

In this selection, Maya Angelou describes her experiences, first in her local high school and then in George Washington High School in San Francisco.

Although my grades were very good (I had been put up two semesters on my arrival from Stamps), I found myself unable to settle down in high school. It was an institution for girls near my house, and the young ladies were faster, brasher, meaner and more prejudiced than any I had met at Lafayette County Training School. Many of the Negro girls were, like me, straight from the South, but they had known or claimed to have known the bright lights of Big D (Dallas) or T Town (Tulsa, Oklahoma), and their language bore up their claims. They strutted with an aura of invincibility, and along with some of the Mexican students who put knives in their tall pompadours they absolutely intimidated the white girls and those Black and Mexican students who had no shield of fearlessness. Fortunately, I was transferred to George Washington High School.

The beautiful buildings (of George Washington High) sat on a moderate hill in the white residential district, some sixty blocks from the Negro neighborhood. For the first semester, I was one of three Blacks in the school, and in that rarefied atmosphere I came to love my people more. Mornings as the streetcar traversed my ghetto I experienced a mixture of dread and trauma. I knew that all too soon we would be out of my familiar setting, and Blacks who were on the streetcar when I got on would all be gone and I alone would face the forty blocks of neat streets, smooth lawns, white houses and rich children.

In the evenings on the way home the sensations were joy, anticipation and relief at the first sign which said BARBECUE or DO DROP INN or HOME COOKING or at the first brown faces on the streets. I recognized that I was again in my country.

In the school itself I was disappointed to find that I was not the most brilliant or even nearly the most brilliant student. The white kids had better vocabularies than I and, what was more appalling, less fear in the classrooms. They never hesitated to hold up their hands in response to a teacher's question; even when they were wrong they were wrong aggressively, while I had to be certain about all my facts before I dared to call attention to myself.

George Washington High School was the first real school I attended. My entire stay there might have been time lost if it hadn't been for the unique personality of a brilliant teacher. Miss Kirwin was that rare educator who was in love with information. I will always believe that her love of teaching came not so much from her liking for students but from her desire to make sure that some of the things she knew would find repositories so that they could be shared again.

She and her maiden sister worked in the San Francisco city school system for over twenty years. My Miss Kirwin, who was a tall, florid, buxom lady with battleship-gray hair, taught civics and current events. At the end of a term in her class our books were as clean and the pages as stiff as they had been when they were issued to us. Miss Kirwin's students were never or very rarely called upon to open textbooks.

She greeted each class with "Good day, ladies and gentlemen." I had never heard an adult speak with such respect to teenagers. (Adults usually believe that a show of honor diminishes their authority.) "In today's *Chronicle* there was an article on the mining industry in the Carolinas (or some such distant subject). I am certain that all of you have read the article. I would like someone to elaborate on the subject for me."

After the first two weeks in her class, I, along with all other excited students, read the San Francisco papers, *Time* magazine, *Life* and everything else available to me. Miss Kirwin proved Bailey right. He had told me once that "all knowledge is spendable currency, depending on the market."

There were no favorite students. No teacher's pets. If a student pleased her during a particular period, he could not count on special treatment in the next day's class, and that was as true the other way around. Each day she faced us with a clean slate and acted as if ours were clean as well. Reserved and firm in her opinions, she spent no time in indulging the frivolous.

She was stimulating instead of intimidating. Where some of the other teachers went out of their way to be nice to me—to be a "liberal" with me—and others ignored me completely, Miss Kirwin never seemed to notice that I was Black and therefore different. I was Miss Johnson and if I had the answer to a question she posed I was never given any more than the word "Correct," which was what she said to every other student with the correct answer.

Years later when I returned to San Francisco I made visits to her classroom. She always remembered that I was Miss Johnson, who had a good mind and should be doing something with it. I was never encouraged on those visits to loiter or linger about her desk. She acted as if I must have had other visits to make. I often wondered if she knew she was the only teacher I remembered. (946 words)

Checking for Understanding

1. What was Ms. Angelou's opinion of the "Negro girls straight from the South"?

   _____

   _____

2. What evidence does the author present in support of her opinion? _____

   _____

3. How did Ms. Angelou feel as she rode the streetcar to George Washington High School? _____

   _____

4. Describe when you have felt the same way. _____

   _____

5. What was Maya Angelou's opinion of the "white kids" at George Washington High? _____

   _____

6. What evidence does the author present in support of her opinion? _____

   _____

7. What was Ms. Angelou's opinion of her teacher Miss Kirwin? _____

   _____

8. What evidence does she present to support her opinion? _____

   _____

9. How did the students in Miss Kirwin's class learn if they never opened their books? How do you know this? _____

   _____

   _____

10. Someone named Bailey told Angelou that "all knowledge is spendable currency, depending on the market." What did he mean by that? Do you agree? Why? Why not? Support your opinion with reasons. _____

    _____

    _____

Reviewing Key Words

Place the words from this list in the appropriate sentence slots.

a. aura   d. elaborate   g. intimidate   j. trauma
b. currency   e. florid   h. invincibility
c. diminished   f. frivolous   i. rarefied

1. The bully tried to _____ me, but I was not afraid of him.

2. There is an _____ of both strength and gentleness about Maya Angelou; her distinctive air makes her stand out among other writers.

3. If you cannot _____ on that topic, tell me what you know about any other related topic.

4. When the wind _____ and the rain stopped, I knew the storm was over.

5. When I traveled in France, I had to learn to use the French _____ , ____ for there are no dollars and cents in that country.

6. Her _____ behavior annoyed us. We wanted to be serious and she acted in the opposite way.

7. She experienced extreme _____ at the death of her father.

8. In the _____ atmosphere of that elite college, I grew restless for the ordinary happenings I was accustomed to at home.

9. I was never convinced of the _____ of our army. As a result, I was not surprised by the defeat.

10. The speaker was so angry that his face became _____ . I feared that he would have a heart attack.

Select several of the new vocabulary words and enter them into your personal vocabulary list to use in writing and speaking.

Writing About Reading

Do you have a teacher whom you remember from elementary or high school? Following Maya Angelou's model, write a paragraph or two describing that teacher. In your paragraph state your opinion of him or her. To help you get started, first jot down any words that come to mind that describe the teacher. Then build your paragraph using those words.

EXTENDING WHAT YOU HAVE LEARNED

Building a Knowledge Base for Reading

Circle the names of these places on the maps in Figures 10.8, 11.2, and 14.3.

USSR	Philadelphia, Pennsylvania
Europe	Paris, France
Holland, Italy, and Spain	Wisconsin and South Carolina

Applying Reading Strategies

Select an editorial or a syndicated column from a newspaper. Record the title, author, date, and newspaper on an index card. Read the column, applying the strategies for reading persuasive writing. On the card, record the main topic of the column, the point of view of the writer, and the evidence the writer cites in support of the point of view. Decide: Does the author make you agree with him or her?

Extending Your Vocabulary

Select several of the words featured in this chapter to record in your personal vocabulary list. Include a model sentence for each. Try to use your chosen words in speaking and writing.

Writing Opinions

1. Think about an issue that is of current interest. Phrase that issue as a question: for example, Should smoking be banned in all public buildings? Should college tuition be raised? Should candidates for public office be judged on the way they handle their private lives? Decide how you feel about the issue. Write a paragraph or two in which you state your opinion and support that opinion with reasons.

2. Write a brief summary of a book you have read or a film that you have seen. Then express your opinion of the book or film and support your opinion by describing specific things about the film or book that you liked.

15

Interpreting Charts, Graphs, and Diagrams

Before reading the chapter, read the title, the stated objective, and the headings and subheadings. Ask yourself: What is the topic of the chapter? In the space above and beside the chapter number, jot down what you already know about that topic. Then in the space below the chapter number, jot down at least two questions you hope to answer through reading the chapter.

OBJECTIVE

In this chapter, you will learn to interpret data presented visually; specifically, you will learn to read charts, graphs, and diagrams.

INTRODUCTION—CHARTS, GRAPHS, AND DIAGRAMS

An integral part of many textbooks is the accompanying figures, or illustrations. You should consider visual matter briefly during your preview survey. At this stage, just read the captions to get a rough idea as to the kinds of data available in the figures. As you later read the text more thoroughly, you should study each figure at the point where it is referenced in the text (e.g., "See Figure 2.5" or "as shown in Figure 12.4"). Usually figures are numbered sequentially; Figure 4.7 is the seventh figure in Chapter 4.

CHARTS AND TABLES

One way that authors present data is the data chart, a gridlike table with labeled rows and columns. An example is shown in Figure 15.1.

To interpret a grid,

- Read the title or caption on the data chart. The title usually tells you the topic of the chart—what it is about.

- Read the labels on the rows and columns, giving particular attention to the labels indicating the units that apply to numerical data (for example, area given in square miles, population given in millions, numbers given as percentages).

- Analyze the data to find relationships within them: Which is the biggest? The smallest? Which is the first? The last? Which is fastest? The slowest? Which feature is common to all the items? Is there a pattern or trend in the data? What is the chart saying to me? How do the data relate to the information given in the textual part?

Figure 15.1 *Populations on the Land (1987)*

	Area in Square Miles	Percent Cultivated	Population in Millions	Percent Forested
United States	3,615,104	20	243.8	28
U.S.S.R.	8,649,498	10	284.0	42
Netherlands	14,405	23	14.6	8
Brunei	2,228	1	0.2	49
India	1,269,340	51	800.3	21
China	3,705,390	11	1,062.0	14
Egypt	386,660	2	51.9	0
Kenya	224,961	4	22.4	6
Brazil	3,286,475	9	141.5	66

Learning the Strategies

Study the data chart in Figure 15.1. Then answer these questions:

1. The chart tells the reader
   a. the way land is used in countries with reference to their populations.
   b. the need for conservation in diverse countries of the world.
   c. the need for population control in different countries of the world.
   d. the relationship between famine and food production in countries of the world.
   e. All of the above are true.

2. The area of the United States is given as 3,615,104. This means that there are
   a. 3,615,104 people in the United States.
   b. 3,615,104 square miles of territory in the United States.
   c. 3,615,104 acres of territory in the United States.
   d. 3,615,104 people in the United States for every square mile of territory.
   e. 3,615,104 people in the United States for every acre of territory.

3. The cultivated area of the United States is listed as 20. This means that
   a. Twenty thousand square miles of territory are under cultivation in the United States.
   b. Twenty million square miles of territory are under cultivation in the United States.
   c. Twenty percent of the land in the United States is under cultivation.
   d. Twenty people live on each square mile of land in the United States.
   e. None of the above are true.

4. The forested percentage of the United States is listed as 28. From this and other information in the chart, you can say that the amount of cultivated land in the United States is
   a. greater than the amount of forested land.
   b. less than the amount of forested land.
   c. about the same as the amount of forested land.

5. The actual area of the United States that is forested is
   a. 3,615,104 square miles.
   b. 723,020.8 square miles.
   c. 1,012,229.12 square miles.
   d. 48,760,000 square miles.
   e. 68,264.000 square miles.

6. The population of the United States is listed as 243.8. This means that
   a. 243.8 people lived in the United States in 1987.
   b. 243,800 people lived in the United States in 1987.
   c. 2,438,000 people lived in the United States in 1987.
   d. 243,800,000 people lived in the United States in 1987.
   e. 243,800,000,000 people lived in the United States in 1987.

Now check your answers to 1 through 6.

1. The answer to the first question is "a." The chart tells the reader the way the land is used in different countries in reference to their population. You

know this from the title of the chart and from the fact that the labels at the heads of the columns are "Population in Millions," "Area in Square Miles," "Percent Cultivated," and "Percent Forested." No data tell you definitively that there is need for conservation or population control. There are no data on famine. If you picked one of the other options in question 1, beware of reading too much into a chart.

2. The answer to question 2 is "b"; there are 3,615,104 square miles of territory in the United States. You get this fact by reading the datum in the row labeled "United States" and the column labeled "Area in Square Miles." The number in this slot of the grid is 3,615,104. In reading that fact, you must affix the numerical label to it—in other words, 3,615,104 square miles. This shows that the numerical labels on the grid are important. They tell you how to interpret the data.

3. The answer to question 3 is "c"; 20 percent of U.S. land is cultivated. Again you get this information by applying the numerical label at the head of the column ("Percent Cultivated") to the number in the row labeled "United States."

4. The answer to question 4 is "b"; 28 percent of U.S. land is forested. Comparing that datum to 20 percent under cultivation, you can conclude that less land is cultivated than is forested. Since both pieces of data are given as percentages, you can make this kind of comparison.

5. The answer to question 5 is "c." To find out the actual amount of land that is forested, you must multiply the total square miles of land in the United States (3,615,104) by the percent forested (28 percent, or .28). Thus, .28 of 3,615,104 square miles is 1,012,229.12 square miles. To multiply by a percentage number, you must first change it to its decimal equivalent. By the term *percent,* we mean "parts of 100." Therefore, you must multiply by .28, which really is 28/100.

Now calculate the amount of land that is under cultivation in the United States. First convert the percentage to its decimal equivalent. Then multiply the total square miles in the United States by that decimal equivalent. Do not use the population datum that is given. It does not relate directly to land under cultivation. Make your calculations in the space provided:

Calculation	Amount of Land under Cultivation in United States

6. The answer to question 6 is "d"; the number of people living in the United States in 1987 was 243,800,000. The label on the column marked "Population in Millions" tells you how to handle data in that column. Each pop-

ulation figure given must be multiplied by 1,000,000 (1 million), because each number is in millions.

$$243.8 \times 1,000,000 = 243,800,000$$

Applying the Strategies

Now apply the principles of data-chart reading you have just learned to answer these questions. Use the data from Figure 15.1.

7. The population of the Netherlands is
   a. 146,000,000.
   b. 14,600,000.
   c. 14,400,000.
   d. 144,000,000.
   e. 1,460,000.

8. The number of square miles of cultivated land in Egypt is
   a. 2,000,000.
   b. 1,038,000.
   c. 386,660.
   d. 7,733.2.
   e. 0.

9. The number of square miles of forested land in Egypt is
   a. 2,000,000.
   b. 1,038,000.
   c. 386,660.
   d. 7,733.2.
   e. 0.

10. The population of Brazil is
    a. 3,705,390.
    b. 2,169,073.
    c. 1,277,100.
    d. 1,415,000.
    e. 141,500,000.

You can also compare countries using the data in Figure 15.1. Questions 11–15 are examples of how you can use charts to make comparisons.

11. The country on the chart with the greatest land area is
    a. China
    b. India.
    c. the United States.
    d. the USSR.
    e. Brazil.

12. The country on the chart with the smallest land area under cultivation is
    a. Brunei.
    b. Egypt.
    c. Kenya.
    d. Brazil.
    e. the Netherlands.

13. The country listed in the chart with the greatest number of square miles of forest lands is
    a. Brunei.
    b. the USSR.
    c. Brazil.
    d. the United States.
    e. China.

14. The country listed in the chart with the largest total population is
    a. the United States.
    b. the USSR.
    c. China.
    d. India.
    e. Brazil.

15. The country with the most cultivated land is
    a. India.
    b. the USSR.
    c. the Netherlands.
    d. China.
    e. the United States.

Now correct questions 11–15. The country with the greatest land area is the USSR, answer "d." The chart gives its area as 8,649,498 square miles. Run your eye down the column labeled "Area Square Miles." No other country comes anywhere near this; the second country in size is China, with a land mass of 3,705,390 square miles.

The answer to question 12 is "a." Brunei has the smallest total land mass—2,228 square miles, and it is the country on the chart with the smallest percentage of cultivated land (1 percent). Although you can multiply 2,228 square miles by .01 to get 22.28, you really do not have to do the calculation. If you multiply the smallest land mass by the smallest percent under cultivation, the number you get will represent the smallest of all the countries listed.

The answer to question 13 is "b"—the USSR. You can use the same reasoning as in question 12 here. The USSR has the largest total land mass. It also has 42 percent of its land in forests. Brunei has a larger percent of land in forest—49 percent. But Brunei is very, very small. There is no way it could have more forest land than the USSR. Brazil has a larger percentage (66 percent) of its land in forest, but its total land mass is under half that of Russia. Again, although you can multiply 8,649,498 by .42 to get the forested land of Russia (3,632,789.16 square miles), and you can multiply 3,286,475 by .66 to get the forested land of Brazil (2,169,073.5 square miles), and you can multiply 2,228 by .49 to get the forested land of Brunei (1091.72), you really don't have to do any calculations. You can reason out the relationships in your head.

The answer to question 14 is "c." The population of China is one billion, sixty-two million (1,062,000,000)! India is second, with a population of a little more than eight hundred million.

The answer to question 15 is "b." The USSR has the largest land mass dedicated to agriculture. You can calculate it by multiplying the total land mass of the USSR (8,649,498 square miles) by the percent under cultivation. The result is 864,949.8—one-tenth of the total land. Although India has 51 percent under cultivation, its land mass is considerably smaller than the USSR's; India has only

647,363.4 square miles of cultivated land—a little more than half its total mass. Again, if you are able to juggle numbers mentally, you can estimate rather than carry out the total multiplication.

You can also get another kind of information from the chart in Figure 15.1—the population density—the population per square mile of territory for each nation listed. To find the number of people per square mile of land mass, you divide the total area by the total population. For example, the population per square mile in Brazil is 43.06.

$$\frac{\text{population}}{\text{area in square miles}} \quad \frac{141,500,000}{3,286,475} \quad = 43.06 \text{ people per square mile}$$

43.06 is the number (on average) living within each square mile of Brazil. Of course, there is a problem with that figure; the population is not spread out evenly across the land mass of Brazil. Many people live tightly together in the cities, whereas the vast forest regions of Brazil are sparsely populated.

What is the population density of these countries? Use a calculator to help you find out.

Brunei $\quad \dfrac{\text{population} = 200,000}{\text{area} = 2,228 \text{ sq. miles}} =$

India $\quad \dfrac{\text{population} = 800,300,000}{\text{area} = 1,269,340 \text{ sq. miles}} =$

China $\quad \dfrac{\text{population} = 1,062,000,000}{\text{area} = 3,705,390 \text{ sq. miles}} =$

the Netherlands $\quad \dfrac{\text{population} = 14,600,000}{\text{area} = 14,405 \text{ sq. miles}} =$

16. Of the countries listed below, which has the greatest average population density?
    a. Brunei
    b. India
    c. China
    d. the Netherlands

17. Of the countries listed below, which has the smallest average population density?
    a. Brunei
    b. India
    c. China
    d. the Netherlands

SELECTION 1: LAND AND POPULATIONS

Figure 15.2 presents data on other countries of the world, similar to what you have been considering already. Use those data to answer these questions.

	Area in Square Miles	Percent Cultivated	Population in Millions	Percent Forested
Ethiopia	471,776	11	46.0	23
Bangladesh	55,598	63	107.1	15
Canada	3,851,792	5	25.9	33
Mexico	761,602	13	81.9	23
United Kingdom	94,525	29	56.8	9
Poland	120,726	47	37.8	28
Australia	2,967,896	6	16.2	14
Djibouti	8,494	0	0.3	0

Figure 15.2   *Land and Populations (1987)*

18. The country listed in Figure 15.2 with the largest population is
    a. Australia.
    b. Bangladesh.
    c. Canada.
    d. Mexico.
    e. the United Kingdom.

19. The country in Figure 15.2 with the smallest population is
    a. Australia.
    b. the United Kingdom.
    c. Djibouti.
    d. Ethiopia.
    e. Poland.

20. The country with the smallest land mass under cultivation is
    a. Australia.
    b. the United Kingdom.
    c. Djibouti.
    d. Ethiopia.
    e. Poland.

21. The country with the smallest amount of forested lands is
    a. Australia.
    b. the United Kingdom.
    c. Djibouti.
    d. Ethiopia.
    e. Poland.

22. The country with largest number of square miles dedicated to farming is
    a. Ethiopia.
    b. Bangladesh.
    c. Canada.
    d. Mexico.
    e. Australia.

23. The country with the largest number of square miles in forest is
    a. Ethiopia.

b. Poland.
c. Canada.
d. Mexico.
e. Australia.

24. The country with the greatest number of people per square mile is
    a. Ethiopia.
    b. Bangladesh.
    c. Canada.
    d. Mexico.
    e. the United Kingdom.

SELECTION 2: THE FIFTY STATES OF THE UNITED STATES

Figure 15.3 contains data on the states within the United States. Use the table to answer the following questions. Read the title and the labels on the rows and columns before answering.

25. The state that has the largest land area is
    a. Alaska.
    b. California.
    c. Colorado.
    d. Montana.
    e. Texas.

26. The state that has the smallest land area is
    a. Connecticut.
    b. Delaware.
    c. Hawaii.
    d. New Jersey.
    e. Rhode Island.

27. The first state to enter the Union was
    a. Delaware.
    b. Georgia.
    c. New York.
    d. South Carolina.
    e. Florida.

28. The first states to enter the Union were generally located
    a. along the Pacific Coast.
    b. along the Atlantic Coast.
    c. along the Gulf of Mexico.
    d. along the Mississippi River.
    e. outside the continental United States.

29. The last two states to enter the Union were located
    a. along the Pacific Coast.
    b. along the Atlantic Coast.
    c. along the Gulf of Mexico.
    d. along the Mississippi River.
    e. outside the continental United States.

State	Area in Sq. Miles	Rank in Area	Entered Union	Entry Order	Population 1980	Pop. Rank 1980	Pop. per Sq. Mile
Alabama	51,609	29	1819	22	3,893,888	22	76.7
Alaska	589,757	1	1959	49	401,851	50	.7
Arizona	113,909	6	1912	48	2,718,425	29	23.9
Arkansas	53,104	27	1836	25	2,286,435	33	43.9
California	158,693	3	1850	31	23,667,565	1	151.4
Colorado	104,247	8	1876	38	2,889,735	28	27.9
Connecticut	5,009	48	1783	5	3,107,576	25	637.8
Delaware	2,057	49	1787	1	594,317	47	307.6
Florida	58,560	22	1845	27	9,746,324	7	180.1
Georgia	58,876	21	1788	4	5,463,105	13	94.1
Hawaii	6,450	47	1959	50	964,691	39	150.1
Idaho	83,557	13	1890	43	944,038	41	11.5
Illinois	56,400	24	1818	21	11,426,518	5	205.3
Indiana	36,291	38	1816	19	5,490,260	12	152.8
Iowa	56,290	25	1846	29	2,913,808	27	52.1
Kansas	82,264	14	1861	34	2,364,236	32	28.9
Kentucky	40,395	37	1792	15	3,660,257	23	92.3
Louisiana	48,523	31	1812	18	4,206,312	19	94.5
Maine	33,215	39	1820	23	1,125,027	38	36.3
Maryland	10,577	42	1788	7	4,216,975	18	428.7
Massachusetts	8,257	45	1788	6	5,737,037	11	733.3
Michigan	58,126	23	1837	26	9,262,078	8	162.6
Minnesota	84,068	12	1858	32	4,075,970	21	51.2
Mississippi	47,716	32	1817	20	2,520,638	31	53.4
Missouri	69,686	19	1821	24	4,916,759	15	71.3

Figure 15.3   *A Data Chart on the States of the United States*

30. The most densely populated state is
    a. Connecticut.
    b. New Jersey.
    c. New York.
    d. Massachusetts.
    e. Rhode Island.

31. The most densely populated states tend to be those admitted to the Union
    a. between 1787 and 1790.
    b. between 1800 and 1850.
    c. between 1851 and 1900.
    d. between 1901 and 1950.
    e. after 1950.

State	Area in Sq. Miles	Rank in Area	Entered Union	Entry Order	Population 1980	Pop. Rank 1980	Pop. per Sq. Mile
Montana	147,138	4	1889	41	786,690	44	5.4
Nebraska	77,227	15	1867	37	1,569,825	35	20.5
Nevada	110,540	7	1864	36	800,493	43	7.3
New Hampshire	9,304	44	1788	9	920,610	42	102.4
New Jersey	7,836	46	1787	3	7,364,823	9	986.2
New Mexico	121,666	5	1912	47	1,302,981	37	10.7
New York	49,576	30	1788	11	17,558,072	2	370.6
North Carolina	52,586	28	1789	12	5,881,813	10	120.4
North Dakota	70,665	17	1889	39	652,717	46	9.4
Ohio	41,222	35	1803	17	10,797,624	6	263.3
Oklahoma	69,919	18	1907	46	3,025,290	26	44.1
Oregon	96,981	10	1859	33	2,633,149	30	27.4
Pennsylvania	45,333	33	1787	2	11,863,895	4	264.3
Rhode Island	1,214	50	1790	13	947,154	40	897.8
South Carolina	31,055	40	1788	8	3,121,833	24	103.4
South Dakota	77,047	16	1889	40	690,768	45	9.1
Tennessee	42,244	34	1796	16	4,591,120	17	111.6
Texas	267,338	2	1845	28	14,229,288	3	54.3
Utah	84,916	11	1896	45	1,461,037	36	17.8
Vermont	9,609	43	1791	14	511,456	48	55.2
Virginia	40,817	36	1788	10	5,346,818	14	134.7
Washington	68,192	20	1889	42	4,132,180	20	62.1
West Virginia	24,181	41	1863	35	1,950,279	34	80.8
Wisconsin	56,154	26	1848	30	4,705,521	16	86.5
Wyoming	97,914	9	1890	44	469,557	49	4.8

Figure 15.3   *continued*

32. The state with the greatest number of people is
    a. Alaska
    b. California.
    c. New York.
    d. New Jersey.
    e. Pennsylvania.

32. The most sparsely populated state is
    a. Alaska.
    b. Arizona.
    c. Hawaii.
    d. North Dakota.
    e. South Dakota.

PICTOGRAPHS

A pictograph is a graph that uses pictures as symbols. Each picture-symbol represents a fixed amount given in the key. Study Figure 15.4. It is a pictograph that shows the population of the key land masses of the world. At the bottom is the key. It tells you that each person symbol on the pictograph stands for one hundred million (100,000,000) people. Incomplete person symbols stand for a part of that number. A half a person symbol stands for fifty million; a quarter of a symbol stands for twenty-five million.

An advantage of a pictograph is that you can make comparisons at a glance because the data are presented visually. A disadvantage is that, when there are parts of a picture symbol, you must interpret the amounts for which they stand. Your interpretation, therefore, is an approximation, not as exact as an answer read from a data chart.

Interpreting a Pictograph

Study the pictograph in Figure 15.4. What is the population of North America, which includes the countries of Canada and the United States? Count the number of symbolic people. There are two people plus a part of a person symbol. That part appears to be larger than a half. Given that each person symbol stands for 100 million people, you would be correct in assuming that the population of North America in 1987 was in the neighborhood of 275 million.

Now read the pictograph to find the following data:

1. the population of Africa _____

2. the population of Latin America _____

3. the population of Asia, excluding China _____

Figure 15.4   *Pictograph of Population of Key Land Masses of the World in 1985*

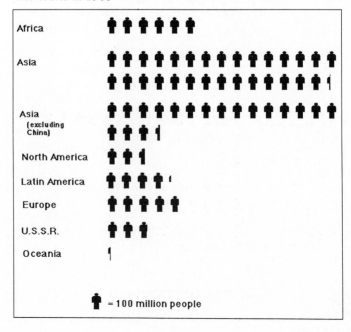

4. the population of China _____

5. the population of Europe _____

6. the population of USSR _____

7. the population of Oceania (which includes Australia and New Zealand) __

8. the land mass with the greatest population _____

9. the land mass with the smallest population _____

Figure 15.5 presents data on the per capita (per person) gross national product (GNP) (in U.S. dollars) for each of the land masses in 1985. Each $ sign stands for $1,000.00. Given that information, you can see that the per capita GNP (which gives a rough idea of the annual wealth of an area) of Oceania is in the neighborhood of 8,300 U.S. dollars. Using Figure 15.5, supply the data required:

10. the per capita GNP of Africa _____

11. the per capita GNP of Latin America _____

12. the per capita GNP of Asia, excluding China _____

13. the per capita GNP of North America _____

14. the per capita GNP of Europe _____

15. the per capita GNP of the USSR _____

16. the land mass with the highest per capita GNP _____

17. the land mass with the lowest per capita GNP _____

Figure 15.5 *Pictograph of Gross National Product (GNP) of Key Land Masses of the World in 1985*

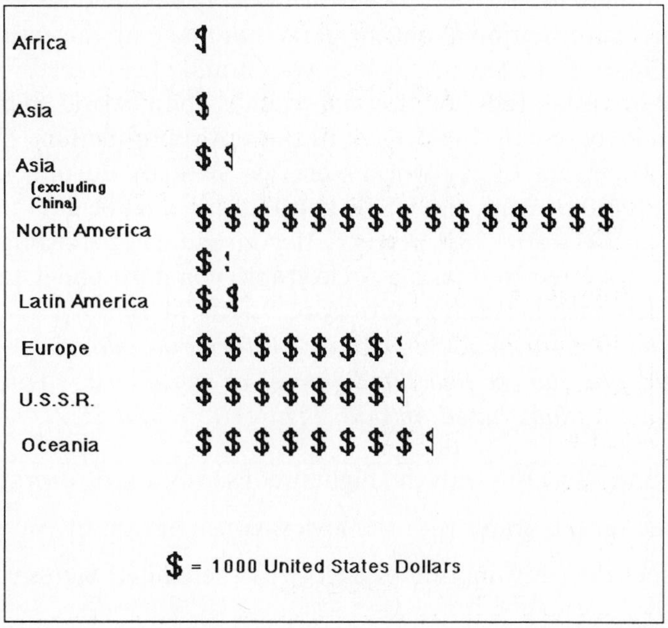

Making a Pictograph

Make a pictograph, using the data in Figures 15.1 and 15.2. To do this, select a symbol to represent what you want to show—perhaps the percent of forested land in a group of countries chosen from the chart. A good symbol in this case is a pine tree. Decide on the percentage of forested land each symbol is to represent. In this case, one pine tree might represent ten percent forested land. Draw your pictograph in the space provided:

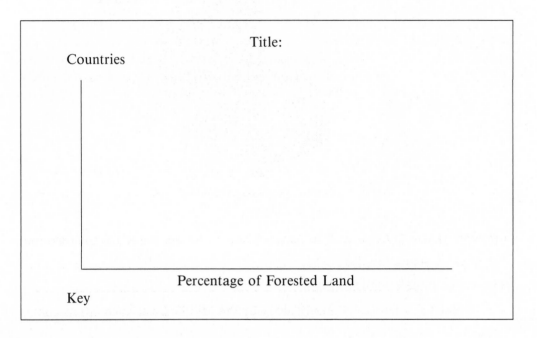

CIRCLE (OR PIE) GRAPHS

A pie graph is a picture that shows percentages. It is based on a circle. The whole circle stands for 100 percent of the data. The individual wedges (or pieces of the pie) give information about the parts that make up the entire pie, or circle.

Study Figure 15.6. The title, which you should always read first when studying any kind of visual, tells you that the graph is about world energy production. The total circle represents 100 percent of the world production. The Middle East produces 19.0 percent of the world's energy, Western Europe 7.4 percent, the United States 23.0 percent, the USSR and Eastern Europe 24.4 percent, and the other areas of the world 26.2 percent. If you add the percentages you get 100 percent. To work effectively with a circle graph, you must understand percentages and realize that each percentage gives you "parts of 100."

Now study Figure 15.7. What kind of information does it give? Yes, reading from the title, you can see that this figure gives world energy consumption data. Answer these questions based on both Figures 15.6 and 15.7:

1. The country or area with the highest consumption of energy _____

2. The area on the graph with the lowest consumption of energy _____

3. How does the consumption of energy by the United States compare with its production? _____

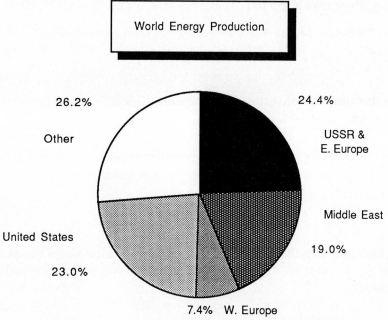

Figure 15.6 *World Energy Production—a Pie Graph*

4. Hypothesize: What does the United States do to get the additional energy resources that it needs? _____

_____

5. How does the consumption of energy by the Middle Eastern countries compare with their production? _____

_____

Figure 15.7 *World Energy Consumption—a Pie Graph*

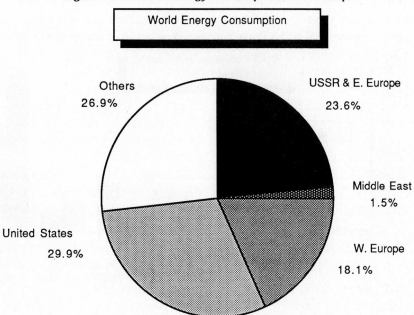

6. Hypothesize: What do the Middle Eastern countries do with the surplus energy they produce? _____

_____

7. Think: What problems can you think of arising from the energy production and consumption situation in the world? _____

_____

As these questions demonstrate, sometimes the reader can go beyond the data presented in a chart or graph to hypothesize and generalize.

BAR GRAPHS

Another way that data are often represented visually is by a bar graph. Each bar on the graph presents a piece of information. Bars can be arranged vertically or horizontally.

Study Figure 15.8. Start by reading the title. What does the graph show? Give the topic of the graph here:

1. _____

Now consider the data. Across the bottom on the horizontal axis are labels that identify the areas of the world for which data are given. Down the left-hand side of the graph on the vertical axis are the numbers (in this case, percentages) that guide you in interpreting each bar. For each country, there are two bars. The solid one gives the population. The dotted one gives food production.

Here is how you read the graph. Asia (excluding the USSR) has about 58 percent of the world's population. It produces 37 percent of the food. A good hypothesis to make at this point is that some areas of Asia will probably have to import food.

Answer these questions based on the graph.

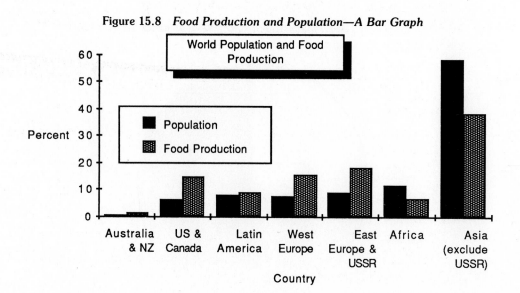

Figure 15.8 *Food Production and Population—A Bar Graph*

2. What percentage of the world's population lives in Australia and New Zealand? _____

3. What percentage of the world's food is produced in Australia and New Zealand? _____

4. Are Australia and New Zealand more likely to be food importers or food exporters? _____

   Explain. _____

   _____

5. What percentage of the world's population lives in Africa?

   _____

6. What percentage of the world's food is produced in Africa?

   _____

7. Are African nations more likely to be food importers or food exporters?

   _____

   Explain your answer. _____

SELECTION 3: IMMIGRATION TO THE UNITED STATES

Read the graph given in Figure 15.9 to get the information to answer the following questions.

1. What kind of information is given in the graph?
   a. world immigration patterns
   b. immigration to the United States 1850–1899
   c. emigration from Europe to the United States, 1850–1899
   d. emigration from Europe and Asia during 1850–1899
   e. All of the above are true.

2. How many people immigrated to the United States during 1890–1899?
   a. 2,000,000
   b. 2,750,000
   c. 3,200,000
   d. 3,650,000
   e. 5,250,000

3. During which decade did the greatest number of people immigrate to the United States?
   a. 1850–1859
   b. 1860–1869
   c. 1870–1879
   d. 1880–1889
   e. 1890–1899

4. During which decade did the smallest number of people come to the United States from other countries?

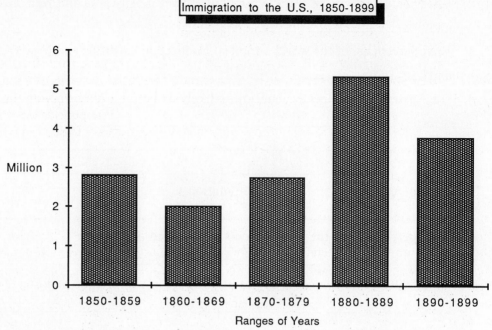

Figure 15.9 *Immigration to the United States—A Bar Graph*

a. 1850–1859
b. 1860–1869
c. 1870–1879
d. 1880–1889
e. 1890–1899

5. How did the number of immigrants to the United States during 1890–1899 compare to the number during 1880–1889?
   a. The number during 1890–1899 was less than that during 1880–1889.
   b. The number during 1890–1899 was greater than that during 1880–1889.
   c. The number during both periods was approximately the same.

6. How did the number of immigrants to the United States during 1850–1859 compare with the number during 1870–1879?
   a. The number during 1850–1859 was much less than that during 1870–1879.
   b. The number during 1850–1859 was much greater than that during 1870–1879.
   c. The number during both periods was approximately the same.

7. Think about the decade in which immigration to the United States was the lowest. Can you account for the low that occurred during that decade? If you can, write a sentence that explains why there was a drop in immigration during that period.

_____

_____

LINE GRAPHS

A line graph is another way of visually representing numerical data, especially data in which there is an element of change that takes place over time. A line graph has two labeled axes, a vertical one and a horizontal one. Figure 15.10 is a line graph showing the same data as the bar graph in Figure 15.9. Note that the number of immigrants is given on the vertical axis, the time periods on the horizontal axis, as in Figure 15.9. Note, too, that it is rather easy to see the ups and downs in immigration on this simple line graph.

Figure 15.11 is another simple line graph. Preview it by reading the title. The topic of the graph is pesticide production in the United States. Look at the labels on the points marked on the vertical axis. They start at the bottom with 100 million pounds of pesticide and extend to 1,600 million pounds of pesticide in even increments of 200 million pounds. That means that there is the same distance on the axis between 200 and 400 million pounds as between 1,400 and 1,600 pounds. Notice that the unit (millions of pounds) is indicated. The author of the graph did not write out the large numbers (e.g., 200,000,000), but used only 200 with the label indicating that each number should be read as "millions of pounds."

Now think about the horizontal axis. It indicates the years for which data are given—in this case, 1947 to 1980. Notice that in general the years are given in increments of five years (1970, 1975, 1980), and that the labeled years are placed beneath marked points on the horizontal axis. Notice again that the space between each marked year point (e.g., between 1970 and 1975 and between 1975 and 1980) is the same.

Figure 15.10   *Immigration to the United States–A Line Graph*

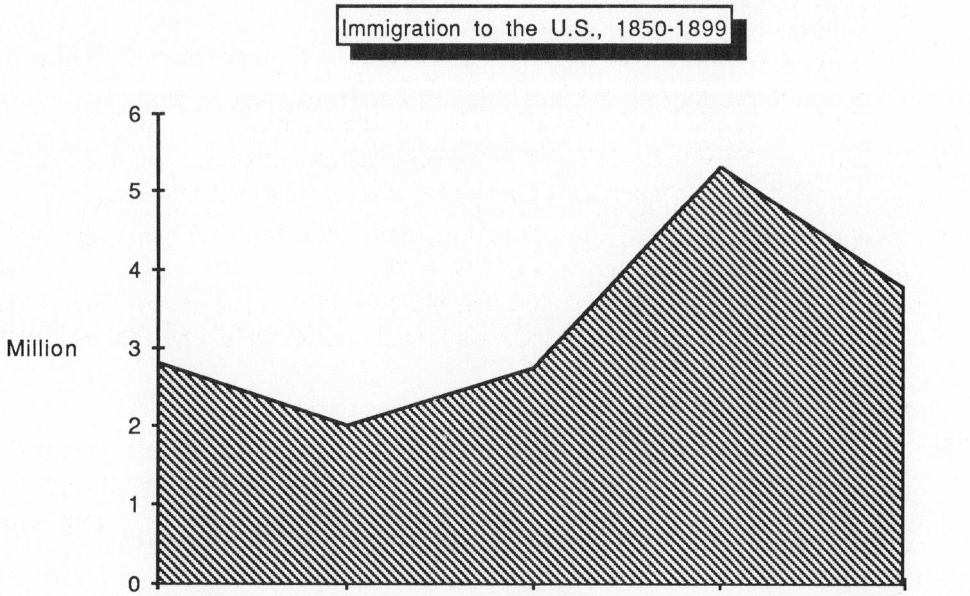

Immigration to the U.S., 1850-1899

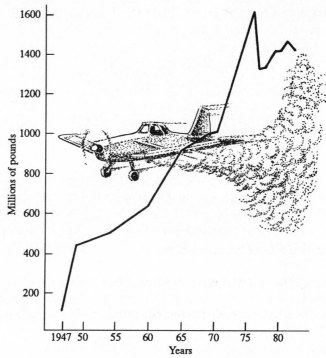

Figure 15.11 *Pesticide Production in the United States—a Line Graph*

Before trying to get information from a line graph, you should read the title and the labels on the axes, including any units indicated.

Now answer these questions based on Figure 15.11:

1. The topic of the graph is
   a. millions of pounds of pesticides.
   b. the United States between 1947 and 1985.
   c. pesticide production in the United States from 1947 to 1985.

2. The 800 written on the vertical axis refers to
   a. 800 people.
   b. 800,000,000 pounds of pesticide.
   c. 800,000,000 people.
   d. 800 pounds of pesticide.

3. The year in which the greatest amount of pesticide was produced in the United States was
   a. 1950.
   b. 1965.
   c. 1974.
   d. 1980.

4. The amount of pesticide produced each year in the United States from 1947 to 1985 tended to
   a. decrease.
   b. increase.
   c. stay the same.

5. The amount of pesticide produced in the United States from 1947 to 1985
   a. went down once during the period.
   b. went down twice during the period.
   c. went down three times during the period.
   d. never went down during the period.

SELECTION 4: WEATHER IN NEW DELHI AND SANTIAGO

Preview the two graphs in Figure 15.12. Read the titles and the labels on the vertical and horizontal axes. Note that each graph has two lines. The top solid line gives the average high temperature in that location. The bottom solid line gives the average low temperature there. Note again that the units on the vertical axis increase in equal increments.

Now study the graph and answer these questions.

1. During what month does the temperature reach its highest point in New Delhi?
   a. April
   b. May
   c. June
   d. July
   e. August

Figure 15.12 *Temperature Highs and Lows in Two Parts of the World—India and Chile*

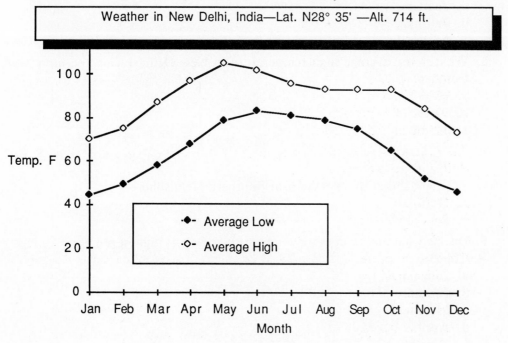

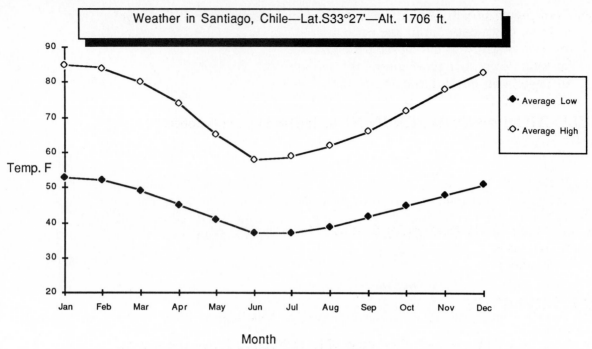

Figure 15.12 *Continued*

2. During what month does the temperature reach its lowest point in New Delhi?
   a. November
   b. December
   c. January
   d. February
   e. March

3. What is the average high temperature in New Delhi during the month of October?
   a. 65°F
   b. 93°F
   c. 105°F
   d. 97°F
   e. 102°F

4. Is New Delhi in the Northern or Southern Hemisphere?
   a. Northern
   b. Southern

5. During what month does the temperature reach its highest point in Santiago, Chile?
   a. January
   b. February
   c. March
   d. April
   e. December

6. During what month does the temperature reach its lowest point in Santiago?
   a. May
   b. June
   c. July
   d. August
   e. September

7. What is the average high temperature in Santiago during October?
   a. 45°F
   b. 66°F
   c. 72°F
   d. 85°F
   e. 83°F

8. Is Santiago in the Northern or Southern Hemisphere?
   a. Northern
   b. Southern

LINE DRAWINGS

As you may have discovered as you tried to answer questions 4 and 8 above, some geographical understanding is helpful in reading and comprehending some graphs. To answer those questions correctly, you had to know that the hottest months are June, July, and August in the Northern Hemisphere. The hottest months are December, January, and February in the Southern Hemisphere. In short, the Northern and Southern Hemispheres experience summer at opposite times of the year.

Study Figure 15.13. It is a line drawing that shows why there are seasons. Answer the following questions based on it.

1. When it is summer in the Northern Hemisphere, the direct rays of the sun strike the
   a. Arctic Circle.

Figure 15.13 *Diagram Showing the Seasons*

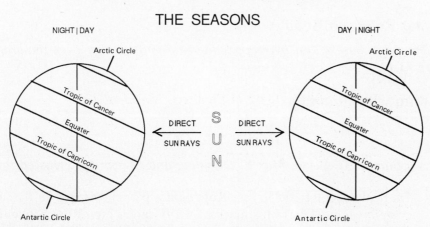

THE SEASONS

SUMMER SOLSTICE. NOON SUN IS DIRECTLY OVERHEAD ON THE TROPIC OF CANCER AT 23-1/2° NORTH LATITUDE. JUNE 21. LONGEST DAY OF THE YEAR FOR THE NORTHERN HEMISPHERE.

WINTER SOLSTICE. NOON SUN IS DIRECTLY OVERHEAD ON THE TROPIC OF CAPRICORN AT 23-1/2° SOUTH LATITUDE. DECEMBER 21. SHORTEST DAY OF THE YEAR FOR THE NORTHERN HEMISPHERE.

    b. Tropic of Cancer.
    c. Equator.
    d. Tropic of Capricorn.
    e. Antarctic Circle.
 2. When it is winter in the Northern Hemisphere, the direct rays of the sun strike the
    a. Arctic Circle.
    b. Tropic of Cancer.
    c. Equator.
    d. Tropic of Capricorn.
    e. Antarctic Circle.
 3. Figure 15.13 indicates that
    a. the earth rotates on its axis.
    b. the earth revolves around the sun.
    c. the earth is tilted on its axis.
    d. All of the above are true.

There is no one strategy to use to understand line drawings. Each drawing has characteristics that make it unique. However, general steps to take include these:

- Read the title.
- Carefully study all labels.
- Explain the drawing to yourself in your own words.

SELECTION 5: ROSE VERSUS COBB

Expanding Your Vocabulary for Reading

You will find the word *era* in this selection. An era is the period of time to which something belongs. For example, you could say that a particular time period was the rock and roll era. An abbreviation you will encounter is *vs.* It stands for the word *versus,* which in sports is used to denote a contest between two players. The word is also used in reference to court cases, such as in the case *Brown* v. *Board of Education, 1954.* In this case, versus is abbreviated as *v.*

Getting Ready to Read

Preview the selection by reading the title and looking over the graphs in Figure 15.14.

Reading with Meaning

ROSE VS. COBB
Samuel C. Certo, Max E. Douglas, and Steward W. Husted

On September 11, 1985, Pete Rose won a permanent spot in baseball history by breaking Ty Cobb's mark of 4,191 career hits. Rose broke the record with two hits (a single and a triple), giving him 4,193 in his twenty-third major league season.

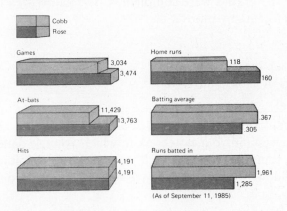

Figure 15.14   *Rose vs. Cobb*

But the career-hit record is just one statistic. How does Rose compare to Cobb in other career statistics? The bar charts below highlight a few of the major areas of comparison. These data were gathered just before Rose broke Cobb's record.

Rose certainly had more opportunities to hit, since he played over 400 more games and was at the plate 2,334 more times than Cobb. Cobb's batting average of .367 seems far greater than Rose's .305. Cobb also surpassed Rose in RBI's.

Many baseball historians claim that you cannot accurately compare players from different eras. It is like comparing Bing Crosby to Bruce Springsteen. For example, in Cobb's era, players' gloves were mittens—compared to the "baskets" that are used today. How many diving catches were made in the 1920s? Today's professional baseball player may face four or five pitchers, since relief specialists have become a vital part of the game. In Cobb's day, relief pitchers were considered mop-up men. Rose also pointed out that he faced the best players of his era, but in Cobb's time black players were excluded from the game.

Needless to say, the comparison of the bar charts [in Figure 15.14] needs to be framed in proper perspective. What about the effect of night games? Longer travel schedule? Better training techniques? This list could go on. How do *you* interpret these statistics?

Checking for Comprehension

1. Who had the greater number of home runs?
   a. Rose
   b. Cobb
2. In terms of one statistic, at the time the graphs were compiled Rose and Cobb had comparable records. What statistic was that?
   a. games played
   b. runs batted in
   c. hits
   d. at-bats

3. At the time the graphs were compiled, Cobb had batted in more runs than had Rose. How many more?
   a. 42
   b. 440
   c. 676
   c. 62

4. Who was the greater player? You decide based on the information in the graphs and any other information you know about these ball players. Then write a paragraph in your notebook in which you use data from the graphs. Start with a topic sentence in which you state your opinion as the main idea. Use your follow-up sentences to give data to support your opinion.

EXTENDING WHAT YOU HAVE LEARNED

Going from Visuals to Words—Part I

Locate a bar or line graph. Study it. Then write a paragraph in which you summarize what the graph is saying. Be ready to share what you have written.

Going from Visuals to Words—Part II

Locate a line drawing. Study it. Then write a paragraph in which you summarize the data presented in the drawing. Be ready to share what you have written.

Going from Visuals to Words—Part III

Locate a map with information of interest to you. Study it. Then write a paragraph in which you summarize the data from the map. Be ready to share what you have written.

Extending Your Knowledge Base

Scan the material in this chapter, including the charts and graphs. Circle on the map in Figures 5.4, 7.2, 11.2, 12.3, 13.2, and 14.2 each place mentioned or listed in the chapter.

Summation

Reading
with Meaning

What have you learned about reading with meaning? In the area surrounding the title on this page, record words, phrases, sentences, and reading strategies that come to your mind.

Calculating Your Reading Rate: Reading Rate Tables and Explanations

To calculate your reading rate:

1. Record your starting time in hours, minutes, and seconds; for example, you might have started at

10 o'clock   55 minutes   31 seconds

2. Read the selection and record your ending time; for example, you might have finished reading at

11 o'clock   5 minutes   10 seconds

3. Subtract your starting time from your ending time to find the time it took you to read the selection:

11 o'clock   5 minutes   10 seconds
<u>10 o'clock   55 minutes   31 seconds</u>
9 minutes   39 seconds

4. Convert your time to a decimal by rounding up to the nearest quarter of a minute, as follows:

60 seconds = 1 minute
45 seconds = .75 minutes
30 seconds = .50 minutes
15 seconds = .25 minutes

In this case, 9 minutes and 39 seconds becomes 9.75 minutes.

5. To find your reading rate, divide the number of words in the selection by your reading time given in minutes—for example:

$$\frac{750 \text{ words}}{9.75 \text{ minutes}} = 77 \text{ reading rate (words per minute)}$$

Or use Table A to find your reading rate. To use the table,

- Locate your reading time in the left-hand column.
- Locate the number of words in the selection in the top row.
- Find your reading rate at the intersection of the selected column and row on the chart.

Reading Rate

						NO.	OF	WORDS																			
		140	160	180	200	220	240	260	280	300	320	340	360	380	400	420	440	460	480	500	520	540	560	580	600	620	640
	2	70	80	90	100	110	120	130	140	150	160	170	180	190	200	210	220	230	240	250	260	270	280	290	300	310	320
	2.25	62	71	80	89	98	107	116	124	133	142	151	160	169	178	187	196	204	213	222	231	240	249	258	267	276	284
	2.5	56	64	72	80	88	96	104	112	120	128	136	144	152	160	168	176	184	192	200	208	216	224	232	240	248	256
	2.75	51	58	65	73	80	87	95	102	109	116	124	131	138	145	153	160	167	175	182	189	196	204	211	218	225	233
	3	47	53	60	67	73	80	87	93	100	107	113	120	127	133	140	147	153	160	167	173	180	187	193	200	207	213
	3.25	43	49	55	62	68	74	80	86	92	98	105	111	117	123	129	135	142	148	154	160	166	172	178	185	191	197
	3.5	40	46	51	57	63	69	74	80	86	91	97	103	109	114	120	126	131	137	143	149	154	160	166	171	177	183
	3.75	37	43	48	53	59	64	69	75	80	85	91	96	101	107	112	117	123	128	133	139	144	149	155	160	165	171
	4	35	40	45	50	55	60	65	70	75	80	85	90	95	100	105	110	115	120	125	130	135	140	145	150	155	160
	4.25	33	38	42	47	52	56	61	66	71	75	80	85	89	94	99	104	108	113	118	122	127	132	136	141	146	151
	4.5	31	36	40	44	49	53	58	62	67	71	76	80	84	89	93	98	102	107	111	116	120	124	129	133	138	142
	4.75	29	34	38	42	46	51	55	59	63	67	72	76	80	84	88	93	97	101	105	109	114	118	122	126	131	135
	5	28	32	36	40	44	48	52	56	60	64	68	72	76	80	84	88	92	96	100	104	108	112	116	120	124	128
TIME	5.25	27	30	34	38	42	46	50	53	57	61	65	69	72	76	80	84	88	91	95	99	103	107	110	114	118	122
	5.5	25	29	33	36	40	44	47	51	55	58	62	65	69	73	76	80	84	87	91	95	98	102	105	109	113	116
	5.75	24	28	31	35	38	42	45	49	52	56	59	63	66	70	73	77	80	83	87	90	94	97	101	104	108	111
IN	6	23	27	30	33	37	40	43	47	50	53	57	60	63	67	70	73	77	80	83	87	90	93	97	100	103	107
	6.25	22	26	29	32	35	38	42	45	48	51	54	58	61	64	67	70	74	77	80	83	86	90	93	96	99	102
	6.5	22	25	28	31	34	37	40	43	46	49	52	55	58	62	65	68	71	74	77	80	83	86	89	92	95	98
DECIMAL	6.75	21	24	27	30	33	36	39	41	44	47	50	53	56	59	62	65	68	71	74	77	80	83	86	89	92	95
	7	20	23	26	29	31	34	37	40	43	46	49	51	54	57	60	63	66	69	71	74	77	80	83	86	89	91
	7.25	19	22	25	28	30	33	36	39	41	44	47	50	52	55	58	61	63	66	69	72	74	77	80	83	86	88
MINUTES	7.5	19	21	24	27	29	32	35	37	40	43	45	48	51	53	56	59	61	64	67	69	72	75	77	80	83	85
	7.75	18	21	23	26	28	31	34	36	39	41	44	46	49	52	54	57	59	62	65	67	70	72	75	77	80	83
	8	18	20	23	25	28	30	33	35	38	40	43	45	48	50	53	55	58	60	63	65	68	70	73	75	78	80
	8.25	17	19	22	24	27	29	32	34	36	39	41	44	46	48	51	53	56	58	61	63	65	68	70	73	75	78
	8.5	16	19	21	24	26	28	31	33	35	38	40	42	45	47	49	52	54	56	59	61	64	66	68	71	73	75
	8.75	16	18	21	23	25	27	30	32	34	37	39	41	43	46	48	50	53	55	57	59	62	64	66	69	71	73
	9	16	18	20	22	24	27	29	31	33	36	38	40	42	44	47	49	51	53	56	58	60	62	64	67	69	71
	9.25	15	17	19	22	24	26	28	30	32	35	37	39	41	43	45	48	50	52	54	56	58	61	63	65	67	69
	9.5	15	17	19	21	23	25	27	29	32	34	36	38	40	42	44	46	48	51	53	55	57	59	61	63	65	67
	9.75	14	16	18	21	23	25	27	29	31	33	35	37	39	41	43	45	47	49	51	53	55	57	59	62	64	66
	10	14	16	18	20	22	24	26	28	30	32	34	36	38	40	42	44	46	48	50	52	54	56	58	60	62	64
	10.3	14	16	18	20	21	23	25	27	29	31	33	35	37	39	41	43	45	47	49	51	53	55	57	59	60	62
	10.5	13	15	17	19	21	23	25	27	29	30	32	34	36	38	40	42	44	46	48	50	51	53	55	57	59	61
	10.8	13	15	17	19	20	22	24	26	28	30	32	33	35	37	39	41	43	45	47	48	50	52	54	56	58	60
	11	13	15	16	18	20	22	24	25	27	29	31	33	35	36	38	40	42	44	45	47	49	51	53	55	56	58
	11.3	12	14	16	18	20	21	23	25	27	28	30	32	34	36	37	39	41	43	44	46	48	50	52	53	55	57
	11.5	12	14	16	17	19	21	23	24	26	28	30	31	33	35	37	38	40	42	43	45	47	49	50	52	54	56
	11.8	12	14	15	17	19	20	22	24	26	27	29	31	32	34	36	37	39	41	43	44	46	48	49	51	53	54
	12	12	13	15	17	18	20	22	23	25	27	28	30	32	33	35	37	38	40	42	43	45	47	48	50	52	53
	12.3	11	13	15	16	18	20	21	23	24	26	28	29	31	33	34	36	38	39	41	42	44	46	47	49	51	52
	12.5	11	13	14	16	18	19	21	22	24	26	27	29	30	32	34	35	37	38	40	42	43	45	46	48	50	51
	12.8	11	13	14	16	17	19	20	22	24	25	27	28	30	31	33	35	36	38	39	41	42	44	45	47	49	50
	13	11	12	14	15	17	18	20	22	23	25	26	28	29	31	32	34	35	37	38	40	42	43	45	46	48	49
	13.3	11	12	14	15	17	18	20	21	23	24	26	27	29	30	32	33	35	36	38	39	41	42	44	45	47	48
	13.5	10	12	13	15	16	18	19	21	22	24	25	27	28	30	31	33	34	36	37	39	40	41	43	44	46	47
	13.8	10	12	13	15	16	17	19	20	22	23	25	26	28	29	31	32	33	35	36	38	39	41	42	44	45	47
	14	10	11	13	14	16	17	19	20	21	23	24	26	27	29	30	31	33	34	36	37	39	40	41	43	44	46
	14.3	10	11	13	14	15	17	18	20	21	22	24	25	27	28	29	31	32	34	35	36	38	39	41	42	44	45
	14.5	10	11	12	14	15	17	18	19	21	22	23	25	26	28	29	30	32	33	34	36	37	39	40	41	43	44
	14.8	9	11	12	14	15	16	18	19	20	22	23	24	26	27	28	30	31	33	34	35	37	38	39	41	42	43
	15	9	11	12	13	15	16	17	19	20	21	23	24	25	27	28	29	31	32	33	35	36	37	39	40	41	43
	15.3	9	10	12	13	14	16	17	18	20	21	22	24	25	26	28	29	30	31	33	34	35	37	38	39	41	42
	15.5	9	10	12	13	14	15	17	18	19	21	22	23	25	26	27	28	30	31	32	34	35	36	37	39	40	41
	15.8	9	10	11	13	14	15	17	18	19	20	22	23	24	25	27	28	29	30	32	33	34	36	37	38	39	41
	16	9	10	11	13	14	15	16	18	19	20	21	23	24	25	26	28	29	30	31	33	34	35	36	38	39	40
	16.3	9	10	11	12	14	15	16	17	18	20	21	22	23	25	26	27	28	30	31	32	33	34	36	37	38	39
	16.5	8	10	11	12	13	15	16	17	18	19	21	22	23	24	25	27	28	29	30	32	33	34	35	36	38	39
	16.8	8	10	11	12	13	14	16	17	18	19	20	21	23	24	25	26	27	29	30	31	32	33	35	36	37	38
	17	8	9	11	12	13	14	15	16	18	19	20	21	22	24	25	26	27	28	29	31	32	33	34	35	36	38
	17.3	8	9	10	12	13	14	15	16	17	19	20	21	22	23	24	26	27	28	29	30	31	32	34	35	36	37
	17.5	8	9	10	11	13	14	15	16	17	18	19	21	22	23	24	25	26	27	29	30	31	32	33	34	35	37
	17.8	8	9	10	11	12	14	15	16	17	18	19	20	21	23	24	25	26	27	28	29	30	32	33	34	35	36
	18	8	9	10	11	12	13	14	16	17	18	19	20	21	22	23	24	26	27	28	29	30	31	32	33	34	36
	18.3	8	9	10	11	12	13	14	15	16	18	19	20	21	22	23	24	25	26	27	28	30	31	32	33	34	35
	18.5	8	9	10	11	12	13	14	15	16	17	18	19	21	22	23	24	25	26	27	28	29	30	31	32	34	35
	18.8	7	9	10	11	12	13	14	15	16	17	18	19	20	21	22	23	25	26	27	28	29	30	31	32	33	34
	19	7	8	9	11	12	13	14	15	16	17	18	19	20	21	22	23	24	25	26	27	28	29	31	32	33	34
	19.3	7	8	9	10	11	12	14	15	16	17	18	19	20	21	22	23	24	25	26	27	28	29	30	31	32	33
	19.5	7	8	9	10	11	12	13	14	15	16	17	18	19	21	22	23	24	25	26	27	28	29	30	31	32	33
	19.8	7	8	9	10	11	12	13	14	15	16	17	18	19	20	21	22	23	24	25	26	27	28	29	30	31	32
	20	7	8	9	10	11	12	13	14	15	16	17	18	19	20	21	22	23	24	25	26	27	28	29	30	31	32
	20.3	7	8	9	10	11	12	13	14	15	16	17	18	19	20	21	22	23	24	25	26	27	28	29	30	31	32
	20.5	7	8	9	10	11	12	13	14	15	16	17	18	19	20	20	21	22	23	24	25	26	27	28	29	30	31
	20.8	7	8	9	10	11	12	13	13	14	15	16	17	18	19	20	21	22	23	24	25	26	27	28	29	30	31
	21	7	8	9	10	10	11	12	13	14	15	16	17	18	19	20	21	22	23	24	25	26	27	28	29	30	30
	21.3	7	8	8	9	10	11	12	13	14	15	16	17	18	19	20	21	22	23	24	24	25	26	27	28	29	30
	21.5	7	7	8	9	10	11	12	13	14	15	16	17	18	19	20	20	21	22	23	24	25	26	27	28	29	30
	21.8	6	7	8	9	10	11	12	13	14	15	16	17	17	18	19	20	21	22	23	24	25	26	27	28	29	29
	22	6	7	8	9	10	11	12	13	14	15	15	16	17	18	19	20	21	22	23	24	25	25	26	27	28	29
	22.3	6	7	8	9	10	11	12	13	13	14	15	16	17	18	19	20	21	22	22	23	24	25	26	27	28	29
	22.5	6	7	8	9	10	11	12	12	13	14	15	16	17	18	19	20	20	21	22	23	24	25	26	27	28	28
	22.8	6	7	8	9	10	11	11	12	13	14	15	16	17	18	18	19	20	21	22	23	24	25	25	26	27	28
	23	6	7	8	9	10	10	11	12	13	14	15	16	17	17	18	19	20	21	22	23	23	24	25	26	27	28
	23.3	6	7	8	9	9	10	11	12	13	14	15	15	16	17	18	19	20	21	22	22	23	24	25	26	27	28
	23.5	6	7	8	9	9	10	11	12	13	14	14	15	16	17	18	19	20	20	21	22	23	24	25	26	26	27
	23.8	6	7	8	8	9	10	11	12	13	13	14	15	16	17	18	19	19	20	21	22	23	24	24	25	26	27
	24	6	7	8	8	9	10	11	12	13	13	14	15	16	17	18	18	19	20	21	22	23	23	24	25	26	27
	24.3	6	7	7	8	9	10	11	12	12	13	14	15	16	16	17	18	19	20	21	21	22	23	24	25	26	26
	24.5	6	7	7	8	9	10	11	11	12	13	14	15	16	16	17	18	19	20	20	21	22	23	24	24	25	26
	24.8	6	6	7	8	9	10	11	11	12	13	14	15	15	16	17	18	19	19	20	21	22	23	23	24	25	26
	25	6	6	7	8	9	10	10	11	12	13	14	14	15	16	17	18	18	19	20	21	22	22	23	24	25	26

Reading Rate

					NO.	OF	WORDS																				
		660	680	700	720	740	760	780	800	820	840	860	880	900	920	940	960	980	1000	1020	1040	1060	1080	1100	1120	1140	1160
	2	330	340	350	360	370	380	390	400	410	420	430	440	450	460	470	480	490	500	510	520	530	540	550	560	570	580
	2.25	293	302	311	320	329	338	347	356	364	373	382	391	400	409	418	427	436	444	453	462	471	480	489	498	507	516
	2.5	264	272	280	288	296	304	312	320	328	336	344	352	360	368	376	384	392	400	408	416	424	432	440	448	456	464
	2.75	240	247	255	262	269	276	284	291	298	305	313	320	327	335	342	349	356	364	371	378	385	393	400	407	415	422
	3	220	227	233	240	247	253	260	267	273	280	287	293	300	307	313	320	327	333	340	347	353	360	367	373	380	387
	3.25	203	209	215	222	228	234	240	246	252	258	265	271	277	283	289	295	302	308	314	320	326	332	338	345	351	357
	3.5	189	194	200	206	211	217	223	229	234	240	246	251	257	263	269	274	280	286	291	297	303	309	314	320	326	331
	3.75	176	181	187	192	197	203	208	213	219	224	229	235	240	245	251	256	261	267	272	277	283	288	293	299	304	309
	4	165	170	175	180	185	190	195	200	205	210	215	220	225	230	235	240	245	250	255	260	265	270	275	280	285	290
	4.25	155	160	165	169	174	179	184	188	193	198	202	207	212	216	221	226	231	235	240	245	249	254	259	264	268	273
	4.5	147	151	156	160	164	169	173	178	182	187	191	196	200	204	209	213	218	222	227	231	236	240	244	249	253	258
	4.75	139	143	147	152	156	160	164	168	173	177	181	185	189	194	198	202	206	211	215	219	223	227	232	236	240	244
	5	132	136	140	144	148	152	156	160	164	168	172	176	180	184	188	192	196	200	204	208	212	216	220	224	228	232
TIME	5.25	126	130	133	137	141	145	149	152	156	160	164	168	171	175	179	183	187	190	194	198	202	206	210	213	217	221
	5.5	120	124	127	131	135	138	142	145	149	153	156	160	164	167	171	175	178	182	185	189	193	196	200	204	207	211
	5.75	115	118	122	125	129	132	136	139	143	146	150	153	157	160	163	167	170	174	177	181	184	188	191	195	198	202
IN	6	110	113	117	120	123	127	130	133	137	140	143	147	150	153	157	160	163	167	170	173	177	180	183	187	190	193
	6.25	106	109	112	115	118	122	125	128	131	134	138	141	144	147	150	154	157	160	163	166	170	173	176	179	182	186
	6.5	102	105	108	111	114	117	120	123	126	129	132	135	138	142	145	148	151	154	157	160	163	166	169	172	175	178
DECIMAL	6.75	98	101	104	107	110	113	116	119	121	124	127	130	133	136	139	142	145	148	151	154	157	160	163	166	169	172
	7	94	97	100	103	106	109	111	114	117	120	123	126	129	131	134	137	140	143	146	149	151	154	157	160	163	166
	7.25	91	94	97	99	102	105	108	110	113	116	119	121	124	127	130	132	135	138	141	143	146	149	152	154	157	160
MINUTES	7.5	88	91	93	96	99	101	104	107	109	112	115	117	120	123	125	128	131	133	136	139	141	144	147	149	152	155
	7.75	85	88	90	93	95	98	101	103	106	108	111	114	116	119	121	124	126	129	132	134	137	139	142	145	147	150
	8	83	85	88	90	93	95	98	100	103	105	108	110	113	115	118	120	123	125	128	130	133	135	138	140	143	145
	8.25	80	82	85	87	90	92	95	97	99	102	104	107	109	112	114	116	119	121	124	126	128	131	133	136	138	141
	8.5	78	80	82	85	87	89	92	94	96	99	101	104	106	108	111	113	115	118	120	122	125	127	129	132	134	136
	8.75	75	78	80	82	85	87	89	91	94	96	98	101	103	105	107	110	112	114	117	119	121	123	126	128	130	133
	9	73	76	78	80	82	84	87	89	91	93	96	98	100	102	104	107	109	111	113	116	118	120	122	124	127	129
	9.25	71	74	76	78	80	82	84	86	89	91	93	95	97	99	102	104	106	108	110	112	115	117	119	121	123	125
	9.5	69	72	74	76	78	80	82	84	86	88	91	93	95	97	99	101	103	105	107	109	112	114	116	118	120	122
	9.75	68	70	72	74	76	78	80	82	84	86	88	90	92	94	96	98	101	103	105	107	109	111	113	115	117	119
	10	66	68	70	72	74	76	78	80	82	84	86	88	90	92	94	96	98	100	102	104	106	108	110	112	114	116
	10.3	64	66	68	70	72	74	76	78	80	82	84	86	88	90	92	94	96	98	100	101	103	105	107	109	111	113
	10.5	63	65	67	69	70	72	74	76	78	80	82	84	86	88	90	91	93	95	97	99	101	103	105	107	109	110
	10.8	61	63	65	67	69	71	73	74	76	78	80	82	84	86	87	89	91	93	95	97	99	100	102	104	106	108
	11	60	62	64	65	67	69	71	73	75	76	78	80	82	84	85	87	89	91	93	95	96	98	100	102	104	105
	11.3	59	60	62	64	66	68	69	71	73	75	76	78	80	82	84	85	87	89	91	92	94	96	98	100	101	103
	11.5	57	59	61	63	64	66	68	70	71	73	75	77	78	80	82	83	85	87	89	90	92	94	96	97	99	101
	11.8	56	58	60	61	63	65	66	68	70	71	73	75	77	78	80	82	83	85	87	89	90	92	94	95	97	99
	12	55	57	58	60	62	63	65	67	68	70	72	73	75	77	78	80	82	83	85	87	88	90	92	93	95	97
	12.3	54	56	57	59	60	62	64	65	67	69	70	72	73	75	77	78	80	82	83	85	87	88	90	91	93	95
	12.5	53	54	56	58	59	61	62	64	66	67	69	70	72	74	75	77	78	80	82	83	85	86	88	90	91	93
	12.8	52	53	55	56	58	60	61	63	64	66	67	69	71	72	74	75	77	78	80	82	83	85	86	88	89	91
	13	51	52	54	55	57	58	60	62	63	65	66	68	69	71	72	74	75	77	78	80	82	83	85	86	88	89
	13.3	50	51	53	54	56	57	59	60	62	63	65	66	68	69	71	72	74	75	77	78	80	82	83	85	86	88
	13.5	49	50	52	53	55	56	58	59	61	62	64	65	67	68	70	71	73	74	76	77	79	80	81	83	84	86
	13.8	48	49	51	52	54	55	57	58	60	61	63	64	65	67	68	70	71	73	74	76	77	79	80	81	83	84
	14	47	49	50	51	53	54	56	57	59	60	61	63	64	66	67	69	70	71	73	74	76	77	79	80	81	83
	14.3	46	48	49	51	52	53	55	56	58	59	60	62	63	65	66	67	69	70	72	73	74	76	77	79	80	81
	14.5	46	47	48	50	51	52	54	55	57	58	59	61	62	63	65	66	68	69	70	72	73	74	76	77	79	80
	14.8	45	46	47	49	50	52	53	54	56	57	58	60	61	62	64	65	66	68	69	71	72	73	75	76	77	79
	15	44	45	47	48	49	51	52	53	55	56	57	59	60	61	63	64	65	67	68	69	71	72	73	75	76	77
	15.3	43	45	46	47	49	50	51	52	54	55	56	58	59	60	62	63	64	66	67	68	70	71	72	73	75	76
	15.5	43	44	45	46	48	49	50	52	53	54	55	57	58	59	61	62	63	65	66	67	68	70	71	72	74	75
	15.8	42	43	44	46	47	48	50	51	52	53	55	56	57	58	60	61	62	63	65	66	67	69	70	71	72	74
	16	41	43	44	45	46	48	49	50	51	53	54	55	56	58	59	60	61	63	64	65	66	68	69	70	71	73
	16.3	41	42	43	44	46	47	48	49	50	52	53	54	55	57	58	59	60	62	63	64	65	66	68	69	70	71
	16.5	40	41	42	44	45	46	47	48	50	51	52	53	55	56	57	58	59	61	62	63	64	65	67	68	69	70
	16.8	39	41	42	43	44	45	47	48	49	50	51	53	54	55	56	57	59	60	61	62	63	64	66	67	68	69
	17	39	40	41	42	44	45	46	47	48	49	51	52	53	54	55	56	58	59	60	61	62	64	65	66	67	68
	17.3	38	39	41	42	43	44	45	46	48	49	50	51	52	53	54	56	57	58	59	60	61	63	64	65	66	67
	17.5	38	39	40	41	42	43	45	46	47	48	49	50	51	53	54	55	56	57	58	59	61	62	63	64	65	66
	17.8	37	38	39	41	42	43	44	45	46	47	48	50	51	52	53	54	55	56	57	59	60	61	62	63	64	65
	18	37	38	39	40	41	42	43	44	46	47	48	49	50	51	52	53	54	56	57	58	59	60	61	62	63	64
	18.3	36	37	38	39	41	42	43	44	45	46	47	48	49	50	52	53	54	55	56	57	58	59	60	61	62	64
	18.5	36	37	38	39	40	41	42	43	44	45	46	48	49	50	51	52	53	54	55	56	57	58	59	61	62	63
	18.8	35	36	37	38	39	41	42	43	44	45	46	47	48	49	50	51	52	53	54	55	57	58	59	60	61	62
	19	35	36	37	38	39	40	41	42	43	44	45	46	47	48	49	51	52	53	54	55	56	57	58	59	60	61
	19.3	34	35	36	37	38	39	41	42	43	44	45	46	47	48	49	50	51	52	53	54	55	56	57	58	59	60
	19.5	34	35	36	37	38	39	40	41	42	43	44	45	46	47	48	49	50	51	52	53	54	55	56	57	58	59
	19.8	33	34	35	36	37	38	39	41	42	43	44	45	46	47	48	49	50	51	52	53	54	55	56	57	58	59
	20	33	34	35	36	37	38	39	40	41	42	43	44	45	46	47	48	49	50	51	52	53	54	55	56	57	58
	20.3	33	34	35	36	37	38	39	40	40	41	42	43	44	45	46	47	48	49	50	51	52	53	54	55	56	57
	20.5	32	33	34	35	36	37	38	39	40	41	42	43	44	45	46	47	48	49	50	51	52	53	54	55	56	57
	20.8	32	33	34	35	36	37	38	39	40	40	41	42	43	44	45	46	47	48	49	50	51	52	53	54	55	56
	21	31	32	33	34	35	36	37	38	39	40	41	42	43	44	45	46	47	48	49	50	50	51	52	53	54	55
	21.3	31	32	33	34	35	36	37	38	39	40	40	41	42	43	44	45	46	47	48	49	50	51	52	53	54	55
	21.5	31	32	33	33	34	35	36	37	38	39	40	41	42	43	44	45	46	47	47	48	49	50	51	52	53	54
	21.8	30	31	32	33	34	35	36	37	38	39	40	40	41	42	43	44	45	46	47	48	49	50	51	51	52	53
	22	30	31	32	33	34	35	35	36	37	38	39	40	41	42	43	44	45	45	46	47	48	49	50	51	52	53
	22.3	30	31	31	32	33	34	35	36	37	38	39	40	40	41	42	43	44	45	46	47	48	49	49	50	51	52
	22.5	29	30	31	32	33	34	35	36	36	37	38	39	40	41	42	43	44	44	45	46	47	48	49	50	51	52
	22.8	29	30	31	32	33	33	34	35	36	37	38	39	40	40	41	42	43	44	45	46	47	47	48	49	50	51
	23	29	30	30	31	32	33	34	35	36	37	37	38	39	40	41	42	43	43	44	45	46	47	48	49	50	50
	23.3	28	29	30	31	32	33	34	34	35	36	37	38	39	40	40	41	42	43	44	45	46	46	47	48	49	50
	23.5	28	29	30	31	31	32	33	34	35	36	37	37	38	39	40	41	42	43	43	44	45	46	47	48	49	49
	23.8	28	29	29	30	31	32	33	34	35	35	36	37	38	39	40	40	41	42	43	44	45	45	46	47	48	49
	24	28	28	29	30	31	32	33	33	34	35	36	37	38	38	39	40	41	42	43	43	44	45	46	47	48	48
	24.3	27	28	29	30	31	31	32	33	34	35	35	36	37	38	39	40	40	41	42	43	44	45	45	46	47	48
	24.5	27	28	29	29	30	31	32	33	33	34	35	36	37	38	38	39	40	41	42	42	43	44	45	46	47	47
	24.8	27	27	28	29	30	31	32	32	33	34	35	36	36	37	38	39	40	40	41	42	43	44	44	45	46	47
	25	26	27	28	29	30	30	31	32	33	34	34	35	36	37	38	38	39	40	41	42	42	43	44	45	46	46

Reading Rate

			NO.	OF	WORDS																						
		1180	1200	1220	1240	1260	1280	1300	1320	1340	1360	1380	1400	1420	1440	1460	1480	1500	1520	1540	1560	1580	1600	1620	1640	1660	1680
	2	590	600	610	620	630	640	650	660	670	680	690	700	710	720	730	740	750	760	770	780	790	800	810	820	830	840
	2.25	524	533	542	551	560	569	578	587	596	604	613	622	631	640	649	658	667	676	684	693	702	711	720	729	738	747
	2.5	472	480	488	496	504	512	520	528	536	544	552	560	568	576	584	592	600	608	616	624	632	640	648	656	664	672
	2.75	429	436	444	451	458	465	473	480	487	495	502	509	516	524	531	538	545	553	560	567	575	582	589	596	604	611
	3	393	400	407	413	420	427	433	440	447	453	460	467	473	480	487	493	500	507	513	520	527	533	540	547	553	560
	3.25	363	369	375	382	388	394	400	406	412	418	425	431	437	443	449	455	462	468	474	480	486	492	498	505	511	517
	3.5	337	343	349	354	360	366	371	377	383	389	394	400	406	411	417	423	429	434	440	446	451	457	463	469	474	480
	3.75	315	320	325	331	336	341	347	352	357	363	368	373	379	384	389	395	400	405	411	416	421	427	432	437	443	448
	4	295	300	305	310	315	320	325	330	335	340	345	350	355	360	365	370	375	380	385	390	395	400	405	410	415	420
	4.25	278	282	287	292	296	301	306	311	315	320	325	329	334	339	344	348	353	358	362	367	372	376	381	386	391	395
	4.5	262	267	271	276	280	284	289	293	298	302	307	311	316	320	324	329	333	338	342	347	351	356	360	364	369	373
	4.75	248	253	257	261	265	269	274	278	282	286	291	295	299	303	307	312	316	320	324	328	333	337	341	345	349	354
	5	236	240	244	248	252	256	260	264	268	272	276	280	284	288	292	296	300	304	308	312	316	320	324	328	332	336
TIME	5.25	225	229	232	236	240	244	248	251	255	259	263	267	270	274	278	282	286	290	293	297	301	305	309	312	316	320
	5.5	215	218	222	225	229	233	236	240	244	247	251	255	258	262	265	269	273	276	280	284	287	291	295	298	302	305
	5:75	205	209	212	216	219	223	226	230	233	237	240	243	247	250	254	257	261	264	268	271	275	278	282	285	289	292
IN	6	197	200	203	207	210	213	217	220	223	227	230	233	237	240	243	247	250	253	257	260	263	267	270	273	277	280
	6.25	189	192	195	198	202	205	208	211	214	218	221	224	227	230	234	237	240	243	246	250	253	256	259	262	266	269
	6.5	182	185	188	191	194	197	200	203	206	209	212	215	218	222	225	228	231	234	237	240	243	246	249	252	255	258
DECIMAL	6.75	175	178	181	184	187	190	193	196	199	201	204	207	210	213	216	219	222	225	228	231	234	237	240	243	246	249
	7	169	171	174	177	180	183	186	189	191	194	197	200	203	206	209	211	214	217	220	223	226	229	231	234	237	240
	7.25	163	166	168	171	174	177	179	182	185	188	190	193	196	199	201	204	207	210	212	215	218	221	223	226	229	232
MINUTES	7.5	157	160	163	165	168	171	173	176	179	181	184	187	189	192	195	197	200	203	205	208	211	213	216	219	221	224
	7.75	152	155	157	160	163	165	168	170	173	175	178	181	183	186	188	191	194	196	199	201	204	206	209	212	214	217
	8	148	150	153	155	158	160	163	165	168	170	173	175	178	180	183	185	188	190	193	195	198	200	203	205	208	210
	8.25	143	145	148	150	153	155	158	160	162	165	167	170	172	175	177	179	182	184	187	189	192	194	196	199	201	204
	8.5	139	141	144	146	148	151	153	155	158	160	162	165	167	169	172	174	176	179	181	184	186	188	191	193	195	198
	8.75	135	137	139	142	144	146	149	151	153	155	158	160	162	165	167	169	171	174	176	178	181	183	185	187	190	192
	9	131	133	136	138	140	142	144	147	149	151	153	156	158	160	162	164	167	169	171	173	176	178	180	182	184	187
	9.25	128	130	132	134	136	138	141	143	145	147	149	151	154	156	158	160	162	164	166	169	171	173	175	177	179	182
	9.5	124	126	128	131	133	135	137	139	141	143	145	147	149	152	154	156	158	160	162	164	166	168	171	173	175	177
	9.75	121	123	125	127	129	131	133	135	137	139	142	144	146	148	150	152	154	156	158	160	162	164	166	168	170	172
	10	118	120	122	124	126	128	130	132	134	136	138	140	142	144	146	148	150	152	154	156	158	160	162	164	166	168
	10.3	115	117	119	121	123	125	127	129	131	133	135	137	139	140	142	144	146	148	150	152	154	156	158	160	162	164
	10.5	112	114	116	118	120	122	124	126	128	130	131	133	135	137	139	141	143	145	147	149	150	152	154	156	158	160
	10.8	110	112	113	115	117	119	121	123	125	127	128	130	132	134	136	138	140	141	143	145	147	149	151	153	154	156
	11	107	109	111	113	115	116	118	120	122	124	125	127	129	131	133	135	136	138	140	142	144	145	147	149	151	153
	11.3	105	107	108	110	112	114	116	117	119	121	123	124	126	128	130	132	133	135	137	139	140	142	144	146	148	149
	11.5	103	104	106	108	110	111	113	115	117	118	120	122	123	125	127	129	130	132	134	136	137	139	141	143	144	146
	11.8	100	102	104	106	107	109	111	112	114	116	117	119	121	123	124	126	128	129	131	133	134	136	138	140	141	143
	12	98	100	102	103	105	107	108	110	112	113	115	117	118	120	122	123	125	127	128	130	132	133	135	137	138	140
	12.3	96	98	100	101	103	104	106	108	109	111	113	114	116	118	119	121	122	124	.126	127	129	131	132	134	136	137
	12.5	94	96	98	99	101	102	104	106	107	109	110	112	114	115	117	118	120	122	123	125	126	128	130	131	133	134
	12.8	93	94	96	97	99	100	102	104	105	107	108	110	111	113	115	116	118	119	121	122	124	125	127	129	130	132
	13	91	92	94	95	97	98	100	102	103	105	106	108	109	111	112	114	115	117	118	120	122	123	125	126	128	129
	13.3	89	91	92	94	95	97	98	100	101	103	104	106	107	109	110	112	113	115	116	118	119	121	122	124	125	127
	13.5	87	89	90	92	93	95	96	98	99	101	102	104	105	107	108	110	111	113	114	116	117	119	120	121	123	124
	13.8	86	87	89	90	92	93	95	96	97	99	100	102	103	105	106	108	109	111	112	113	115	116	118	119	121	122
	14	84	86	87	89	90	91	93	94	96	97	99	100	101	103	104	106	107	109	110	111	113	114	116	117	119	120
	14.3	83	84	86	87	88	90	91	93	94	95	97	98	100	101	102	104	105	107	108	109	111	112	114	115	116	118
	14.5	81	83	84	86	87	88	90	91	92	94	95	97	98	99	101	102	103	105	106	108	109	110	112	113	114	116
	14.8	80	81	83	84	85	87	88	89	91	92	94	95	96	98	99	100	102	103	104	106	107	108	110	111	113	114
	15	79	80	81	83	84	85	87	88	89	91	92	93	95	96	97	99	100	101	103	104	105	107	108	109	111	112
	15.3	77	79	80	81	83	84	85	87	88	89	90	92	93	94	96	97	98	99.7	101	102	104	105	106	108	109	110
	15.5	76	77	79	80	81	83	84	85	86	88	89	90	92	93	94	95	97	98.1	99.4	101	102	103	105	106	107	108
	15.8	75	76	77	79	80	81	83	84	85	86	88	89	90	91	93	94	95	96.5	97.8	99	100	102	103	104	105	107
	16	74	75	76	78	79	80	81	83	84	85	86	88	89	90	91	93	94	95	96.3	97.5	98.8	100	101	103	104	105
	16.3	73	74	75	76	78	79	80	81	82	84	85	86	87	89	90	91	92	93.5	94.8	96	97.2	98.5	99.7	101	102	103
	16.5	72	73	74	75	76	78	79	80	81	82	84	85	86	87	88	90	91	92.1	93.3	94.5	95.8	97	98.2	99.4	101	102
	16.8	70	72	73	74	75	76	78	79	80	81	82	84	85	86	87	88	90	90.7	91.9	93.1	94.3	95.5	96.7	97.9	99.1	100
	17	69	71	72	73	74	75	76	78	79	80	81	82	84	85	86	87	88	89.4	90.6	91.8	92.9	94.1	95.3	96.5	97.6	98.8
	17.3	68	70	71	72	73	74	75	77	78	79	80	81	82	83	85	86	87	88.1	89.3	90.4	91.6	92.8	93.9	95.1	96.2	97.4
	17.5	67	69	70	71	72	73	74	75	77	78	79	80	81	82	83	85	86	86.9	88	89.1	90.3	91.4	92.6	93.7	94.9	96
	17.8	66	68	69	70	71	72	73	74	75	77	78	79	80	81	82	83	85	85.6	86.8	87.9	89	90.1	91.3	92.4	93.5	94.6
	18	66	67	68	69	70	71	72	73	74	76	77	78	79	80	81	82	83	84.4	85.6	86.7	87.8	88.9	90	91.1	92.2	93.3
	18.3	65	66	67	68	69	70	71	72	73	75	76	77	78	79	80	81	82	83.3	84.4	85.5	86.6	87.7	88.8	89.9	91	92.1
	18.5	64	65	66	67	68	69	70	71	72	74	75	76	77	78	79	80	81	82.2	83.2	84.3	85.4	86.5	87.6	88.6	89.7	90.8
	18.8	63	64	65	66	67	68	69	70	71	73	74	75	76	77	78	79	80	81.1	82.1	83.2	84.3	85.3	86.4	87.5	88.5	89.6
	19	62	63	64	65	66	67	68	69	71	72	73	74	75	76	77	78	79	80	81.1	82.1	83.2	84.2	85.3	86.3	87.4	88.4
	19.3	61	62	63	64	65	66	68	69	70	71	72	73	74	75	76	77	78	79	80	81	82.1	83.1	84.2	85.2	86.2	87.3
	19.5	61	62	63	64	65	66	67	68	69	70	71	72	73	74	75	76	77	77.9	79	80	81	82.1	83.1	84.1	85.1	86.2
	19.8	60	61	62	63	64	65	66	67	68	69	70	71	72	73	74	75	76	77	78	79	80	81	82	83	84.1	85.1
	20	59	60	61	62	63	64	65	66	67	68	69	70	71	72	73	74	75	76	77	78	79	80	81	82	83	84
	20.3	58	59	60	61	62	63	64	65	66	67	68	69	70	71	72	73	74	75.1	76	77	78	79	80	81	82	83
	20.5	58	59	60	60	61	62	63	64	65	66	67	68	69	70	71	72	73	74.1	75.1	76.1	77.1	78	79	80	81	82
	20.8	57	58	59	60	61	62	63	64	65	66	67	67	68	69	70	71	72	73.3	74.2	75.2	76.1	77.1	78.1	79	80	81
	21	56	57	58	59	60	61	62	63	64	65	66	67	68	69	70	70	71	72.4	73.3	74.3	75.2	76.2	77.1	78.1	79	80
	21.3	56	56	57	58	59	60	61	62	63	64	65	66	67	68	69	70	71	71.5	72.5	73.4	74.4	75.3	76.2	77.2	78.1	79.1
	21.5	55	56	57	58	59	60	60	61	62	63	64	65	66	67	68	69	70	70.7	71.6	72.6	73.5	74.4	75.3	76.3	77.2	78.1
	21.8	54	55	56	57	58	59	60	61	62	63	63	64	65	66	67	68	69	69.9	70.8	71.7	72.6	73.6	74.5	75.4	76.3	77.2
	22	54	55	55	56	57	58	59	60	61	62	63	64	65	65	66	67	68	69.1	70	70.9	71.8	72.7	73.6	74.5	75.5	76.4
	22.3	53	54	55	56	57	58	58	59	60	61	62	63	64	65	66	67	67	68.3	69.2	70.1	71	71.9	72.8	73.7	74.6	75.5
	22.5	52	53	54	55	56	57	58	59	60	60	61	62	63	64	65	66	67	67.6	68.4	69.3	70.2	71.1	72	72.9	73.8	74.7
	22.8	52	53	54	55	55	56	57	58	59	60	61	62	62	63	64	65	66	66.8	67.7	68.6	69.5	70.3	71.2	72.1	73	73.8
	23	51	52	53	54	55	56	57	57	58	59	60	61	62	63	63	64	65	66.1	67	67.8	68.7	69.6	70.4	71.3	72.2	73
	23.3	51	52	52	53	54	55	56	57	58	58	59	60	61	62	63	64	65	65.4	66.2	67.1	68	68.8	69.7	70.5	71.4	72.3
	23.5	50	51	52	53	54	54	55	56	57	58	59	60	60	61	62	63	64	64.7	65.5	66.4	67.2	68.1	68.9	69.8	70.6	71.5
	23.8	50	51	51	52	53	54	55	56	56	57	58	59	60	61	61	62	63	64	64.8	65.7	66.5	67.4	68.2	69.1	69.9	70.7
	24	49	50	51	52	53	53	54	55	56	57	58	58	59	60	61	62	63	63.3	64.2	65	65.8	66.7	67.5	68.3	69.2	70
	24.3	49	49	50	51	52	53	54	54	55	56	57	58	59	59	60	61	62	62.7	63.5	64.3	65.2	66	66.8	67.6	68.5	69.3
	24.5	48	49	50	51	51	52	53	54	55	56	56	57	58	59	60	60	61	62	62.9	63.7	64.5	65.3	66.1	66.9	67.8	68.6
	24.8	48	48	49	50	51	52	53	53	54	55	56	57	57	58	59	60	61	61.4	62.2	63	63.8	64.6	65.5	66.3	67.1	67.9
	25	47	48	49	50	50	51	52	53	54	54	55	56	57	58	58	59	60	60.8	61.6	62.4	63.2	64	64.8	65.6	66.4	67.2

Glossary:
Words Featured
in the Text

Explanation:

- The guide words at the top of each page tell you which words are located on that page. For example, the guide words for the first page are *aa* and *autocrat*. Words that come alphabetically after *aa* but before *autocrat* are found on the page.

- Within parentheses after each entry, the word is marked to show pronunciation. Use the marks (called diacritical marks) to help you pronounce the words.

ă	act, cat	o͞o	ooze
ā	ace, cape	ou	out, cloud
â	air, care	ŭ	up
ä	arm	ū	use, flute
ĕ	egg, fed	û	urn, turn
ē	equal, feed	ə	occurs in unaccented
ĭ	it, lit		syllables and is pro-
ī	ice, line		nounced as follows:
ŏ	fox, lot		a aloud
ō	over, so		e item
ô	order		i pencil
oi	oil, toy		o atom
o͝o	took, put		u circus

The symbol (′) as in fre′dəm marks the primary stress, or accent. The syllable preceding it is pronounced with greater emphasis than other syllables. The symbol (′) as in tel′ə fon′ marks the secondary stress, or accent. The syllable preceding the secondary accent (′) is pronounced with less emphasis than the one marked (′).

A

a·a (ä ′ ä ′), *noun,* blocky, angular lava. Some Hawaiian lava fields are made of *aa.* (Chap. 6)

ab·er·ra·tion (ăb′ə rā ′ shən), *noun,* lapse from the normal or usual. The planet's orbital path showed an *aberration* from what the astronomers expected. (Chap. 14)

ab·hor (ăb hôr ′), *verb,* loathe; feel disgust for. The talented artist *abhorred* the cheap copies of his paintings. (Chap. 10)

a·byss (ə bĭs ′), *noun,* a great depth; a bottomless pit. The deep ocean floor is called an *abyss.* (Chap. 2)

ac·cess (ăk ′ sĕs), *noun,* approach to something or somebody; admittance. The reporters were unable to gain *access* to the private meeting. (Chap. 13)

ad·her·ent (ăd hĭr ′ ənt), *noun,* supporter or follower of a cause or leader. Jesse Jackson had many *adherents* during his presidential campaign. (Chap. 13)

aes·thet·ic (ĕs thĕt ′ ĭk), *adjective,* artistic; having a sense of beauty. The graceful ballet appealed to her *aesthetic* sensitivity. (Chap. 2)

a·gil·i·ty (ə jĭl ′ ə tē), *noun,* ability to move quickly and easily. The horse showed its *agility* as it jumped over the wall. (Chap. 2)

a·kin (ə kĭn ′), *adjective,* related; similar. We both liked Dixieland; our tastes in music are *akin* to one another. (Chap. 5)

al·ien·a·tion (āl′yə nā ′ shən), *noun,* withdrawal of affection; estrangement. The Pilgrims developed an *alienation* to England. (Chap. 14)

al·le·vi·ate (ə lē ′ vĭ āt′), *verb,* lessen; mitigate; make easier to bear. The rescue squad was able to *alleviate* the patient's pain. (Chap. 2)

al·li·ance (ə lī ′ əns), *noun,* a connection or agreement between nations or parties for some special purpose. During World War I, the United States made an *alliance* with Great Britain and France against Germany. (Chap. 13)

al·loy, (ăl ′ oi), *noun,* a composition of two or more metals melted together. Stainless steel is an *alloy* of steel and chromium that resists rust. (Chap. 6)

an·o·nym·ity (ăn′ə nĭm ′ ə tĭ), *noun,* having no name recognition as an author. The author enjoyed his state of *anonymity* because no one bothered him to get his autograph. (Chap. 6)

an·tag·o·nist (ăn tăg ′ ə nĭst), *noun,* an opponent in any kind of contest. The actor played the role of the *antagonist* in the play. He was the one who made trouble for the hero. (Chap. 7)

an·te·date (ăn ′ tə dāt′), *verb,* to be an older date than; happen before in time. The arrival of Columbus in the New World *antedates* that of the pilgrims in Plymouth. (Chap. 3)

an·thro·pol·o·gist (ăn′thrə pŏl ′ ə jĭst), *noun,* one who studies the origins, development, cultures, and beliefs of human beings. The *anthropologist* was able to rebuild a clay bowl from the fragments that were unearthed. (Chap. 3)

an·ti·bi·ot·ic (ăn′tĭ bī ŏt ′ ĭk), *noun,* a substance produced by molds, yeast, or bacteria that kills or weakens germs. The *antibiotic* was used to kill the bacteria. (Chap. 3)

an·ti·war (ăn′tĕ wôr ′), *adjective,* against or opposed to war. Pacifists are *antiwar.* (Chap. 3)

an·to·nym (ăn ′ tə nĭm), *noun,* a word that means the opposite of another word. The word "large" is an *antonym* of the word "small." (Chap. 3)

aq·ua·pho·bi·a (ăk′wə fō ′ bĭ ə) *noun,* a fear of water. His *aquaphobia* prevented him from benefiting from swimming lessons. (Chap. 3)

arch (ärch), *adjective,* most important; sly, cunning. Among several, he was the *arch* rival. (Chap. 7)

ar·chae·ol·o·gy (är′kē ŏl ′ ə jē), *noun,* the study of customs, life, and things of ancient times by excavating the remains of structures and cities. Because he wanted to know more about Greek buildings, he studied *archaeology.* (Chap. 2)

a·ris·to·crat·ic (əřis′tə krăt ′ ĭk), *adjective,* belonging to an upper class; considered superior. Because of his intelligence, fame, and culture, he appeared *aristocratic* to some. (Chap. 10)

ar·tic·u·la·tion (är tĭk′yə lā ′ shən), *noun,* a jointed state. The House and Senate committees worked smoothly together; they had good *articulation.* (Chap. 3)

as·pire (ə spīr ′), *verb,* seek; aim for. We *aspire* to achieve our dreams. (Chap. 10)

as·tro·nom·i·cal (ăs′trə nŏm ′ ək əl), *adjective,* having to do with astronomy. Galileo made *astronomical* measurements with his telescope. (Chap. 3)

au·ra (ôr ′ ə), *noun,* distinctive character or manner. The procession had an aura of beauty and dignity. (Chap. 14)

au·to·crat (ô ′ tə krăt′), *noun,* a ruler who holds absolute power. Some kings were *autocrats* who thought their power was a given right. (Chap. 6)

av·id (ăv ′ ĭd), *adjective,* extremely eager, keen. Many writers start out as *avid* readers. (Chap. 12)

B

bi·cam·er·al (bī kăm ′ ər əl), *adjective,* having two chambers. Our United States Congress is *bicameral.* (Chap. 4)

bi·cen·ten·ni·al (bī sĕn tĕn ′ ē əl), *noun,* a 200th anniversary. In 1977 the United States celebrated the *bicentennial* of the Constitution. (Chap. 3)

brac·ing (brās ′ ĭng), *verb,* preparing; putting oneself in readiness. They were *bracing* the tent against the expected winds. (Chap. 2)

brood (brüd), *verb,* dwell moodily in thought; to ponder at length. He *brooded* about his errors; he could not bring himself to correct them. (Chap. 2)

C

cam·ou·flage (kăm ′ ə fläzh′), *verb,* coloring or screening objects so that they blend into their background. The spots on the bird eggs *camouflaged* them so that the predator walked by without seeing them. (Chap. 12)

ca·price (kə prēs ′), *noun,* change of mind with no apparent reason. Because directions were given by *caprice,* the workers did not know what to do next. (Chap. 7)

car·ni·vore (kär ′ nə vōr′), *noun,* an animal that eats meat. The *carnivorous* eagle ate the fish. (Chap. 3)

cas·cade (kăs kād ′), *noun,* a waterfall over rocks. We saw a rainbow through the spray thrown up by the cascade. (Chap. 2)

cat·a·ract (kăt ′ er ăkt′), *noun,* a waterfall over a steep cliff. The water of the *cataract* spashed hundreds of feet down the face of the rocks. (Chap. 2)

cen·ten·ni·al (sĕn tĕn ′ ē əl), *noun,* a 100th anniversary. A parade and fireworks marked the town's *centennial.* (Chap. 3)

cir·cum·nav·i·gate (sûr′kəm năv ′ ə gāt′), *verb,* sail around. In the early 1400s, Chinese ships *circumnavigated* southeast Asia and sailed to India and the Persian Gulf. (Chap. 3)

clar·i·fy (klăr ′ ə fī), *verb,* make clear. His summary *clarified* what he said. (Chap. 3)

cleave (klēv), *verb,* split open; split or cut with a blow. The cook *cleaved* the chops off the roast one by one. (Chap. 2)

co·los·sal (kə lŏs ′ əl), *adjective,* huge; gigantic. The pyramids of Egypt are *colossal* structures. (Chap. 1)

co·los·sus (kə lŏs ′ əs), *noun,* anything huge or gigantic. The legendary statue of Apollo known as the *Colossus* of Rhodes was one of the Seven Wonders of the World. (Chap. 1)

com·mis·sion (kə mĭsh ′ ən), *noun,* a task or job; a grant of authority. Goethals received a *commission* to engineer the building of the Panama Canal. (Chap. 10)

com·pact (kŏm ′ păkt), *noun,* an agreement; a contract. In 1867, Secretary of State Seward made a *compact* with Russia to purchase Alaska. (Chap. 7)

com·pat·i·ble (kəm păt ′ ə bəl), *adjective,* able to exist in harmony. The *compatible* children enjoyed playing together. (Chap. 7)

com·pla·cent (kom plā ′ sənt), *adjective,* self-satisfied with one's advantages. *Complacent* citizens may find that their rights become limited by ignoring bad acts of officials. (Chap. 14)

con·cen·tra·tion (kŏn′sən trā ′ shən), *noun,* the amount of a substance in a given area or volume. His soft drink had a high *concentration* of sugar. (Chap. 12)

con·cep·tu·al (kən sĕp ′ chŏŏ əl), *adjective,* pertaining to concepts. The scientist arranged his thoughts into a *conceptual* scheme. (Chap. 6)

con·se·crate (kŏn ′ sə krāt′), *verb,* declare sacred, dedicate for a purpose. The ceremony *consecrated* the new temple. (Chap. 11)

con·sign (kən sīn ′), *verb,* hand over; deliver. His arrest forced him to *consign* his expensive car to the courts. (Chap. 13)

con·tempt (kən tĕmpt ′), *noun,* the feeling one has about something or someone regarded as unworthy or mean; scorn; disdain. She felt *contempt* for the selfish group who thought only of themselves. (Chap. 2)

con·ti·nen·tal di·vide (kŏn′tə nən ′ təl dĭ vīd ′), *noun,* a line of mountaintops across a continent that separates stream flows to oceans on either side. The pioneers found passes across the *continental divide.* (Chap. 5)

co·or·di·nate (kō ôr ′ də nĭt), *adjective,* of equal rank; equal in importance. Generals of the army and admirals of the navy have *coordinate* positions. (Chap. 8)

cor·ner·stone (kôr ′ nər stōn′), *noun,* stone built into the corner of an important building and usually hollowed out to contain documents. Before it was cemented in place, newspapers and pictures were placed in the *cornerstone.* (Chap. 13)

coup (ko͞o),   *noun,* unexpected achievement. It was a *coup* to achieve an A in that difficult course. (Chap. 10)

crust (krust),   *noun,* the solid outer rock layers of the earth. The oil well drill penetrated deep into the earth's *crust.* (Chap. 2)

cu·ren·cy (kûr ′ ən sē),   *noun,* money; medium of exchange. The *currency* he tried to deposit was counterfeit. (Chap. 14)

D

daunt·ing (dônt ′ ĭng),   *adjective,* bold; courageous; daring. Climbing Mt. Everest was a *daunting* adventure. (Chap. 7)

de·ba·cle (dā bä ′ kəl),   *noun,* a rout; sudden collapse or overthrow. The dam break was a *debacle;* water flooded the town. (Chap. 5)

de·com·po·si·tion (dē′kŏm pə zĭsh ′ ən),   *noun,* act of decomposing; taking apart. Bacteria help in the *decomposition* of wastes. (Chap. 6)

de·fault (dĭ fôlt ′),   *noun,* failure to pay a financial debt. If its obligations are not paid, the bank will *default.* (Chap. 11)

de·gen·er·ate (dĭ jĕn ′ ə rāt′),   *verb,* decline, deteriorate. Drugs made him *degenerate* mentally and physically. (Chap. 11)

de·grad·ing (dĭ grā ′ dĭng),   *adjective,* lowering in dignity. Being pushed to the rear was a *degrading* experience. (Chap. 10)

dep·re·ca·tion (dĕp′rə kā ′ shən),   *noun,* disapproval of; protestation against. No one likes his or her work to be subject to *deprecation* by others. (Chap. 14)

de·rive (di rĭv ′),   *verb,* obtain from some source. The chemist *derived* the scent from the rose petals. (Chap. 6)

der·ma·tol·o·gy (dûr′mə tŏl ′ ə jē),   *noun,* the science of the skin and its diseases. The *dermatologist* gave him an antibiotic for his rash. (Chap. 3)

des·ig·nate (dĕz ′ ig nāt),   *verb,* point out; mark. He was told to park his car in the zone *designated* for students. (Chap. 2)

de·tract (dē trăkt ′),   *verb,* take away; withdraw value or reputation. All the nasty remarks did not *detract* from his fine reputation. (Chap. 11)

dev·as·tate (dĕv ′ ə stāt′),   *verb,* destroy; lay waste. The arsonist *devastated* the buildings with fire. (Chap. 5)

dis·crep·an·cy (dĭs krĕp ′ ən se),   *noun,* difference; inconsistency. There was a large *discrepancy* between what she said and what she meant. (Chap. 14)

di·min·ish (dĭ mĭn ′ ĭsh),   *verb,* make smaller; reduce. His interest *diminished* when he learned there was little in it for him. (Chap. 14)

di·vulge (dĭ vulj ′),   *verb,* reveal; make known. The mechanic *divulged* his technique for repairing the special part. (Chap. 13)

dom·i·nant (dŏm ′ ə nənt),   *adjective,* controlling; ruling. The characteristics of *dominant* genes usually show in the offspring. (Chap. 6)

dwin·dle (dwĭn ′ dəl),   *verb,* become smaller and smaller. He sat and did nothing; he let his vacation time *dwindle* away. (Chap. 10)

E

e·col·o·gy (ē kŏl′ ə jē),   *noun,* the branch of biology that deals with living things and their relationships to the environment. *Ecologists* have found that weeds can tolerate poor environmental conditions. (Chap. 3)

e·co·nom·ic (ē′kə nŏm ′ ĭk),   *adjective,* having to do with production, distribution and use of wealth. Adam Smith formulated *economic* principles in the 1700s. (Chap. 14)

ed·i·fice (ĕd ′ ə fis),   *noun,* large or imposing building. The Lincoln Memorial in Washington is a grand *edifice.* (Chap. 6)

e·ject (ĭ jĕkt ′),   *verb,* expel; force out. The unruly were *ejected* from the meeting. (Chap. 6)

e·lab·or·ate (ĭ lăb ′ ə rāt′),   *verb,* add details. Dickens *elaborated* on all the characters in his novels. (Chap. 14)

e·lite (ĭ lēt ′),   *noun,* select; best part. The nobility thought they were *elite* persons. (Chap. 10)

e·mas·cu·late (ĭ măs ′ kyə lāt ′),   *verb,* castrate; remove testes or ovaries. Steers are bulls that have been *emasculated.* (Chap. 6)

em·bod·y (ĕm bŏd ′ ē),   *verb,* to invest with a body; to give real form to. The Constitution *embodies* principles in which we all believe. (Chap. 2)

em·bo·lus (ĕm ′ bəl əs),   *noun,* clot or undissolved mass carried in the circulatory system. Sometimes the body can dissolve an *embolus* in the bloodstream. (Chap. 12)

en·sure (ĕn shŏŏr ′),   *verb,* make sure; make certain. Her special care *ensured* the safety of her children. (Chap. 4)

en·voy (ĕn ′ voi),   *noun,* a diplomatic representative. An *envoy* is next in rank below an ambassador. (Chap. 13)

er·a (ĭr ′ ə),   *noun,* a significant period of time or history. The Industrial Revolution occurred during the *era* from the mid 1700s to the mid 1800s. (Chap. 7)

es·chew (ĕs chŏŏ ′),   *verb,* avoid, shun. The shy couple *eschewed* publicity. (Chap. 4)

es·sence (ĕs ′ əns),   *noun,* important elements; that which makes a thing what it is. I got the *essence* of his speech but could not follow the details. (Chap. 2)

e·voke (ĭ vōk ′),   *verb,* produce memories or feelings. Vivid memories were *evoked* when she saw the old photograph. (Chap. 2)

e·volve (ĭ vŏlv ′),   *verb,* develop or change gradually. Fossils indicate that horses *evolved* from ancestors the size of dogs. (Chap. 12)

ex·ag·ger·a·tion (ĭg zăj ′ ə rā′shən),   *noun,* an overstatement; a description beyond the truth. Her remarks about the importance of her job were an *exaggeration.* (Chap. 2)

ex·pe·di·tion (ĕks′pə dĭsh ′ ən),   *noun,* a journey, or voyage, made for exploration, scientific study, or another special purpose. John Powell and nine other men started an *expedition* to explore the Green and Colorado rivers in 1869. (Chap. 2)

ex·plic·it (ĕk splĭs ′ ĭt),   *adjective,* clearly stated; definite. Her directions were *explicit;* no one misunderstood. (Chap. 2)

ex·ploi·ta·tion (ĕks′ploi tā ′ shən),   *noun,* selfish use for one's own advantage. The invaders *exploited* the peasants and took most of their harvest. (Chap. 7)

ex·tinc·tion (ĭk stĭngk ′ shən),   *noun,* dying out of a biological line. We have caused the *extinction* of many plant and animal species. (Chap. 10)

F

fa·cade (fə säd ′),   *noun,* the front face of a building. Some pioneer western towns had fancy *façades* with only simple buildings behind. (Chap. 13)

fes·tive (fĕs ′ tĭv),   *adjective,* merry, lively. The family gathering was a *festive* reunion. (Chap. 10)

flor·id (flôr id),   *adjective,* ruddy in cheeks or complexion. Their faces were *florid* from exposure to the intense sun. (Chap. 14)

for·ay (fôr ′ ā),   *noun,* a raid for plunder. The horse troop made a *foray* through the town to take food and livestock. (Chap. 13)

for·bear·ance (fôr bâr ′ əns),   *noun,* patience. The mother had *forbearance* as the child struggled to dress himself without help. (Chap. 13)

for·tu·i·tous·ly (fôr tū ′ ə təs lē),   *adverb,* by chance; accidentally. *Fortuitously,* the rain stopped in time for the outdoor ceremonies. (Chap. 4)

fraught (frôt),   *adjective,* full of; involving. The government is *fraught* with a legacy of debt. (Chap. 7)

fren·zy (frĕn ′ zē),   *noun,* wild agitation; excitement. The fox caused a *frenzy* in the chicken coop. (Chap. 10)

fres·coe (frĕs ′ kō),   *noun,* a picture painted in wet plaster. The *frescoes* on the façade of the building were known for their detail and color. (Chap. 13)

friv·o·lous (frĭv ′ ə ləs),   *adjective,* with lack of sense; trivial; of little importance. His objections were *frivolous;* people paid no attention. (Chap. 14)

fu·ror (fyŏŏr ′ ôr),   *noun,* outburst of excitement; rage. The referee's poor decision caused a *furor* in the grandstand. (Chap. 2)

G

gar·goyle (gär ′ goil),   *noun,* a rainspout on a roof gutter often made in the shape of an ugly animal or human head. When it rained, the *gargoyles* spouted water from their mouths. (Chap. 13)

ge·net·ic (jə nĕt ′ ĭk),   *adjective,* dealing with genetics, the science of heredity. Mendel worked with *genetic* traits but did not use the word *gene.* (Chap. 3)

ge·ol·o·gy (jē ŏl ′ ə jē),   *noun,* the science that deals with the earth, the rocks that compose it, and its changes. In *geology* class, we identified rocks that we collected. (Chap. 2, 3)

graph·ic (grăf ′ ĭk),   *adjective,* lifelike; vivid; pertaining to drawing or painting. The boy's *graphic* description of the accident was very clear. (Chap. 3)

guise (gīz),   *noun,* general appearance; assumed appearance. The spy got into the building under the *guise* of a repairman. (Chap. 14)

H

hal·low (hăl ′ o), *verb,* make holy; consecrate. Lincoln did not think he could *hallow* a battlefield. (Chap. 11)

hap·haz·ard (hăp′hăz ′ ərd), *adjective,* at random; by chance. His notes were haphazard; he had trouble organizing them for study. (Chap. 12)

heir (âr), *noun,* one who inherits property of a deceased person. She was the *heir* to her mother's few keepsakes. (Chap. 11)

he·mo·sta·sis (hē′mə stā ′ sĭs), *noun,* condition of blood stoppage. Two Greek words meaning ''blood'' and ''standing'' are put together to make the word *hemostasis.* (Chap. 12)

herb·i·vore (hûr ′ bĭv ôr), *noun,* an animal that eats plants. Cows and horses are *herbivores.* (Chap. 3)

hi·er·o·glyph·ic (hī′ər ə glĭf ′ ĭk), *adjective,* pertaining to a picture writing system where symbols stand for words. Egyptian *hieroglyphic* writing includes pictures of birds and tools. (Chap. 7)

hig·gle·dy-pig·gle·dy (hĭg ′ əl dē-pĭg ′ əl dē), *adverb,* confused jumble. After the crowd left, the chairs were left scattered *higgledy-piggledy* around the room. (Chap. 13)

hor·rif·ic (hô rĭf ′ ĭk), *adjective,* causing horror. Being caught in a fire is a *horrific* experience. (Chap. 5)

hy·brid (hī ′ brĭd), *noun,* the offspring of two animals or plants of different varieties or species. A mule is a *hybrid* resulting from the mating of a female horse and a male donkey. (Chap. 6)

hy·per·ac·tive (hī′pər ăk ′ tĭv), *adjective,* overactive; easily excited. The *hyperactive* child was constantly moving about. (Chap. 3)

hy·po·thet·i·cal (hī′pə thĕt ′ ə kəl), *adjective,* not well supported by evidence; conditional; supposed. His argument was *hypothetical;* it was not based on fact. (Chap. 2)

I

i·dol (ī ′ dəl), *noun,* an image representing a diety. Some *idols* are worshipped, fed, and clothed as if they were alive. (Chap. 11)

ig·ne·ous (ĭg ′ nĭ əs), *adjective,* fire-formed; produced under intense heat. *Igneous* rocks form from molten material. (Chap. 6)

im·pend·ing (ĭm pĕn ′ ding), *adjective,* about to happen. We ran inside to avoid the *impending* thunderstorm. (Chap. 13)

im·per·cep·ti·ble (ĭm′pər sĕp ′ tə bəl), *adjective,* not noticeable; very slight. Any defects in the fine carving were *imperceptible.* (Chap. 4)

im·prov·i·sa·tion (ĭm′prəv ĭ zā ′ shən), *noun,* something provided on the spur of the moment. The musician did an *improvisation* when the song title was announced. (Chap. 2)

in·ad·vert·ent·ly (ĭn′əd vûr ′ tənt lē), *adverb,* unintentionally. He fell after he *inadvertently* stepped on an icy spot. (Chap. 6)

in·au·di·ble (ĭn ô ′ də bəl), *adjective,* not capable of being heard. The machinery was so quiet that it was *inaudible* to the workers. (Chap. 2)

in·con·clu·sive (ĭn ′ kən klōō ′ sĭv), *adjective,* not settled. The experiment did not settle anything; it had *inconclusive* results. (Chap. 13)

in·cum·bent (ĭn kŭm ′ bənt), *noun,* The holder of an office. The newcomer challenged the *incumbent* president in the election. (Chap. 5)

in·ex·tri·ca·bly (ĭn eks ′ trə kə blē), *adverb,* cannot be taken apart. The cables were tangled *inextricably.* (Chap. 11)

in·no·va·tion (ĭn′ə vā ′ shən), *noun,* something new or different introduced. The invention of the transistor was an *innovation* that made modern computers possible. (Chap. 3)

in·sem·in·ate (ĭn sĕm ′ ə nāt), *verb,* implant; impregnate. Animal breeders *inseminate* cows with semen from bulls that have desirable traits. (Chap. 6)

in·sur·rec·tion (ĭn′sə rĕk ′ shən), *noun,* a revolt; open resistance against civil authority. Shay's Rebellion in 1786 was an *insurrection* by farmers to prevent debt judgments against them. (Chap. 6)

in·ten·si·ty (ĭn tĕn ′ sə tē), *noun,* great strength; power; violence. The *intensity* of the heat from the furnace was great enough to burn their faces. (Chap. 2)

in·ter·state (ĭn′tər stāt ′), *adjective,* between states. The railroad carrying goods from Missouri to California was involved in *interstate* commerce. (Chap. 3)

in·ter·vene (ĭn′tər vēn ′), *verb,* come between; be between. The referee *intervened* in the dispute between the two teams. (Chap. 4)

in·tim·i·date (ĭn tĭm ′ ə dāt′), *verb,* make timid, cow. The others were *intimidated* by his outspoken sureness. (Chap. 14)

in·tol·er·able (ĭn tŏl ′ ər ə bəl), *adjective,* unbearable; unendurable. Patrick Henry found the rule of the king to be *intolerable.* (Chap. 14)

in·tra·state (ĭn′trə stāt ′), *adjective,* within one state. The inspector's duties were *intrastate;* he took water samples only in Georgia. (Chap. 3)

in·un·date (ĭn ′ ən dāt′), *verb,* overflow; flood; deluge. After heavy rains, some rivers *inundate* nearby towns. (Chap. 5)

in·vin·ci·bil·i·ty (ĭn vĭn′sə bĭl ′ ə tē), *noun,* status of not being able to be conquered or overcome. The ignorant soldiers were told their *invincibility* protected them against bullets. (Chap. 14)

i·ron·y (ī ′ ər nē ′), *adjective,* outcome of events opposite to that expected. There was *irony* in that the journalist who advocated gun control used an unregistered pistol. (Chap. 10)

isth·mus (ĭs ′ məs), *noun,* narrow neck of land connecting two larger land areas. The *isthmus* of Suez connects Asia and Africa. (Chap. 5)

J

jos·tle (jŏs ′ əl), *verb,* push or shove rudely against. The pickpocket *jostled* the victim to draw his attention away from the thieving action. (Chap. 11)

K

keen (kēn), *verb,* wail for the dead. They *keened* loudly and made everyone aware of the tragedy. (Chap. 10)

Ko·ran (Kō rän ′), *noun,* Islamic sacred scripture. The *Koran* is believed by Muhammadans to contain revelations by Allah. (Chap. 11)

L

lan·guish (lăng ′ gwĭsh), *verb,* lose vigor, strength; become weak. The battle survivors *languished* from their wounds. (Chap. 11)

leg·a·cy (lĕg ′ ə sē), *noun,* something handed down by a predecessor or ancestor. Free speech and press are a *legacy* from our Founding Fathers. (Chap. 7)

leg·end·ar·y (lĕj ′ ən dĕrē), *adjective,* in regard to a story handed down by tradition. Although *legendary* stories have no proof of truth, they are often accepted as having happened. (Chap. 10)

leg·is·la·tive (lĕj ′ ĭs lā ′ tĭv), *adjective,* having the function of making laws. Our national *legislative* body sits in Washington. (Chap. 4)

lei·sure·ly (lē ′ zhər lē), *adjective,* without haste; taking plenty of time. The couple strolled *leisurely* along the beach. (Chap. 2)

lit·er·ate (lĭt ′ ər ĭt), *adjective,* able to read and write. He was barely *literate;* he could hardly read the highway signs. (Chap. 14)

M

man·i·fest (măn ′ ə fĕst), *verb,* make plain; show clearly. John Hancock *manifested* his belief in independence by his large, bold signature. (Chap. 2)

me·di·ate (mē ′ dĭ āt′), *verb,* try to bring agreement between disputing groups or persons. The mediator was called to *mediate* the differences between labor and management. (Chap. 13)

mem·o·ra·ble (mĕm ′ ər ə bəl), *adjective,* worthy of remembering; notable. Memorial Day, May 30, is a *memorable* date in memory of dead war veterans. (Chap. 3)

mere·ly (mĭr ′ lĭ), *adverb,* only; nothing more; simply. She thanked him *merely* as a matter of form and meant nothing else. (Chap. 6)

met·a·mor·phic (mĕt′ə môr ′ fĭk), *adjective,* having change in form or structure. Heat and pressure can change sedimentary rocks into *metamorphic* rocks. (Chap. 6)

mi·grate (mī ′ grāt), *verb,* move from one country or region to settle in another. Many of us have ancestors that *migrated* here from another country. (Chap. 13)

mil·len·ni·um (mĭ lĕn ′ ē əm), *noun,* one thousand years. There are trees that have lived more than a *millenium.* (Chap. 3)

mire (mīr), *verb,* stuck in soft, deep mud or slushy snow. Spinning the wheels only *mired* the car more deeply. (Chap. 5)

mul·ti·tude (mŭl ′ tə tōōd), *noun,* a crowd; a great many. The hungry *multitude* gathered around the food truck. (Chap. 3)

mus·ter (mŭs ′ tər), *verb,* summon; gather together. The new miners *mustered* their courage before entering the deep mine shaft. (Chap. 5)

mu·til·ate (mū ′ tə lāt′), *verb,* disfigure; destroy a body part. She was *mutilated* in the car accident. (Chap. 14)

N

nat·ur·al·ist (năch ′ ər ə lĭst), *noun,* a person who studies plants and animals. John Muir was a *naturalist* who crusaded for national parks and nature reservations. (Chap. 6)

neg·li·gi·ble (nĕg ′ lə jə bəl), *adjective,* can be neglected. Because their differences were *negligible,* they came to an agreement on the contract. (Chap. 13)

niche (nich), *noun,* in ecology, the role or position and function of an animal or plant in the natural community. The monkey's *niche* was to live and feed in the tops of trees. (Chap. 3)

nov·ice (nŏv ′ ĭs), *noun,* one without experience; one new to the position. He was a *novice* with hammer and saw, but the carpenter would train him. (Chap. 2)

O

o·a·sis (ō ā ′ sĭs), *noun,* a desert place where water is available. In an *oasis,* ground water comes near or to the surface and allows some plants to thrive. (Chap. 11)

ob·jec·tive (əb jĕk ′ tĭv), *adjective,* unbiased; free from personal feelings. While interpreting the data, the chemist made an effort to be *objective.* (Chap. 4)

ob·liv·i·on (ə blĭv ′ ĭ ən), *noun,* condition of being forgotten by the world. Some early civilizations have passed into *oblivion.* (Chap. 6)

ob·scu·ri·ty (əb skyo͞or ′ ə tē), *noun,* condition of being unknown; dimness. The original meanings of the markings on the monument have faded into *obscurity.* (Chap. 7)

ob·ses·sion (əb sĕsh ′ ən), *noun,* a persistent idea or dominating influence that a person cannot escape. Columbus was driven by an *obsession* to reach India by sailing westward. (Chap. 7)

om·in·ous (ŏm ′ ə nəs), *adjective,* threatening; portending evil. The funnel-shaped cloud was *ominous;* it meant a tornado. (Chap. 10)

om·nip·o·tent (ŏm nĭp ′ ə tənt), *adjective,* having unlimited power or authority. Many ancient kings were *omnipotent* in their kingdoms. (Chap. 3)

om·ni·pres·ent (ŏm ′ nə prĕz ′ ənt), *adjective,* all present; being or existing everywhere. God, in many religions, is thought to be *omnipresent.* (Chap. 3)

op·er·a·tive (ŏp ′ ər ā ′ tĭv), *adjective,* exerting influence; being in effect. The rules *operative* when he played the game have since been changed. (Chap. 2)

or·ni·thol·o·gist (ôr ′ nə thŏl ′ ō jĭst), *noun,* one who studies birds. The *ornithologist* found that the bird ate thousands of harmful insects. (Chap. 2)

or·tho·dox (ôr ′ thə dŏks ′), *adjective,* conventional; correct in doctrine. His unwavering, rigid views were called *orthodox.* (Chap. 14)

o·ver·all (ō ′ vər ôl ′), *adjective,* from one extreme of a thing to the other. The *overall* length of the car was fifteen feet. (Chap. 2)

P

pa·hoe·hoe (pä hō ′ ā hō ′ ā), *noun,* lava that looks like coils of heavy rope. Some Hawaiian lava fields are made of *pahoehoe.* (Chap. 6)

pa·le·on·tol·o·gy (pâ ′ lē ən tŏl ′ ə jē), *noun,* the science of extinct forms of life as represented by fossil plants and animals. We have learned about dinosaurs through *paleontology.* (Chap. 3)

pan·the·on (păn ′ thĭ ŏn ′), *noun,* temple dedicated to the gods. Hadrian erected a domed *pantheon* that today is used as a church. (Chap. 14)

par·a·mount (păr ′ ə mount ′), *adjective,* above all; superior in authority. His *paramount* concern was to make his car payment. (Chap. 13)

pa·tron (pā ′ trən), *noun,* one who supports art, music, science, or other worthy endeavors. The *patron* covered the cost of the free concert. (Chap. 10)

per·il·ous·ly (pĕr ′ əl əs lē), *adverb,* in a dangerous manner. The sure-footed goats walked *perilously* close to the edge of the cliff. (Chap. 2)

per·pet·u·ate (pər pĕch ′ o͞oāt ′), *verb,* make perpetual; make endless or of long duration. Our constitution was designed to *perpetuate* our form of government. (Chap. 7)

per·ti·na·cious (pûr ′ tə nā ′ shəs), *adjective,* holding tightly to a course of action, purpose, or belief. The *pertinacious* writer kept revising the article until it was accepted. (Chap. 6)

pet·u·lant (pĕch ′ ə lənt), *adjective,* showing irritation. The *petulant* crowd shouted and booed when the player made slight errors. (Chap. 13)

pho·tom·e·ter (fō tŏm ′ ətər), *noun,* an instrument

for measuring light intensity. The camera had a built-in *photometer.* (Chap. 3)

pho·to·syn·the·sis (fō′tə sĭn′thə sĭs), *noun,* process used by plants to build sugar molecules starting with water and carbon dioxide and with the aid of chlorophyll and light. Plants need sunlight to furnish energy for the process of *photosynthesis.* (Chap. 6)

pic·to·graph (pĭk′tə grăf′), *noun,* a chart or record that has amounts shown by picture symbols. The three bundles of wheat in the *pictograph* stood for three thousand bushels. (Chap. 15)

plas·ma (plăz′mə), *noun,* liquid part of blood in which blood cells are suspended. Blood *plasma* is about 90 percent water. (Chap. 12)

Pleis·to·cene (plīs′tə sēn′), *noun,* glacial epoch that lasted one million years and included the last four ice ages. During the *Pleistocene* epoch, ice sheets extended southward to the valleys of the Missouri and Ohio rivers. (Chap. 7)

pol·y·the·ism (pŏl′ĭ thē ĭzəm) *noun,* belief in many gods. The ancient Greeks believed in *polytheism.* (Chap. 13)

post·war (pōst′wôr′), *adjective,* after a war. The *postwar* period was a time for rebuilding. (Chap. 3)

pre·ce·dent (prĕs′ə dənt), *noun,* a preceding example that may serve as justification for a later case. The lawyer cited a *precedent* to support his case. (Chap. 13, 14)

pre·da·tion (prē dā′shən), *noun,* act of hunting and seizing animals for food. Many reptiles, insects, and mammals feed on other animals by *predation.* (Chap. 6)

pre·em·i·nent (prē ĕm′ə nənt), *adjective,* superior to others; distinguished above others. The *preeminent* authors and scientists were honored at the ceremony. (Chap. 13)

pre·side (prĭ zīd′), *verb,* hold the place of authority; have charge of a meeting. The committee chairperson *presided* at the meeting. (Chap. 4)

pres·tige (prĕs tēzh′), *noun,* distinction; reputation, based on abilities, achievements or rank. Those awarded the Nobel prize have great *prestige* in the world. (Chap. 4)

prod·i·gy (prŏd′ə jē), *noun,* person having extraordinary talents. Isaac Newton was a *prodigy* in mathematics. (Chap. 10)

pro·found (prə found′), *adjective,* extreme; intense; going far beyond the obvious. He made a

profound discovery that was to have far-reaching importance. (Chap. 2)

prom·is·so·ry note (prŏm′ə sôr ē nōt), *noun,* a written promise. A *promissory* note may be written with payment due at a certain time or on demand. (Chap. 11)

prop·o·si·tion (prŏp′ə zĭsh′ən), *noun,* proposal; plan; scheme. The business *proposition* meant a large order for the salesperson. (Chap. 11)

pro·tag·o·nist (prō′tăg′ə nĭst), *noun,* leading character in a play. Macbeth was both *protagonist* and title of a tragedy written by Shakespeare in 1606. (Chap. 7)

pro·to·type (prō′tə tīp′), *noun,* a model or example from which something is formed. Others copied the *prototype* that he had developed. (Chap. 3)

pseu·do·sci·ence (soō′dō sī′əns), *noun,* false; sham science. Astrology is a *pseudoscience;* it is not based on systematic truths showing general laws. (Chap. 3)

pum·ice (pŭm′ĭs), *noun,* porous, glassy form of lava. Finely ground *pumice* is used as an abrasive cleanser. (Chap. 6)

py·ro·clas·tic (pī′rə klăs′tĭk), *adjective,* firemade from volcanoes. The *pyroclastic* rock fragments made a cone around the volcano. (Chap. 6)

Q

quad·ri·cen·ten·ni·al (kwŏd′rĕ sĕn tĕn′ē əl), *noun,* a 400th anniversary. A *quadricentennial* marks the completion of 400 years. (Chap. 3)

quest (kwest), *noun,* a search or pursuit. Don Quixote made a number of unsuccessful *quests.* (Chap. 11)

quin·tu·plet (kwĭn′tə plĭt), *noun,* one of five offspring born at a birth. If identical *quintuplets* are born, all five are of the same sex. (Chap. 3)

quo·rum (kwôr′əm), *noun,* number of members of a body required to be present for business to be conducted legally. In the House and Senate, a majority constitutes the *quorum* to do business. (Chap. 4)

R

rad·i·cal (răd′ə kəl), *adjective,* drastic; thoroughgoing. Moving from stagecoach to railroad was a *radical* change in transportation. (Chap. 3)

ral·ly (răl′e), *verb,* bring together; bring to order.

Washington *rallied* his dispirited troops at Valley Forge. (Chap. 10)

rare (râr), *adjective,* unusual; uncommon. Some *rare* animals and plants are on an endangered species list. (Chap. 12)

rar·e·fied (râr ′ ə fīd ′), *adjective,* less gross; refined. The stunning furnishings made the room appear *rarefied.* (Chap. 14)

ra·tion·al (răsh ′ ən əl), *adjective,* reasonable; having good sense; sane. His screaming and thrashing about showed he was *irrational.* (Chap. 14)

re·af·firm (rē ′ ə fûrm ′), *verb,* again state as true. The presidents *reaffirmed* their economic agreement. (Chap. 7)

re·ces·sive (rē sĕs ′ ĭv), *adjective,* hereditary character usually having less biological activity than a present dominant character. If shortness is a trait *recessive* to tallness, hybrids will probably be tall. (Chap. 6)

rel·e·vant (rĕl ′ ə vənt), *adjective,* connected to, or bearing upon, the matter at hand. His directions were *relevant* to repairing the broken chair. (Chap. 2)

rem·i·nisce (rĕm ′ ə nĭs ′), *verb,* to recall past experiences. The World War II veterans *reminisced* about the battles in Normandy. (Chap. 7)

re·pu·di·ate (rĭ pū ′ dē āt), *verb,* refuse to accept; cast off; disown. The country *repudiated* the debts owed to other nations. (Chap. 7)

res·o·nant (rĕz ′ ə nənt), *adjective,* echoing; resounding. The sounds of the organ were *resonant* throughout the cathedral. (Chap. 4)

rev·e·la·tion (rĕv ′ ə lā shən), *noun,* act of revealing, disclosing. The *revelation* disclosed that undercover agents were checking the criminal activities. (Chap. 13)

rev·er·ie (rĕv ′ ə rĭ), *noun,* daydream; dreamy musing. Her *reveries* brought back pleasant memories of childhood. (Chap. 6)

round·ly (round ′ lē), *adverb,* severely; vigorously. He beat the rug *roundly* to get the dirt out. (Chap. 14).

S

sa·gac·i·ty (sə găs ′ ə tĭ), *noun,* soundness of judgment; sharpness of mind. Albert Einstein was admired for his *sagacity.* (Chap. 6)

sa·li·ent (sā ′ lē ənt), *adjective,* prominent; conspicuous. The fireworks were the *salient* event in the celebration. (Chap. 4)

scaf·fold (skăf ′ əld), *noun,* temporary platform structure. A *scaffold* might be erected for workers and materials or to serve as a stage for exhibits. (Chap. 10)

sce·nic (sē ′ nĭk), *adjective,* having to do with natural scenery. The *scenic* wonders of our national parks attract many visitors. (Chap. 2)

scheme (skēm), *noun,* a plan; design; project. John Roebling had a grand *scheme* for building the Brooklyn Bridge. (Chap. 6)

score (skōr), *noun,* set of twenty. Lincoln spoke of four *score,* or eighty years. (Chap. 11)

sco·ri·a (skōr ′ ĭ ə), *noun,* volcanic rock with saclike holes. The *scoria* had the appearance of a mass of hardened bubbles. (Chap. 6)

scru·tin·y (skrōō ′ tə nē), *noun,* a careful examination; a detailed search. The people crossing the border were given close *scrutiny* by the guard. (Chap. 2)

sed·i·men·ta·ry (sĕd ′ ə mĕn ′ tər ē), *adjective,* formed from deposits of sediment. Some *sedimentary* rocks show layers of different colors. (Chap. 6)

shroud (shroud), *noun,* something that hides or conceals like a garment. The trees were *shrouding* the deer from the hunter's view. (Chap. 2)

siege (sēj), *noun,* the surrounding of a fortified place to capture it by cutting off supplies or help. The army kept bombarding the fort while keeping it under *siege.* (Chap. 13)

sig·ni·fy (sĭg ′ nə fī ′), *verb,* be a sign of. The arrow in the road sign *signifies* a curve. (Chap. 10)

sit·u·a·tion (sĭch ′ ə wā ′ shən), *noun,* state of affairs at any given time. In winter camp at Valley Forge, Washington's men were in a desperate *situation.* (Chap. 5)

sov·er·eign (sŏv ′ ĭ rĭn), *noun,* monarch; king or queen. The *sovereign* had his portrait put on all the coins and stamps. (Chap. 14)

spate (spāt), *noun,* sudden onset or outpouring. Desert flowers bloom after a *spate* of rain. (Chap. 6)

spec·ter (spĕk ′ tər), *noun,* ghost; visible spirit. In Dickens' "A Christmas Carol," Scrooge was frightened by several *specters.* (Chap. 6)

spec·u·late (spĕk ′ yə lāt ′), *verb,* form or express opinion without sufficient evidence. They *speculated* about the weather for the next game. (Chap. 6)

spew (spū), *verb,* to discharge contents; to vomit.

Old Faithful geyser *spewed* water and steam into the air. (Chap. 2)

stag·ger·ing (stăg ′ ər ĭng), *adjective,* heavy, as to cause falling or tottering. The *staggering* load on his back made him fall down the stairs. (Chap. 10)

stal·wart (stôl ′ wərt), *adjective,* strongly built; firm; steadfast. The defenders of the Alamo were *stalwart* to the end. (Chap. 4)

ster·ile (stĕr ′ ĭl), *adjective,* without life; free of germs; barren. Heating the needle over a bare flame made it *sterile*. (Chap. 14)

struc·tur·al (strŭk ′ chər əl), *adjective,* having to do with structure; pertaining to how parts are put together. *Structural* steel made up the framework of the building. (Chap. 3)

sub·lime (sə blīm ′), *adjective,* inspiring; impressing the mind. Lincoln's *sublime* address at Gettysburg did not impress the people at the time he spoke but inspires awe today. (Chap. 2)

sub·se·quent (sŭb ′ sə kwənt), *adjective,* following in order; coming later. The playoff game was *subsequent* to the regular season games. (Chap. 2)

sub·tle (sŭt ′ l), *adjective,* delicate; likely to avoid perception. The mouse never noticed the *subtle* movements of the owl. (Chap. 2)

su·per·in·ten·dent (so͞o ′ pər ĭn tĕn ′ dənt), *noun,* one who directs or oversees an institution or enterprise. The *superintendent* was in charge of the blueprints for the new bridge. (Chap. 3)

sur·vive (sər vīv ′), *verb,* continue to live or exist. The plant *survived* through the extreme cold spell. (Chap. 2)

sym·bol (sĭm ′ bəl), *noun,* something standing for something else. Highway *symbols* that show curves, railroad, and deer crossings are warnings that the motorist should heed. (Chap. 2)

syn·thet·ic (sĭn thĕt ′ ĭk), *adjective,* made by putting components together; made, rather than formed naturally. *Synthetic* fabrics take the place of cotton and wool. (Chap. 14)

syn·the·sis (sĭn ′ thə sĭs), *noun,* a building of simpler parts into a complex organization. Plants make sugar by *synthesis* of small molecules. (Chap. 6)

T

te·di·ous (tē ′ dĭ əs), *adjective,* lengthy and tiresome. Westward pioneers made *tedious* journeys. (Chap. 6)

tel·e·graph (tel ′ ə grăf), *noun,* a device for sending coded messages over long distances. Marconi invented a wireless *telegraph* and was the first to send a message across the Atlantic Ocean. (Chap. 3)

tes·ta·ment (tĕs ′ tə mənt), *noun,* a formal declaration or statement, usually written. The Declaration of Independence was a *testament* of the founders' beliefs. (Chap. 4)

the·o·ret·i·cal (thē ′ ə rĕt ′ ək əl), *adjective,* dealing with theories; not practical. *Theoretical* knowledge of the universe is obtained from examining changes in stars. (Chap. 3)

throm·bus (thrŏm ′ bəs), *noun,* blood clot. Fibrin molecules of the plasma together with blood cells make a clot called a *thrombus*. (Chap. 12)

trance (trăns), *noun,* a dazed condition; a half-conscious state. She stood *trance*like and seemed totally unaware of others moving around her. (Chap. 2)

tran·quil·i·ty (trăng kwĭl ′ ə tē), *noun,* peacefulness; calmness. They rested in the *tranquility* of the early morning. (Chap. 11)

trans·con·ti·nen·tal (trăns ′ kŏn tə nən ′ təl), *adjective,* extending across a continent. When tracks from the Pacific coast and from Omaha were joined near Ogden, Utah, in 1869, the first *transcontinental* railroad was completed. (Chap. 3)

trau·ma (trô ′ ma), *noun,* violent bodily injury; shock. The word *trauma* can mean physical harm or severe shock to mental well-being. (Chap. 14)

trea·tise (trē ′ tĭs), *noun,* a formal book or paper on some subject. Asa Gray wrote a *treatise* on plant identification. (Chap. 6)

tri·lat·er·al (trī lăt ′ ər əl), *adjective,* having three sides. The three electric companies have a *trilateral* agreement to share power when one has a shortage. (Chap. 3)

triv·i·al (trĭv ′ ĭ əl), *adjective,* unimportant; commonplace. His problems were *trivial;* he soon forgot them. (Chap. 6)

trust (trŭst), *noun,* a monopoly; an organization in restraint of trade. Anti*trust* laws now regulate the powers of trusts. (Chap. 14)

ty·rant (tī ′ rənt), *noun,* an oppressive ruler. In countries where *tyrants* rule, free speech or press is not possible. (Chap. 7)

U

u·nan·i·mous (ū năn ′ ə məs), *adjective,* agreed; in complete accord. They all agreed; the vote was *unanimous*. (Chap. 4) u•nique (ū nēk ′),   *adjective,* sole; being the only one of its kind. Something unique has no like or equal; we should not say something is very *unique.* (Chap. 13)

un•ruly (un rü ′ lē),   *adjective,* difficult to control; not conforming to rule. The chairperson had difficulty in maintaining order during the *unruly* meeting. (Chap. 13)

un•scru•pu•lous (ŭn skrōō ′ pyə ləs),   *adjective,* having no principles or no conscience. The *unscrupulous* salesperson took advantage of their ignorance. (Chap. 10)

V

ver•i•ta•ble (vĕr ′ ə tə bəl),   *adjective,* genuine; real; true. The experiment was carefully repeated so that the scientist could see whether its results were *veritable.* (Chap. 6)

ves•i•cle (vĕs ′ ə kəl),   *noun,* cavity; sac; small bladder. The sponge was filled with *vesicles.* (Chap. 6)

vic•e ver•sa (vī ′ sə vûr ′ sə),   the other way around. The abstract painting should have been hung *vice versa.* (Chap. 10)

vir•tu•al (vûr ′ chōō əl),   *adjective,* being in force or in effect but not actually expressed as such. The general was the *virtual* power behind the throne; he told the king what to do. (Chap. 5)

vis•cous (vĭs ′ kəs),   *adjective,* sticky; gummy. The *viscous* grease dripped from the roasting pan. (Chap. 6)

W

wal•low (wŏl ′ ō),   *verb,* roll the body around in; indulge in. The children contentedly *wallowed* in the new snow. (Chap. 11)

wrest (rĕst),   *verb,* pull away by force. The thief tried to *wrest* the jewelry from the woman. (Chap. 2)

Glossary compiled by George Hennings

Acknowledgements

Reading on page

6—Henry Graff, *This Great Nation.* Copyright 1985 by Riverside Publishing Company. Reprinted by permission of the publisher.

12—Adapted from Helena Curtis and N. Sue Barnes, *Invitation to Biology,* Copyright 1985 by Worth Publishers. Reprinted by permission of the publisher.

16—Emma Lazarus, "The New Colossus," from the pedestal of the Statue of Liberty.

22—Sentences are from Leo Fay, et al., *Riverside Reading Program, Level 15.* Copyright 1989 by Riverside Publishing Co. Reprinted by permission of the publisher.

23 and the objectives and chart, pp. 141–42—Charles Cazeau, Robert Hatcher, and Francis Siemankowski, *Physical Geology: Principles, Processes, and Problems.* Copyright © 1976 by Harper and Row Publishers, Inc. Reprinted by permission of Harper & Row, Publishers, Inc.

25—Corcoran Gallery of Art, "Niagara" (Washington, D.C., 1986).

29—Excerpt pp. 6–7 from *Living with Computers* by Patrick G. McKeown, copyright © 1986 by Harcourt Brace Jovanovich, Inc., reprinted by permission of the publisher.

44, 181—Alan Mandell, *The Language of Science.* Copyright 1974 by the National Science Teachers Association. Reprinted by permission of the National Science Teachers Association.

48—Stefi Weisburd, "Brushing Up on Dinosaurs," *Science News,* 130 (October 4, 1986), pp. 216–220. Reprinted with permission from *Science News,* the weekly newsmagazine of science, copyright 1986 by Science Service Inc.

51—Daniel D. Chiras, *Environmental Science* (Menlo Park, Calif: Benjamin/Cummings, 1985), p. 62.

66—The ten paragraphs on this and following pages are from Hubert Pryor, "Summer of Destiny," *Modern Maturity* (February/March 1987), p. 60. Copyright 1987 by American Association of Retired Persons. Reprinted by permission.

72—William Ecenbarger, "James Michener," *Modern Maturity* (February–March 1985, pp. 24–26. Reprinted with permission. Copyright 1985 American Association of Retired Persons.

80—From *The Constitution of the United States of America* by Sam Fink. Foreword copyright © 1985 by James Michener. Reprinted by permission of Random House, Inc.

86—The paragraphs on this and following pages are from William Ecenbarger, "James Michener," *Modern Maturity* 28 (August/September 1985), p. 24.

92—Lee Sheridan, "The Bridge They Said Couldn't Be Built," *In Concert,* published 1989 by Riverside Publishers, Chicago. Reprinted with permission of Carole Palmer and Riverside Publishing.

97—George Cruys, "The Dream of Panama," *Skald* (Spring/Summer 1986), pp. 2–7. Copyright 1986 by Royal Viking Line. Reprinted by permission of the Royal Viking Line.

114—The seven paragraphs quoted on pages 114–121 are from Chester R. Longwell, Adolph Knopf, and Richard Flint, *Physical Geology* (New York: John Wiley, 1948), pp. 347–348.

124—The four paragraphs quoted on pages 124–127 are from Jay Pasachoff, Maomi Pasachoff, Roy Clark, and Marlene Westermann, *Physical Science Today.* Copyright 1987 by Prentice Hall. Reprinted by permission of the publisher.

130, 242–50—Pamela Camp and Karen Arms, *Exploring Biology* 2d ed. (Philadelphia: Saunders, 1984), pp. 2–5. Copyright © 1984 by Saunders College Publishing, a division of Holt, Rinehart and Winston, Inc., reprinted by permission of the publisher.

145—John J. Patrick, "The Bicentennial of the Northwest Ordinance of 1787," *Social Education,* 51:5 (September, 1988). Reprinted with permission of the National Council for the Social Studies and the author.

155, 332—Samuel C. Certo, Max E. Douglas, and Stewart W. Husted, *Business,* 2d ed. Copyright © 1987 by Allyn and Bacon, Inc. Reprinted with permission.

159—Daniel Politoske, *Music,* 4th ed. © 1988, pp. 510–12. Reprinted by permission of Prentice Hall, Inc., Englewood Cliffs, NJ.

163—Richard Rodriquez, *Hunger of Memory: The Education of Richard Rodriguez.* Copyright © 1981 by Richard Rodriguez. Reprinted by permission of David R. Godine, Publisher.

170—Nila Smith and H. Alan Robinson, *Reading Instruction for Today's Children,* 2d ed. Copyright 1980 by Prentice Hall, Inc. Reprinted by permission of the publisher.

172 and 174—Thomas Brock, David Smith, and Michael Madigan, *Biology of Microorganisms,* 4th ed. Copyright 1984 by Prentice Hall. Reprinted by permission of the publisher.

176—Eudora Welty, *One Writer's Beginnings* (Cambridge, Mass.: Harvard University Press, 1984), pp. 29–30. Copyright 1983, 1984 by Eudora Welty. Reprinted by permission of the publisher.

179—Robert Wiggins, "Complex Insecurity: Big Brother Is Watching You," *MacUser,* 4 (April 1988), p. 47. Reprinted from MacUser, April 1988. Copyright © 1988 Ziff Communications Company.

182—Brock, Smith, and Madigan, *Biology of Microorganisms,* 4 ed. Copyright 1984 by Prentice Hall, Inc. Reprinted by permission of the publisher.

187—Jean Berko Gleason, *The Development of Language.* Copyright 1985 by Charles E. Merrill. Reprinted by permission of the publisher.

193—Richard Erdoes and Alfonso Ortiz, ed., *American Indian Myths and Legends* Reprinted by permission of Pantheon Books, a division of Random House, Inc.

202—Roger Kamien, *Music: An Appreciation* (New York: McGraw-Hill, 1980), pp. 208–212. Used by permission.

214—Nikki Giovanni, "the drum," from *Spin a Soft Black Song,* by Nikki Giovanni. Copyright © 1971, 1985 by Nikki Giovanni. Reprinted by permission of Hill and Wang, a division of Farrar, Straus and Giroux, Inc.

216—Abraham Lincoln, "Address at the Dedication of the Gettysburg National Cemetery," November 19, 1863.

220—Martin Luther King, Jr., "I Have a Dream." Reprinted by permission of Joan Daves. Copyright © 1963 by Martin Luther King, Jr.

226—Langston Hughes, "Dreams" and "The Dream Keeper," *The Dream Keeper and Other Poems* (New York: Alfred Knopf, 1932). Copyright 1932 and renewed 1960 by Langston Hughes.

226—"Dream Dust," *The Panther and the Lash* (New York: Alfred Knopf, 1947). Copyright 1947 by Langston Hughes. Reprinted from *The Panther and the Lash* by Langston Hughes by permission of Alfred A. Knopf.

232—Excerpts on pages 232 to 240 are from John W. Hole, Jr., *Human Anatomy and Physiology.* Copyright 1979 by William C. Brown. Reprinted by permission of the publisher.

257—William Tracy, "Middle West Meets Middle East," *Aramco World Magazine,* 38:5 (September–October 1987), p. 3. Used by permission.

260—Anne Marshall Zwack, "Florence, the Magnificent," *Travel and Leisure,* 17:4 (April 1987), pp. 103–114, 162. Reprinted by permission of *Travel and Leisure* and of the author.

274—Paul Lunde and John A. Sabini, *ARAMCO and Its World: Arabia and the Middle East.* Copyright 1980 by Arabian American Oil Company. Reprinted by permission of ARAMCO.

290—Harry Truman, "The 8 Best Presidents—and Why," *Parade Magazine,* April 3, 1988, pp. 4–5. From *More Plain Speaking,* by Harry S. Truman, edited by Margaret Truman and Scott Meredith. Reprinted by permission of the author and Scott Meredith Literary Agency, Inc., 845 Third Avenue, New York, NY 10022 and with permission from *Parade.* Copyright © 1988.

298—William Pfaff, "Soviet Reform Reflects Tragedy of the Revolution." © 1988, Los Angeles Times Syndicate. Reprinted by permission.

304—Maya Angelou, *I Know Why the Caged Bird Sings,* Copyright © 1969 by Maya Angelou. Reprinted by permission of Random House, Inc.

Index

Names of authors of selections are given in *italics*. Names of selections are in **bold**.

A

Achievement of Desire, The, 163–164
Activating what you know before
    reading, 2–3, 137
Affixes, 35, 39–43
Alliteration, 213
Allusions, literary, 214
American Indian Myths and Legends,
    192–200
Anatomy and Physiology, 232–233
Angelou, Maya, 304
Antonyms, using to unlock the mean-
    ing of words, 20, 21
Arms, Karen, 130, 243, 248
Assigned reading, dealing with, 3
Attacking Words in Science, 44–45
Author's purpose, 2, 231, 255, 286

B

Ball-park figure, 88
Bias in writing, detecting, 286–288
Big Brother Is Watching You, 179–
    181
Black Folk Music, 157–161, 162
Bridge They Said Couldn't Be Built,
    The, 92–95
Brock, Thomas, 172, 174, 182
Brushing Up on Dinosaurs, 48–50

C

Camp, Pamela, 130, 243, 248
Can Chimpanzees Learn to Speak?
    187–188
Cause/effect, recognizing, 122–123,
    270–271
Cazeau, Charles, 23–24
Cell Membrane, The, 234
Charts, interpreting data, 61–65
Charts and tables, interpreting, 310–
    320
Charts for gathering data, 188, 189,
    194, 203
Chiras, Daniel, 51–52
Chronology, comprehending, 267–
    270

Chunks of meaning, 169–176
Clue words, following, 110–135
Comparing, strategy for, 187–188,
    191
Comparisons and contrasts, recogniz-
    ing, 118–120
Computer as Mind Tool, The, 29
Concentrating while reading, 169
Concluding, 189–191, 192
Conditional relationships, recogniz-
    ing, 120–122
Connotation, 287–288
Context clues to unlock the meaning
    of words, 19–33
Critical thinking, 186–210
Cruys, George, 97
Curtis, Helena, 12–14

D

Data chart, recording opinions with,
    289, 300
Data charts as a before reading strat-
    egy, 140
Data gathering chart, 188, 189, 194,
    203
Deductive paragraphs, 63
Definitions, comprehending, 231–239
Definitions, using to unlock the
    meaning of words, 20, 21
Denotation, 287–288
Descriptions, comprehending, 255–
    266
Details, comprehending, 57–64, 85–
    109
Dickinson, Emily, 258 (*see also* **Emily**
    Dickinson)
Dictionary, using to unlock the mean-
    ing of words, 20
Diffusion and Osmosis, 235
Directional changes, recognizing,
    115–118
Distractions and reading, 169
Drawings, line, 331–332
Dream at Panama, The, 95–107
Dream Dust, 227
Dream Keeper, The, 226

Dreams, 226
drum, the, 214

E

Eagle, The, 257
Early Presidents of the United States,
    61–65
Ecenbarger, William, 72
Eight Best Presidents and Why, The,
    289–295
Elements Known to Ancient Civiliza-
    tions, 124–127
Emily Dickinson, 269–270
Energy Value of Food, 237–239
Equations, using for interpreting def-
    initions, 232, 233
Erdoes, Richard, 193
Essay questions, 165–166
Evolution by Means of Natural Selec-
    tion, 243–246
Examinations, preparing for (*see* Test
    taking)
Examples, recognizing, 113–115
Explanations, comprehending, 239–
    253
Explanations, using to unlock the
    meaning of words, 20, 21

F

Fifty States of the United States, The,
    317–318
Figures of speech, 214, 256–259, 265–
    266
Florence the Magnificent, 259–265

G

Germ Theory of Disease, The, 174–
    175
Getting ready to read, 1–4, 17–18,
    137–141
Gettysburg Address, The, 216–218
Giovanni, Nikki, 214
Gleason, Jean, 187
Glossary, using to unlock the meaning
    of words, 20, 340–351

Graff, Henry, 6–9
Graphs:
  bar, 324–326
  circle, 322–324
  line, 327–331
  pictograph, 320
  pie, 322–324
Great Constructions of the World, 89–91
Grids, interpreting (*see* Charts and tables)

H

Haydn and Mozart, 200–209
Headings and subheadings, 2, 137–138, 139–140
Hennings, George, 111
Heterotrophs and Autotrophs, 51–52
Highlighting a text, 155
Hole, John, 232, 233, 234, 235
Hughes, Langston, 226–227
Hypothetical Cell, A, 233–234

I

I Have a Dream, 218–222
I Know Why the Caged Bird Sings, 304–306
Idea webbing, 4–5, 12, 16, 97, 140, 142, 143
idea, main, *see* Main idea
Idea-cluster webs as a before reading strategy, 140
Illustrations, use of in previewing, 2–3, 310
Imagery, 214
Immigration to the United States, 325–327
Inductive paragraphs, 63
Inferring, 188–189, 190, 192
Introductory sections of a chapter, 138

J

James Michener, 71–77
Judging, 191, 192
Judgments, assessing the validity of, 288

K

Kamien, Roger, 202
Key on graphs, 320
King, Martin Luther, 220
Knowledge base for reading, 2

L

Land and Populations, 310–317
Language and Communication, 181–182
Lazarus, Emma, 16–17
Leading Cloud, Jenny, 193
Lincoln, Abraham, 216
Lunde, Paul, 274

M

Main idea, 56–84
Maya Angelou's School Thoughts, 303–306
Mandel, Alan, 44–45
Maps:
  Central America, 109
  Italy, 261
  Little Big Horn region, 195
  Middle East, 275
  northeastern United States, 11
  Northwest Territories, 151
  USSR, 302
Mapping a selection, 58–59, 82, 112, 114, 116
Mapping a summary for writing, 156–157, 158, 162, 247, 251
Mapping ideas for writing, 107–108, 127–128, 281–282
McKeown, Patrick, 29
Metaphor, 214, 256–259, 265–266
Michener, James, 80–81, see also **James Michener**
Microbial Environment, The, 182–184
Microscope and Microorganisms, The, 172–173
Mind talk as part of reading, 154–156, 240–241, 288
Mood, definition, 215
Moon, 258
Muhammad the Prophet, 272–281

N

Narrative, definition of, 255
Narratives, comprehending, 266–284
Nation on the Move—America Moves West, A, 6–9
Natural Selection—The Peppered Moth, 246–251
Nature of Scientific Investigation, The, 129–135
New Colossus, The, 16
Niagara, 25–26
Northwest Ordinance of 1787, The, 142–151
Notetaking in a text (*see* Highlighting)

O

On Geology, 23–24
One Writer's Beginnings, 176–179
Opinions, comprehending, 285–308
Outlines of chapters, 137–138

P

Paragraph, structure of (*see* Structure of a paragraph)
Paragraphs, writing, 64–65, 107–108, 127–128
Paraphrasing, 231–232
Patrick, John, 145
Personal reading, 3
Persuasive writing, 286
Pfaff, William, 297, 298, 300–301
Phyllis Wheatley, 267
Physical Geology, 141–142
Pictographs, interpreting, 320
Poetry, interpreting, 15–17, 214, 225–228, 257, 258
Politoske, Daniel, 159
Predicting:
  how many items will be discussed, 111–113
  whether a comparison or contrast is coming, 118–120
  whether a conditional relationship is being established, 120–122
  whether an example is coming, 113–115
  whether a reason is going to be given, 122–123
  whether there will be a change in direction, 115–118
Predicting based on clue words, 111–135
Predicting before reading, 141
Prefixes, 35, 39–42
Previewing before reading 2–3, 17–18, 139–141
Print type, using, 2
Pryor, Hubert, 65
Punctuation and sound effects, 213
Purpose, author's, 2, 231, 255, 286
Purpose, reader's, 2, 3
Purposes and Objectives of Business, 155–156

Q

Question-types, examination, 165–166
Questioning before reading, 140

R

Rapid reading, 168–185
Rate of reading (*See* Reading rate)

pose, 2, 3
185
Reading rate:
 calculating, 336
 charts for finding, 337–339
 discussion of, 168–185
Reading, definition of, 2, 111
Reasons, recognizing, 122–123
Reciting as part of reading, 154–156
Reference points from history, 268
Relating events, 271–272
Reviewing after reading, 156–157
Rodriguez, Richard, 163
Roots, charts of common, 36, 46
Root words, 34–35, 36–39
Ross Vs. Cobb, 332–334

S

Sabini, John, 274
Secret of Ameria, The, 78–82
Semantic webbing, (see Idea webbing)
Sentence, topic (see Topic sentence)
Setting a purpose for reading, 2, 3
Sheridan, Lee, 92
Short-answer questions, 166–167
Significance of events, determining, 271
Signs of Life, The, 12–15
Simile, 214, 256–259, 265–266
Sound, repetitive use of, 213
Soviet Reform Reflects Tragedy of the Revolution, 296–301
Special text features, 140–141
SQ3R, 136–167
Strategy for:
 comparing, 187–188, 191
 comprehending chronology, 268–269, 270
 comprehending definitions, 231–235
 comprehending descriptions, 255–257

comprehending explanations, 241–242
comprehending narratives, 272
comprehending opinions and judgments, 286–288
concluding, 188–189, 190
detecting bias, 286–288
differentiating fact from opinion, 286–288
distinguishing between general and specific, 57–61
getting at implied meanings, 88–89
getting ready to read, 1–3, 17–18, 139–141
increasing reading rate, 168–185
inferring, 188–189, 190, 192
interpreting charts and tables, 310
interpreting graphs, 320–331
interpreting line drawings, 331–332
judging, 191, 192
making main ideas while reading, 65
preparing for a test, 164–167
sorting significant from less significant details, 61–62
studying, 136–167
surveying before reading, 2–3, 139–141
unlocking the meaning of unfamiliar words, 54
working with details, 89
Structure of a paragraph, 62–65
Structure of a text, 136–152
Style:
 definition of, 213
 elements of, 213–214
 reading to determine, 214–215
Suffixes, 35, 42–43
Summaries, writing after reading, 138, 156–157, 158, 162, 247, 251
Summer of Destiny, 65–71
Surveying before reading, 2–3, 139–141
Symbols on graphs, 320
Synonyms, using to unlock the meaning of words, 20, 21

T

Tennyson, Alfred, 256–257
Test taking, 164–167
Thinking along, 240–241, 288
Thinking aloud, 240–241
Thoreau, Henry David, 255
Three Classes of Rocks, The, 111
Time, words signalling passage of, 269
Time lines as a before reading strategy, 140
Time lines, using for comprehending chronology, 267–270
Timed reading, 169–185
Tone, definition of, 215
Topic, determining, 2–3, 57
Topic sentence, 57
Truman, Harry S., 290

V

Visual appearance of a selection, 213
Visualizing, 231–232, 255–257
Vocabulary, developing, 19–55
Vocabulary lists, using, 140–141

W

Walden Pond, 255–256
Weather in New Delhi and Santiago, 329–330
Webbing (see Idea webbing)
Weisburd, Stefi, 48–50
Welty, Eudora, 176
What's Involved in Rapid Reading, 170
Wiggins, Robert, 179
Word parts, 34–35, 36–39
Word structure clues, 34–55
Writing:
 mapping a selection before writing, 107–108, 127–128
 using clue words, 127–128
 using idea maps, 127–128

Z

Zwack, Anne, 260–265

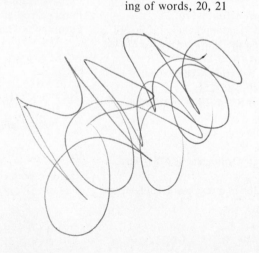